Studia Fennica
Folkloristica 8

The FINNISH LITERATURE SOCIETY (SKS) was founded in 1831 and has, from the very beginning, engaged in publishing operations. It nowadays publishes literature in the fields of ethnology and folkloristics, linguistics, literary research and cultural history.

The first volume of the Studia Fennica series appeared in 1933. Since 1992, the series has been divided into three thematic subseries: Ethnologica, Folkloristica and Linguistica. Two additional subseries were formed in 2002, Historica and Litteraria. The subseries Anthropologica was formed in 2007.

In addition to its publishing activities, the Finnish Literature Society maintains research activities and infrastructures, an archive containing folklore and literary collections, a research library and promotes Finnish literature abroad.

EDITORIAL OFFICE
SKS
P.O. Box 259
FI-00171 Helsinki
www.finlit.fi

Myth and Mentality

Studies in Folklore and Popular Thought

Edited by Anna-Leena Siikala

Finnish Literature Society · Helsinki

Studia Fennica Folkloristica 8

The publication has undergone a peer review.

VERTAISARVIOITU
KOLLEGIALT GRANSKAD
PEER-REVIEWED
www.tsv.fi/tunnus

The open access publication of this volume has received part funding via
a Jane and Aatos Erkko Foundation grant.

A digital edition of a printed book first published in 2002 by the Finnish Literature Society.
Cover Design: Timo Numminen
EPUB: Tero Salmén

ISBN 978-951-746-371-3 (Print)
ISBN 978-952-222-849-9 (PDF)
ISBN 978-952-222-848-2 (EPUB)

ISSN 0085-6835 (Studia Fennica)
ISSN 1235-1946 (Studia Fennica Folkloristica)

DOI: https://dx.doi.org/10.21435/sff.8

A free open access version of the book is available at https://dx.doi.org/10.21435/sff.8 or by scanning this QR code with your mobile device.

Contents

Foreword 7

MYTH, BELIEF AND WORD VIEW

Anna-Leena Siikala
What Myths Tell about Past Finno-Ugric
Modes of Thinking 15

Lauri Harvilahti
Očy Bala
A Mythological Epic Heroine 33

Vilmos Voigt
Cosmographical Maps (on Stars) 42

Mihály Hoppál
Linguistic and Mental Models for Hungarian
Folk Beliefs 50

Laura Stark-Arola
The Dynamistic Body in Traditional
Finnish-Karelian Thought
Väki, vihat, nenä, and *luonto* 67

WITCHES AND DEVILS

Éva Pócs
World View, Witch Legend, Witch Confession 107

Ülo Valk
The Devil's Identity
On the Problem of His Pre-Christian Prototype in Estonian
Mythology 122

Pasi Klemettinen
Many Faces of Evil 130

Ulrika Wolf-Knuts
Two Discourses about the Devil 148

VALUES AND COLLECTIVE EMOTIONS

Satu Apo
Alcohol and Cultural Emotions 171

Henni Ilomäki
Narratives of Ethnicity
Karelian War Legends 207

Pekka Hakamies
Proverbs and Mentality 222

EXPRESSIONS OF LOVE AND SEXUALITY

Anneli Asplund
Changing Attitudes to Love in Finnish Folk Songs 233

Seppo Knuuttila and Senni Timonen
If the One I Know Came Now 247

Tarja Kupiainen
The Forbidden Love of Sister and Brother
The Incest Theme in Archangel Karelian Kalevala Meter Epic 272

Annikki Kaivola-Bregenhøj
Sexual Riddles
The Test of the Listener 301

Foreword

The genres of folklore which arise in the process of oral communication are discourse practices endowed with cultural meanings. Folkloristic research has not only examined their metadiscursive meanings but has also traced out what they tell us about the themes and motifs, and poetic style and substance, of traditional narratives and songs. If we wish to determine not only what oral tradition says but also what it tells us about, then the field of topics covered by folkloristic research broadens considerably. We may ask ourselves what oral tradition tells us about the thoughts and feelings of its performers. What sorts of beliefs, values and attitudes, emotions and memorised experiences come across in traditional songs and narratives? Folklorists have long been intrigued by the world view and beliefs reflected in oral tradition. The broadening of this perspective to cover cultural awareness, personal experiences and emotions is, however, a relatively new development. The study of folk thinking draws upon the insights afforded by the study of mentalities and cognitive studies of culture.

The concept of mentality has recently been rediscovered and continues to thrive despite the criticism levelled at it from time to time. There are two reasons for the ambivalent attitude, the more important being the notions implied by the term *mentality*. Although mentality is a serviceable heuristic tool, its conceptual confines are often so wide and vaguely defined that scholars in search of precise cognitive tools have tended to avoid it. Another source of criticism was the political use of the concept for nationalistic purposes in the Germany of the 1930s. The study of mentality may even be said to have split into two opposing research traditions: one inspiring national images for use in the public domain and the other highlighting ways of thinking and experiencing either hidden from or rejected by the public eye. Representing the latter is the research tradition founded by the Annales school in France that gave the concept of mentality a new sense and established its use in the European disciplines interested in folk thinking.

The history of mentalities, represented by such scholars as Jacques Le Goff, Emmanuel Le Roy Ladurie, Fernand Braudel and Lucien Febvre, turned its gaze on the everyday life and thought of centuries past. The Annalists strove to probe the collective mind set, experiences and thought processes of a particular era; in other words, an area overlooked by conventional historical research concentrating on politics and the ruling class. In addressing mentalities, historians in fact hit upon a subject that had long been examined by researchers in folk tradition: the world of the ordinary man, or what Le Goff called a mental universe at once both stereotypical and chaotic.

The concept of mentality has also been used in referring to the collective psychological disposition of a people, in speaking of the national character. German culture research in the 1930s tried to describe the German character, its mentality, by comparing it with that of neighbouring peoples. Among other cultural sources, it used as its material folklore such as proverbs, as

7

expressions of national values. This research school with its political objectives gave the concept of mentality a negative stigma, and debates regarding national characters died out during the maelstrom of the Second World War. Recalling that humanistic disciplines such as folkloristics which investigate collective values and beliefs always serve particular ideologies, it is possible to undertake a critical analysis of the application of the mentality concept in its various social contexts. From the perspective of the research history of folkloristics, debates regarding national character illuminate the political ties of the discipline in Europe during the 1930s.

As a heuristic concept, mentality seems to still occupy a key role in the debate on nationality and national identity today. This was conspicuous during the process of integration taking place in Europe in the early 1990s, in which examination of national state projects and of the relationship between the national and the European was one of the leading trends in the humanities and social sciences. Thus both the Swedish and Finnish national characters have been held up for inspection from many new angles, many of them drawing on the concept of mentality.

The concept of mentality established by the French Annalists refers to the thought and experience of the ordinary man and woman, to everyday, collective cultural representations. In referring to collective mental contents it is comparable to the concept of world view favoured by folklorists, even though the latter is, in emphasising the cognitive aspect, more limited in scope. Carol Ginzburg, in speaking of mentality, has drawn attention to the hazy, subconscious dimension of world view: the archaisms, emotional and irrational elements embedded in it. The concept is most commonly used to refer to attitudes to life, values and emotions, and to collective modes of thought and experience which guide everyday activities. Since all of these find expression in folklore, the concept of mentality has proved a useful tool in folkloristic research.

While the concept of mentality has proven helpful in referring to the broad domain of world view and folk thought, values and emotions, on the other hand it has been found wanting in the examination of specific thematic topics, since it is abstract and only vaguely definable. Finnish folkloristics has in fact developed a more cogent methodology for the study of mentalities by exploiting the theory borrowed from cognitive research regarding the storage and processing of observations and data. Mentalities can thus be conceived of as cognitive, emotional and action-determining models for viewing the world. Cognitive anthropology uses the expressions 'cultural model' and 'mental model' to refer to these semantic structures (see Anna-Leena Siikala, *Suomalainen šamanismi: Mielikuvien historiaa*, Finnish Literature Society, 1992). This study works from the premise that the cultural models which shape mentality create and order visible expressions of culture such as the folkloristic genres and motifs. They also become embedded in folkloristic representations and are handed down with them from one generation to the next.

The encoding of folk thinking, human experience, emotions and beliefs in oral tradition was of special interest to Finnish folklorists in the 1990s. One reason for this heightened interest was the growing awareness of the

8

value and usefulness of the Finnish tradition archives. The Folklore Archives of the Finnish Literature Society, containing material collected from the early 19th century onwards, contain over four million texts. Since these items are the work of not only scholars but also of amateur collectors, tradition performers and their audiences, they provide new avenues for the researcher seeking to answer questions surrounding popular mentalities. This research trend has itself combined and incorporated a number of different perspectives. Since many important works have appeared in Finnish only, I will mention only a few of them here. Professor Seppo Knuuttila (University of Joensuu), who has discussed many of the conceptual problems of mentality and world view in a number of publications, examines humour as a testing-ground for the 'reality' of concepts belonging to the folk world view in his *Kansanhuumorin mieli: Kaskut maailmankuvan aineksina* (Finnish Literature Society, 1992).

One dominant feature of contemporary Finnish folkloristics is the meeting between research into popular thought and a gendered perspective. Professor Satu Apo (University of Helsinki) has pioneered this field of research with her book *Naisen väki* (Hanki ja jää, 1995), which works from the premise that the archival texts born of folk discourse afford a perspective on the way people in the past understood the world of women, corporeality and family relations. At its broadest, the spectrum of women's studies in Finnish folkloristics can be seen in *Gender and Folklore: Perspectives on Finnish and Karelian Culture*, edited by Satu Apo, Aili Nenola and Laura Stark-Arola (Studia Fennica Folkloristica 4, 1998). This volume examines not only contemporary phenomena connected with the gender system, womanhood and girlhood but also the determination of gender in the traditional Finnish-Karelian world view. In his book *Jätkän synty* (Finnish Literature Society, 1997), Dr. Jyrki Pöysä (Joensuu Folklore Archive) discusses the differences represented in folklore from the male perspective. Finnish lumberjack lore also provides insights into folk humour and the communal conditions which give rise to it.

The study of popular thought, experience and emotion is a field of research with many branches. It is here approached by examining various aspects of cultural awareness, beginning with myths, world views and beliefs and proceeding to expressions of values and emotions. The section headed *Myth, Belief and World View* contains five articles addressing their topics from a broad temporal and geographical perspective. The opening article by Anna-Leena Siikala (Academy Professor, University of Helsinki), *What Myths Tell about Past Finno-Ugric Modes of Thinking*, examines the concept of mentality and what mentality history has to offer folkloristics. The focus of the article is, however, on the collective mythical models and images of speakers of Finno-Ugric languages and the re-contextualisation of mythic tradition in the identity processes of today's increasingly globalised world. The contribution *Očy Bala. A Mythological Epic Heroine* by Professor Lauri Harvilahti (University of Helsinki) points out the organic link between myth and epic. Mythical motifs and images can be described as the lasting semantic constructs that have survived thanks to the skill of its performers and the ability of epic poetry to interest audiences. The study of mythic semantic constructs and the examination of the formal features of poetic performance thus complement each other.

Cosmological and cosmographic knowledge is one of the fundamental elements of mythic traditions. In his article *Cosmographical Maps (on Stars)* Professor Vilmos Voigt (University of Budapest) examines European maps of the 16th and 17th centuries that reflect the changing contemporary concept of the world. In his research Voigt applies principles from semiotics, as does Dr. Mihály Hoppál (European Folklore Centre), a scholar focusing on the Hungarian belief system, in his article *Linguistic and Mental Models for Hungarian Folk Beliefs*. Dr. Hoppál does not confine himself to merely describing the mental models for folk beliefs, but also views beliefs as models which guide action. In an article entitled *The Dynamistic Body in Traditional Finnish-Karelian Thought*, Docent Laura Stark-Arola (University of Helsinki) examines concepts of the body/self and the forces seen to threaten it. The Western habit of categorising the body and mind as two separate components of the human entity is not, in her opinion, necessarily appropriate in the study of other cultures. In underlining the dynamic nature of the human body in Finnish folk thought, she notes that conceptions of body and illness are closely interconnected, two sides of the same coin.

Research into mentalities has traditionally been concerned with beliefs and magic in particular. The reason for this lies in the nature of the source material at the disposal of historians. The witch trials of the 16th, 17th and 18th centuries yielded a wealth of detailed information on the images associated with witchcraft. The section *Witches and Devils* is devoted to this field of research – a field shared by mentality historians and folklorists. In her article *World View, Witch Legend, Witch Confession*, Dr. Éva Pócs (Hungarian Academy of Sciences) uses some of the same sources as historians in drawing on texts yielded by the witchcraft prosecutions. Going through the narratives of witnesses, prosecutors and the accused as they appear in the court records, she shows how the nature of the narratives changed as the trials progressed, which to her mind reflects the shifting conflicts behind the accusations.

The witch trials provide modern-day researchers with valuable insights into images connected to the Devil. In *The Devil's Identity: On the Problem of His Pre-Christian Prototype in Estonian Mythology*, Professor Ülo Valk (University of Tartu) indicates that Christian concepts of the Devil were founded on both ethnic features of European origin and features derived from the high religions of the East. Dr. Pasi Klemettinen (Folklore Archives of the Finnish Literature Society) also addresses concepts of the essence of evil in his *The Many Faces of Evil*, based on his doctoral dissertation *Mellastavat Pirut* (Finnish Literature Society, 1997) which deals with poltergeist phenomena. The article by Professor Ulrika Wolf-Knuts (Åbo Akademi, Turku), *Two Discourses about the Devil*, is likewise based on her doctoral research *Människan och djävulen* (Åbo, 1991). Wolf-Knuts stresses that the images of the Devil created by the teachings of the Church on the one hand, and the folk mentality on the other, belong to two discourses that were emphasised in different ways but nonetheless constitute a single entity, despite echoing different voices.

The section *Values and Collective Emotions* turns away from folk belief to values, attitudes and emotions. The shift is not as radical as it may seem from the perspective of today's secularised world. Here in Europe folk morality engaged in a dialogue with the teachings of the Christian Church; imaginary beings, the Devil included, were appealed to as a way of sanctioning misdeeds. In Finnish folk culture, alcohol possessed powerful cultural connotations. The recent in-depth study by Professor Satu Apo, *Viinan voima* (Finnish Literature Society, 2001), examines folk attitudes toward alcohol and alcohol-related behaviours provides a picture of unusual breadth stretching from prehistory to the present day of the Finnish beliefs, concepts and experiences surrounding alcohol. In her contribution to this volume, *Alcohol and Cultural Emotions*, she debates the meanings and collective emotions attached to alcohol in Finnish folk culture and the concepts upon which the Finnish national alcohol policy is founded. She also presents a methodological model for research on cultural models and emotional attitudes based on multiple folklore genres.

Images of the enemy contained in historical narratives provided Licentiate Henni Ilomäki (Finnish Literature Society) with the point of departure for her article *Narratives of Ethnicity: Karelian War Legends*, which discusses the folk concept of ethnicity. The enemy, the Other, is described as lacking a sense of right and wrong and being capable of atrocities. *Cynocephalus* images link stereotypes of the enemy with mythical images of the Devil. The interesting thing is that folk visions of the enemy such as those revealed in folktales were revived in narratives regarding the wars of the 20th century, as demonstrated by Docent Ulla-Maija Peltonen in her doctoral dissertation *Punakapinan muistot* (Finnish Literature Society, 1996) which examines the oral tradition surrounding the abortive attempt at revolution in Finland 1917–1918. Sayings and proverbs reflecting cultural values are popular tools for debating national character. Docent Pekka Hakamies (Karelian Research Institute, University of Joensuu), in *Proverbs and Mentality*, analyses the relationship between proverbs, values and attitudes and looks into the use of the mentality concept in paremiological research. In a comparison of proverbs characterising the Russians and the Finns, he points out perceived differences in the ways the two nations think which also recur in other forms of cultural discourse as well.

The four articles in the section *Expression of Love and Sexuality* are based on Finnish folklore archive materials. The opening article, *Changing Attitudes to Love in Finnish Folk Songs*, by Licentiate Anneli Asplund (Folklore Archives of the Finnish Literature Society) describes the attitudes to love and sexuality portrayed in various vocal genres. Since the spread of ballads and roundelays in the Finnish-Karelian region can be dated approximately, the article also follows the changes that have taken place in the concepts of love and sexual relations. Joint authors Professor Seppo Knuuttila and Licentiate Senni Timonen (Folklore Archives of the Finnish Literature Society) take an in-depth look at one lyrical song (*If the one I know came now*) in Kalevalaic metre. The portrayal of passionate love in this song is unique to Balto-Finnish lyric poetry in this metre; the poem has been translated into 467 languages, and into German by none other than Goethe.

11

This rare poem aroused the interest of scholars nearly two centuries ago. Knuuttila and Timonen present some of its earliest interpretations and stress the corporeal nature of the emotion expressed in the poem.

Incest is usually defined in Kalevala-metre poetry as a relationship between sister and brother or mother and son, unlike in, for example, Indo-European oral tradition, where the father-daughter relationship tends to be emphasised. Licentiate Tarja Kupiainen (University of Joensuu), in *The Forbidden Love of Sister and Brother: The Incest Theme in Archangel Karelian Kalevala Meter Epic*, examines cultural concepts surrounding incest and the picture of it given by Karelian poetry from the viewpoint of the victimized girl.

Riddles, a well-known medium of erotic fantasy, are silent on the subject of love. In *Sexual Riddles: The Test of the Listener*, Professor Annikki Kaivola-Bregenhøj (University of Turku), traces out the sexual imagery of riddles collected over a span of more than a hundred years. Although attitudes towards sexuality have fundamentally changed during this period, sexual riddles still occupy a place of their own in modern culture. Folk eroticism has elicited relatively little interest among folklorists, though the way was opened for further studies in Finland by Satu Apo's work *Naisen väki* (1995) mentioned above. The same theme is taken up in the anthology *Amor, Genus & Familia* (Finnish Literature Society, 1998) edited by Jyrki Pöysä and Anna-Leena Siikala, which addresses folk eroticism and representations of love as described in folklore.

This collection of articles is published in the frame of the "Myth, History and Society" -project financed by the Finnish Academy.

The process of editing and translating the articles of this book into English has been a lengthy one, subject to numerous delays. I am grateful to the authors for their patience. The articles were translated by Leila Virtanen, MA and Docent Laura Stark-Arola. Satu Lehtinen, MA, Saara Paatero, BA and Dr. Anastasios Daskolopoulos assisted with the editing. Technical assistant Pirkko Hämäläinen has been responsible for solving a number of problems involved in the editing and processing of the final text. I wish to express my warmest thanks to all who contributed to the book in some way or another for their valuable assistance.

Espoo, 25th November 2001

Anna-Leena Siikala

Myth, Belief and Word View

ANNA-LEENA SIIKALA

What Myths Tell about Past Finno-Ugric Modes of Thinking

Myths establish a link to immutable principal events in the past and in doing so establish a social whole united by notions of common origin. They have the uncanny power of self-definition and are therefore suitable for political uses. Myths have played and still play an important role in social movements attempting to create group unity on national or ethnic grounds. Myths address both cultural and existential questions. Therefore, research into mythical traditions has been vital in analysing both the shaping of our common European history as well as the construction of national identities. The former explains the extent of classical mythology studies (see Detienne 1981), while the latter led, among other things, to the compilation of the *Kalevala* and ensuing research on its underlying source materials (Honko 1990). The study of myths has played a special role in establishing a common background for the Finno-Ugric peoples even if interest in this project had waned by the middle of this century. Since the 1980s, the study of mythical traditions has again grown in importance due mainly to the establishment of the European Union and the subsequent need to strengthen European identity. In the United States the new wave of myth research has been inspired by the ethnonationalism of the postcolonial era. Similar tendencies can be observed in the field of the Uralic mythologies: new interests both in historical and field based studies of myth are evident in different countries.

Myth, Mentality and Slowly-transforming Structures of Thought

The interest in myth studies depends on the central position of myths in world view and on its possibility to illuminate past modes of thought. By codifying the structures of a world view, myths carry mental models of the past; they are one structural manifestation of *longue durée* of culture. In addressing the prerequisites of human and social existence, the mythologies of the world revolve around the same key questions, even though the solutions may vary from culture to culture. Thus the mythologies of different cultures are not the same. Ways of seeing the world and analysing it, even making empirical judgements and thus ascribing meanings to perception vary across

Myth and Mentality
Studia Fennica
Folkloristica 8, 2002

cultures. Notions concerning the world and its phenomena are structured in different systems of knowledge and mental imagery. The most fundamental areas of cultural consciousness are related to the community's world view and basic values; mythology is constructed as a representation of precisely such basic structures of consciousness.

Discrete cultural materials and oral traditions can easily cross national boundaries. Unlike these surface elements, the structures of consciousness needed to sustain a world view and to resolve contradictions are more deeply rooted and conservative. Hence, mythology is one of the most tenacious forms of mental representation. In fact, we can even view mythology as a "long-term prison" – as Fernand Braudel characterises mentalities – which endures even the most radical historical changes and continuously carries the past into the present. Nevertheless, myths are interpreted within the framework of each culture and continually transformed according to the social context (Vernant 1992:279). The life of a mythical tradition is characterised by the inherently conservative nature of its basic structures and even themes, but at the same time these structures and themes are constantly reinterpreted in social practice (Sahlins 1985).

The line of research initiated by the Annales school in France and known as the history of mentality, aims at getting to the heart of the world of human experience and thought. Jaques Le Goff defines its scope as follows: "The history of mentalities operates on the level of the everyday and the authentic. It attacks the area not covered by history centering on the individual – it reveals the non-personal substance of the individual's thought, the substance shared by Caesar and the last of his legionaries, Saint Louis and the peasant on his land, Columbus and the sailors on his ship." (Le Goff 1978:247– 248.) It is worth pointing out that mentality historians have been interested in folk thought and in particular the field of folk belief and magic. (Cf. Ginzburg 1985/1966; Ginzburg 1988/1976; Gurevich 1990; Le Roy Ladurie 1985/1975; Thomas 1971).

The mentality historian is interested in what goes on in the minds of people in a particular era. The worlds of human experience and thought are, among other things, factors pointing to the concept of mentality. A comprehensive and uniform definition of mentality is not, however, easy to find. According to Le Goff the French *mentalité* is used in English philosophy to denote the nature of the collective mind of a people or group of peoples (1978:250). The Finnish *kansanluonne*, or "national character", is akin to the English term mentality but has gone out of use since it became charged with political undersirable overtones in the 1930s. Le Goff also mentions that the German *Weltanschauung*, which refers "to a mental universe that is at the same time both stereotyped and chaotic", comes close to the concept of mentality. A similar line is adopted by Aron Gurevich in his studies of the medieval folk mentality focusing on the world view and collective psychological disposition of medieval man. (Gurevich 1990:xvi). Instead of clear-cut theories and ideas, he is interested in implicit models of consciousness and behaviour. Also close to the concept of mentality is that of world view, although it is, due to its concentration on the cognitive aspect, more narrowly defined (Knuuttila 1989:187–196).

According to Carlo Ginzburg, the history of mentalities has been interested in the enigmatic, unconscious aspect of world view, relics of the past, archaisms, the emotional and the irrational (Ginzburg 1976:20). In this case, the scope of mentality studies approaches that of mythology studies. Michel Vovelle, in turn, prefers the formulation of Robert Mandarou: mentality refers to "visions of the world", but he admits that this attractive formulation is undeniably vague. He states that "we have progressed from a history of mentalities which, in its beginning, essentially stuck to the level of culture, or clear thought, to a history of attitudes, forms of behaviour and unconscious collective representations" (Vovelle 1990:5).

It becomes evident upon examining the multitude of definitions for "mentality" that this term is a problematic concept if we wish to use it in analytic work. It hints – as does the term world view – at a totality, an integrated whole which is not easily resolved into meaningful elements. For this reason, mentality as a concept serves most often as a heuristic tool for an interpretative mind interested in shared forms of thought and experience as well as attitudes toward life, values and emotions. The concept refers to the mental contents that guide the everyday actions of ordinary individuals and that are sometimes conscious, sometimes unconscious. Lucien Febvre gives them the name "mental equipment".

Mentality thus comes close to the collective consciousness of Émile Durkheim that has moulded the course of research. The representations of collective consciousness are, according to Durkheim, social in their origin (1980:32). To Durkheim 'social' also means 'historical':

> The collective representations are the outcome of a vast process of working together with a temporal and not only a spatial dimension; in order to form them, numerous minds have combined, compounded and classified ideas and sentiments; in them many generations have stored their experiences and their knowledge (1980: 37).

One possible approach – as I have myself realised – to unravelling the conceptual entity of mentality has been the application of cognitive theory. Mentality, mental equipment, can then be conceived of as a set of cognitive, phenomenal, action-governing models for analysing the world. Cognitive anthropology refers to these models by using the terms cultural model, folk model and mental model (Siikala 1992). Mentality or collective awareness can be regarded as consisting of these models. By means of cultural models, mentality or collective awareness organises and creates the manifestations evident in culture; it also becomes fixed and transmitted along with these visible representations.

Historians of mentalities have pointed out the supra-individual nature of mentalities. In accordance with the Durkheimian tradition, the Annalists conceived of mental forms as a set of collective obligations and norms linking individuals together into a community (Hagen 1984:7). Collectivity is in the abstract sense nevertheless something of a problem. Carlo Ginzburg has drawn attention to the generalising way in which the historians (and Lucien Febvre in particular) have, with no concern for social strata, brandished the concept of collective mentality (Ginzburg 1988:20–21). We may well ask "whose mentality?"

In addition to the collective nature of mentalities, researchers have stressed their resistance to change. Jaques Le Goff points out that the history of mentalities is the history of the slowness of history (1978:257). Mentality researchers have been interested in the continuities involved in history – in tradition, thought and modes of behaviour which appear to be spontaneous but which have their origins in the distant past and which reflect the philosophical outlook of bygone eras (Le Goff 1978: 249). E. Le Roy Ladurie speaks of "mental barriers" which cannot be crossed by thought, while Fernand Braudel calls mental structures "long-term prisons" (Peltonen 1988:277). Being slow to change, he says, mental structures pose "obstacles and limitations" which man and his experience is incapable of overcoming (Manninen 1989:66). Jaques Le Goff concretises the mode of existence which drags the past along in its wake as follows: "Man uses the machines he has created, yet at the same time preserves the mentality he had before them. The motorist speaks in the words of the horseman and the 19th century factory worker has the peasant mentality of his fathers and forefathers." (1978:249.)

Elsewhere, however, Le Goff observes that the history of mentality is not only the history of the slowness of history but also the history of change (1978:257). Instead of emphasising the static nature of the factors characterising mentality, it would be more in order to debate the way in which they change. The slow pace at which mentalities change does not surprise the folklorist as much as it does the scholar studying the history of thoughts and ideas. One of the characteristic features of popular world view is syncretism, which involves a multiplicity of origins, the peaceful coexistence of numerous ideals, beliefs and concepts – some of them contradictory – assimilated from different sources and different times (cf. Redfield 1989:54; also Bloch 1968:129).

One important observation as regards mythology and folk belief studies concerns the longevity of the belief tradition and the slow rate at which it changes. Changes in mentalities may be concretely observed by interpreting the cultural products generated by them. Both written and oral texts offer insights into the minds of people representing different eras. Mythic traditions have been slow to change; they carry voices from the ancient past to the present day. We can try to trace the roots of our world view by listening to this voice. Research in Uralic and Finno-Ugric mythology has attempted to map out ancient modes of thought by analysing the common features of materials collected over the past two hundred years among the ethnic groups in question. Recent developments in linguistics and archaeology have provided new tools for this work. We may ask, what was the world view or mentality of the early Finno-Ugric or Uralic peoples, what were the mythic models of thought among the linguistic ancestors of the Finns?

Common Roots of the Finno-Ugric Mentality

The multidisciplinary symposium entitled *Suomen väestön juuret* ("The origin of the Finnish people") held at Lammi on 8–10 November 1997 challenged established notions within studies of Finnish mythical traditions.

The interdisciplinary consensus connecting Finno-Ugric speakers with East-European Comb-pit Ceramic archaeological cultures (Häkkinen 1996:73) and above all the location of the early Indo-European language speakers in the neighbouring areas on the Russian steppes provide new substance for reconstructing the background of the Finno-Ugric mythical tradition. An analogous case for the study of Uralic and Finno-Ugric prehistory is provided by comparative and multidisciplinary research on Austronesian cultures in which the research, based previously on archaeology and linguistics, has expanded to include the examination of cultural and social phenomena, genetics and surviving historical documentary materials.

Comparative studies have demonstrated that the mythical motifs found in the Kalevalaic epics which depict the emergence, structure and creation of different cultural phenomena are part of a widespread international tradition. Parallels can be found both in Uralic and Indo-European, as well as in more distant Asian and even Native American cultures. The significance of these parallels for the understanding of pre-Christian cultures and their world view is a difficult research problem. Nevertheless, mythology consisting of narrative motifs, mythical imagery, symbols and significant concepts can be regarded as a type of language or system of coding which has its own characteristics. This notion opens up the possibility to analyse, through comparative research of mythical traditions and their motifs, imagery and concepts, a strata of traditions extending in different directions which corresponds to the subgroupings of languages based on the results of comparative linguistics.

While many fundamental questions remain under discussion, including where the Uralic languages were spoken and over how large an area, a common vocabulary reveals quite clearly what kind culture speakers of early Uralic and Finno-Ugric languages possessed. As Kaisa Häkkinen has pointed out, pan-Uralic vocabulary fragments indicate "a language used by a society living in the relative North which practised hunting and fishing at a Stone Age level of development" (1990:176). In seeking the roots of Finnish shamanism on the basis of comparative research (Siikala 1992), I came to the conclusion that the oldest layer of religious imagery does not represent an Arctic but a Subarctic culture, existing in the milieu of the northern "taiga" type. It was a culture, furthermore, in which waterways occupied an crucial role. This is well suited to the framework of the vocabulary presented by Häkkinen, even if it must be kept in mind that the meaning of a word may shift in the course of cultural or ecological change. In so far as we interpret Uralic and Finno-Ugric vocabulary on the basis of information concerning northern hunting and fishing cultures, whose environment and subsistence modes make them useful points of comparison, we can attempt to describe these ancient cultures in more detail.

It is characteristic of the hunting and fishing cultures of northern Eurasia that they exhibit a vast range of detail within surprisingly similar basic structures. The variety of detail can be traced back to traditional orality and the absence of a codified educational system, while the structural resemblance is connected to similarities in subsistence modes and ecological conditions, but can also be seen to derive from highly archaic models of thought. Early

Uralic hunting and fishing cultures can be assumed to have contained similar cosmological structures and mental models regarding the other world, the nature of humans and their relationship to their environment, as well as animal ceremonialism and shamanistic practices.

Cosmological concepts

Concepts and images regarding the structure of the cosmos are some of the oldest common legacies in the Eurasian area. The Northern person observing their world from the centrality of their own vantage point saw the fixed point of the cosmos in the stationary North Star, around which revolved the redundant constellations. Finnish terms for the Polar Star – the "navel of the sky" (*taivaan napa*), the "pivot of the North" (*pohjan tappi*) and the "nail of the North" (*pohjan naula*) (Harva 1948:43) – which find parallels in the Sami language (Pentikäinen 1995:130) show that the North Star was thought to fix the sky in place. The concept shared among the Sami, Nganasan (Gračeva 1989:234; Kort & Simchenko 1985:179, 246) and Finns, according to which the sky was held up by an enormous pillar reaching from the earth to the center of the sky, often precisely to the North Star, is known in many areas of Eurasia.

In northern Eurasian and Native America, we encounter two different but often variously intertwined concepts of the structure of the universe. According to the vertical model, the cosmos consists of three primary levels. The upper and lower worlds are themselves divided up into levels whose numbers vary from culture to culture. What unites these cosmic levels and provides passage between them is the central axis of the universe, the world pillar, world tree or world mountain, beneath which is located the lower world, and from whose top or peak begins the road to the upper world (Harva 1920; Eliade 1964:367 ff). In Central and Northern Asia, as in India and Northern Europe, it was believed that the center of the world was located in the North. There also lay the extreme edge of the human world, which was conceived of as an ocean, river or the abrupt end of the earth (Harva 1948:42–51; Eliade 1964:270–271).

According to the horizontal model, the world inhabited by humans was thought to be a sort of disc-shaped surface, similar to the floor of a circular tent, over which the sky curved like the dome of a tent cover. Izmail Gemuev (1990), an expert in Mansi culture, has interpreted the *kota* with its central pillar as the model for the structure of the cosmos. Within the microcosm of the *kota*, the central support pole corresponded to the world pillar, the roof of the *kota* to the celestial dome, and the different parts of the *kota* to the four points of the compass. One reached the other world from the point at which the earth and sky converged as if from underneath the tent-flap. Uno Harva considerered the multi-level view of the world to be a borrowing by Western Turkic peoples from more southern civilizations. Harva, however, does not take note of the fact that this view of the world known from Finnic tradition is also found among the Arctic Nganasan (Gračeva 1989:237) and Chukchi (Bogoras 1904–1909:331). Both models of the structure of the universe, the vertical and the horizontal, are widely distributed in Europe and are part of a world view which, in its essential features, is probably extremely ancient. In reconstructing the Proto-Uralic world view, V.V. Napolskikh (1992) started out, like Aleksandra Ajkhenvald, Eugene Helimsk and Vladimir Petrukhin (1989:157) from a multilayered view of the universe. Napolskikh (1992:11–13) also combines the vertical and horizontal models of the cosmos. The position and epithets he reconstructs for the Proto-Uralic underworld correspond to later concepts among the Evenk: it is situated in the North, at the mouth of a river, in the cold sea, and is located underground. The upper world is situated to the south, at the source of a river, on a mountain, or in the heavens. Shamans and spirits could slip into the lower world through a hole located at the world's center, at the base of a pole corresponding to the central vertical pillar of the tent. According to the Evenk, this passage to the lower world could be found in whirlpools formed by river currents, for instance.

In Northern hunting and fishing cultures, the horizontal level was not a flat, undifferentiated surface but was composed of cardinal points and the directions of the winds, each with its own cultural meaning. Galina Gračeva (1989:233–235), for example, sees the horizonal aspect as emphasized in the world view of the Nganasan, in which the world is conceived of as four-cornered. The north-south and east-west divisions are apparent among the Nganasan in how they utilize space in the *kota*, and in norms and taboos related to movement and location. In terms of symbolism regarding life and death, these crucial north-south and east-west axes structure the world view of other Uralic groups as well. The stress laid on the four points of the compass, and the importance of the sun among Arctic peoples is also reflected in the images of the cosmos which decorate the heads of Sami shamans' drums (Manker 1938, 1950; Sommarström 1987).

The plotting of cardinal directions intrinsic to the horizontal level is also linked to the careful depiction of the roads, paths and passages of the other world commonly found in Siberian shamanism, a precision which reflects a hunting and fishing way of life. The conceptual geography of the "other side" is reminiscent of the topography of the human world. Among the Nganasan, the directions of these paths are determined by the cardinal points and directions of river flow (Gračeva 1989). The paths taken by celestial objects in the night sky, and the flow-direction of major rivers emptying into the Arctic Ocean are an important part of Arctic peoples' experiences of space and time.

The direction of death, soul-concepts and the land of the dead
Among the peoples of northern Eurasia, the location of the land of the dead was primarily the cold and dark North, while more southerly groups had their land of the dead in the direction of the setting sun, or the West. But Arctic peoples are known to have sometimes located their land of the dead in the West as well (Gračeva 1989). Unlike shamans, the dead did not have to rely on finding the road to the other world themselves. Different waterways, rivers and lakes, formed the route to the other world among Western Siberian peoples (Harva 1933:15, 232; Veres 1989:166 ; also Lehtisalo 1924:133). The water route leading to the other world, particularly the land of the dead, may be a feature shared by all Uralic groups. The concept is also found

among the Balto-Finnic groups and the Komi (Semonov 1985:173–174) as well the Ob-Ugrians, for whom the land of the dead was located on an underwater island in the Arctic Ocean at the mouth of the River Ob. The use of the boat as a coffin is based on the idea of the deceased person's journey over the water to the other world (Karjalainen 1918:105–106; Napolskikh 1992:7). It was natural, following this line of thought, that the dead would be buried near waterways (compare Finnish island cemeteries, of which there are mentions in 17th century Savo court records, for instance).

In addition to the concept of the distant land of the dead, it was typical of Northern hunting and fishing cultures in Siberia that there existed a vast array of dwelling places for the deceased. Thus it is possible that Finno-Ugric peoples, too, had their own unique beliefs concerning a heavenly land of the dead even before the advent of Christianity. In a hunting and fishing culture, it was not desirable for the dead person to linger long near the grave site. If the transition was difficult, the shaman might accompany the dead person's soul on its journey to the land of the dead. The relationship of hunting peoples to their dead is clearly more filled with fear and dread than in the case of farming peoples. The graves of the Comb-Ceramic culture (Pihlman 1981) were characterised by the use of red ochre, fire, stone structures and the practice of covering the deceased's head with stones, all of which may represent self-protective measures (Gračeva 1989:234). It is also interesting that the bodies in the graves were positioned with their feet pointing north, and that the graves were located along waterways. These features refer to the aforementioned concepts of the direction and nature of the land of the dead. Among the Nganasan, a living person was not allowed to lie down with their feet pointing north or west, the directions of death (Gračeva 1989:234).

In the grave, the covering of one part of the body, for example, the head, with stones, points to the complex concept of the soul typical of Northern hunting and fishing cultures. Within the concepts of different groups, the parts of the soul, the number of souls, and their location in the body varied. But what these hunting and fishing cultures of northern Eurasia nonetheless had in common was the idea of a soul that could leave the body and move about independently during sleep, trance or illness. On the other hand, there was also a soul that remained within the body: the Hanti word *is-*, the Mordvin *eś*, Komi *ač*, Sami *(j)ieš* and Finnish *itse* all show that these groups once possessed a dualistic concept of the soul (Häkkinen 1990:185). The Mansi term *is* means a shadow, for example the shadow of a tree or a house, but also the "ghost" or spirit of both a living being and a dead person. The Finnish word *itse* has narrowed to refer to "self, consciousness". The underlying notion here is that the mobile part of the soul or the spirit which detaches from the person during dreaming, for example, represents a person's conscious self or ego (Harva 1948:249–251). The term which referred to the corporeal soul, or soul element vital to sustaining life, was *löyly* ("sauna steam" in modern Finnish). The word *löyly*, which originally meant "breath" or "spirit" (compare Sami *liew'lâ*, Komi *lov*, Udmurt *lul*, Mansi *lili*, and Hungarian *lélek*; Häkkinen 1990:183) is of Finno-Ugric origin. This so-called dualistic, or better yet, pluralistic concept of the soul belongs to the most archaic and fundamental layer of thought and forms a background for animal ceremonialism and shamanistic rites rooted in the Paleolithic Era. In the Finno-Ugric region, the most common form adopted by the soul travelling to the other world was the bird (Haavio 1950). Concepts of the soul-bird form one cornerstone of bird mythology.

The direction of life and bird mythology

Numerous researchers have taken note of the decorations which adorn containers produced by the Comb-Ceramic culture, decorations which appear to depict waterfowl. In Northern areas, the return of migratory birds heralded the arrival of spring, and even today, the Northern Hanti celebrate the return of the birds in one of the most important gatherings of the winter-spring period. In the beliefs of the Ob-Ugrians, the wintering place of migratory birds, which they reached by slipping under the edge of the sky (Karjalainen 1918:399), has parallels among the Chukchi (Bogoras 1904–1909:237) and numerous other groups in northern Siberia. The Finnish concept of the *Lintukoto*, which is located in the South or Southwest, and to which birds migrate in the winter, is one variant of the image complex held by Finno-Ugric peoples concerning the southernly wintering land of the birds (Harva 1948:58–61).

The migration of water birds, which marked the coming of spring and was important for subsistence, is also immortalized in astral mythology. The Milky Way, for example, was known to Finno-Ugric peoples as the Course of the Bird (*Linnunrata*) or Path of the Wild Goose (Napolskikh 1992:6–10). The symbolic value of birds varies somewhat among different peoples; nonetheless the swan occupied a central role in the mythologies of many Uralic peoples. The importance of the migration of water birds in astral mythology suggests the antiquity and cultural significance of bird symbolism.

Mythology concerned with birds and the World Tree is linked to descriptions of life-sustaining forces. A significant feature in the mythologies of the Uralic peoples has been the role of the female as ruler over life, death, and the directions which symbolize them, south and north (Siikala 1996; Napolskikh 1992). The information collected by Vladimir Napolskikh concerning mythology among the Mansi, Nganasan, Selkup and Volga-Finnic groups shows that the complex of images and concepts dealing with the southern abode of the birds is associated not only with the life-giving Mother figure, who very often represents the sun, but also with a variant of the World Tree, the Tree of Life, which among many peoples is depicted as a birch. For many Uralic groups, this image complex includes the reservoir of unborn children's souls awaiting birth in the other world, as well as a mythical bird as incubator and then transporter of these souls; these models of thought are known from throughout Siberia (cf. Friedrich-Buddruss 1955:156). The antiquity and importance of the *south – sun – mother – birch – water/ migratory birds – soul repository* image complex can be seen from the fact that the terms *koivu* (birch) and *suvi* (summer, thaw) are among the few terms representing the common vocabulary of the Uralic peoples (Häkkinen 1990:170). The common Finno-Ugric vocabulary, on the other hand, contains the "pochard" (*sotka*) of the world creation myth, whose cognates among related peoples refer to other diving birds such as mallards and mergansers (Häkkinen 1990:180). Among the Finns, the southern land of the sun could perhaps, in addition to *Lintukoto*, also be *Päivölä*. It seems natural to consider the obstacle in Lemminkäinen's journey to the banquet at Päivölä farm, the giant birch on whose top perched an eagle, as linked to the aforementioned themes, even if the topos has shifted to a depiction of the dangers lurking on the road to the other world. In Finland, however, the female sun-deity *Päivätär* was not the focus of a cult, as she may have been replaced in the Middle Ages with the Virgin Mary, who represented life force and was called upon for aid in childbirth.

The Uralic myth *The Theft of the Sun and Moon,* which deals with the problematics of cosmos and chaos; is associated with solar and lunar mythology in general (Ajkhenvald, Helimski & Petrukhin 1989:159) and was preserved in Kalevalaic poetry in two versions: one which adhered to the older Balto-Finnic ethnic religion, and a Christianized version. The counterforce to the Mother of Life, that is, the ruler of death and illness, is also depicted among Uralic peoples as female. The clearest example of a northerly realm of bitter cold, death and illness is the Land of the North *(Pohjola)* encountered in Kalevalaic epic and incantation, whose ruler is the female *Loveatar* or *Louhi.*

Myths of world creation, according to which the cosmos was born from the pieces of a broken egg or from mud dredged from beneath the waters by a water bird, are associated with bird mythology. Juha Pentikäinen makes a connection between the World Egg Myth of Kalevalaic poetry and the petro-glyphs near Lake Onega (1995:109). The World Egg Myth is not, however, part of the oldest Finno-Ugric tradition. The creation of the world from the broken shell of a primeval egg is a myth widely dispersed throughout the world, whose links to Indian tradition were demonstrated by Herman Kellgren already in 1849 and by Otto Donner in 1863. The myth is also known from the Avesta. Pentti Aalto (1987:85–86) points out that only in the Iranian and Finnish myths is the World Egg associated with a bird, and he therefore judges the myth to be a legacy from the Proto-Aryan period. The Proto-Uralic tradition, on the other hand, according to studies made by Vladimir Napolskikh, has included an even more broadly distributed myth – stretching across Siberia and to the Americas – that of the Diver-Bird, in which the creator god asks a water bird to bring Earth up from the bottom of a primordial sea.

Beings which regulate human life
The critical supernatural beings from the perspective of people in Northern hunting and fishing cultures are relatively similar in their basic nature and classification, even if features and names of individual beings vary. The highest beings, which function at the greatest distance from humans, are associated with natural phenomena and points of the compass. Of these, the one with the broadest influence is the ruler of the heavens, which over the last centuries has taken on the attributes of the Christian God, but who may have earlier been the personification of the sky itself. Ajkhenvald, Helimski

ja Petrukhin (1989:159) have pointed out the supposition according to which the Mansi term *numi* "higher, heavenly" (cf. Numi-Torəm), the Hanti *num*, (cf. Num-Jelam) and the Samoyed **num* "God, heavens, weather" can be traced back to the Proto-Uralic name for the sky god.

The names for supreme deities (demiurge, the lord of the heavens, weather god) which derive from the Finno-Ugric proto-language are the Finnish *Ilmarinen*, the Udmurt *Inmar*, the Komi *Jen(m)*, and the Hanti *Num-Jelam*, all of which can be traced back to words meaning "sky", "air" or "weather". Ajkhenvald, Helimski ja Petrukhin (1989:158–159) consider it significant that between the Finno-Ugric **(j)ilma* and the Volga-Finnic terms referring to god or supreme god (Finnish *jumala*, Estonian *jumal,* Sami *ibmel,* Mordvin *jumi-si-paz,* Mari *jumo*) an alliterative consonance predominates. However, it is not clear whether these terms reflect an Aryan source (an established epithet for Indra is *dyuman* "bright, clear"). The authors propose, in fact, that in both Proto-Uralic and Proto-Finno-Ugric mythology the sky god and supreme god have been counterbalanced by opposing, evil forces. It is interesting that the former group of names discussed above are ancient indigenous words, while the latter are adopted from outside groups and represent an apparently competing religious system.

The earliest concepts connected to the thunder deity may have been represented in Eurasian and American images of the thunderbird. V.V. Ivanov and V.N. Toporov (1974) have shown that the thunder god tradition in Europe has received influences from the Baltic and Slavic cultures. The Finnish thunder god *Ukko,* and *Horagalles* of the Scandinavian Sami have been shaped not only by Baltic influences but also by Scandinavian images. *Tiermes,* known among the Sami living in Kuola and on the Ruija coast, may be related to the names of the Hanti god *Turem* and the Mansi god *Torem.*

In the Uralic language area, the sky god was seen to have a less immediate and concrete impact on people's lives than nature spirits, animal spirits and the spirits of deceased ancestors, which even today occupy an important status in the life of many ob-Ugrian and Samoyed groups. The anthropomorphic idols discovered in Finnish archeological sites can most often be interpreted as nature spirits and guardian spirits of home and kingroup. It is worth noting that clay idols in human form produced by the Comb-Ceramic culture (Huurre 1979:62) may have been dressed in animal furs.

Animal ceremonialism and astral mythology
Not only sacrificial offerings but also the bones of hunted game animals were brought to the place dedicated to the guardian spirit of a particular animal species. The notion underlying this practice was that the existence of a species of animal could be safeguarded by returning the slaughtered animal to the spirit responsible for watching over that species. The return of certain parts of the animal's body meant the return of the soul to its original home so that it could be born anew. The most important ritual manifestation of animal ceremonialism is the complex of myths and rites surrounding bear-killing among the Finns, Sami and Ob-Ugrians. The return of the animal's bones and other body parts to its guardian spirit in order to promote its

rebirth diverges in terms of its underlying motivation from sacrifice proper, even if these two types of ritual may be very similar in terms of formal features. In fact, this ancient legacy of hunting rituals later survived in the context of sacrificial ceremonies. Rituals known from northern Eurasia to North America which ended by returning the bones of slaughtered animals, were repeated whenever a large or rare game animal was killed (Paproth 1976). Such animals included the bear and elk. Herd animals such as the deer, on the other hand, became the objects of ritual handling during hunting only when they were the hunting season's first kill or the first animal from its herd to be brought down.

The guardian spirits responsible for the continued existence of game animals might appear to people in the form of the species they protected. The guardian spirit of the most powerful and most important game animals might develop into a figure known to protect all species of forest fauna. In hunting and fishing cultures, animal ceremonialism is connected to totemism. The totemic animal is described in Ob-Ugrian myths, for example, as the progenitor and protector of the entire kin group.

The astral mythology of hunting and fishing cultures is animal-oriented. Its events, immortalized in the constellations of the night sky, depict the activities most vital to the continuance of life. The special status of the bear and the elk in the mythology of the Uralic peoples, as among Siberian hunting cultures more generally, can be seen in the important role they play in astral mythology. Jouko Hautala (1947) has shown that the theme *The Ski-Chase to Catch the Hiisi-Elk is* based on the northern Asian and American myth of Orion. The Sami mythology related to the same theme can be compared to the Finnish-Karelian myth, which includes the making of the skis and the skiing episode which follows. According to J.A. Friisi, the Sami *Kalla barnek*, or Sons of Kalla are the mythical inventors of the ski. The Finnish-Karelian tradition, however, does not contain the theme of taming the elk encountered in Sami mythology. The Sami not only link this cosmic theme of the elk chase to the constellation of Orion, but to the Pleiades and Arcturus as well (Pentikäinen 1995:137).

Shamanism
Within those cultures characterized by the religious system described above, one of the best-known institutions is shamanism. The shaman's role was to be in direct communication with supranormal beings in order to resolve crisis situations. Central tenets of shamanism include the concept of a soul which can move freely outside the body, the shaman's alliance with helper-spirits, his ability to shape-shift, and his journey to the other world while in a state of trance (Siikala 1992). These features also apply to the early shamanistic institutions of the Uralic peoples. The Finno-Ugric word *nojta*, which has cognates in Mansi (*najt*), Sami (*noai'de*), Estonian (*noid*) and Finnish (*noita*), means a shaman capable of achieving trance and communicating with spirits. The Finnish tradition, too, contains depictions of shamanistic journeys to the other world. Many features of Finnish shamanism point to the shamanistic complex of subarctic forested regions (Siikala 1992:292–293), for instance the shamanic institution of the Evenks.

Common features can also be found from Arctic shamanism, however, and some of these features were transmitted through the Sami. Hallmarks of the Sami *noai'de* institution include the central role played by visionary trances, the journey of the soul, and helper spirits in animal form, as well as the broad functions of the shamanistic institution and its cultural importance (Hultkrantz & Bäckman 1978). As such, the Sami institution differs markedly from shamanistic practices in the coniferous forest zone. Arctic features include a scarcity of information concerning the shaman's costume, and the practice of untying the belt and other fastened pieces of clothing during the shamanic session. The anthropomorphic helpers of the Sami *noai'de* who live in the mountains or in a two-bottomed lake may be indigenous to the Sami, although the idea of a mountain as a dwelling place in the other world is considered a Scandinavian loan. Both *Saivo* or *Bisse*, the holy mountain in which the helper spirits known as *gadse* resided, and the totemistic context of the eastern Sami *kaddz* spirits (Pentikäinen 1995:148) may have been part of an ancient Arctic tradition which was transformed under the influence of pan-Scandinavian thinking concerning *spiritus familiares*.

The Structure of Uralic Mythology and the Transformation of Tradition

I have characterized the Finno-Ugric hunting and fishing cultures as fitting the framework of the Comb-Ceramic and Pit-Ceramic cultures of Eastern Europe and the Urals. The earlier Uralic-language culture was, in its general outlines, a similar sort of Northern hunting and fishing culture. Thus the structural hallmarks of the mythology characteristic of such Uralic and Finno-Ugric cultures are linked to the demands of a nature-oriented way of life and observation of both nature and the paths and positions of the stars in the night sky. For many cosmological myths and images documented among Uralic peoples, analogous forms have been discovered from such a broad area that these traditions have been considered age-old, stretching back in time as far as the Stone Age. Thus they can also be considered in all likelihood to have been part of the culture of those peoples speaking the early Proto-Uralic language.

In addition, Uralic mythology as a whole appears to form a world view built on intertwined complexes of mental images and reflecting the mentality of hunters and fishers. Its cosmographic features include a world view centered on the North Star, the syncretic fusion of horizontal and vertical models of the world, an emphasis on the north-south axis as well as the importance of waterways in linking this world and the next. The north-south axis is also emphasized in depictions of the forces associated with life and death. The centrality of (water) birds reflected in astral mythology is connected to the cult of the sun as well as a female life-giver, whose attribute is the birch, a variant of the world tree. Categories of the supranormal have undergone continuous alteration under the influence of neighboring religions, so that it is difficult to identify divine beings leading directly back to the Uralic period. Beliefs held in common, however, include the concept of the sky-god, female deities having power over life and death, and above all the nature spirits and animal spirits essential to a hunting and fishing culture. Uralic peoples have also shared the fauna-centered astral mythology peculiar to Eurasian hunting and fishing cultures as well as the complex view of the soul which underlies both animal ceremonialism and the shamanic institution.

Elements of a mentality reaching back to early hunting and fishing cultures were best preserved among those groups for whom these modes of subsistence were of continued economic importance. The most significant rupture in this mode of thinking occurred during the transition to agriculture. The transition was nonetheless so gradual, and left ample room for the continuation of hunting as a supplementary form of subsistence, that the foregoing themes and images of mythology survived for millenia. Even if many features of livelihood and habits in the Finnish-Karelian culture area were fairly modern, seers, hunters and fishermen maintained age-old traditions found among other Finno-Ugric and Uralic cultures. The basic elements of Uralic mythologies were preserved, for example, in the Finnish-Karelian epic and incantation poetry: these included cosmological beliefs, animal ceremonialism, especially bear rituals and myth, astral mythology (involving the elk and bear), bird mythology and the female mistress of sun and south, features of shamanism, among others.

Cultural contact and dominant religions transform mythic traditions by eradicating the old and introducing new elements. But the way in which change occurs in models of mythology and folk belief – both the Uralic and others – still remains a problem. The issue at stake is basically the relationship between the birth, establishment and transformation of factors characterising mentality and other structures of culture. The three-level scheme of the Annalists, in which the third level – culture – is viewed as the outcome of the social and economic level, is too mechanical to suffice on its own as an explanation for the changes encountered by mentalities (Darnton 1984:250–251). Conceiving of mentalities as "fragments of past ideologies" operating at a deeper spiritual level than the mere ideologies themselves has led scholars to view them as autonomous.

The complete absence of history in mental structures such as this is not supported by the results of comparative anthropology and ethnology. On the contrary, despite the stubborn conservatism of collective awareness, mentalities seem to differ in communities with different social and economic structures. This is evident if we look at the differences in the mythic traditions of different Finno-Ugric and Uralic groups. There are, in fact, many more differences than similarities and these reflect the history and economic and social conditions of different groups. Le Goff does indeed point out that "mentalities stand in a complex relationship to social structures, but not apart from them." The complexity of this relationship is reflected in the fact that attitudes may change in times of relative stability but remain constant in times of change (Darnton 1984:51).

We could examine the transformation of myth tradition as a dialectic process in which cultural change and new cultural contacts offer new concepts and images to replace the old ones. The mental models inherited from the past, on the other hand, provide cognitive frameworks into which these new elements are placed. The adoption of new elements thus occurs on the terms dictated by existing cultural knowledge. This can be seen particularly in concepts regarding divinities and the land of the dead. Another prominent feature of folk belief and mythology is the multiplicity of parallel images and ideas. New images combine easily with those generated on the basis of tradition.

The more vital and deeply rooted the values, attitudes and beliefs, the broader the transformation required in the culture as a whole to renew them. Elements of religion and mythical world view may have persisted despite opposition through various cultural eras. But their meanings may not necessarily have remained the same: the motifs may have been re-interpeted and re-fashioned within the confines of new cultural frames.

Recontextualisation of the Ancient Heritage in Present Day

The meanings ascribed to mythical images and poetic metaphors have varied in different cultural contexts. Mythic images, concepts and motifs derived from different epochs constitute loosely structured networks open to constant reinterpretation. The nature of mythical discourse defines the possibilities of recontextualisation (Hanks 1996:274–277) but, despite constant variation, tradition has a historical continuity. It would appear that the mental models guiding observations do not become "long-term prisons" until they have been established in a process of a constant re-interpretation as a subconscious cultural legacy or have acquired the status of a ritually revered tradition. A close relationship with nature and especially the symbolically important animals, such as the elk and bear, have preserved the important role of mythology in the context of the changing cultural atmosphere experienced by most Uralic peoples. The Finno-Ugric peoples are seen to be, for example, descendants of the bear, as suggested by the title of a book published by Pekka Hakamies in 1998. Indeed, bear rituals function as identity symbols among the present day Khanti and Mansi. They even seem to have a certain symbolic value in modern Finland, where bear rituals have been revived by students and theatre groups.

The role of myth research in creation of these "long term prisons" in our self awareness, pictures of our mythic heritage, is of course crucial and as such is an important object of study. On the other hand, the interest in mythology among artists and ethno-futurists of different Finno-Ugrian groups is a phenomenon of the modern globalising world and at the same time a mark of ethnic revival. We have to remember that the studies made on relics of the past and the creation of ideologies and movements of the present day are not separated by a gulf but are in a complex dialogue with each other. During the last century, the study of myth had an ideological function in the building of the nation state because of the special value attached to its object. Today myths give substance to different local, ethnic, social and gender groups in creating metaphors and symbols for their self awareness and identity. It is possible to obtain an insight into the nature of mythical thinking and mythic-historical discourse through fieldwork. The new field materials on Uralic mythologies open up possibilities to analyse the processes of reconstruction, recontextualisation and constant variation characteristic of mythic-historical discourse. The continuing negotiative process concerning the mythic-historical tradition leaves room for the creative imagination, which uses doubt and deviation as well as stereotypic reproduction, borrowed elements and their assimilation and adaptation to produce unique performances and new forms of art relevant to the present day. The study of the recontextualisation of heritage in these processes will be as important in future as the examination of the character of myth or the past phases of myth traditions.

Translated by Laura Stark-Arola.

NOTE

The article was first published in the volume of plenary papers of the Congressus Nonus Internationalis Fenno-Ugristarum 7.–13.8.2000. Tartu, (Pars I).

BIBLIOGRAPHY

Aalto, Pentti 1987: Connecetions between Finnish and Aryan Mythology. Studies in Altaic and Comparative Philology, A Collection of Professor Pentti Aalto' s Essays in Honour of his 70th Birthday. Studia Orientalia 59. Helsinki.

Ajkhenvald, Aleksandra – Helimski, Eugene – Petrukhin, Vladimir 1989: On Earliest Finno-Ugrian Mythologic Beliefs: Comparative and Historical Considerations for Reconstruction. M. Hoppál – J. Pentikäinen (eds) Uralic Mythology and Folklore. Ethnologica Uralica 1. Budapest

Anisimov, A.F. 1963: Cosmological Concepts of the Peoples of the North. H.N. Michael (ed.) Studies in Siberian Shamanism. Arctic Institute of North America, Translations from Russian Sources 4. Toronto, Canada.

Bloch, Marc 1968: La Société féodale. Paris.

Bogoras, Waldemar 1904–1909: The Chukchee. F. Boas (ed.) The Jesup North Pacific Expedition. Memoir of the American Museum of Natural History VII. Leiden, New York.

Carpelan, Christian 1995: Kirsi Korpela, Mistä tulit, suomalainen? Tiede 2000 4.

Darnton, Robert 1984: The Great Cat Massacre and Other Episodes in French Cultural History. London.

Detienne, Marcel 1981: The Creation of Mythology. Chicago and London.

Durkheim, Émile 1980: Uskontoelämän alkeismuodot. Australian toteemijärjestelmä. (Original 1912). Helsinki.

Eliade, Mircea 1964: Shamanism. Archaic Technique of Ecstasy. London.

Friedrich, Adolf – Buddruss, Georg 1955: Schamanengesichten aus Sibirien. München-Palnegg.

Gemuev, I.N. 1990: Mirovozzrenie mansi: Dom i kosmos. Novosibirsk.

Ginzburg, Carlo 1976: Il formaggio e i vermi: Il cosmo di un mugnaio del =500. Torino.

– 1985: Night Battles, Witchcraft & Agrarian Cults in the Sixteenth & Seventeenth Centuries. (Original 1966). Penguin Books. New York.

– 1988: Osten och maskarna. (Original 1976, see above). Stockholm.

Gračeva, G.N. 1989: Nganasan Shaman's Ways and World view. M. Hoppál – J. Pentikäinen (eds) Uralic Mythology and Folklore. Ethnologica Uralica 1. Budapest.

Gurevich, Aron 1990: Medieval Popular Culture. Problems of Belief and Perception.

Cambridge Studies in Oral and Literature Culture 14. Cambridge.

Haavio, Martti 1950: Sielulintu. Kalevalaseuran vuosikirja 30. Porvoo.

Hagen, R. 1984: Historien om mentaliteterna. Häften för kritiska studier, 1.

Hajdú, Péter 1975: Sukulaisuuden kielellistä taustaa. P. Hajdú (ed.) Suomalais-ugrilaiset. Pieksämäki.

Hakamies, Pekka 1998: Ison karhun jälkeläiset. Suomalaisen Kirjallisuuden Seura. Helsinki.

Hanks, William F. 1996: Language and Communicative Practices. Westview Press: Boulder, Colorado, USA & Oxford, England.

Harva, Uno 1920: Elämänpuu. Helsinki.

– 1933: Altain suvun uskonto. Porvoo.

– 1948: Suomalaisten muinaisusko. Porvoo.

Hautala, Jouko 1947: Hiiden hirven hiihdäntä: vertaileva kansanrunoudentutkimus. Helsinki.

Holmberg, Uno 1915: Lappalaisten uskonto. Porvoo.

Honko, Lauri 1990: Religion, Myth, and Folklore in the World's Epics. The Kalevala and its Predecessors. Mouton de Grüyter. Berlin & New York.

Hultkrantz, Åke 1962: Die Religion der Lappen. Ivar Paulson, Åke Hultkrantz – Karl Jettmar, Die Religionen Nordeurasiens und der amerikanischen Arktis. Die Religionen der Menschheit 3 (Herausgegeben von Christel Matthias Schröder). Stuttgart.

Hultkrantz, Åke – Bäckman, Louise 1978: Studies in Lapp Shamanism. Acta Universitatis Stockholmiensis. Stockholm Studies in Comparative Religion 16. Stockholm.

Huurre, Matti 1979: 9000 vuotta Suomen esihistoriaa. Helsinki.

Häkkinen, Kaisa 1990: Mistä sanat tulevat. Suomalaista etymologiaa. Helsinki.

– 1996: Suomalaisten esihistoria kielitieteen valossa. Tietolipas 147. Helsinki.

Ivanov, V.V. – Toporov, V. N. 1974: Issledovanija v oblasti slavjanskikh drevnostej. Moskva.

Kannisto, Artturi 1951: Wogulische Volksdichtung 1. Texte mytischen Inhalts. Mémoires de la Société Finno-ougrienne CI. Helsinki.

Karjalainen, K.F. 1918: Jugralaisten uskonto. Porvoo.

Kharuzin, N. 1890: Russkie lopari (ocherki prošlogo sovremennogo byta). Moskva.

Kort, I.R. – Simchenko, Yu. B. 1985: Wörterverzeichnis der nganasanischen Sprache. Berlin.

Knuuttila, Seppo 1989: Kansanomainen maailmankuva. M. Enwall – S. Knuuttila – J. Manninen (eds) Maailmankuva kulttuurin kokonaisuudessa. Jyväskylä.

Le Goff, Jacques 1978: Mentaliteterna, en tvetydig historia. J. Goff – P. Nora (eds) Att skriva historia. Stockholm.

Le Roy Ladurie, Emmanuel 1985: Montaillou, ranskalainen kylä 1294–1324. (Original 1975). Keruu.

Lehtisalo, Toivo 1924: Entwurf einer Mythologie der Jurak-Samojeden. Mémoires de la Société Finno-ougrienne 90. Helsinki.

Manker, Erns 1938: Die lappische Zaubertrommel 1. Acta Lapponica I. Stockholm.

– 1950: Die lappische Zaubertrommel 2. Acta Lapponica VI. Uppsala.

Manninen, Juha 1989: Tiede, maailmankuva, kulttuuri. M. Enwal – S. Knuuttila – J. Manninen (eds) Maailmankuva kulttuurin kokonaisuudessa. Jyväskylä.

Napolskikh, Vladimir 1989: The Diving-Bird Myth in Northern Eurasia. M. Hoppál – J. Pentikäinen (eds) Uralic Mythology and Folklore. Ethnologica Uralica 1. Budapest.

– 1992: Proto-Uralic World Picture: A Reconstruction. M. Hoppál – J. Pentikäinen (eds) Northern Religions and Shamanism. Ethnologica Uralica 3. Budapest.

Paproth, Hans-Joachim 1976: Studien über das Bärenfeste bei den tungusischen Völkern I. Bärenjagdriten und Bärenfeste bei den tungusischen Völkern. Skrifter utgivna av Religionshistoriska institutionen i Uppsala (hum.fåk.) genom C.-M. Edsman 15. Uppsala.

Peltonen, Matti 1988: Johtolankoja ja tiheää kirjausta. Mitä uutta mentaliteettien historia on tuomassa? Historiallinen aikakauskirja 4.

Pentikäinen, Juha 1995: Saamelaiset. Pohjoisen kansan mytologia. Helsinki.

Pihlman, Sirkku 1981: Esihistorialliset ruumiskuoppahautaukset uskonnon kannalta tulkittuina. Esitelmä arkeologian lisensiaattiseminaarissa 15.12.1981. Turun yliopiston kulttuurien tutkimuksen laitos. Turku.

Redfield, Robert 1989: Peasant Society and Culture. R. Redfield (ed.) The Little Community and Peasant Society and Culture. Chicago.

Sahlins, Marshall 1985: Islands of History. Chicago & London 1985.

Semonov, V.A. 1985: Nekotorye arkhaičnye predstavlenija komi po materialam pogrebal'nogo obrjada. Voprosy etnografii naroda komi. Syktyvkar.

Šimkevic, P.P. 1896: Materialy dlja izučenija šamanstva u gol'dov. Zapiski priamurskogo otdela Russkogo geograficeskogo obščestva I, 2. Habarovsk.

Siikala, Anna-Leena 1992: Suomalainen šamanismi. Mielikuvien historiaa. Helsinki.

– 1996: Kalevalaisen mytologian nainen. P. Hakamies (ed.) Näkökulmia karjalaiseen perinteeseen. Suomi 182. Helsinki.

Sommarström, Bo 1987: Ethnoastronomical Perspectives on Saami Religion. T. Ahlbäck (ed.) Saami Religion. Scripta Instituti Donneriani Åboensis XII. Uppsala.

Thomas, Keith 1971: Religion and the Decline of Magic. New York.

Veres, Peter 1989: The Mythological Background to Ethnic Names of the Ob-Ugrian. M. Hoppál – J. Pentikäinen (eds) Uralic Mythology and Folklore. Ethnologica Uralica 1. Budapest.

Vernant, Jean-Pierre 1992: Mortals and Immortals. Collected Essays. Princeton University Press. Princeton, New Jersey.

Vovelle, Michel 1990: Ideologies & Mentalities. The University of Chicago Press & Polity Press. Cambridge.

LAURI HARVILAHTI

Oču Bala

A Mythological Epic Heroine

The heroic poems about woman-warriors are a peculiar phenomenon in Altai epics. Oču Bala tells about the exploits of two heroic sisters *Oučyra-Manjy* and Oču Bala, a warrior heroine and a hunter. They find a place to settle down on the "hub of the Altai". As usually in the Altai epics, the prosperous life of the people and the "white cattle" are threatened by a hostile khan, in this case *Kan-Taajy-Bij*, messenger of Erlik, the ruler of the underworld. Most of the epic consists of battle scenes. First Oču Bala fights against *Kan-Taajy-Bij*'s son *Ak-Jalaa*. The most impressive is the fantastic description of the fight against the gigantic blue bull sent by Erlik. Only after the bull is conquered, *Oču Bala* finds a way to the domain of *Kan-Taajy-Bij*. The heroine transforms herself into a maid, and wins the khan by making the gigantic antagonist get drunk. The people are free and the golden era returns. The descriptions of the heroine are quite different from the ones of their male counterparts:

Tolo ajdy čyrailu,	Full-moon faced
Soloŋydy kačarlu	Rainbow-cheeked
Körgön pojy kök čolmondy,	Starry blue eyes
Köörkij pojy su-altyndy paatyr-kys	A fair and golden heroine
Ermektengen ermegi,	Uttering her words
Agyn suunyŋ šylyrtyndy	Babbling brooks flow
Kuučyndagan kuučyny	Speaking her speech
Pijik tuudyŋ köbygindi.	Mountain tops glisten.

Oču Bala (Gacak e.a. 1997), verses 1121–1131

It is important to mention that in Altai language there is no linguistic category for gender, except of pronouns, of course. The utmost "masculine" word *paatyr*, 'hero' can be used for both sexes, the male and female hero/heroine. Sometimes a noun denoting female gender may be added, as in the example above *paatyr-kys*, "hero-girl". This means that the same formulas and patterns can be used in various epics, although the description of the appeal of the heroine clearly indicates the gender (as above).

For the first time the epic of Oču Bala performed by Altai master singer Aleksej Kalkin was written down already in 1949 by E.I. Babaeva, an elementary school teacher from Kalkin's home district of Pasparta, and by

Myth and Mentality
Studia Fennica
Folkloristica 8, 2002

I.P. Kučijak the same year. The manuscripts were lost, but the texts were published in 1951 in Gorno-Altajsk.[1] Kalkin's version of the epic was thereafter recorded or written down five more times. The longest version recorded on tape (3622 verses) is the one published in the volume of 1997, after some cosmetic emendations it comprised a total of 3496 verses.[2] Our group (the writer of this article, the Academician V.M. Gacak and local Altai researchers Zoja Kazagačeva, Tamara Sadalova and Mira Tolbina) made the last recordings in 1996, but the singer was only able to perform short fragments. Even so, the last recordings and interviews are as such valuable. This master of the vanishing, archaic culture was documented in video at the eleventh hour with high quality equipment.

An Interview with A.G. Kalkin

In 1996 Kalkin was still able to sing short passages of the traditional heroic songs, but due to his old age and illness he was not fully able to produce the unique sound of Altai epic singing. This was the last time his songs were recorded, and the last time he performed epic songs. His son Elbek has learned the singing style, and he is interested in carrying the tradition forward to his son.

Mira Tolbina makes the following interview in Altai language. The questions were always formulated beforehand in our group meetings or in short consultations before the field work period.

Mira Tolbina: Aleksej Grigorevič, how do you keep a song in your memory?

A.G. Kalkin: Well, I do not perform only one epic song, but forty-two. All of them I know by heart. I don't perform only one song! In spite of those forty-two epics that I am able to perform, I know folktales. I perform various songs from different districts in different voices (= dialects).

Mira Tolbina: From whom have you learned to sing *kay*?

A.G. Kalkin: My father was a *kayčy*[3]. I used to sit next to him and listen. Then amongst my friends of the same age I started to tell stories myself and performed *kay*. That's the way I learned.

Mira Tolbina: Which epic was the first that you performed?

A.G. Kalkin: That was a tale called *Taptalgang*, then another one called *Bašparang*, then *Maaday-Kara*, and *Ösküs uul*. Then my father, relatives, elder people and *kayčy's* said: "Aleksej, from now on don't leave the tales anymore, keep on telling them to the children, so you'll learn how to sing and perform". And so I did learn. Then in the hospital of Gorno-Altajsk I met Ulagašev. I was singing a tale to the children, and he said: "If you will not stop singing the tales, you may earn your living that way". I was glad about his nice words, and I did not stop performing the tales. Then my songs were published in the form of books: *Očy-Pala* and *Maaday-Kara*. Somehow I felt that I became a sort of useful man for the people.

Mira Tolbina: As for the forty-two songs, is it so that all of them have not been written down, nor recorded?

A.G. Kalkin: Not all of them. Among those not recorded it would be necessary to write down *Temene-Koo, Talay-Kaan, Karaty-Kaan, Kaan Altyn, Ejen-Boodo Kaan*. But I am mostly interested only in the tales like *Boodoy-Koo, Očy-Pala, and Maaday-Kara*, those that are written in books, or published on gramophone records.

Before starting his performance Kalkin tunes his instrument and talks: "One has to give praise to the *topšuur*. There are many praise songs for the *topšuur*. And after that the tale itself follows. If you praise the instrument as is appropriate, the song proceeds well. When the great *kayčy*'s are performing *Maaday-Kara*, they always begin from his horse, the land, his two eagles, his two watch dogs, encampments, the home-country, the mountains surrounded by forest, the land, and so on. Then the song continues with other parts."

> Mira Tolbina: When your father taught you how to sing, did he tell you that you should always perform the tale until the end, the whole story?
> A.G. Kalkin: Of course he did! But when I was just beginning my training as a singer, my father went to the war. He came back with 12 wounds, with two crutches, without legs. But he returned, and continued performing the *kay*, until his death.

Kalkin tunes his instrument, and finally he is ready to start to sing *Oč̌y-Bala*. After a while he stopped playing and started to blame his instrument: "The voice of the *top* does not come out properly. And as for myself, my voice does not come either, it seems. What happened, my throat is somehow blocked? But what can you do, that's what happened". Kalkin again starts tuning the *topšuur*, and starts from the beginning the song *Oč̌y Bala*.

Oč̌y Bala by A.G. Kalkin

In the following I shall analyse a small chapter of the two performances recorded in 1996 from the beginning of the epic song *Oč̌y Bala*, performed by A.G. Kalkin. In the archives of the Upper Altai Research Centre for the Humanities there are four texts of this epic performed by A.G. Kalkin. In *The Altai Heroic Tales* published in 1997 this epic consists of 3497 verses. The following short passages from the beginning of the song are very typical of Altai epics. 1) Kalkin begins his performance by dedicating the whole song to the goddess of the mountain, and refers to her in the song as *Palam*, lit. "My child". He expresses with subtle words his wish to perform the song for the spirit. The singer assures that the song will have renewing and positive mental effects. In the lines following this dedication, 2) the narration is transferred to the mythical sphere, to the dawn of time, when none of the people living now was alive. Then 3) the singer turns to the topos of the narrative – describes the elements of the landscape, the mountains, the mythical river. In the next chapter 4) the sphere of the main hero's (in this epic as a rule, the heroine's) activities is described. In our text below the old singer used nouns that clearly refer to a male hero. The formulas of that part of the text are in fact among the most common ones in Altai epics, and the seriously ill singer was not able to pay attention to the choice of words. These "errors" serve, however, as examples of the peculiar verbalization process of an epic singer.

One of the tasks of the hero/heroine is to settle his people in places where there is enough firewood and pastures for the cattle. With symbolic formulas he thus creates a picture of the cultural sphere which has been there in the bygone days, and forms a continuum with our times in the Altai region. At the end of the short introductory part of the song 5) the singer once again stresses with a number of common epithets the mightiness of the hero (again using "male" nouns), and refers to the nomadic people's way of life. Since time immemorial the settlements and camps have left traces in the landscape.

According to Bahtin, the epics as a genre may be characterized with three features: 1) the main object is the national past. Bahtin refers to the term "absolute past" – a term used by Goethe and Schiller. 2) The point of departure for the epics is the cultural heritage, tradition, and not personal experience or invention. 3) The epic world is separated from the present time, from the time of the singer and his/her audience by means of the "absolute epic distance".[4] In his essay Bahtin discusses literary and national epics, but in many senses the categories presented above also can apply to oral epics. I should like to add that at the same time that the "absolute past" and the "absolute distance" is created, a bridge is built between the past and the present, the distance and the attendance.[5]

I shall first give in the following the English translation of the two versions performed on the same day, and thereafter the original Altai text. The variation of the formulas or parallel lines is indicated in the text by keeping similar or equivalent verses on the same line, whereas there is a blank space if in either of the versions occur differing formulas, parallel verses or additional chapters. Italics indicate minor lexical variation.

A.G. Kalkin
Oču Bala I
1.
O-o-o
Making the long night *short*
I'll perform kay – listen, my pala
Forget about heavy thoughts,
I will sing kay, may I, my pala,
Making the short dawn long,
I will sing kay, listen, my pala
Illuminating the dark thoughts
I'll perform Ülger, may I, my pala.
2.
In bygone, bygone, bygone *time*
When the people did not exist,
In early, early, early time
When none of us was here
3.
At the junction of the earth and sky
In the loins of seven mountains
On the side of a flowing-not-flowing white river,
On the plain shore,
On the side of a streaming-not-streaming blue river
On the broad branching river

A.G. Kalkin
Oču Bala II
1.
O-o-o
Making the long night *long*
I'll perform kaj – listen, my pala
Forget about heavy thoughts,
I will sing kay, may I, my pala,

2.
In the bygone, bygone, bygo-o-ne.
When these people did not exist,
In early, early, early time
When we weren't here
3.
At the junction of the earth and sky

Paatyr-hero was living.
4.
Where pasture, he placed his cattle
Where firewood, he placed his tribe
At his jurt he fed the cattle,
A tall, great kezer he was.
At his door he fed the people,
5.
He was a big man, a paatyr,
Leaving traces on the earth,
From ancient times he lives.

On the shore of seven rivers
At the base of seven mountains
Paatyr-hero was living.
4.
Where pasture, he placed his cattle
Where firewood, he placed his tribe
At his jurt he fed the cattle,

At his door he fed the people,

A.G. Kalkin
Oču-Bala I
1.
O-o-o
Usun Tündi-i *kyskartyp*
Men kailajyn tynda la, palam
Uur sanaa undukui, de[p]
[Men] kailajyn ji-be, palam.//
Kyska taŋdy mu uzadyp,
Men kailajyn tyŋda la,palam.
Karaçui sagyšyŋ jaryda
Ülger aidajyn ji-be palam.//
2.
Ozo, ozo, ozo *čakta*
Oturgan ulus jok tušunda.
Erte-erte, erte öidö
Emdigiler jok tušunda
3.
Jer-teŋeri peltirinde
Jeti taiga koltugunda-a-a,
Agar-akpas ak talaidyŋ
Ajaŋ polgon jaradynda,
Jylar-jylbas kök talaidyŋ
Jajylyp akkan peltirinde

Paatyr kiži jurtap jatty//
4.
Odorluga malyn salgan,
Odynduga jonyn salgan,
Ulaasynaŋ uilar ičken,
Ulu jaan kezer bolgon.
Ešigineŋ elder ičken,
5.
Erlü jaan paatyr bolgon.
Erčil üstün kese pasy[p]
Jebren öigö jurtai pertir//

A.G. Kalkin
Oču-Bala II
1.
O-o-o
Usun tündi *uzadyp*
Men kailajyn, tyŋda la, palam.
Uur sanaa undukui, dep
Men kailajyn ji-be, palam

2.
Ozo-ozo-ozodo -o-o,
Oturar ulus jok tušunda,
Erte-erte, erte öidö,
Emdi-i pister [jok] tušunda-a,
3.
Jer-teŋeri peltirinde,

Jeti talai jaradynda,
Jeti taiga edeginde
Paatyr kiži jurtap jatty.
4.
Odorluga malyn salgan,
Odynduga jonyn salgan,
Ulaasynaŋ uilar ičken,

Ešigineŋ elder ičken//

Already in this short passage we are able to follow the central features of the inauguration part of this archaic epic song: the dedication to the gods, the transition to the mythical beginning of the times, and (related to that) allegories, metaphors and concrete details that describe the mythical topos and the beginnings of the human activities in the bygone days. This all combines to make a bridge between the myth and the present time. That was the way everything started, and this world is a continuum of those distant times. In the third passage above the narration is placed in a mythical landscape by using traditional formulas: *at the junction of the earth and sky*, *on the shore of seven rivers* or *in the loins of seven mountains*. It is essential to pay attention to the variation in these two versions recorded on the same day. Kalkin uses in both cases the same core-formula *Jer-teŋeri peltirinde*, 'In the junction of the earth and sky', otherwise he varies the lexical elements, although the basic formulaic patterns remain the same. The following verses serve as example: *Ajaŋ polgon jaradynda*, "On the plain shore" *Jeti talai jaradynda*, "On the shore of seven rivers", and *Jeti taiga koltugunda* "In the loins of seven mountains" and *Jeti taiga edeginde* "At the base of seven mountains". In two cases the latter half of the verse – the word *jaradynda* 'on the shore' occurs exactly in the same lexical and morphological form. In the two latter verses the first half is repeated: *Jeti taiga* 'Seven mountains'. In all verses one important combining feature is the four-foot meter, which is the prevalent metrum in the tradition of "the school" of A.G. Kalkin.[6] Additionally, in all of these verses a common feature is morphological parallelism, the locative case *-da/-de* in the 4-syllabic noun forms: *peltirinde*, *jaradynda, koltugunda, edeginde*, "in the junction? "on the shore", "in the loins", at the base". In both versions the concluding formula of the 3rd passage is a common marker-type cliché *Paatyr kiži jurtap jetty*, 'Paatyr-hero was living'. It is possible to find countless examples of these kinds of formulas. The next passage describes the settlement of the people in places where there is plenty of firewood, rich pastures for the cattle and horses, an ideal landscape of the Altai region. At the same time, in just a few strokes this passage characterizes the traditional way of living and sources of livelihood: *Odorluga malyn salgan, Odynduga jonyn salgan, Ulaasynaŋ uilar ičken, Ešigineŋ elder ičken*, "Where pasture, he placed his cattle, where firewood, he placed his tribe, at the jurt (-base) he fed his cattle, at his door the people were fed".

In the above verses we also find the most typical primary poetic features of Upper Altai epics 1) two or more verses are combined with the same phoneme, syllable or lexical unit at the very beginning of the verses (anaphora): **O***dorluga malyn salgan,* **O***dynduga jonyn salgan,* 2) repeated occurrence of the same phonemes, or combinations of vowels and consonants at the beginning of two or more consecutive words in the same verse (alliteration): *Ulaasynaŋ* **u***ilar ičken,* **E***šigineŋ elder ičken,* 3) lexical, and/ or morpho-syntactical parallelism of two or more consecutive verses, sometimes with exact repetition of lexical units, as in our example:

Odorluga malyn salgan,
Odynduga jonyn salgan,
Ulaasynaŋ uilar ičken,
Ešigineŋ elder ičken.

The languages of Altai are, as other Turkic and Mongolian languages, agglutinative. In the following I will give an impression about the parallel structure of the above verses, not going into a detailed analysis of the affixes, possessive suffixes, case endings and verbal forms:[7]

Odor-lu-ga = 'to the (place) with pastures'
Odyn-du-ga = 'to the (place) with firewood'
mal-y-n = 'his cattle'
jon-y-n = 'his people'
+ sal-gan = 'he left'

Ulaa-sy-naŋ = 'from the corner of his jurt'
Eši-gi-neŋ = 'from his door'
ui-lar = 'the cows'
el-der = 'the people'
+ ič-ken = 'drank', or 'ate'

Turkic and Mongolian Ethnopoetic Models

This type of parallelism is very characteristic of the Turkic and Mongolian oral tradition. The study of Turkish and Mongolian traditions reveals parallels which can be traced to earlier Central Asian layers of mythical epic or to later cultural borrowings. Often it is impossible to distinguish these layers from one another and some of the parallels may exist due to purely typological similarities. In numerous Mongolian epic poems there exist reflected stages of development of hundreds of years: cosmogony, shamanism, history of the Mongol tribes and the cultural influence of Iran, India and Tibet. The best known of these traditions are Džangar and Geser, songs that belong to the most widespread epic traditions of the world. The epic Džangar is known among the Oirats in Northwest China, among the Kalmyks in the Volga region, in Mongolia and also among the Buriats living around Lake Baikal. Geser is mainly spread within Tibetan populations in Tibet, Mongolia, among the Buryats, but also in Nepal, Bhutan, Sikkim and Ladakh. The influence of Mongolian epics is quite substantial in the Altai area as well. Both Džangar and Geser are known as great heroes, and there are many similarities in plot structure and also on the level of lexical borrowings and poetic diction.

Similar to some of the large-scale Turkic heroic epics, the Mongolian great epics describe fights against mythical monsters, with one of the popular themes being also wooing journeys and contests. Different kinds of transformations, voyages to the Underworld and resuscitation of the deceased hero tell about parallels of the archaic nature of this epic poetry culture. Such parallels include the similarities found among depictions of basic plot development in epic poetry. From the level of basic plot structure to that of micro poetic features, the mythological Altai epic, Buryat heroic poetry, Evenk heroic legends, the Olonho poems of the Yakutians, as well as the Halha Mongol and Oirat traditions share many common traits.[8] Nevertheless, the layers of influence are many. For the most part, Altaic epic imagery derives from Siberian shamanistic traditions and hunting culture. Nekljudov provides an interesting picture of the Mongolian poetry tradition; the number of lines in the versions produced may range from more than twenty thousand among western Buryats to less than a thousand in the epic poems of the Khalkhas.[9] Buryat epic poetry has also more archaic mythical features than that of the Khalkhas and Oirats. In light of these, it should be mentioned that the longest versions of Yakut epics *olonkho* comprise 10,000 to 15,000 lines. There are even longer Yakut epic poems (or artificial conglomerates), for example the *Nürgun Bootur* by P.A. Ojunskij, a collation of 37,000 lines.[10]

The descriptions of herds of cattle and horses to symbolize the wealth of the heroes belong to a later layer of Altai (and Mongolian) heroic poetry. Many of the poems begin with a mythical golden age. The hostile khan's attack brings this happy era to an end. The hero's beloved, kin and entire community are forced to become subjects of the enemy. The loss of happiness equated with the wife, subjects, livestock and land lies at the heart of the epic conflict; reclaiming this property is thus a return to the original and harmonic world order. Although various phases of development can be discerned in nomadic epics, the fundamental pattern remains the same, except that the mythical antagonists appear (rendered with a profusion of hyperbolic images) as hostile khans closely associated with Erlik, Lord of the Underworld.

As for the analysis of the prehistory of epic plot and genres, the earliest forms are found in the "heroic folktale".[11] The heroic folktale has two key themes: 1) heroic courtship and 2) the battle against a ferocious beast or another tribe. Nevertheless, the term "heroic folktale" is misleading. An examination of several Eurasian archaic epic traditions proves that particularly heroic courtship (often based on astral mythology) and battles against mythical monsters or antagonistic tribes are general Eurasian epic poetic traditional narrative models, not only folktale elements.[12]

According to Nekljudov, on the basis of historical, typological and regional divisions one can discern three Turkish – Mongolian epic areas of distribution: 1) western (Central Eastern, the Volga region, the Caucasus, the Middle East, and the Crimean area), 2) eastern (Altaic tradition, Oirat, Halha, east and south Mongolian epic) and 3) the northern (Yakutian and Buryat epics). Nekljudov asserts that, based on the features of various stages, Mongolian epic has preserved an older layer than has the Turkic poetic tradition. According to him, the archaic nature of the Yakutian epic is more likely a result of secondary archaization. I would state that the mythologically-based epic poetry expressing the archaic world view of the Yakutians, Ehirit-Bulagat Buryats and Altaians is far more abundant (and not necessarily secondary) when compared to that of other Turkic and Mongolian peoples.[13]

NOTES

1   Surazakov 1973:442; Kazagačeva 1997:579.
2   Kazagačeva 1997:579; Gacak & Kazagačeva 1997:74.
3   A singer, using the *kay* style, a peculiar type of overtone singing.
4   Bahtin 1986:401.
5   Cf. Katašev 1995:7
6   Cf. Katašev 1988:163–165.
7   See in detail Reichl 1992:171–181.
8   Cf. Nekljudov 1984:133–139; See also Hatto 2000:131–144
9   Nekljudov 1984, e.g. p. 83
10   Puhov 1975:16
11   See Žirmusnkij 1974:337 passim.
12   See e.g. Siikala 1994:250–297. Harvilahti 1992:97–98. Finnish Kalevala meter poetry, the Šubabc epics of the Evenk's, and many other Eurasian traditions serve as examples.
13   Nekljudov 1995:10. According to Nekljudov, the roots of the Yakutian and Buryat archaic epic extend to the settlement history of their ancestors from Southern and Eastern Siberia (dating back to the 9th century). The epics of these peoples have retained all the themes found in heroic folktales, although stronger elements are that of heroism during war and collective pathos in the narrative; plot dynamics are replaced by long epic descriptions. The remarkable length of Yakutian and Buryat poetic and prose epics is also characteristic.

BIBLIOGRAPHY

Bahtin, M.M. 1986: Èpos i Roman. Bočarov, S.G. & Kožinov, V.V. (sost.): M.M. Bahtin – Literaturno Kritičeskie stat'i. Hudožestvennaja literatura. Moskva.

Gacak, V.M. – Kazagačeva, Z.S. 1997: Tekstologičeskie principy i procedury izdanija. – Gacak, V.M. (otv. red.): Altajskie geroičeskie skazanija. Pamjatniki fol'klora narodov Sibiri i Dal'nego Vostoka, T. 15. Nauka, Novosibirsk.

Harvilahti, Lauri 1992: Kertovan runon keinot. Inkeriläisen runoepiikan tuottamisesta. SKS. Helsinki.

Hatto, Arthur T. 2000: Textology and epics from Siberia and beyond. L. Honko (ed.) Textualization of Oral Epics. Mouton de Gruyter. Berlin & New York.

Katašev, S.M. 1988: Poètika altajskogo geroičeskogo èposa. Gacak, V.M. (otv. red.): Fol'klornoe nasledie narodov Sibiri i dal'nego vostoka. GANIIJALI. Gorno-Altajsk.

– 1995: Hudožestvennoe osobennosti altajskogo geroičeskogo èposa. Sadalova, T.M. (otv. red.): Gorno-Altajskij Institut Gumanitarnyh Issledovanii. Gorno-Altajsk.

Kazagačeva Z.S. 1997: (Perevod tekstov, podgotovka tekstov, stat'i o skaziteljah, primečanija, kommentarii, slovar', ukazateli imen i toponimov). Gacak, V.M. (otv. red.): Altajskie geroičeskie skazanija. Pamjatniki fol'klora narodov Sibiri i Dal'nego Vostoka, T. 15. Nauka, Novosibirsk.

Nekljudov, s. Ju. 1984: Geroičeskij èpos mongol'skih narodov. Nauka. Moskva.

– 1995: Zametki ob èpose central'noaziackih narodov. Nikulin, N.I. (otv. red.): Èpičeskie tradicii afro-aziackih narodov. Nasledie. Moskva.

Puhov I.V. 1975: Geroičeskij èpos tjurko-mongol'skih narodov Sibiri. Gacak, V.M. (otv. red.): Tipologija narodnogo èposa. Nauka, Moskva.

Reichl, Karl 1992: Turkic Oral Epic Poetry. Traditions, Forms, Poetic Structure. Garland. New York & London.

Siikala, Anna-Leena 1994: Suomalainen šamanismi. Mielikuvien historiaa. SKS, Helsinki.

Surazakov S.S. 1973: (zapis' teksta, perevod, priloženija): Maadaj-Kara. Altaj kaj čörčök. Nauka, Moskva.

Žirmunskij, V.M. 1974: Tjurkskij geroičeskij èpos. Nauka. Leningrad.

VILMOS VOIGT

Cosmographical Maps (on Stars)

Astronomical* – more precisely cosmographical – maps and other forms of charts, and globes are superb indicators of world view and its development. Notions like "above" and "below", "center", versus "periphery" or even "sphere", and "hemisphere" can be derived from such charts. As for the traditional European world view, from Ancient Greece to the Renaissance, the so-called Ptolemaic system was dominant: the Earth was the center or fixed point of the Universe, around which the heavenly bodies (stars, planets, and of course, both Sun and Moon) moved. A new system, the so-called Heliocentric system was first fully presented by Nicolaus Copernicus. His major work *De revolutionibus orbium coelestium* was printed in Nuremberg in 1543. According to his theory, the planets revolve around the Sun, and the turning of the Earth on its axis accounts for the apparent rising and setting of the stars in the sky. The same idea was expressed by Johannes Kepler in his most important book *Harmonices Mundi* (1619), which was criticized but admired and silently accepted as a theorem by Galileo Galilei in his *Dialogi sopra i due massimi sistemi del mondo* (1632). The century between Copernicus and Galileo was often characterized as one of the decisive times of change in world model paradigms in Europe. Not only the titles of some major publications, but the tone and style of these clearly show the aim to give not only a strictly astronomic or mathematic study, but also to find a universal (sometimes metaphorical) key for understanding the whole world system.[1]

Astronomical and cosmographical maps of the 16th and 17th centuries reflect the changing world models. Epistemological studies in astronomy, physics, philosophy or mapping often deal with those maps, stressing the importance of these in shaping old or new models.[2] However, to the best of my knowledge, no serious attempt has been made to interpret the maps within the framework of semiotics. Since "actual" maps of the countries and stars may be more or less accurate, I think the semiotical aspects are more obvious if we deal with clearly arbitrary sign systems. That is the reason I choose constellation maps for my first analysis.

Stars and constellations can be represented in the form of a globe. The Greek philosopher, Anaximander (6th century B.C.) spoke about the theoretical framework of such representation. Eudoxus of Cnidos, a pupil

Myth and Mentality
Studia Fennica
Folkloristica 8, 2002

of Plato, one of the most famous astronomers in the 5th century B.C., argued for a global spheric world model, with the sun, moon and the five known planets "fixed" and at the same time "moving" within that sphere. The famous marble sculpture *"Atlas Farnese"* (the only copy existing today is in Museo Nazionale in Naples, dates from the 1st-2nd centuries B.C., and follows an earlier version from the 3rd century B.C.) shows a figure of a giant holding a 68 cm wide sky-globe. From Rome we have less evidence; but from Byzantium and from the Middle Ages in Western Europe there are numerous references to such globes. There are a dozen medieval Arabic sky-globes known to us. The oldest one among them is kept at the Bibliothéque Nationale in Paris – a small one, 18 cm diameter, made by an unknown master about 1080 A.D. The end of the 15th century marked a new beginning for the golden age of such globes. Nicolaus Cusanus (Nicholaus of Cues) made a small globe –17 cm diameter –1440 in Nuremberg (today at the Kusanus-Museum in Kues) with 44 stars on it. The diameter of the globes from the 1480s is usually 40–50 cm. The famous sky-globe by Gerard Mercator (1551) was a parallel to his earth-globe. The famous astronomer and mechanic, Jost Bürgi made various astronomic globes. Two of them (by 1582/6 and 1592/4) are today in Kassel, at the astronomical-physical exhibit. All the globes present the constellations by their recognized forms and names. An early attempt was made by the Dutch theologian, P. Plancius, in 1598 to introduce new constellation figures: partly drawn from the Bible, partly of exotic animals, e.g. giraffes, unicorns among others. The illustrations were cut by Jodocus Hondius, who soon took over all the properties of the world-famous Mercator map drawings. Dutch explorers just before that time had made the first good map of the constellations of the southern hemisphere, thus Plancius could aim at a general figural reshaping of the constellations. The most famous globe of this type was made (1602) by Wilhelmus Janssonius Blaeu (1571–1638), founder of the most famous institution in old cartography, Officina Blaviana, 1603. This globe has a diameter of 34 cm, with stars of the southern hemisphere as well. Blaeu, who was a student of the world famous astronomer Tycho Brahe, in his larger globe (1616, diameter 68 cm) made a perfect world model, directly influenced, according to many historians, by the then rediscovered *Atlas Farnese* sculpture. Later, in a Baroque style, new attempts were made to reshape the constellations with figures of the coats of arms of the European ruling dynasties, or with scenes from the Bible.

Another method for charting the sky was with flat maps, first drawn and later printed. Maps were better known and accepted than globes, because it was easier to produce a two-dimensional chart than a spherical globe.

For maps and globes a common list of stars is always needed. The first major list, with names and constellation figures used in our days is usually attributed to the Alexandrian astronomer, Ptolemy (2nd century A.D.), known by the title of its Arabic and Latin translations, *Almagest*, which contains data on about 48 constellations. European scholars continued to enlarge, correct and publish it until the end of 16th century, when Tycho Brahe's new, updated list (1600) of northern hemisphere constellations appeared. For the southern hemisphere two Dutch astronomers, P. D. Keyser and F.

De Houtman compiled the first general list of stars (1595–1597). For centuries these lists served as astronomical maps, until new and richer data were collected by more modern astronomical instruments.

Names and figures for the stars are well known from all cultures of the world: for example 36 stars for Enlil, Anu and Ea from Mesopotamia, or the constellation pictures at the Hathor-Temple in Old Egypt. Greek and Roman authors refer to various stars as naming the constellations. The highly developed Arabic – and, in general, Muslim – astronomy gave names to many bright stars. There is no doubt that medieval Europe had names for most of the visible stars. Astrology contributed much to the complicated naming systems and tried to "decipher" the influence of most of the heavenly bodies.[3]

It is surprising how late the current constellation scheme was accepted in Europe – most probably in the first half of the15th century. A century later, the first printed star maps (first of all the so-called *eccliptic planiglobes* by Johannes Stabius and Conrad Heinfogeil, Nuremberg 1515) with the woodcut constellation figures drawn by Albrecht Dürer served to fix our visual image of the heaven.

Following these developments comes the work of others: Johannes Honterus, a Saxonian scholar from Transylvania, who first compiled *Rudimenta Cosmographica* (1532, printed in 1541, in Basle), the German cartographer Petrus Apianus and his *Images Syderum Coelestium* (Ingolstadt 1536), followed by his chief work *Astronomicum Caesareum* (Ingolstadt 1540); the Italian, Alessandro Piccolomini with his *De la Sfero del Mondo e Delle Stelle Fisse* (first published in 1540 with many subsequent reprints and French editions).

The most complete description was published by Johannes Bayer (Augsburg 1603, *Uranometria omnium asterismorvum* ... and various later editions), with 51 constellation figures, including also a fairly accurate description of the southern hemisphere. German, French and English astronomers of the second half of the 17th century added much to the picture of the sky.

One of the most important and perhaps the most beautiful star maps was made by the Dutch mathematician and geographer, Andreas Cellarius (working between 1656 and 1702). His publication *Harmonia macrocosmica seu Atlas universalis et novus*, first published in Amsterdam 1660, then in various reprints until 1708, is an individual variant of cosmographic descriptions. He followed the German Julius Schiller (died 1627) in attributing Biblical motifs to the stars and constellations.

Johannes Hevelius, John Seller and the famous English astronograph, John Flamsteed followed the same way. A curiosity is the *Coelum Heraldicum* by the German Erhard Weigel (published first in Jena 1688), which associates the constellations with European coats of arms. By the time of the Enlightenment and French Revolution, suggestions for new nomenclatures of the stars came into light. This time period is sadly out of the confines of the present survey.[4]

The splendid illustrations in Cellarius' work serve different purposes.[5] He gives very elaborate illustrations both for the Ptolemaic and the

Copernican system, and explains in other illustrations the Zodiac and the phases of the moon. For constellations he offers three different semiotic transcriptions. In two maps, *Hemisphaerium stellatum boreale antiquum* and *Hemisphaerium stellatum australe antiquum*, he draws the well known constellations, mostly from "Greco-Roman mythologizing" tradition; however, these are arranged from east to west – the opposite direction, to which we are used today, – and with some old names for some constellations. More important for him was to present a Christian map of the constellations –again in two maps: *Coeli stellati Christiani Hœmisphœrium posterius* and *Coeli stellati Christiani hœmisphœrium prius*, which depict Old Testament and New Testament scenes and figures from the history of the church. Noah's Ark, King David playing the cithara, the Magi, apostles and archangels, St. Helena with the Holy Cross, Pope Sylvester and St. Benedictus occur among other ecclesiastical motifs. A third interpretation is by projecting the stars' sphere on to the earthly globe. *Hemisphœrii borealis coeli et terrœ sphaerica scenographia* unites the constellations of the northern hemisphere with the outlines of the continents. *Hœmisphœrium scenographicum australe coeli stellati et terrœ* unites the constellations of the southern hemisphere with the continents of America and a very large space for "Terra Australis Incognita". Two very accurate "political" maps, with boundaries of states and territories follow that: *Hœmisphœrium stellatum boreale cum subiecto hœmisphœrio terrestri*, for northern continents and constellations, and *Hœmisphœrium stellatum australe aequali sphœrarum proportione*, attempting the same for the southern hemisphere and continents.

The ideology of Cellarius' attempt is clear and direct. The sky is a map of the earth, and terrestrial geography is represented by the constellations. And if we propose Greek and Roman myths for explaining the curious shapes of the constellations, we should also Christianize the figures of the sky-map. It is very important for us that in the same work we meet three "interpretations" of the same star distributions: an ancient (pagan, Greco-Roman), a modern (Christian) and a secular (geographic). It is like a translation of the same message in three different languages. It is difficult to imagine a better sample for the famous definition of signs: *aliquid stat pro aliquo*. In the case of geographical maps, the items exist in fact, can be explored, and are visible for the actual visitors. If in old maps Paris or Rome has a singular shape, seas and islands are spread by a special proportion, then visitors or cartographers can check the maps. The stars are far, and in fact nobody can imagine that they represent small or big she-bears (*Ursa minor, Ursa major*), the poetic horse (*Pegasus*) or the dragon-killing hero (*Perseus* and *Andromeda*). All those figures and names are but signs.

The pragmatic aspect of constellation signs is a well known phenomenon: they are maps for identifying stars and groups of stars, important for traveling, especially for navigation. It is not by chance that the same theories were made for terrestrial and celestial cartography, and that the famous cartographers of both domains were the same too.

It is easy to characterize the syntactic aspect of constellation signs. Individuals, performing simple acts (e.g. pouring water, stretching a bow with an arrow), are dominant among the visual representations. The contrasting brightness of the stars seems to be of secondary importance. Bright stars are placed on unimportant features of the pictures, and uneven representation between symmetrical picture parts (e.g. in *Cancer, Scorpius, Libra*) are very common. The syntax of the stars is not similar to that of human constructions, like houses or machines, where all the details must serve the same practical purpose. It is more akin to fantasy pictures or poems, where the next moment has a firm tie with previous one, but it is still unpredictable as to how and what comes next.

For the semantic aspects the threefold mapping (ancient, christian, geographical) is of great importance. It becomes self evident that there is no single decipherment, no unique meaning of the stars: we always face alternatives in attributing semantics to any utterance. The three semantic interpretations conflict and coincide with one another. And because the stars are finally useless, far away and silent, there is no way to demonstrate which interpretation is more or less valid. This is again a difference from geographic maps, where in principle there could be achieved a "better" semantics.

Behind this kind of "primary" semiotics of the astronomical maps, there lies in them another dimension of semiosis.

The double title of Cellarius' work (*Harmonia macrocosmica seu Atlas universalis et novus*) refers to both dimensions. The map is at the same time a "primary" picture (named here by a symbolic denomination as *Atlas*, from the giant in Classical mythology compelled to support the heavens on his shoulders, and known at least since the "*Atlas Farnese*" in European tradition), and on a "secondary" level it depicts the "Harmony of the Macrocosm". The harmony of the universe is a very old and widespread notion, known already in the Ptolemaic system, often labeled as the "Harmony of the Spheres". Pythagoreanism, with its ideas on the transmigration of the soul and belief in numbers as the ultimate elements of the universe, the theological symbolism of the heavens throughout the Middle Ages, and even musicology have frequently used the "harmonical" code of the universe. There are various ways of shaping a "harmonical system of the world". A founder of modern solmization (*solfeggio*), Bartolomeus Ramus (Bartolomé Ramos de Pareja) professor at the universities in Salamanca and Bologna, in his work *De musica practica* (written 1472, published 1482) combines "mundus et musica" in a world map. The famous German humanist Agrippa von Nettesheim in his summarizing work *De occulta philosopia sive de magia* (1531–1533) refers to music in a constant and elaborated symbolic language. Kepler's *Harmonices Mundi* (1619) is a summary of centuries' old trends in physics, astronomy, mathematics, musicology and theology. In the book he gives the musical notes of Jupiter, Mars, Mercury and that of the music of the spheres. He never revoked his early, astrological work *Mysterium Cosmographicum* (1596).[6]

Thus we can easily demonstrate that astronomical maps also present a "secondary modelling system".

Three final semiotical remarks should be made, as pointers for further, thorough research.

1. We have said at several times that "a sign" does not exist – only "systems of signs" are conceivable. For astronomical charts a very elaborate and special

grammar was needed, more complicated than that of geographical maps. For constellations, groups of stars were bound together, and in attempts to describe the movement of the heavenly bodies, it was necessary to develop a very complicated mathematical-geometrical system. One of the most industrious "sign systems" was made for the stars.

2. If we understand properly the notion of "sign system" it must be of the same level of logical complexity when we create a *significans* for the *significatum*. In maps of the heavens we must introduce the same complexity as is found in geographical maps. Only the whole world could serve as a sign for another world. When Cellarius uses in the series of his maps the term *scenographia*, or the expression "*aequali proportione*" he refers to that world model quality of the maps. In a provocative short sentence we could say that the only perfect sign system for the world is a celestial global map projected upon the geographical global map. The "harmony of the macrocosm" is due to the logical equivalence between world model *A* and world model *B*. It is not so often that we can see a perfect world model, a perfect sign system of the world. Some astronomical maps fulfill that criterion.

3. Mapping and systems of the universe are common topics in any general semiotics. Still it would be important to outline a Peircian astronomical semiotics. Everybody who is familiar with such seminal papers by Peirce as, for example, *The Fixation of Belief* (1877), mentioning as "the early scientists" Copernicus, Tycho Brahe, Kepler and Galileo; or *How to Make Our Ideas Clear* (1878), mentioning the nine different ways for measuring the velocity of light, expressing a deep knowledge of history of astronomical physics; or *The Architecture of Theories* (1891) which stresses the importance of the inauguration of dynamics to the modern scientific thought by Galileo – anyone familiar with these writings should notice how deeply Peirce understood the philosophical and methodological connotations in developing systems for the universe. Biographical data explain his keen interest of the topic. His father, Benjamin Peirce, was professor of astronomy and mathematics at Harvard. Peirce himself, working for the Coast and Geodetic Survey, at that time the chief scientific agency of the United States Government, which entrusted him with astronomical tasks, e.g. to make a trip to the Mediterranean to observe the 1870 December eclipse of Sun. The second and largest European trip of Peirce (1875–1876) was also devoted to scientific commitments: to complete photometric studies of the stars of a region of our galaxy, with a view to a more accurate determination of the shape of the galaxy. During this trip he examined medieval and renaissance manuscripts of Ptolemy's star catalogue in several European libraries. Peirce's only book published during his life time is the *Photometric Researches* (Leipzig 1878), with his own, updated edition of Ptolemy's catalogue. And if we add that before he entered the Coast Survey, he helped his father in geodetic and astronomic investigation, and served as an assistant in the Harvard Observatory, we can say that much of Peirce's life was under the signs of the stars.[7] We should construct indeed a Percian astrosemiotics, perhaps under the auspicies of an actualized macrocosmical harmony.[8]

NOTES

*   Another version of my paper was presented at the ISI Conference, 1990 in Imatra, and published in: Center and Periphery in Representations and Institutions. Edited by Eero Tarasti. (Acta Semiotica Fennica 1). I acknowledge with gratitude the permission to include into the present collection of papers too.

[1]   Because I am referring to well-known books and facts, I will give detailed source references only when necessary.

[2]   See the data in any of the handbooks of the history of mapping, e.g. Kretschmer et al. 1986. Vol.1. 293–301, with further references.

[3]   On astrology a separate study is needed. The major work on the ideological and philosophical problems of world models is still the ten bulky volumes of Duhem (1913–1959).

[4]   There is a long list of publications devoted to the history of sciences before and during the French revolution. A summarizing collective volume, with summaries of previous researches is Rashed (ed.) 1988.

[5]   For illustration I used the 1990 edition of the illustrations of Cellarius from a copy kept at the Hungarian National Library (Széchényi Library). Budapest Patay 1990.

[6]   It is interesting to notice that Eco in his sketch for a history of semiotics lists very few persons or works with astronomical connotations (Eco 1983:84): for example, under the label *"Repressed"* theories we find: Nicholaus of Cues: the system of the world as unlimited semiosis – Giordano Bruno's world – Scientific language in Galileo and the semiotics of new mathematical sciences. Astrology occurs in his checklist of terms, astronomy and mapping are absent.

[7]   Relevant data about Peirce is available in various publications. For convenience I refer here only to Fisch 1981.

[8]   In my present paper it was not my intention to give a detailed summary of cartographical semiotics. Two remarks, however, should be made. "Mapping" as a new term in semiotics – e.g. in Eco 1979:245–258, and the entry "Mapping" by Wulf Rehder in the *Encylopedic Dictionary of Semiotics* (Sebeok ed. 1986. Volume I., 481–482 etc.) refers to the relation of algebra and logics, and not to cartography. It is more important that Martin Krampen in his very informative entry "Cartography" to the above mentioned *Encyclopedic Dictionary* (Sebeok ed. 1986. Vol.1. 98–99) stresses the importance of the topic, mentioning the first suggestions to study maps from a semiotic point of view by Bertin (1967) and Palek (1980). Among his historical references early works by Bühler and Korzybski occur, and he also mentions Peirce's theoretical interest in maps. Both Krampen and the authors quoted by him worked on maps generally, and not on astronomical maps in particular, thus the topic is still unjustifiably neglected by semioticians.

BIBLIOGRAPHY

Bertin, J. 1967: Sémiologie graphique: Les diagrammes les réseaux, les cartes. La Haye. Mouton.
–   1974: Graphische Semiologie. Diagramme – Netze – Karten. Ukvests nacheder 2. Frankrisizcken Edition von 9 fenoch. Berlin.
Duhem, Pierre 1913–1959: Le système du monde: histoire des doctrines cosmologiques de Platon Copernic. Hermann. Paris.
Eco, Umberto 1979: A Theory of Semiotics. Indiana University Press. Advances in Semiotics. Bloomington.
–   1983: Proposals for a History of Semiotics. In Semiotics Unfolding. Proceedings of the Second Congress of the International Association for Semiotic Studies, Vienna, July 1979 Tasso Borbé (ed.), Vol. 1, 75–89. Mouton de Gruyter. (= Approaches to Semiotics 68). Berlin.

Fisch, Max H. 1981: Peirce as Scientist, Mathematician, Historian, Logician, and Philosopher. Proceedings of the C. S. Peirce Bicentennial International Congress. K. L. Ketner – J. M. Ransdell – C. Eisele – M. H. Fisch – C. S. Hardwick (eds) Graduate Studies Texas Tech University No. 23. September 1981, 13–34.

Kretschmer, Ingrid – Dörflinger, Johannes – Wawrik, Franz (bearbeitet von) 1986: Lexikon zur Geschichte der Kartographie. Band 1: A-L. Die Kartographie und ihre Randgebiete. Enzyklopädie. Redigiert und herausgegeben von Erik Arnberger. Band C/1/. Franz Deuticke. Wien.

Palek, Bohumil 1980: An Analysis Of Map Signs. Paper for the Conference held at the Symposium on Theoretical Semiotics: Verbal Signs – Visual Signs. Warsaw, September 23–24, 1980.

Patay, Klára 1990: Csillagtérképek 1990: Budapest. Képzomuvészeti Kiadó.

Rashed, Roshi (ed.) 1988: Sciences à l'époque de la Révolution française. Paris. A. Blanchard.

Sebeok, Thomas A. (ed.) 1986: Encyclopedic Dictionary of Semiotics. Vol. 1–3. Mouton de Gruyter. Approaches to Semiotics 73. Berlin – New York – Amsterdam.

MIHÁLY HOPPÁL

Linguistic and Mental Models for Hungarian Folk Beliefs

"Now faith is the assurance of things hoped for, the conviction of things not seen." Thus the Bible (Hebrews 11.1) aptly defines one of the indirectly acting, highly elusive phenomena of culture. The world of opinions, knowledge, cognition, insights, assumptions, prejudices, faiths and beliefs plays a crucial role in every culture, their operation pervading every moment in the life of the individual. In this paper I focus on how the belief system functions. Within the theoretical framework of (ethno-) semiotics the present paper might be described as one which is concerned with pragmatics, i.e., the use of signs, how beliefs are used. The material for analysis comes from the world of the traditional peasant. These examples, I believe, have the validity of the model and are thus suitable for illustrating the mechanics of the whole system.[1]

Among the cultural sign mechanisms governing the functioning of the community, a peculiar place is assigned to the phenomena of cognitive processes. Earlier, Marxist social science devoted little attention to the systematic study of the concepts of everyday consciousness, social consciousness, world view, faith and belief, as they were simply deemed unimportant factors in the molding of social processes. That one-sided attitude has been proven wrong by life itself. In the mid-70s, a joint conference was organized involving Hungarian researchers in the fields of the humanities and the social sciences. These sociologists, linguists, anthropologists, psychologists, historians and aestheticians then addressed the complex problem of belief systems and social consciousness. Approaching the question from the vantage point of their respective scholarly fields, the participants at that interdisciplinary symposium described and analyzed the regularities of this peculiar form of consciousness. Thanks to their discussions, *belief*, as a scientific term, was at last firmly established in the theoretical vocabulary of Hungarian social sciences.[2]

Although the collection and systematic presentation of beliefs has a long tradition in Hungarian folklore studies, it was not until the late 1960s that, at the initiative of Vilmos Diószegi, some truly methodical and thorough collecting projects were undertaken. The work continued even after his death and the monographs on folk belief which had been prepared in the meantime were all duly published, rescuing a wealth of material on the beliefs of Hungarian ethnic groups and Hungarians living outside their mother country.

Myth and Mentality
Studia Fennica
Folkloristica 8, 2002

Also completed were a few theoretical studies – ones which scrutinized the inner dynamics of the world of beliefs, trying to establish the rules of the organization of the texts.[3]

The theoretical orientation of recent Hungarian research owes much to Russian semiotics, that is, the theory that the mythology built on language is a secondary sign system, with this peculiar form of collective consciousness forming part of the over arching canopy of the belief system. Another influence can be traced to research done in American cultural anthropology whereby a system could be reconstructed by collecting the beliefs deemed part of the world view and folk knowledge (folk ideas).[4] The world view (*Weltanschauung*)[5] characteristic of a culture is possible through the transmission, appropriation, and reproduction of folk ideas and knowledge, that is the belief system of the entire society. In culture, sign systems, especially the secondary sign systems, are articulated in language.[6]

Socially distributed character is highly important, as it partly accounts for the extremely durable nature of cultural systems,[7] (including constituent systems such as beliefs).

Common to the definitions is the conception of belief as a state of consciousness that impels one to action without possession of first-hand evidence of its truth. This definition has two essential implications for further discussion: one concerns the property of beliefs, that they play a crucial role in triggering our actions (something we will consider later on); while the other important feature of beliefs is that we accept them as valid guides to action even when we are uncertain of their truth. More precisely, truth is not a prerequisite of their validity and influence. We use beliefs without raising the question of truth – that is, we employ them in the same way as we do signs and symbols; in certain life situations such beliefs are regarded as culturally appropriate.

According to another, more comprehensive definition, the belief system is, in fact, the entire universe of the individual's views on the physical world. In other words, it is nothing other than our everyday knowledge relating to the environment surrounding us, in which, at several points, we see a twilight zone between faith or belief and well-grounded knowledge. That is partly to be attributed to the fact that the "knowledge" serving as the basis for routine actions of daily life – i.e., our belief that we are acting correctly – is acquired during the earliest stages of socialization, with the process continuing into our later life. We absorb and assimilate it simultaneously with the emergence of the personality and the acquisition of language, long before questions arise concerning the authenticity of the symbols acquired. As with signs, beliefs are authenticated by collective consensus and are imprinted by acceptance.

Belief Systems

Studies centered on day-to-day life have established that the knowledge, cognition, and beliefs regulating daily actions – which are, at the same time, elements in the entire system of culture – make up an inter-connected, coherent system.[8] Time and time again the monographic literature shows us the interdependence of the assumptions, beliefs, knowledge and cognition that we are equipped with when formulating the behavior of our daily living; rather than occurring in a random, chaotic fashion, they form a latent system. Let us take a few simple examples, the predictions of dreams. Let me cite some examples from my field notes.

"When we dreamt something it always had some kind of meaning: troubled water – sickness; rain – crying; fire – danger."

"Soldier: rain.
Ring: separation.
Extraction of a tooth: a dead person, a near relative".

"Whoever dreams about a pigeon is going to receive a letter."
"If someone dreamt about geese, it meant they were about to hear good news."
"If you dream about a horse, you are going to receive a letter from a long way away."[9]

By radically simplifying the structure of beliefs and placing the signs on the left-hand side with the meanings arranged into a column on the right side, we get the following series on the basis of the above examples:

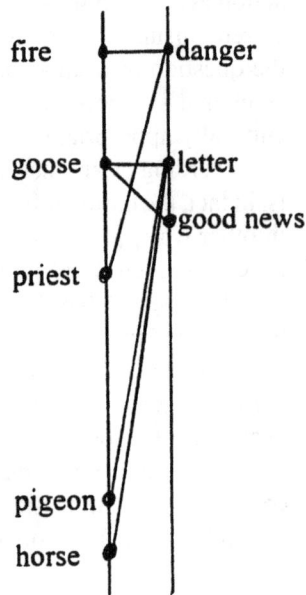

Leaving aside the immediate, non-recurrent associations, we can see that some of the signs, even in these few texts, have several meanings associated with them, while some of the meanings have several signs associated with them (e.g. the arrival of a letter is signalled by a goose, pigeon, and horse seen in one's dream). Therefore, the net or web[10] seems to be the most apt image for conveying the systematized nature of beliefs.

"If someone had an itch in their mouth, it meant that they were going to be kissed"

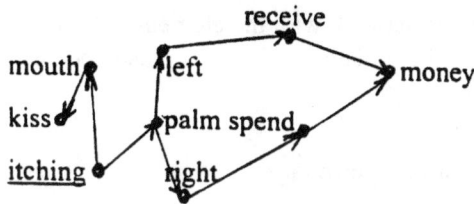

According to the belief, itching, as a sign, calls to mind the above associative relationships. Naturally, in the case of longer texts, the net of interconnections shows an even more intricate picture. A description of this nature is in full concordance – not only in terms of form but also regarding its basic theoretical idea – with modern methods for describing textual meaning.[11] Let us see a few slightly more complicated examples:

"... Or if someone who was pregnant and had not yet reached the half-way point of their pregnancy had something fall on them, a mark was left there. My daughter too has a mark here. I was with an old woman; we were on our way to weave hemp. She says: "Come in. I shall shake some plums for you from the tree; but don't stand under the tree, in case a plum falls on you and leares your child with a mark." No sooner had she finished saying this than I looked up and a plum fell on me here. And, sure enough, my daughter has a black plum-like spot here on her neck. That's how it happened. We did the washing in the brook as well; this is how we beat the clothes. But no one was allowed to borrow another's beetle – that is, a woman couldn't have two beetles because then she would have two children. One mustn't eat a plum that is stuck together, and a pregnant woman was not permitted to carry two hoes, because then she was going to have twins."[12]

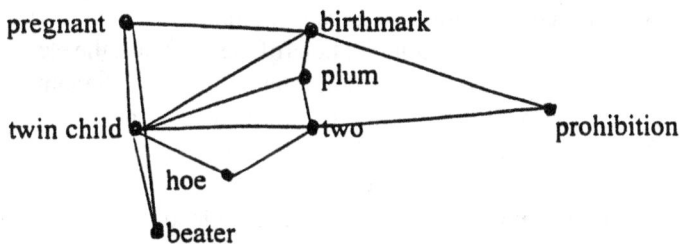

By properly ordering the elements belonging to the same grammatical categories, we can better survey the "net". Thus, for instance, separate columns will be formed by objects (hoe, beetle, rosary, table, knife etc.), by parts of the body (palm, mouth, tooth, eye, etc.), by particular points of time (midnight, before sunrise, after sunset, midday, full moon, Friday etc.), by locales of magic actions (threshold, dunghill, gate, ditch in the cemetery, grave, crossroads etc.), by numbers (three, seven, nine), by personages and beings possessing supernatural power (wizard, witch, incubus, gipsy woman etc.) and a large number of various other categories. On the basis of different systems of classification, there can exist cultures in which special importance adheres to sacred or consecrated objects, or round or moving objects as opposed to stationary ones.[13] The classes of the elements, the categories, form main filaments of the "net" or network with the elements featuring as the individual nodes[14] within in them. This could be represented in the following highly simplified scheme:

objects   parts of   points   locales   personages   actions   numbers

the body   of time

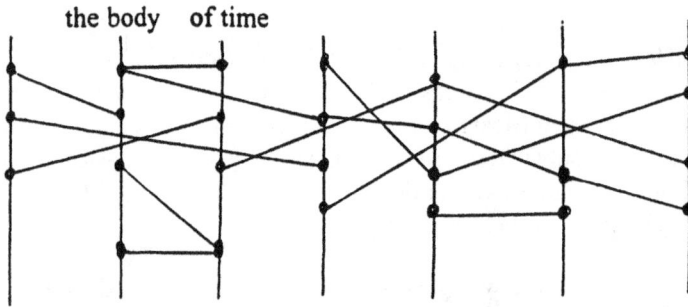

This mutual interconnection greatly contributes to the stability of belief systems.[15] When writing in the nodes of the belief web in this fashion, those information-carrying elements, (which, in the form of words, regularly recur in the texts), which play a part in building up the system, were taken into account. Just as language is made up of words, the communications of the belief code – of which the texts quoted have been exponents – are built up of those elements. Certain elements can have only certain elements attached to them, because only in this way can "meaningful" belief texts result. In this network, the order of the connections preserves the grammar of the belief system, i.e., the possible combinations of elements, just as in spoken language there are permissible and forbidden – i.e., incorrect – combinations of elements. The sign system or cultural text under examination can invariably be characterized by the permissible combinations of the elements, the elementary signs being used. From a general semiotic standpoint, this phenomenon corresponds to the traditionally determined coordination of the basic signs of folk dress (the articles of clothing) or the ingredients of dishes or, for that matter, the decorations on wooden graveposts.[16]

The order of the elements and the connections collectively, that is, the plotting of the network, the form varying – form culture to culture – of its regularities, the internal organization of the belief-system essentially correspond to, and model, the structure of social consciousness, which, when placed among some categories deemed particularly important, will trace out the culture's world view. The world-view, as a kind of filter, determines how we might see the world more exactly, how we should arrange our perceptions, and how new experience is to be slotted into the already existing categories.[17] That becomes clear if we think of the great difficulty that students of a foreign culture encounter when trying to establish correspondences between the two systems: for instance, Russian *domovoy* ("brownie", "goblin") has no exact equivalent in Hungarian folk belief, which therefore can, at best, render it by a descriptive paraphrase ("házimanó"). By the same token, the spirits of the pagan Ob-Ugrians were translated by Russian missionaries simply with the word *tshort* which corresponds to "devil", originating from the Christian world of beliefs. To use a more graphic image, we might say that the nodes in the respective belief-system network of the two cultures are not congruent, the structures of the two are divergent – although it is certain that the principal cases of the elements are almost identical; yet, they differ in the connections, in terms of which elements may interlock.

The frequent references to the spoken language thus far are hardly coincidental. It is important to emphasize the intimate interconnections between the belief system and the natural language. After all, the mother tongue occupies a central place in the system,[18] as it is the most highly structured among the sign systems used by human beings. The range of religious beliefs plays an vital role in every culture, especially in the organization of festive behavior, but it also informs the beliefs of everyday life. The great world religions hedge themselves round with an array of systematized doctrines and rituals. And what is perhaps a more important characteristic of the constituent system of religious beliefs is the fact that, in most cultures, it is this subsystem that stores the value judgements of the given community, in many cases in the form of precise religious customs and rules. The closed elements of the religious system fasten more rigidly to one another; therefore, on the whole, the religious system changes more slowly than the more open system of everyday beliefs anchored in daily events.

In life, man strives to formulate – at the everyday level, precisely by means of his belief system – his place in and attitude to the world. The most important function of a society's everyday ideological system is to help provide an answer to the questions that arise, such as "What is the structure of the world like?" and "Where is man's place in the world?" Within the belief system, it is the cosmological beliefs that provide the answer to all the questions that relate to the internal structure of the world view. Undoubtedly, these beliefs in the world view are highly significant, as they can be used for a typological characterization of cultures and mythologies in comparative research. The individual inherits and accepts beliefs no differently than he does his mother tongue.

The cohesive force is looser at the periphery of the system among everyday beliefs. Naturally, language also exerts an influence on everyday beliefs. But beyond primary linguistic articulation, it is in the codes of the various verbal folklore genres that beliefs gain a definitive form – for instance, in the form of the myth, the tale, the proverb or the saying or, as the case may be, in that of the simple words of advice or prohibition. Language preserves for us in its vocabulary words like "fairy", "witch", "nightmare", "magic steed", "spell" – words whose belief contents, now being slowly obscured, it incorporates into the expressions used in contemporary life: "the *bogey* (*mumus* in Hung.) of economic crisis"; "he was flying like a *magic steed* (*taltos*)"; "that old woman is a *witch* (*boszorkány*)". Rather than being mere metaphorical expressions, these are, in fact, instances of the language's living use of the traditional belief system. Of course, it is very difficult to decide whether or not we are simply dealing with ordinary similes. In my opinion, it is, in both cases, the implied reference to the original belief that is essential. We are all aware of the fundamental proposition of modern linguistics: language holds a whole range of implicit assumptions, items of knowledge and information, and beliefs that are conceptualized in our utterances. For example, upon hearing the Hungarian expression *"gólya szàllt a hàzra"* ("a stork has alit on the house"), one immediately translates it for oneself into "a child has been born"; thus the expression conveys the old belief linking the stork with the birth of a child.

Rarely used linguistic forms preserve beliefs, and the belief contents of certain words help preserve linguistic formulas. Such a close interdependence between the belief system and the language system means that the linguistically grounded structural nature of the belief system is complemented by another, secondary regularity, resulting from the belief code itself, which we shall come back to in the next section of this article.

We can also posit our beliefs as making up a system because that system possesses a clearly definable armory of elements, and those elements can be connected with each other only in a specified order. Moreover, within the system of everyday beliefs, several subsystems can be found which likewise correspond partially to each other and influence each other's functioning, as, for instance, the knowledge and superstitions of folk healers or the beliefs relating to farming and the weather. In the case of everyday beliefs, then, we are dealing with the mutually penetrating operations of structures grounded on one another (linguistic + religious + everyday belief structures). And in the course of the reconstruction of the system, not one of the subsystems can be ignored. Here we may detect the operation of a latent structure which influences and invisibly moves the actions of our daily lives. We might say that the belief system operates as the program, as construed in the cybernetic sense of the word, of everyday behavior. Let us think of what wide-ranging knowledge was needed for the *"well-formed"*[19] organization – *well-formed* to be taken in the social sense of the word, signifying 'concordant with the value-system of the community' – of a wedding or a funeral. It embraced everything from the art of cooking to the particular details of the custom itself, such as acquaintance with the songs and the dances, and an accurate evaluation of the kinship relations, – which as has been seen – has a most important role in, for instance, determining the seating order. All these minute details may be conceived of as subsystems of the entire culture, and only in the light of the connections can the individual phenomena really be understood.

Regarding the various phenomena of culture as a system, post-modern anthropology, adopting an ethno-semiotic approach, has introduced a new element by recognizing the close interdependence that exists between the particular groups of phenomena. The individual elements and phenomena explain one another by their relationships.

Perhaps the reason why the traditional belief system operated so effectively was that it provided a definite plan of action for all the minute details of life, helping the individual with ready-made patterns for decision-making. This will be illustrated with a few examples in the following part, as I believe that it may serve as a model for understanding everyday behavior in general, our daily living encumbered with prejudices.

The Functioning of Beliefs

According to researchers of belief systems, one of the most important of the multitude of features displayed by beliefs   one of the most important, that is, for studies scanning the mechanisms of daily social practice   is the following: beliefs are inseparable from the action sequences governing them and thus ordering individual behavior. [20]

There are two ways in which beliefs impel the believer to action. One type of action takes place merely on a lingistic level when we generate texts expressly designed to communicate the contents of our belief. This happens, for example, when, requested by the anthropological field-worker, the informants relate stories about a wizard or an incubus will-o'-the-wisp. (The Hungarian word *lidérc* carries the triple meaning of "incubus"; "nightmare"; and "will-o'-the-wisp" or *ignis fatuus*.)[21]

"For three weeks one has to carry under one's armpit an egg from a black hen. The person who's hatched it, that man or woman, has every wish of his or hers fulfilled. If a woman has hatched it, a rooster hatches out; if a man has hatched it, a pullet hatches. They live like husband and wife. The rooster sleeps with the woman. It's impossible to get rid of it. It must be made to carry out an impossible task, that will cause it to run away. On the snow, let them fetch water from the Bodrog river, sand in a rope, daylight in a sack." [22]

"The incubus lies on the chest of the sleeper. When this occurs the sleeper can neither speak nor move. To ward it off, nine cloves of garlic are placed at the four corners of the bed."

"The will-o'-the-wisp indicates that there is some treasure there. It purifies itself every seven years. It appears in the form of a flame."[23]

"The incubus used to go in to the women through the chimney. Because it was like a star. Because I myself saw one when I was at school. I saw it once, but no more. It was a kind of star and it had a long tail. It used to visit those harlot women. To them it would bring everything – so then it made them comfortable."[24]

"The will-o'-the-wisp is a spirit that frightens one; by night, it shines with a bright light; when it walks it shits fire."[25]

"The will-o'-the-wisp walks on the surface of the water in the grove; it has long legs and it gives off light."

After an analysis of the texts, we can record the stock of elements of the texts dealing with the particular forms of *lidérc* /incubus/nightmare/will-o'-the-wisp/

lidérc ———— "lamp" ┌→light ———→flies ———→by night
                    └→ flame ┌→ rustles
                             ├→ frightens
                             ├→ haunst
                             └→leads

lidérc —→lidérfény ┌→flame →indicates —→treasure ┌→every ↗swamp
                   │   ├→seven│
                   │   └→years│
(will-o'- └→light ┌→purifies ——————————————————————→marsh
the-wisp)   └→shoots up   └→meadow

lidérc —— "fiery star" star ┌—has a tail ┬→flies away ┌→fire
                            │   ├→flies up   ├→spark
                            │   ├→scatters→ │
                            └   └→shits ——————

lidérc —— "fiery man" ┌→man ———→wanders ———→by night —→is damned
                      ├→"engineer" ┌→walks
                      └→soul   └→sizes up
                              ↘→flames

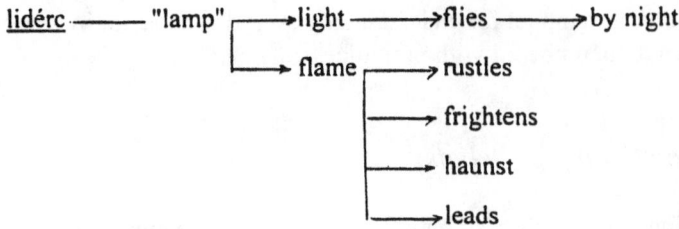

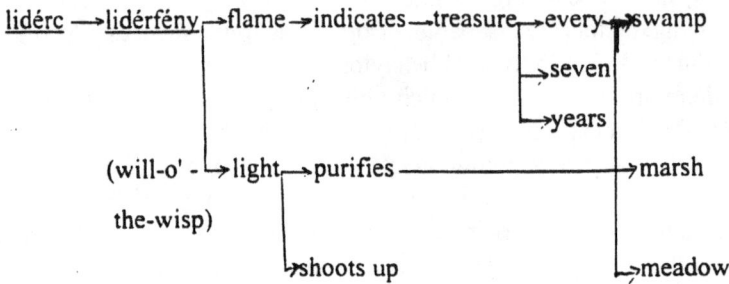

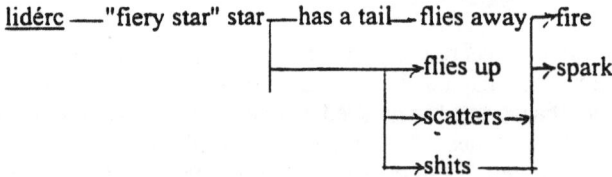

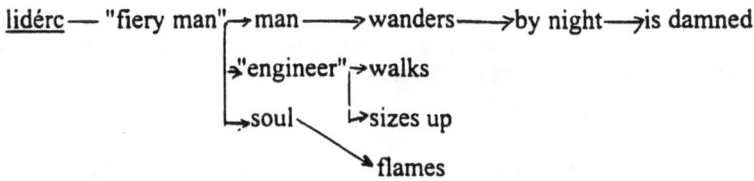

If we extract from the above texts the elements that are important from the standpoint of the belief system and write these elements side by side according to the order of where they possibly join, we can then obtain a semantic model of the range of beliefs of Hungarian *lidérc*:

```
Lidérc ——— living ——— man ——— adult
                                  └— child
                      animal ——— bird (chicken)
                              ╲— non-bird (horse)
        inanimate —— light ——— lamp
                              ╲— will-o'-the-wisp
                              ╲ hay-pole
                              ╲ fiery star
                      spirit ——— nightmare (dream)
                              ╲ "wandering soul"
                              ╲ the souls of the dead
                              ╲ devil
```

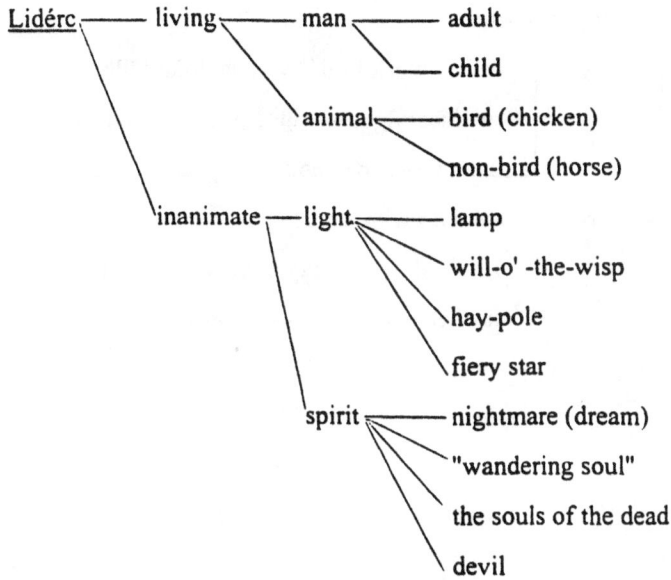

This simple model serves to show the variety of forms in which the being called *lidérc* may "appear" in Hungarian folk belief (e.g. in the form of man or beast, a luminous phenomenon or some kind of indefinable spirit).

It is apparent from the above diagram which elements must join themselves to each other for "correctly" formulated *lidérc* stories to result. What we are seeing is essentially the semantic tree of a single word, which, however, carries within it the possibilities of generating the texts of belief legends of varying length. A single word appears to contain the entire text, the elements and the rules of generation.

The above examples allow us to observe this property of cultural texts, from which the available stock of elements – obviously not infinite – the individual may freely choose. Moreover, of the possibilities of linguistic formulation too, he/she freely chooses the one best suited to her/his individuality and abilities. It is the fact, or rather, the possibility of choice that needs to be underscored. This is by no means merely a question of style, but rather this property of culture, within the system, ensures the individual the possibility of choice between the equivalent elements, (or paradigms, to use a more technical term). Folkloric texts provide good examples to prove that proposition. A semantic diagram can be prepared for each of the elements of the belief system. Here is a description of the *garabonciás* from a paper by Zoltán Fejös[26] (*garabonciás* = a figure of folk belief; a wizard disguised as a travelling student, believed to be able to raise a storm):

garabonciás→his figure——man
———beast—black bird; "winged, long-tailed"
———mythical figure—táltos (sorcerer, wizard)
———natural phenomenon—fiery tail
→his properties—is born with teeth
his food— milk, egg of young chicken
his helper ——————————→dragon
→his activity——carries away children →snake
→destruction (rain of fire, thunderstorm, rain
→ smashes things to pieces)
→would run away into the forest

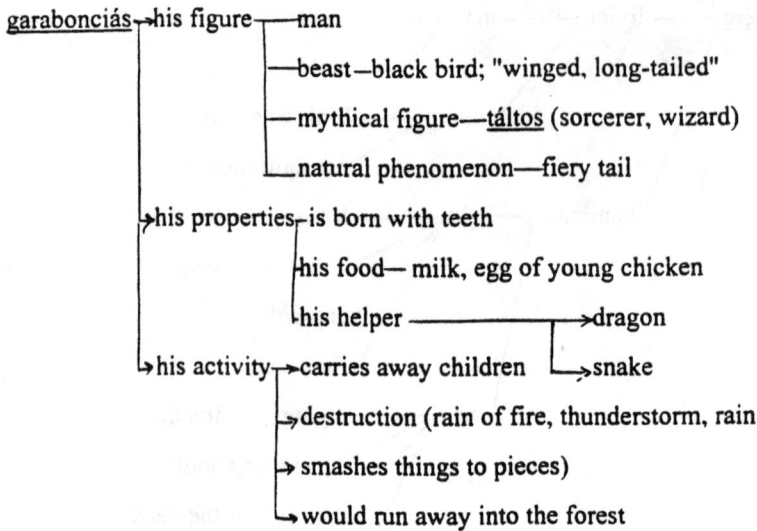

Beliefs also prompt the individual to act in the real sense of the word. Our next example comes from a range of our everyday beliefs, more specifically, the beliefs connected with a highly important area of knowledge, i.e., ethnomedicine. I have chosen, accordingly, a text that bears on a fairly general phenomenon of old village life – namely, the range of beliefs relating to the *evil eye*, supposedly responsible for sudden illnesses in small children, and the preparation of 'coaly water.'

"We used to make *coaly* water, too, and I used to pick herbs. That kind of herb is found on fallow land. It is sort of tall, with a round flower head at the end; it was sort of prickly. When I walked across the fallow I would go to pick some. When I found one, I pulled it out. When a small child was suffering from the influence of the *evil eye*, I would brew these herbs. Before sunrise, I would fetch water from three wells, and I would prepare the brew before sunrise. Then I would bathe the child in it once before sunrise; I would bathe it a second time at midday and for a third time as the sun was going down but was still up. And it did really work."[27]

In the village, in Nógrád County, where the above text was recorded, similar treatments involving three baths were reported, in identical fashion, by about ten more women. Additional materials indicate its function as a general behavioral model in the village as old and young alike were, almost without exception, able to recount the relevant beliefs. Clearly, there existed, and there still survives, a program in the consciousness of the community on how these actions must be performed in a specified order for the healing process against the *evil eye* to work.

Let us see another example, a piece of information dating back a hundred years. The poet János Erdélyi, who spent his childhood in Zemplén County, derived one of the scenes in his poem *A'siri hang* (A Voice from the Grave) from a folk belief of that particular region.[28] In it, the hero, while passing the graveyard, hears the sound of crying. He approaches the sound, and from the grave an unchristened child who was killed by its mother speaks to him.

He baptizes the child, so that it may find eternal rest. Here 'baptism' must be understood as 'placing a small wooden cross over the grave'. This action the soldier duly performed (The Hungarian word for "baptize", "christen" *(megkeresztel)* contains the root of *kereszt* (= "cross"), allowing the literal interpretation of "marking with a cross").

In 1973, in a small village in Nógrád County, I tape-recorded the following story as it was told by an old shepherd:

"This again is a true story; it's something that happened to me. I was coming home here in the graveyard ditch; it was getting dark, too. There was a footpath leading across the graveyard, and I used to walk that way. Suddenly I heard something like the crying of a child in the ditch of the graveyard. I go near and have a look ... as I was going in the ditch ... I listen ... well, this is where it's crying! You could hear it crying beneath the ground! I strike a match so that I can see better – well, there is a small grave there, but it was overgrown with weeds. God only knows how old it could have been. Well, I baptized it – this is what they say: "I baptize you to God! (If you are a girl, let your name be Eve!) If you are a boy, let your name be Adam!" – And, sure enough, I haven't heard anything since then; but it's certain that it was the crying of a child. I heard from old people back in the old days that children who were born earlier and were not baptized cried every seven years."[29]

This belief narrative is an excellent example of how the belief system really operated, how a given belief triggered an entire chain of actions. Let us recapitulate the events as they happened. Hearing the "voice from the grave", as a sign, activated the belief. At the time of the story, in the 1920s, a man of about twenty years of age is walking across the cemetery. According to the beliefs of our forebears, the cemetery is a place of special importance, since it is the realm of the dead, another world set apart from the village; all of which is particularly true of the cemetery ditch, it being the place where suicides and those who died unbaptized used to be buried. A possible hallucination, the darkness, weariness or fear set in motion some of the beliefs possibly linked to the cemetery. Of these, the following two form an interconnected associative sequence of beliefs: 1) the crying of unbaptized children can be heard every seven years; 2) unbaptized children are normally buried in the ditch of the cemetery. If, therefore, the sound of crying is heard from the ditch at the edge of the cemetery, it can only be an unbaptized child, in which case, the obligatory action to be performed is as follows: the little dead soul must be baptized, by the recitation of a prescribed formula. As is clear from the story, our informant, who was still a young shepherd boy at the time, was not only familiar with this element of the belief system, but he also recognized the imperative of the obligatory performance of the conventionalized actions enjoined by the elements. In other words, he knew *what* was to be done and *how* it was to be done. The belief system, to use a metaphor from linguistics, functioned like a set of rules for generating correct belief sentences, as a kind of deep structure engendering the perceptible sign sequences of the surface structure. In the above case, this was a specific action, i.e., the baptizing.

Even in the early 1970s, in the Örség region, I found and photographed a milk-jug whose neck was "adorned" by an X-sign. At the beginning of the

1940s, László Kardos recorded the following custom as practiced in Öriszentpéter:

> "... the reason why no milk is served after sunset is that the cows start kicking then and they do not yield milk ... but the progress of milk served during the daytime is not without its hazards, either. Therefore, prior to sending it on its way, the mistress of the household dips a finger in the pot of milk and draws an X on the kitchen wall ... to prevent good luck from leaving the milk."[30]

The tilting cross, the X sign, used to be a well-known magic apotropaic symbol[31] throughout Europe, includings slavic regions; but the same sign would often be drawn with garlic over the stable door by the Palots inhabitants of Nógrád County, who employed it as a cross designed to ward off the evil eye.

A sign dictated by beliefs used to be made by simply placing a broom upside down. In the early 1970s, while making an ethnographic film in Örhalom, I had the opportunity of observing an old woman turn the broom "with the brush of birch upwards" when leaving home. Asked why she did this, she replied that it was "to signal that nobody was at home".[32]

> "To prevent a witch from entering the house, a broom was placed by the corner of the door."[33]

> "When a little child was left alone in the house, a birch-broom was placed upside down against the door."[34]

We know from other data, too, that, according to ancient belief, the birch-broom – and birch in general – was credited with magic powers. Moreover, inversion, in beliefs, always conveyed magic powers: a garment worn inside-out was believed to ward off evil. It is apparent from the examples listed that the belief assumed shape in specific actions.

Another vivid example of everyday beliefs is connected with the dead; it is one which, in the form of a prohibition, served as a program of expected behavior:

> "As a rule, the bath water was not poured out where we came and went. If, in the evening, someone poured out some water, she – I mean my father's mother – used to say: "My daughter, if you pour out some water in the evening, do it only where the water drains from the roof; or if you want to pour it out in the courtyard, call out, Whoever stands there stand back, because I'm pouring water!" This is because the dead return home, and whoever pours out the water after sunset douses his own dead relative, because the dead keep coming back."[35]

There is a clear reference to the belief being transmitted by the older generation, the grandmother, who did not only formulate the canons of correct behavior, but also explained the meaning of the action, or rather the prohibition, relating to respect for the dead, the ancestors. The belief that the dead return determined a daily action, i.e., the manner in which the dirty water was poured out.

Now here is another example of how the belief system, conceived as a fabric of reticulations, has been superimposed, as it were, on the actions of everyday life and how it regulates them. The following semi-pagan prayer used to be known in the region inhabited by the Palots people; its recitation, as an action, was prompted by the appearance of the new moon, as a sign:

"When they saw the new moon they always kneeled down and said: "New moon, new king / It's you I salute / With a living head, with a dead soul / With the word of the Blessed Virgin' – this they would repeat three times and they would cross themselves."[36]

The Hungarians of Gyimesvölgy used to say the prayer to the moon like this: "We were taught that the sign of the cross was to be made on seeing the new moon in the sky for the first time:

Good day, New moon, new king
good months
in good months, good weeks
in good weeks, good days
in good days, good hours
in good hours, good minutes
in good minutes, good moments!
– he makes the sign of
the cross and says a prayer."[37]

The prayer is also an example of how we literally act with words, and, at the same time, of how we act by beliefs as with 'speech acts'. It is, moreover, an example of the survival, in Hungarian folk belief and oral tradition, of highly archaic, medieval or even older elements – a fact which has been revealed by Zsuzsanna Erdélyi's collection of folk prayer texts,[38] in which she explores their relevant sources. These are important facts from the standpoint of the entire body of Hungarian folklore, signalling, as they do, the strength of the belief system, which, in the dual anchorage of faith and poetic language, has survived for centuries on the lips and in the memory of prayers. And here we must refer again to the codes of culture that operate parallel with one another, as the gesture of the hands folded in prayer, the posture of kneeling, the text of sweeping rhythm, and, underlying all these, the signs and symbols of faith – the world view – all combined to engender *prayer*, as a genus of the cultural "text".[39]

The beliefs described in terms of the codes reveal the fundamental reciprocities between the beliefs and the behavior, also describing the behavior formats most characteristic of the individual groups. To put it in a schematic fashion: the beliefs and knowledge making up a human conception of the universe, themselves internalized during the practice of day-to-day life, help one adjust to one's environment.

Having said that, it is important to underscore once again that, as attested by the above examples, too, beliefs invariably are attached to some kind of action. In other words, the belief functions as a program, and it regulates the lives of individuals, "guiding our desires and shaping our actions".[40] This was given a clear formulation over a hundred years ago by the classic author of American semiotics, C.S. Peirce, writing on beliefs as a conditioning mechanism: it "put us in such a condition that we shall behave in a certain way, when the occasion arises".[41]

Translated by Orsolya Frank.

NOTES

1. On the semiotic approach to believing see Parret, ed.1983; on ethnosemiotics Hoppál 1992.
2. Frank – Hoppál (eds) 1980, see also Parret (ed.) 1983.
3. Fejős 1983, Hoppál 1974, Bosnyák 1982, Pusztainé1967.
4. Dundes 1971. – See D'Andrade 1995 for a critical review of cognitive anthropology, and Workshop 1993.
5. Smart 1983, Gothóni 1991, Lindquist 1995, Helve 1993, Voigt 1996.
6. Hoppál 1978.
7. Szalay 1984, Connerton 1989.
8. Hahn 1973, Hoppál 1979, Szalay – Maday 1973, 1983; Szalay 1984.
9. Collected by M. Hoppál (1968) Gyöngyösvisonta (Northern Hungary). On dreams Kaivola-Bregenhøj 1993.
10. Szalay – Maday 1983:112, Wallace 1989:525, Hoppál 1979.
11. Melchuk 1974.
12. Collected by M. Hoppál (1972) Varsány (Northern Hungary).
13. Witherspoon 1971.
14. On nodes and cognitive mapping, see Szalay 1984:73, Wallace 1989:518, D'Andrade 1995:138, on network, Darányi 1996.
15. On the categories: Szalay et alii 1979; on social memory Connerton 1989:6–36, and McNamara 1992.
16. For more details Hoppál 1992.
17. Very few studies has been completed on this topic but see Szalay et alii 1979 and Helve 1993.
18. Hoppál 1979:272.
19. A basic concept in text-linguistics – see Petöfi 1974.
20. Parsons – Shils 1962:169.
21. Hoppál 1974, with more texts.
22. The text collected by V. Diószegi (1962).
23. Collected by M. Hoppál (1968). Tiszafüred.
24. Collected by V. Diószegi (1961). Gyuró.
25. Collected by M. Hoppál (1968). Gyimesközéplak.
26. Fejős 1983:97.
27. Collected by M. Hoppál (1973). Varsány.
28. Erdélyi 1844:140.
29. Collected by M. Hoppál (1973). Varsány.
30. Kardos 1943:138.
31. Gunda 1941.
32. Collected by M. Hoppál (1971). Örhalom.
33. Pusztainé 1967:85.
34. Collected by M. Hoppál (1967). Pusztafalu.
35. Collected by M. Hoppál (1967). Visonta.
36. Collected by M. Hoppál (1967). Visonta.
37. Bosnyák 1982:73.
38. Erdélyi 1974.
39. On ritual speech acts – see Lovász 1996, on narrating Kaivola-Bregenhøj 1996.
40. Maranda – Köngäs-Maranda 1979:253.
41. Peirce 1877:14–1.

BIBLIOGRAPHY

Bosnyák, Sándor 1982: A gyimesvölgyi magyarok hitvilága. Folklór Archivum 14:68–157.

Connerton, Paul 1989: How Societies Remember. University Press. Cambridge.

D'Andrade, Roy 1995: The Development of Cognitive Anthropology. University Press. Cambridge.

Darányi, Sándor 1996: Formal aspects of Natural Belief Systems, Their Evolution and Mapping: A Semiotic Analysis. Semiotica 108:1–2:45–63.

Dundes, Alan 1971: Folk Ideas as Units of Worldview. A. Dundes (ed.) Every Man His Way 401–424. Englewood Cliffs. Prentice Hall.

Erdélyi, János 1844: Költeményei. Budán.

Erdélyi, Zsuzsanna 1974: Hegyet hágék, l töt lépék (Archaic folk prayers) Kaposvár.

Fejős, Zoltán 1983: Hiedelemrendszer, szöveg, közösség (Belief System, Text, Community) in: Néprajzi Közlemények vol. XXVII. Néprajzi Múzeum. Budapest.

Frank, Tibor – Mihály Hoppál (eds) 1980: Hiedelemrendszer és társadalmi tudat. (Belief System and Social Mind) vol. I–II. Masscommunication Institute. Budapest.

Gothóni, Renè 1991: Worldview and Mode of Life Orthodox and Theravada Monastic Life Compared. Temenos 27:41–59.

Gunda, Béla 1941: A kereszt, mint mágikus jel az agyagedényeken. (Cross as Magic Sign on Pottery). Ethnographia LII:66–67.

Hahn, Robert 1973: Understanding Beliefs: an Essay on the Methodology of the Description and Analysis of Belief Systems. Current Anthropology 14:3:207–224.

Hamill, James F. 1990: Ethno-logic: the Anthropology of Human Reasoning. Champaign. University of Illinois Press.

Helve, Helena 1993: The World View of Young People. A Longitudinal Study of Finnish Youth Living in a Suburb of Metropolitan Helsinki. Suomalainen Tiedeakatemia. Helsinki.

Hoppál, Mihály 1974: Ein semantisches Modell des ungarisches Alpglaubens. Acta Linguistica 24:167–181.

– 1978: Mythology as a Sign-System. S. Gentili – G. Paioni (eds) Il mito greco. Atti del convegno internazionale 349–364. Ateneo-Bizzari. Roma.

– 1979: On Belief Systems. W. Burghardt – K. Hölker (eds) Text Processing-Textverarbeitung 236–253. de Gruyter. Berlin.

– 1992: Etnoszemiotika (Ethnosemiotics) Debrecen: Kossuth L. Tudományegyetem.

Ipolyi, Arnold 1854: Magyar Mythologia. Pest: Heckenast (reprint Budapest: 1987).

Kaivola-Bregenhøj, Annikki 1993: Dreams as Folklore. Fabula 34:211–224.

– 1996: Narrative and Narrating. Helsinki: FF Communications No. 261.

Kardos, László 1943: Az rség népi táplálkozása (Folk Foodways). A Magyar Táj-és Népismeret könyvtára. Budapest.

Lindquist, Galina 1995: Travelling by the Other's Cognitive Maps or Going Native and Coming Back. Ethnos 60:1–2:5–40.

Lovász, Irén 1996: Boundaries between Language and World. Archaic World Concept. L. Petzold (ed.) Folk Narrative and World View 463–468.

Maranda, Pierre – Elli-Kaija Köngäs-Maranda 1979: Myth as a Cognitive Map. V. Burghardt – K. Hölker (eds) Textprocessing – Textverarbeitung 253–272. de Gruyter. New York.

McNamara, Patrick 1992: A Transpersonal Approach to Memory. The Journal of Transpersonal Psychology 24:1:61–78.

Melchuk, Igor A. 1974: Opyt t'eorii lingvisticheskikh mod'elei: 'smysl' i 'tékst'. (On the theory of linguistic models: 'mind' and 'text') Nauka. Moskva.

Parret, H. (ed.) 1983: On Believing. Epistemological and Semiotic Approaches. de Gruyter. Berlin – New York.

Parsons, Talcott – Shils, E.A. 1962: Towards a General Theory of Action. Harper. New York.

Peirce, C.S. 1877: Chance, Love, and Logic. Kegan Paul. London.

Petöfi, S. János 1974: New Trends in Typology of Texts and Text Grammars. General

Report delivered at the First Congress of the International Association for Semiotic Studies. Milano.

Pusztainé Madaras, Ilona 1967: Sárrétudvari hiedelmek. (Folk Beliefs) Néprajzi Közlemények XII:1–2:23–225.

Smart, Ninian 1983: Woldviews: Crosscultural Explorations of Human Beliefs. Scribner's. New York.

Szalay, Lorand B. 1984: An Indepth Analysis of Cultural/Ideological Belief Systems. The Manking Quarterly XXV:1–2:71–100.

Szalay, Lorand B. – Maday, Bela C. 1973: Verbal Associations in the Analysis of Subjective Culture. Current Anthropology 14:151–173.

– 1983: Implicit Culture and Psychocultural Distance. American Anthropologist 85:1:110–118.

Szalay, Lorand B. et al. 1979: Iranian and American Perceptions and Cultural Frames of Reference. Washington D.C.: Institute of Comparative Social and Cultural Studies.

Voigt, Vilmos 1996: Views and Worlds of World View Studies. In: Petzoldt, Leander (Hrsg.) Folk Narrative and World View 813–822. Innstbruck: Peter Lang, Europäischer Verlag der Wissenschafte.

Wallace, Ron 1989: Cognitive Mapping and the Origin of Language and Mind. Current Anthropology 30:4:518–526.

Witherspoon, B. 1971: Navaho Categories of Objects at Rest. American Anthropologist 73:110–127.

Workshop on Language, Cognition and Computation. 1993 Barcelona: Fundació Catalana per a la Recerca.

LAURA STARK-AROLA

The Dynamistic Body in Traditional Finnish-Karelian Thought

Väki, *vihat*, *nenä*, and *luonto*

Introduction

Conceptions of the physical body vary through time and across cultures.* Our modern image of the immune system, for instance, and with it our view of the body's relationship to its (threatening) environment which is specific to the Western world, is mere decades old.[1] Numerous anthropologists, historians, folklorists and sociologists have suggested that in other cultures and historical periods, bodies and selves have been seen as more flexible, fluid and dynamic than they are in Western society today.[2]

Scholarly literature on body concepts through European history has tended to focus on official or elite perspectives. Our picture of how the body was perceived and experienced among the semi-literate peasant majority in pre-modern Europe, on the other hand, is riddled with gaps. The present article examines archival materials which reflect the centuries-old, possibly millennia-old world view of hunters, fishers and small-scale peasant farmers prior to the modern era. A brief survey of the Finnish Literature Society Folklore Archives Ethnomedical Index is sufficient to show that many archaic body concepts represented in 19th century Finnish-Karelian oral tradition offer perspectives on corporeality which differ radically from our modern, Western view of the body.[3] These included the belief that menstruation could be transferred to men (Stark-Arola 1998a), that supernatural force emanated from the female vagina,[4] that a newborn child could be born with bristles on its back (*harjakset*, see Keinänen 1996), and that the limits of the body/self did not end at the outer boundary of the skin but rather, that the dimensions of the person were broader and fuzzier than in our modern view (Kurki 1996:28). All suggest the need for further research on how the capabilities, boundaries and limitations of the body in traditional Finnish-Karelian thought diverged from conceptions of the body in modern biomedicine.

In this paper I explore part of the magico-mythical world view held (in varying degrees) by the agrarian population of 19th-century Finland.[5] Variations across regions are ignored for the sake of utilizing available source materials to describe a broad pattern of cultural thought. The model I propose of this Finnish-Karelian world view is composed of a large number of sub-models, which, like their component *schemata*, or "knowledge structures"[6]

Myth and Mentality
Studia Fennica
Folkloristica 8, 2002

should not be seen as necessarily coherent in terms of their internal logic.[7] Some of these sub-models include belief in the evil eye,[8] laws of sympathy and contagion, and various mechanisms of magical harm such as curses and "spoiling". Some of this knowledge was general knowledge possessed by most ordinary persons, while some of it was the province of a ritual specialist with the abilities of a seer, healer and sorcerer, known in the vernacular as the *tietäjä*, literally "one who knows". In the realm of the *tietäjä's* expertise, we find the magical power of the word, as well as a complex, historically-layered system of knowledge regarding helper-spirits, animal spirits, and the topography of the other world (see Siikala 1992). Within the *tietäjä's* knowledge can be further distinguished a separate sub-model dealing with the nature, relationships and effects of dynamistic *väki*-forces which were seen to cause illness and were used in magic and healing rites. These dynamistic forces, and particularly the mechanisms by which they were seen to affect the human body, are the focus of the present paper.

Dynamism

In their classic form, the dynamistic theories proposed in the early 20th century (e.g. Preuss 1904; Mauss 1974/1904; Marett 1909) find no advocates today. It would be short-sighted, however, to entirely shelve the question of dynamistic forces in the study of Finnish and Karelian ethnic religious beliefs and magic rituals, since belief in *väki* (a type of dynamistic force) is well-documented in traditional Finnish and Karelian thought.[9] It should be made clear, however, that the term *väki* as used in Finnish-Karelian rural communities never denoted an "all-pervading" "immanent" or "universal" force, but rather an impersonal 'power charge' of more limited scope, ascribed to a tangible object or entity in the physical world. Nor can *väki* be seen, in the same way as *mana* in classic dynamistic theory, to be the logical or historical underpinning for all religious or magical beliefs and practices (Mauss 1974/1904; Alles 1987). The term *väki* in Finnish-Karelian folk belief was used specifically in reference to a cosmology or system of belief in which impersonal forces of a supernatural nature were seen to inhabit a wide range of objects and spaces in the natural and cultural environment: forest, water, animals, fire, iron tools, among others.[10] According to this belief, numerous beings and categories of beings carried within themselves power charges, and some of their power charges were thus able to infect human beings. Some of these beings and categories were more dynamistically powerful than others, or their *väki* forces were incompatible (Apo 1998).

In this study I use the term *dynamistic* not according to its classic, early 20th century definition, but in a much more restricted sense, concerning myself only with dynamistic force as it relates to the human body. The human body was at the center of *väki* belief. The dynamistic potential of forest, water, animals, fire, iron tools, etc. was important to people only insofar as it manifested itself in some discernible way in the human body. My definition of *dynamistic* is a conceptual system whereby the body was interpreted and explained in terms of force and movement. To understand traditional Finnish-

68

Karelian body beliefs and the folk categories of illness connected to *väki* forces, it is not sufficient to view the body according to the Western model as stable, concrete and bounded. We must turn to concepts borrowed from physics (dynamics and kinetics) – namely *energy, force,* and *movement* to conceive of *a body in flux and motion.* Moreover, the dynamistic system of belief discussed here has important theoretical implications in that it signals a new way of thinking about bodies, objects, agency and motivation. This is where I part company with the cultural relativist position on systems of mythico-magical knowledge which leaves magic to be seen on its own terms, in which it always remains alien, other, ergo "primitive". I seek to make magic understandable in terms of current western epistemology, within frameworks that are legitimated in our current scientific discourse.

In the Finnish-Karelian dynamistic belief system, the body was in many cases seen to "act" upon other bodies or objects, even though no physical contact took place. The human body was seen as capable of a peculiar kind of agency which blurred the boundaries between subject and object, mind and body: a concept which finds a parallel in anthropologist Kirsten Hastrup's (1995) notion of embodied motivation. Hastrup pays attention to the question of bodily presence, a neglected part of anthropological studies of the body, and argues: "the body is never simple presence. In its ecstatic qualities it expands beyond itself and projects itself outwards..." (1995:94). For Hastrup, embodied motivation is when "some kinds of personal presence exert an almost physical force upon others" (ibid. 97). The notion of embodied motivation appears to share many similarities with belief in dynamistic (*väki*) force. Both can be conceived of as energy, and both have the capacity to influence their surroundings (ibid. 96). Both the notion of embodied motivation and the belief in *väki* view the body not as a bounded, discrete entity separate from its surroundings, but as a field of energy emanating from the corporeal center. Likewise, in both orientations the split between mind/body is rejected in favor of a holistic approach to embodied *agency* which links the energy generated by the body to motivation or intention (ibid. 97). As we shall see, agency appears as a key attribute of dynamistic force in the descriptions examined in this paper.

But bodies were not the only actors in the Finnish-Karelian dynamistic world view. Inanimate entities and objects in the body's environment were also perceived to "act" upon the body – and these acts were motivated, meaning that humans attributed to these objects a will to act, that is, intentionality. These motivated acts by objects blur the line between subject and object, between personal and impersonal force, and thus muddy the analytical distinction between dynamistic beliefs (*väkiusko*) and animism (*haltiausko*) made by Finnish scholars in the late 19th and early 20th centuries. I suggest that magical incantations which addressed harmful, *väki*-filled objects as if they were animate agents were not based upon an erroneous understanding of the true nature of phenomena in the world. Rather, they were based upon a set of logical propositions reminiscent of certain postmodern approaches to the theoretical issue of subject-object relations, such as those of Donna Haraway and feminist anthropologist Marilyn Strathern which take a closer look at the agency of meaningful objects.

Haraway, for her part, redefines both the "knowing" subject and "known" object as "material-semiotic actors", thereby blurring the epistemological boundary between subject and object (Haraway 1991; Prins 1993). Objects of knowledge are brought into being by subjects who do the "knowing". But, as soon as these objects are constructed, that is, imbued with meaning, they can become very powerful and effective in constructing other, sometimes unexpected and unintended objects. Meaning-filled objects should therefore not merely be viewed as passive and inert matter to be appropriated, but also as active and meaning-generating in themselves (Haraway 1991:200).

One of the best anthropological examples of such an "active" object is the *gift*. The agency bestowed upon the gift by society was noted already by Mauss[11] and elaborated upon by subsequent scholars. In gift-giving, objects have powers of their own, they take on attributes of persons (Berking 1999:33–34). They may also have the capacity to simultaneously construct persons, for example gendered persons (Strathern 1988).

The work of these scholars raises the entire philosophical question of how we define subjects and objects in Western "rational" thought – and why. It reveals objectification to be the drawing of an illusory, but seemingly "real" and fundamental boundary between the world and the self. Many premises of the Finnish-Karelian mythico-magical world view, and particularly of dynamistic belief systems, dispense with that illusion and operate as if the boundary between the embodied self and the outside world were fluid. Dynamistic orientations to the world do not recognize a fundamental dichotomy between objects and subjects of knowledge, but instead acknowledge the complexity and two-directional nature of subject-object relations. In magical thought, objects have agency.

Folklore Materials and Cognitive Models

The abundant archival materials located in the Finnish Literature Society Folklore Archives are an important source of information concerning body thought in Finnish and Karelian communities. This is because the body, as a constellation of socially-constructed meanings and images, is always mediated by language, by metaphors and meanings that organise and animate our somatic perception and experience.

The *schemata* I discuss in this paper are examples of representational rather than operational models of causation (Holy and Stuchlik 1981:22). Since a representational model cannot be observed in real life, the researcher can access it only through the statements of those who share the model, the members of the culture in question. Researchers interested in a *cultural* model thus require a large number of such statements in order to reconstruct knowledge structures. However, quantity alone is not sufficient for such a reconstruction. Due to the fact that the verbal statements of persons are highly indexical, meaning that they are mere indicators of a wider body of cultural knowledge or logic which persons use in daily life but do not explicitly formulate,[12] researchers must find some way to access either this unseen cultural frame of reference or the informant's own ethno-theories if they wish to construct a model closely approximating the insider's emic knowledge. Of vital importance in this reconstruction are key texts (see Stark-Arola 1998a:68–69), which represent a conscious reflection by informants upon the cultural knowledge of which they are participants: in key texts, informants themselves make explicit the logical links and draw the theoretical conclusions which form the basis of the researcher's models of causality. I therefore utilize, where available, such key texts and have based my analysis of dynamistic mechanisms upon these texts as much as possible.

An important premise of this paper is that cultural knowledge (including models and *schemata*) is unevenly distributed within society.[13] Not all members of 19th century Finnish-Karelian communities believed in or practiced folk healing and magic, and still fewer had knowledge of dynamistic models of causality. It is no coincidence that our richest information (largest number of key texts) concerning dynamistic mechanisms of infection comes from Eastern and Northern Finland, and especially from North Karelia and Archangel Karelia, areas in which the *tietäjä* institution is known to have survived the longest, up to the beginning of the 20th century (Siikala 1992:68). *Tietäjä*s were the highest level of professionals versed in knowledge of folk illness and supranormal entities, and it was they who preserved, in their enormous repertoires of ritual and folk poetry, the knowledge which is in part the legacy of a shamanistic past (Siikala 1992).

The type of *schemata* which best represent the meanings attached to dynamistic concepts are to be found within the "prototype semantics" approach to knowledge representation in the cognitive sciences, also known as "extensional semantics" (Coleman and Kay 1981, Casson 1983:435). Prototype *schemata* are simplified ideal forms which serve as the purest examples or most representative members of a semantic category. Actual members of the category correspond to a greater or lesser extent to this prototype. Membership in semantic categories is thus a matter of degree or nuance, rather than the strict "yes" or "no" which distinguishes so-called "checklist" theories of meaning such as componential analysis in anthropology and linguistics (Sweetser 1987:43; Casson 1983:435).[14]

Prototype sets have blurred or 'fuzzy' edges, which means that at the margins of the category, as instances resemble the prototype less and less, it becomes harder to identify whether something is a member of the category or not. We can explain the fuzzy boundaries which represent knowledge of dynamistic infection mechanisms on the basis of their *grounding in experience*. Dynamistic infection mechanisms are first and foremost categories of causation, and, as Charles Laughlin (1993) argues in his study of phenomenology in cross-cultural ethnology, categories of causation are based on and sketched from experience. Likewise, the initial perception of illness, an "unwanted condition in one's person or self"(Hahn 1995:5), always proceeds from raw experience, direct sensory input, whatever cultural meanings may be subsequently ascribed to this experience. Because raw experience does not come in organized form, "[t]he more a state of consciousness is oriented on direct experience, the more fuzzy will be the categories informing experience" (Laughlin 1993:23).

The most important point about prototype theory for the present analysis, however, is that the core prototypes, i.e., the best examples underlying a concept, are also the *psychologically salient* members of the category, because the prototype schema *corresponds to and produces the meaning of the concept* (Casson 1983:435). I will discuss applications of the prototype theory for dynamistic categories later in this paper.

Väki

The concept of *väki* was first documented by that name in the late 18th century,[15] but was a fundamental part of the Finnish-Karelian mythico-magical world view already long before this (see Vilkuna 1956). *Väki* can be likened to the idea of a mobile energy force whose transference and effect on other entities, as well as the corresponding reactions it receives from other forms of *väki*, were central. Close proximity and a clear, unobstructed path to its target, if not actual physical contact, were thought to be needed for its transference.[16]

There were a number of different entities which were believed to possess *väki* in Finnish-Karelian folk thought. Different type of *väki* included, but were certainly not limited to: cemetery-*väki* *(kalman väki)*, forest-*väki* *(metsän väki)*, water-*väki* *(veden väki)*, earth-*väki* *(maan väki)*, *väki* from the sauna steam *(löylyn väki)*, fire-*väki*, *väki* of the forge *(tulen väki, pajan väki)*, and *väki* of the rock *(kallion väki)* (see Stark-Arola 1998a). Fire-*väki* was often described as the most powerful *väki*,[17] as well as being the youngest of siblings, with water as the eldest.[18] Additional sources of dynamistic force, although not directly referred to as *väki*, included wind, village chapels, holy icons and female sexual organs (see Stark-Arola 1998a; forthcoming).The force inherent in these entities was named only after it had infected the human body, as *nenä-* or *vihat*-illness.

For most types of *väki*, we lack detailed information regarding how *tietäjä*s and healers obtained and made use of this force. An exception is *väki* of the rock, which was used among other things to aid defendants in court proceedings. According to one informant, *väki* of the rock was more difficult to control than other types of *väki*, and elderly men were the only ones who handled it in former times.[19] Another informant from Archangel Karelia[20] described how *väki* of the rock was procured and handled so as not to 'infect' the user: it had to be obtained from a rock which never saw the sun and was perpetually wet, known as a 'crying rock' *(itkevä kallio)*. From this rock one had to find a place where the rock had broken crosswise, and drop 3 silver coins into this crack. After this, one recited an incantation asking the rock for its *väki*, and took small pieces of rock from the crack using an old knife. These pieces were then wrapped up in a bundle so that the sun never shone on them, and the bundle was kept in the user's pocket. According to the informant, all other forms of *väki*, with the exception of water's *väki*, were believed to fear this *väki*. The bundle containing *väki* of the rock could be kept forever as long as the pieces of rock were never exposed to the sun, but if they were, then their owner would fall ill from exposure to this powerful *väki*.

Uno Harva ((Holmberg) 1916:8) was the first to point out that some types of *väki* could neutralize other, opposing types, and that certain types of *väki* could be used by a *tietäjä* to drive out other forms of *väki*. Some of these *väki*-forces were seen to be stronger and some weaker, some mutually compatible and some antagonistic (Apo 1998:71).

Water-*väki*, cemetery-*väki* and fire-*väki*, for instance, could all be used to drive bears and wolves away from cattle,[21] and fire-*väki* could be used to defeat forest-*väki*, (embodied in the bear) when bear-hunting:

> *Väki* of the forge (*pajan väki*) is good for killing bears. Whoever has *väki* of the forge can make a bear freeze in place with a single word, so that it stands motionless. *Väki* of the forge is stronger than forest *väki*.
> (SKVR I₄:1197. Katoslampi. 1888. – Mikko Vasiljus, heard from older hunters, had himself tried the magic dozens of times and had seen its effectiveness for himself).

Fire-*väki* was also useful in expelling or neutralizing other types of *väki* as well:[22]

> Fire-*väki* (*valkeanväki*) is the most powerful and fastest of all. It can be used to drive out other *väkis*.
> (Kinnula. 1946. Otto Harju 3624. – Toivo Turpeinen, b. 1889).

> In former times, every place was full of *väki*. In the water was a particular "water's *väki*", which might start to torment some person…Water-*väki* was driven out using fire-*väki*. When the healer was asked how it was that he could grasp hot stones with his bare hands, he answered: "Fire does not burn an old friend".
> (Lohtaja. 1936. K. Hakunti 74. – Sofia Nissilä, farm mistress, 83 years).

According to one informant from Archangel Karelia, one could use fire-*väki* so long as one paid for it, in other words, dropped silver coins onto the place from which one had taken dust and ashes in the blacksmith's forge: "the spirit of the forge (*pajan haltija*) receives the silver pieces as payment for its *väki*".[23]

Fire-*väki* and cemetery-*väki* (also known as church-*väki* or *keikkaat*) were particularly incompatible:

> If one person has fire-*väki* and another person has *keikkaat*, then they don't mix. They can't be together even for one night, the rooms start to pop and crackle like a severe cold snap. One man was carrying church-*väki* (*keikkaat*), he came here for the night. But it started to crackle so badly that he had to leave, did not get any peace. "I'm not able to be here", he said, and left.
> (Kajaani. 1915. Paulaharju 7658. – Kaisa Reeta Tornulainen).

Fire-*väki* was useful in protecting oneself against cemetery-*väki* when going to the cemetery to do magic or to return cemetery-*väki* back to its original place after the agreed period of time.[24] But if fire-*väki* taken from the forge, for instance, became damp or wet, then the *väki*-user him/herself was in danger of being infected by the *väki*. In that case, water-*väki* could come in handy to protect the magic-user while taking the ruined fire-*väki* back to its source: "water-*väki* is a safeguard when taking fire-*väki* (*pajanväki*) back to its place."[25] This was possibly because, according to one informant from Archangel Karelia, water-*väki* was more powerful than forest-*väki* ("*vein väki kuin on vahvempi kuin metsän väki...*"):[26]

Information on dynamistic incompatibility can also be found from spoken incantation formulas, for example formulas uttered when taking water-*väki* from a whirlpool formed in river rapids: "Be my support, my safeguard, against all *väki*!";[27] or when taking fire-*väki* in the form of shavings and ashes from various parts of the blacksmith's forge (*pajanväki*) in order to staunch blood: "I request aid against all types of *väki*, only not against water-*väki*."[28]

Luonto

The term *luonto* was used in ritual descriptions to refer to a dynamistic force present in humans which derived from the self and acted upon the outside environment. *Luonto* is etymologically related to idea of agency (> *luoda* 'to create, make' (SKES:108). According to information from folk belief sources, all persons were thought to have some kind of *luonto*, which in its non-raised state was thought to be either hard (= strong) or soft (= weak). A person with a soft or weak *luonto* could be easily frightened and infected by outside *väki* forces in the form of *nenä* illness (see below). Ordinary persons could make their *luonto* harder or stronger through contact with more powerful, *väki*-filled (*väekäs*) sources. Raised *luonto*, sometimes referred to as a *haltia*,[29] on the other hand, represented a different state, one usually only achieved by *tietäjä*s, who were normally supposed to have hard *luonto* as long as they still had their teeth. In order to perform magic, a *tietäjä's luonto* needed to be "rugged" (*karkea*), "strong, solid" (*luja*) or "rock-hard" (*kivikäs*).

Luonto could be raised deliberately or in some cases unintentionally, as when a *tietäjä* saw a bad dream,[30] or began to brag and boast.[31] *Luonto* was raised by physically grinding one's teeth and jumping up and down, clapping one's hands, spitting, coughing, and being angry.[32] Physical manifestations of successfully raised *luonto* were most commonly the *tietäjä's* hair standing on end: "when he grinds his teeth, then his *luonto* rises and his hair stands on end"[33] (see also Siikala 1992:207–208). Raising one's *luonto* through these means was not always successful, however, and the incantation motif "rise, my *luonto*, from the *lovi* (*nouse luontoni lovesta*)" appears to have been used in cases when the *tietäjä's luonto* did not rise as expected: "...if the *tietäjä* senses that his *luonto* is not rising in the right way, then he begins his incantation thus: 'Rise my *luonto* from the *lovi*, from the undergrowth, my *haltija*...".[34]

As can be seen from such incantation verses, *haltia* or *haltija* was often a parallel concept for *luonto* (Siikala 1992:213–214). *Haltia* beliefs differed between northern Finland/Karelia on the one hand, and South Karelia/ Ostrobothnia on the other, but in both cases they were associated with the semantic field of *luonto*: "If there was a person with such a hard *luonto* (*kovaluontoin*), then it was said that that person has a hard *haltia*".[35]

74

According to the information given by one informant in South Karelia, one difference between the concepts of *luonto* and *haltia* was that unlike *luonto*, the *haltia* was seen as able to exist outside the body, albeit in proximity to it, and move ahead of it or behind it.[36] A person's *haltia* could also warn of dynamistic danger: in one text recorded by Samuli Paulaharju in 1916, a female informant "mumbled" something about how her *haltia* began to move inside her when she was in danger of infection from forest-*nenä* (= forest-*väki*):

Forest-nenä
I came across three squirrels, first a rabbit, then three squirrels then after that a reindeer – the forest-*nenä* is on the move (I thought), but it didn't infect me. My *haltia* began to stir inside me. The wife of Miina Kliimo had performed sorcery – the squirrels screeched and screeched. The forest was set in motion, that is certain... The old woman had visited our place and performed sorcery so that...
(1916. Latvajärvi. Paulaharju 7807. – "Mumblings of a woman from Latva-järvi").

This idea of the *haltia* stirring of its own volition inside the body when faced with danger may be associated with the idea expressed by some informants in which a *tietäjä*'s *luonto* "announced" to the *tietäjä* that a snake had been sent through sorcery to bite him[37] or "told" him that he could cure a patient's illness.[38]

Even after death, it was believed that the *haltia* of the deceased remained within the corpse for some time (see also Harva (Holmberg) 1916:15): "It is said that the dead person (*pokoniekka*) has a *haltija*. People are afraid of it."[39] This may explain why it was believed that ordinary persons could increase the strength of their own *luonto* by touching or approaching a corpse,[40] or by biting the twitching juglar vein (*elohiiri*) of a slaughtered animal.[41]

In some cases, a *tietäjä*'s *luonto* was depicted as having a will of its own, beyond the *tietäjä*'s own control:[42] *luonto* raised by sitting on a stone in the center of rapids, for instance, especially in a "black-blooded" (= dark complexioned) person, was believed to become so violent and frenzied that its owner could no longer control it.[43]

Luonto also apparently had a gender component – hard or raised *luonto* could linked to manliness[44] and male sexual potency, as in the example below:

Restoring a young man's potency
The young man is placed on his stomach over the mouth of the well, his shoulders are pushed down with a cowlstaff and the following is said:

Nouse nyt, *luonto*s, lovesta,	Rise now, your *luonto*, from the *lovi*,
Vielä haltiis havahek	What's more, awaken, your *haltia*,
Kerallas keikkumaan,	To sway with you,
Kansas kavehtimaa(n)!	To work magic with you!

(SKVR VII₂:4935. Tohmajärvi. 1889. Hakulinen 372. – Pekka Eronen, 73 years).

Having a hard or strong *luonto* apparently aided men in handling powerful and therefore dangerous types of *väki*. According to one informant, "*väki* of the rock (*kallionväki*) is taken from a mountain. It is more difficult to control than other types of *väki*. In former times, old men handled it."[45] According to Heikki Meriläinen (as interviewed by L. Merikallio in 1909–1910), female *tietäjä*s rarely attempted to control *väki*-forces.[46] This was corroborated by a woman from Paltamo who stated that "a woman cannot manage to control any kind of *väki*."[47] Women who could raise their *luonto* were seen to be exceptional, as can be seen in the following *luonto*-raising incantation:

Nouse, *luonto*ni, lovesta,	Rise, my *luonto*, from the *lovi*,
ha'on alta, haltijani,	From the undergrowth, my *haltija*,
*luonto*ani nostattele,	I raise my *luonto*,
haltiani haastattele,	Summon my *haltia*,
*luonto*ni kiven kovuinen,	My *luonto* as solid as stone,
karvani rauan karkiainen,	My *karva* as hard as iron,
vaikk'oon vaimonen eläjä,	*Although I am a wifely being,*
vaikk' oon vyötty naisten vyöllä,	Although girded with a woman's belt,
pantu naisten palkimilla,	*Fastened with a woman's buckle,*
jotta Hiiet himmeneisi,	So that the Hiisis would fade,
maan kamanat kaippeneisi	the earth's evils diminish
minun liikutellessani,	When I try to move them,
minun järkytellessäni!...	When I try to shake them!...
(SKVR VII$_5$:4697)	

Those women who were considered to have a hard *luonto* (*luonnokas, kovaluontoinen*) and thus extra agency ("and what she wills, it happens"[48]), sometimes also displayed male secondary sexual characteristics such as a beard or moustache.[49]

Nenä

The term *nenä* referred to a human illness (known variously as *heittäytymi-nen, hinkautuminen, nakkautuminen,* and *vigahine*) caused by infection from *väki*-forces in the environment which "attacked" human victims. In some cases, the victim was thought to have offended or angered the supernatural *väki*-agent. Kaarina Åstedt (1960:320–321) has suggested that the term *nenä*, "a mysterious illness which results from infection by the forest, water, cemetery, etc.," is linked etymologically to a wider field of meanings associated with "taking offence, becoming angered, being indignant, etc." (cf. Finnish *nenäkäs*) and thus refers to the concrete result of the nature spirit or dead person being offended or angry. The various symptoms complained of by *nenä* sufferers included toothaches, stomach aches, aching pains in leg, hand, joints, back, eyes, and ears, vomiting, a swollen tongue, bluish lips, eczema or a rash, feeling light-headed or dizzy, and general weakness and poor health. These physical complaints form no coherent class of symptoms and there is no indication from the available information that a diagnosis of *nenä* was ever made on the basis of *the symptoms alone.*

Nenä-type illnesses can be divided into two prototypical categories based on their mechanism of infection. In the first category, the illness agent was seen to infect the human body because the agent was "angered" (*suuttui, niipustui, snieppaantui*) by a transgression or offence perpetrated by the infected victim. Informants specifically mentioned the *väki*-agent's anger as the cause of illness in numerous cases. For instance, in Olonets Karelia it was explained that "the well in Radila village in Kolatselkä is a very angry well. One can easily be infected with illness (*maahinen*) from it."[50] Another informant from Ladoga Karelia gave the following account:

> *Concerning offerings and illnesses caused by places*
> In former times, several places were considered to become angry and offended if they were approached at an improper time or manner. They sent diseases into people, they "became angry" (*snieppaantuivat*) and many eye and skin diseases were caused by this… It was also the custom to give offerings of pieces of bread to the river running through the village of Palomylly in Suistamo when it "became angry".
> (Suistamo. 1935. Eino Toiviainen KRK 154:193. – Julia Särkkälä).

But although some folk informants explained *nenä* illness as arising from human wrongdoing, in actuality a large number of events thought to lead to *nenä* illness do not fit this category. Three occurrences in particular which led to *nenä* illness are interesting because they were accidental, non-deliberate acts: (1) being frightened or startled, (2) falling down, and (3) thinking about infection. Why should unintentional mental processes or loss of bodily control offend the nature spirits and dead capable of infecting with *nenä* illness? I suggest that this lack of agency was seen as the loss of distinction between self and "other". Being in contact with the ground in a horizontal position, for instance, seems to have been seen as a dangerous state. Part of the distinction between human beings and the natural environment is that humans stand vertically to the horizontal plane of the ground: to do otherwise represents a lack of agency. When humans are lying down, they are most often sleeping, sick, injured or dead, all cases characterized by a non-capacity to act, to exert one's conscious will over one's surroundings. The dangerous nature of such a state may explain why persons had to ritually ask permission from the ground before lying down to sleep (on the floor) even in their own homes, and why travellers in the forest had to ask permission from the ground and surrounding nature when wanting to sleep in the open.[51] "Falling down", therefore, may have represented a negative loss of bodily control and thus a blurring of the boundaries between self and the natural environment, leading to infection or penetration of bodily boundaries by outside *väki* forces:[52]

> *Curing forest-*nenä
> "In former times Reeta Jokela, now deceased, healed bruises that were said to be forest-*nenä*, caused by falling down…"
> (Kestilä. 1936. Sigrid Lämsä 35. – K. Rosinkangas, 54 years).

The earth infects when one lies down in the meadow, it infects so badly that one's face is covered with scabs. Nukuli-Jussa looked at it and spoke. Then he took [the patient] to the sheep pen and there spun a piece of earth using a knife, spit on it and used it to wipe the scabs and said:

Maa puhas, jumalan luoma,	Pure earth, God's creation,
Älä vihaa lastas,	Don't hate your child,
Saat sä sen sittenkin,	You will receive him then
Kun kuolee.	When he dies.

He did this three times and then [the patient] recovered.
(SKVR XII$_2$:5804. Kittilä. 1920. – Juhan Erkki Kauppi, old man of the farm, 76 years).

In addition to falling down, other commonly mentioned causes of *nenä* were related to the patient's inner state of mind and affective responses: these included taking fright when walking through the cemetery or a dark forest, or when recalling that a certain shore was the site of a former drowning (Lintinen 1959). By taking fright when in the forest or on a body of water, the person was seen to allow his/her boundaries to be momentarily "opened" or "blurred": "Forest-*nenä* infects, when one happens to take fright in the forest"[53]; "when you are startled in the forest, the forest-*nenä* intrudes, in other words, '*mehäh hiimosti*', the forest realm begins to make you ill..."[54]

One could also be infected simply by *thinking* of the possibility of infection: as one informant explained concerning wells, "...if one spits into them or otherwise disturbs their water, they infect. Especially if one 'thinks about it'".[55] The role of 'thinking' in *nenä* infection was already pointed out by Ilmari Manninen (1922) in his early study *Die Dämonistichen Krankheiten in Finnischen Volksaberglauben*: "Übrigens spielen die gedanken eine grosse rolle bei der ansteckung" (ibid:15); "Eine ansteckung vom Wasser (*hingaundahine*) kann man auch durch den blossen gedanken an diese möglichkeit bekommen..." (ibid: 88).

Examples from Orthodox Karelia suggest that the transgression of boundaries between the inner body/self and outside environment could be the specific result of internal cognitive processes:[56]

Forest-*nenä* comes, for example, if the wind whistles in the forest and frightens you and you think: "dear me, I caused something bad." "One's own thinking brings it."
(Tulomajärvi. 1943. Helmi Helminen 2349. – Solomanida Petrov, b. 1862).

For this reason, no one broke off branches in the spruce copse, for one will receive cemetery-*nenä* if one "thinks, what will come of it."
(Tulomajärvi. 1944. Helmi Helminen 3864. – Jevdokia Kohlojev, b. 1874).

If for example you happen to tread on cemetery-*väki* (*kalma*) and there you think and regret it, "then it forces its way inside." One should cough, make oneself inwardly stronger. One has to audibly clear one's throat, one must not take fright...
(Tulomajärvi. 1944. H. Helminen 2380. – Olga Fomin, b. 1905).

Incantations spoken during the ritual to heal *nenä* illness also allude to the notion that the cause of the infection was the victim's "thinking" of the possibility of such infection:

Hyvä ilta metsän isännät,	Good evening, forest masters,
hyvä ilta metsän emännät...	good evening forest mistresses
...anna rauha, terveys,	...give peace, health
anna rauha, anna rauha,	give peace, give peace
anna anteeksi,	forgive me
jos on tuhmin tuuminut,	if I have badly pondered,
viärin ajatellut...	wrongly thought...

(Impilahti. 1933. A.V. Rantasalo 160. – master of Jyrkinen farm, approx. 60 years).

Furthermore, several examples explicitly support the idea that if one did *not* "think", did *not* allow any suspicions of *nenä* infection to form in one's mind, then one could not be infected:

Nothing more is needed than that you spit in the yard and at the same time think: "hopefully it doesn't infect me", then wind-*nenä* has already intruded. There are some people into whom no sort of wind-*nenä* nor water-*nenä* nor forest-*nenä* ever intrudes, since they don't think about it.
(Porajarvi. 1943. Helmi Helminen 1485. – Ivan Hermonen, 75 years).

If while walking past the church or chapel one thinks of the cemetery residents[57] without sufficient reverence, the church or cemetery spirit (*snievaija*) may infect and produce some illness, and one is not released from it until one visits the church or cemetery and bows to its residents, until one pays a *proškenja* visit, asks for forgiveness. For this reason one *should not be thinking of anything* when at the church or cemetery, just make the sign of the cross and go past.
(Suistamo. 1900. – Iivo Härkönen 416. Emphasis mine).

How are we to understand the idea of humans being infected because they "thought" wrongly? I suggest that "thinking" of the possibility of infection or being startled represented a *breach in the boundaries of the patient's own body-image*, a rift in the interface between self and the "other world" (*tuonpuoli*), a domain which included supernatural *väki*-agents (see Stark-Arola forthcoming).[58] If these cognitive boundaries of self-awareness began to break down, the breach was expressed on the physical surface of the human body in the form of *nenä* illness. The boundary between self and other was thus the very same *luonto*-boundary which marked the outer limits of one's body image. One's *luonto*-force, in turn, was closely linked to agency and will: when one's capacity to act was diminished, one's *luonto* boundaries could be blurred or breached – and the reverse held true as well. This is supported by certain key texts concerning fright, *luonto* and infection. Not only was sudden fright the most commonly mentioned "cause" of *nenä* infection, it was also connected both to the "loss" of *luonto* or personal *haltia*[59] and to falling down: "When a person takes fright, his/her *haltia* departs and the person falls down..."[60]

The most common causes of *nenä* – falling down, taking fright, inadvertently thinking a thought – were all involuntary acts. Did the very fact of a person's momentary loss of volition open the door for the Other, the wilderness environment, to exert its agency over the now defenceless human victim? Did the concept of *luonto* represent, in some concrete or metaphysical

79

manner, active personhood and strength of will, such that loss of agency was seen to correspond to a weakened *luonto* and vice versa? This hypothesis is supported by descriptions which tell how persons with "soft" or "weak" *luonto* were infected by the wilderness environment, while those with "hard" *luonto* were not:

> Bears contain forest-*nenä*. When a person with a loose *luonto* (*löyhäluontoinen*) startles a bear, then forest-*nenä* infects, begins to torment that person. One must call for a *tietäjä*, who knows how to release the victim.
> (Kuhmo. 1916–1917. Samuli Paulaharju 7622. – old man Lehmivaara).

One informant from Olonets Karelia, when speaking of *nenä* illness, mentioned having been infected many times. According to the collector Helmi Helminen, this informant explained his susceptibility by saying that he had a "soft *luonto*".[61] In another description of a rite to cure infection by water-*väki*, the patient was supposed to hold a stone in his hand and say:

> May my *haltia* be as hard as stone,
> May no more *nenä* infect me ever again.
> (SKVR VII$_4$:3105. Suistamo. 1884. – Irina Paramoona, 70 years).

If *nenä* infection represented both a lapse in the victim's volition or agency and the breaching of the self's boundaries by the wilderness environment, the connection between a "hard" *luonto* and resistance to such a breach suggests that in the older dynamistic mode of thought, one's *luonto* defined the limits of the self as agent. At issue was the importance of one's *luonto* "boundary" for resistance against dynamistic attack.

The struggle between the self-force of *luonto* and the illness agent is suggested by a description of a *tietäjä*'s raised *luonto*: "...then the [*tietäjä*] becomes so filled with *luonto* (*luonnokas*) that when he heals a sick person, the illness flees merely from his raw *luonto*."[62] It can also be seen in a description in which a *tietäjä* performs a rite to counteract the *väki* infection resulting from a lizard bite: "one swells up and speaks angrily, so that the [lizard's] *luonto* grows faint."[63] The notion that fright signified a breached or opened *luonto* boundary in this contest can be seen in the following description of the effects of anger and cursing: "When an (ordinary) person becomes angry and lets out a curse, and the other person is startled, then the *luonto* of the one who utters the curse enters the [startled] person immediately."[64]

To summarize, prototypical penetration mechanisms for *nenä*-illness revolved around two *schemata*: (1) offending and angering an illness-agent and (2) loss of agency through fright, falling down, and "thinking". In the next section I seek to show that the prototypical mechanism by which *vihat* penetrated the body was *entry through physical wounds*, in other words, breaches in the skin-boundary of the body.

Vihat

In much of the scholarly literature on the subject, both *vihat* and *nenä* have tended to be classified as similar types of dynamistically infectious illnesses (Åstedt 1960:322; Kurki 1996:39, 41), or as primarily skin-related illnesses. Uno Harva ((Holmberg) 1916), for example, the first scholar to outline the main features of dynamistic forces, their manifestation in nature and manipulation through magic ritual, made no distinction between *väki* and *vihat*. In her linguistic analysis of the term *viha*, Laura Jokinen (1960) posits an original meaning of "snake venom". According to her, the term was later generalized to cover all manner of dynamistically infectious illnesses. Ilmari Manninen (1922) names both wind-*nenä* and wind-*vihat* as the same skin disease caused by the wind, but this claim is supported by only a few archival texts, since most of his material does not specify the mechanism of infection. His claim that in Western Finland the term *maanvihat*, like *maannenä*, referred to various skin diseases, on the other hand, is borne out by the available data. Manninen's work on Finnish folk concepts of illness was important because he was the first to focus on the diagnostic primacy of the *source of the illness in the patient's environment* rather than on physical symptoms.

In the present article, I take a different approach from the above-mentioned scholars by focusing on *dynamistic mechanisms of infection*, and more specifically the pattern of correspondence between terms used for these illnesses and their infection mechanisms as described by informants. Such an approach reveals that as dynamistic illnesses, *viha*(t) and *nenä* exhibit significant differences. Based on my analysis of these patterns of correspondence, I argue that *vihat* was a specific term used to denote a <u>*väki*</u> *force which entered the body <u>through breaches or breaks in the skin</u>, i.e., the physical boundary separating the body from the environment.*

A survey of the healing incantations published in the 34-volume series *Suomen Kansan Vanhat Runot* ("Ancient Poems of the Finnish People", henceforth *SKVR*) reveals that the vast majority of mentions of *vihat* appear in connection with the infection of wounds caused by bites, cuts and burns. The most commonly mentioned causes of such wounds were (1) bites from snakes, lizards, bears, dogs and other animals, (2) cuts received from rocks, tree branches, claws and fingernails, and iron blades (= knives, axes), (3) burns received from fire or frostbite, and (4) wasp stings. The injury in question was not merely the wound itself, but the *väki*-force of the wounding agent which was thought to have entered the wound. In addition, (5) liquid or gaseous substances (and their accompanying *väki*-force) were seen to be capable of entering pre-existing wounds and causing *vihat* infection.

All of the illness-agents listed above contained *väki*-force which entered the body after the illness-agent broke or corrupted the boundary of the body (skin). I therefore posit that the best canonical exemplar of the *vihat* prototype is *väki*-force transmitted into the human body through physical intrusion via surface breaks caused by *hard* or *sharp* objects: teeth, stings, rock, wood, iron and claws. Fire, because it had the power to penetrate through the surface of the skin, was also, by semantic extension, referred to as "sharp" in at least one incantation:

Vesi on vanhin veljistä,	Water is the eldest of brothers,
Tuli on nuorin tyttäristä.	Fire is the youngest of daughters,
Vesi on vanhin ja väkövin,	Water the eldest and strongest,
Tuli nuorin ja terävin.	Fire the youngest and sharpest.

(SKVR VI₁:3272. Varpaisjärvi. 1885. – Topi Huttunen, 53 years).

The primary and secondary meanings of the term *vihat* in related dialects and Balto-Finnic languages reflect several interrelated semantic fields pertaining to Finnish-Karelian dynamistic world view. The term *vihat* was associated not only with dynamistic force but also with anger: the singular form *viha* in modern Finnish means "anger" or "hostility". In addition to the semantic field related to anger, the word *viha* is etymologically associated with the semantic field of the adjectives "sharp", "biting", and "burning", in other words, capable of breaking the boundary surface of the body (SKES:1732–1733). I will return later to the connections between concepts of anger, hardness, and sharpness in Finnish-Karelian dynamistic thought.

Listed below are the different types of *vihat*- producing entities in healing incantations appearing in the *SKVR* series, grouped according to *mechanism of infection*:

1) cuts or scratches caused by hard, inanimate objects[65] (137 incantation variants in SKVR):[66]
– stones (*kiven vihat*),[67] trees (*puun vihat*),[68] iron (*raudan vihat*),[69] and fingernails and animal claws (*kynnen vihat*).[70]

2) bites or stings received from animals (115 incantation variants in SKVR):
– lizards (*sisiliskon vihat*),[71] frogs (*sammakon vihat*),[72] wasps (*ampiaisen vihat*),[73] bears (*karhun vihat*),[74] hogs (*sian vihat*),[75] dogs (*koiran vihat*),[76] wolves (*suden vihat*),[77] stoats (*kärpän vihat*),[78] and especially snakes (*käärmeen vihat, madon vihat*).[79] Related by analogy to snake's *vihat* were also *vihat* of the toothworm"(*hammasmato*).[80]

3) burns received from extreme temperatures (84 incantation variants in SKVR):
– fire (*tulen vihat*),[81] and frost (*pakkasen vihat, vilun vihat*).[82]

4) substances seen capable of enter pre-existing wounds (45 incantation variants in SKVR):
– sauna steam (*löylyn vihat*),[83] water (*veden vihat*),[84] väki from women's genitals (*vitun vihat*, transferred through sauna steam),[85] earth, soil (*maan vihat*).[86]

Some descriptions of the sources and mechanisms of *vihat* are given below:[87]

Dog-bite:

When an angry (*vihainen*) dog bit one so that blood flowed from the wound, then one was supposed to take a piece of bread and use it to wipe the blood from the wound and then one was supposed to give the bread to the dog to eat and say: "Dog, eat your *viha*".

When the dog ate back its *viha* in this way, then it was believed that the wound made by the dog's bite would probably heal...
(Sortavala. 1936. Juho Hyvärinen 822. – Heikki Saikkonen, b. 1904).

Iron and Steam:

Staunching a wound caused by a iron blade

...The wound is bound with a silk scarf and one recites the "Birth of Iron" over water or alcohol which is then put on the wound, and the iron-*vihat* are removed. And if one fears that *vihat* from the sauna steam will enter the wound while bathing, then when one goes to sit on the bench, he/she puts three leaves from the sauna whisk in his/her mouth and chews on them and spits then on the wound and says...
(SKVR XII$_1$:4384. Pohjois-Pohjanmaa. 1880).

Fire:

Removing fire-*vihat*

One licks the burn and recites:

Tulikulta, aurinkoinen,	Darling fire, sunny one,
Aurinkoisen pojan poika,	Grandson of the sunny one,
Elä viikon vihaa,	Don't hate for a week,
Elä kauvan karvastele,	Don't vex for long,
Ota pois vihas,	Take away your *viha(t)*
Ota pois vihas!	Take away your *viha(t)!*

This formula recited into grease, soured milk or milk does good, if one then rubs the wound with it...
(SKVR VI$_1$:3243. Juva. 1899. – M. Ruottinen, 57 years).

Sauna steam:

In the sauna steam the following can infect the wound: female *vihat*, water-*vihat*, snake-*vihat* and fire-*vihat*. Then the wound begins to swell up and hairs grow around it. One should recite an incantation for all of these *vihat*, if one doesn't know which *vihat* have infected the wound.
(Tohmajärvi. 1889. J.H. Hakulinen 254. – Pekka Eronen, farmer).

The prototypical *vihat* illness, then, displayed two important features: (1) it was assumed to come from a *väki*-filled source (fire, water, forest, etc.), and (2) it entered through lesions on the skin surface. A much smaller number of less prototypical infection mechanisms and illness agents connected to *vihat* exhibited one but not both of these features, and can therefore be seen as more peripheral examples of the prototypical *vihat* categories. Meanings which are not among the most prototypical include: (1) those dealing with scabbing, abscessing or swelling of skin, source of infection not clear (approx. 10 examples), (2) source is the wind and its *väki*, entering the body without lesions in the skin (2 examples); (3) source is *väki*-filled entities, mechanism of infection is shock or fright (5 examples); (4) source is *väki*-filled earth, mechanism of infection is horizontal contact or failure to "greet" the earth (approx. 10 examples, most from Western Finland and Ostrobothnia). In a number of examples (approx. 20 examples), there is no mention of how the dynamistic force in question entered the infected body, I therefore leave them aside.

Note that in cases 3 and 4 above, although the illness is referred to as *vihat*, the mechanisms of infection are those which were prototypical for *nenä*-infection instead. I suggest that the semantic fields of *vihat* and *nenä*, although analytically separable, overlapped at their peripheries (fuzzy boundaries). They tended to overlap in folk consciousness because they shared two features in common: both vihat and nenä were manifestations of harmful dynamistic force in the human body, and both were connected to notions of anger. Several informants, in fact, conflated the semantic fields of *vihat* and *nenä*, as in the following statement: "A conifer branch hit his eye in the forest, and thus forest-*nenä* infected his eye. There are such *vihat* in the forest,"[88] or in the following description of earth-vihat:

> …One receives earth-*vihat*, you see, from sleeping on rough earth or from being startled by something, in a place where a corpse was carried or water used to wash a corpse was thrown out, a person with a weak *luonto* (*heikkoluontonen*) took fright and received earth-*vihat*…
> (SKVR XIII$_4$:12750. Johannes. 1938. – A. Terväinen, 65 years).

Dynamistic Origins

In order to grasp the dynamistic folk model of the human body, it is important to clarify the relationship between *luonto* and other *väki*, and chart out their specific dynamistic mechanisms. For example, *väki* force did not only affect other forms of *väki* in the outside environment or cause human illness. Its could also be used to change the nature of *luonto*-force in the human body. For example the *väki* from rocks, stones, and cliffs was used to raise one's own *luonto* and defeat one's enemies, and if one drank alcohol containing forest-*väki*, thus subsituting forest-*väki* for one's own *luonto*, then the new *luonto* was "angry" or "ill-tempered" (*äkänen*).[89]

At this point it is possible to trace out a general model of the role played by dynamistic forces in the *tietäjä*'s or healer's power over the illness agent (particularly over illness agents responsible for *vihat*-infection):

A) the *tietäjä* raises his/her *luonto*
B) the *tietäjä* is aided in this by utilizing various *väki* forces
C) the *tietäjä* attempts to defeat the *väki* (in the form of *vihat*, for example) of his/her opponent by using knowledge of the opponent's origins, including dynamistic origins.

I have dealt with part A of the above model in the foregoing. I now examine the remaining two points in turn. Numerous archival texts give specific examples of how *väki* from the environment was used to raise or harden a person's *luonto*.[90] *Tietäjä*s might permanently obtain a stronger or harder *luonto* in this way already during their initiation period (Siikala 1992: 217–

84

218). Such "helper-*väki*" or "taken *luonto*" (*ottoväki/ottoluonto*) included *väki* from corpses and cemeteries (*kalmanväki*),[91] *väki* from rock formations and cliffs (*kallionväki*),[92] *väki* from stones (*kivenväki/kivenluonto*),[93] *väki* from thunder and electrical storms (*ukonvoima*),[94] as well as forest-*väki*,[95] water-*väki*[96] and fire-*väki*.[97] Various ritual procedures existed for the borrowing of *väki* or *luonto* from the environment, as the following descriptions make clear:

> Persons raised the vehemence of their *luonto*, which was needful in all magic rites. When a thunderstorm struck, sorcerers were supposed to go to the largest stone in the area, stand on the stone stark naked and look up at the thunderclouds and rake their ears with the fingernails of both hands, but their clothes were supposed to be next to the stone, and then when they took their clothes and left the stone, they were not allowed to look back, and they were supposed to circle the stone in a counter-clockwise direction while grinding their teeth together (namely before leaving) and recite:
>
> Anna minulle oma luontosi   Give me your *luonto*
> Ja ota minulta oma luontoni!   And take from me my *luonto*!
>
> that is to say, the sorcerer exchanged the *luonto* of the stone upon which he stood for his own.
> (SKVR XII₁:3523. Kuusamo. 1883. – Paavo Pringer, approx. 60 years).

> If one measures three times with their outspread arms a drying barn containing a corpse inside, then one's *luonto* increases, whenever it is needed. That kind of *luonto* is called "taken *luonto* (*ottoluonto*)". My late father had done this and he had the sort of *luonto* that his hair stood so much on end that his cap had to be pushed down.
> (Ylikiiminki. 1909–1910. L. Merikallio 121. – M. Meriläinen).

Once the *tietäjä* or healer had raised his or her *luonto*, it was necessary to know the innermost secrets of the illness-agent's essential nature and dynamistic origins in order to prevail against it. This information was encoded and expressed in the form of Kalevala-meter incantations recited during the healing rite (Siikala 1992:219–220). Such incantations of origin were often recited specifically in order to remove *vihat*, according to one healer who recited a 172-line long "Birth of Iron" incantation for collector M. Castrén in 1839.[98] The *tietäjä*'s knowledge included different categories to describe the illness-agent's origins and fundamental features: these categories included *koti* (home), *karva* (color, form, or appearance), *suku* (kin), *rotu* (race, breed), and *synty* (origin). Snakes, for example, were linked to the earth, underground, and hence the Underworld: *"Black snake, from under ground / worm, of the Underworld's karva / One who wriggles through decay / One who threads through tree roots! / Drink your viha in alcohol / Your own evil in beer... "*:[99]

> *Words for bewitching a snake, if it bites a person or animal:*
> Mato musta moan näköinen,   Black snake, resembling the earth,
> Toukka tuonen karvallinen,   Worm, of the underworld's *karva*,
> Tiijan mä sun sukusi,   I know your kin
> Voan en konna karvojasi...   But I do not know your *karva*, you
>   scoundrel...
> (SKVR VI₁:3933. Maaninka. 1932. – J. Raatikainen).

Not only were snakes seen to be linked to the earth in terms of their origins and fundamental nature: the same was also true of humans, iron, stones, lizards and wasps. According to one informant, "humans come from the earth just as does earth-*nenä* (*maan hitunen*)":[100]

Wasp

Moasta synnyt sinä,	From earth you are born,
Moasta synnyn minä,	From earth I am born,
Moasta synty suuremmoiset...	From earth are born the great ones...

(SKVR VI$_1$:3762. Nilsiä. 1892. – Pietari Myöhänen, 60 years).

One puts puffball seeds[101] (*ukon tuhnijoita*) in a wound caused by iron and recites:

...Et sä sillon suuri ollut,	You were not big then,
Kuin sä maitona makasit	When you lay as milk
Nuoren neitosen nisissä,	In the young maiden's breasts,
Utarissa uhkuvissa...	In the brimming udders...

...The maiden is the earth, in whose breasts iron is said to have lain in the form of milk.

(SKVR I41:224. Suurijärvi. 1888. – Ohvo Vaassilaine, heard from his elders).

This sort of knowledge of the illness agent's origins made it possible for the healer to appeal to an illness-agent on the basis of common or shared origins. For example, the *tietäjä* usually referred to him/herself as a *blood relation* of iron (because both human and iron were thought to have originated from earth), but merely the "friend" or "creator" of fire (which did not share the same origins):[102]

Words to Staunch Blood and the Birth of Iron

...Kuin sie vestit veikkoasi,	How could you carve your brother,
Lastusit emosi lasta?	Whittle your mother's child?
Moast' olet sieki,	You, too, are from the earth,
Moast' olen mieki,	I, too, am from the earth,
Moast' olemma myö molemmat...	From the earth are we both...

(SKVR I$_4$:195. Vuonninen. 1911. – Anni Lehtonen).

Iron's vihat *are removed by reciting:*

...Miksis söit sukuas,	...Why did you eat your kin,
Haukkasit haamuas?...	Bite your own spirit?...

(SKVR XII$_1$:4362. Kittilä. 1920. – Aukusti Lomajärvi or Kujala, 41 years).[103]

...Tuli ei polta tuttujansa,	...Fire doesn't burn its friend,
Raut' ei raisko lankojansa...	Iron doesn't ravage its brother-in-law...

(SKVR VI$_1$:3228. Luumäki. 1898. – Maria Mustaparta, 54 years, heard from her father Taavetti Mustaparta, nicknamed Rautava).

The *tietäjä* could also utilize notions of *dynamistic* origin, in other words, whence the illness agent originally derived its *väki* force. Wasps and lizards, for example, were linked dynamistically not only to the earth but also more directly to the snake which was the earth's prototypical representative:

The lizard, he contains snake's *viha*. Only his tail has something of the snake's breed (*rotu*), not the rest of the body.
(Tulomajärvi. 1944. H. Helminen 2482. – Solomanida Petrov, b. 1862).

"The wasp has snake's *vihat*, he has half of the snake's *viha*". One recites a snake incantation over a wasp sting.
(Tulomajärvi. 1944. H. Helminen 2407. – Jevdokia Ivanov, 32 years).

Frogs, on the other hand, were associated with water-*väki*, and were thought to transmit water-*vihat* through biting or scratching:[104]

Mato on muan karvainen,	The snake is of the earth's *karva*
Sammakko veen karvainen.	The frog is of the water's *karva*
Mato syöp muan vihoja,	The snake eats earth-vihat,
Sammakko veen vihoja…	the frog water-vihat…

(SKVR VI₁:4004. Pielavesi. 1917. – Juho Kokkonen, 70 years).[105]

Yet even more elaborate mythic origins can be found for iron's dynamistic force. "Birth of Iron" formulas include motifs reminiscent of creation myths which trace out the dynamistic origins leading to iron-*vihat*. The incantation material reveals two alternative theories to explain why iron is *vihainen* (angry, hostile, containing *vihat*). In the first version, of which there exist numerous recorded examples, the wasp or hornet carries snake-*väki* "from the far end of the North" into a primordial blacksmith's forge, and drops it into the water in which an iron object is to be tempered: "…*It finally threw its* viha / *into the iron's baptismal water / that is what corrupted the iron*"[106] (see also Krohn 1917:82-83). Note that the wasp, the snake and iron were all themselves seen to be closely associated with earth–*vihat*, suggesting that the transfer of *väki* was seen to occur along a chain of entities with similar dynamistic origins:

Mehiläini on meän lintu,	The honey-bee is our bird,
Herheläini on hiijen lintu	The hornet is the bird of Hiisi
Kanto keärmehen kähyjä,	Carried the snake's hissings,
Mavon mussan murhijoita	The black snake's spittings
Pajahe ovettomahe,	Into the doorless smithy,
Ilman ikkunattomahe.	Into the windowless forge.
Ei rauta vihani olisi,	Iron would not be angry,
Kun ei olisi keärmehen kähyjä,	If not for the snake's hissings,
Mavon mussan murhijoita…	If not for the black snake's spittings…
…Moa olet sie, moa olen mieki,	…You are of the earth, I am of the earth,
Moan olemma pojat kumpanenki.	We are both sons of the earth.
Miksi vestit velleäsi,	Why did you cut your brother,
Lastusit emosi lasta?	Carve your mother's child?

(SKVR I₄:132. Miinoa. 1894. – Passa Hukkani, heard from her father).

The second version, of which I have located only two examples, is linked to a broader series of origins which also appear to explain the *väki*-force contained in stones and the sky. In this version, the frog, associated with water-*väki*, contaminates the water with its *vihat*. The forged iron then becomes itself tainted by the frog's *vihat* when tempered in the water. In this second explanation of iron's dynamistic origins, the sky is depicted as having been made hard by its contact with the wind, and stone as having been made hard by its contact with the earth. But I suggest that because the purpose of the incantation was to recount the origins of väki-force or *vihat* in the cosmos and particularly in iron, the terms *kova* and *karkea* ("hard"), like their parallel term *vilu* ("cold", "chilly"), do not refer to physical characteristics but to a concentration of dynamistic force, to dynamistic hardness:

Birth of Iron

...Tuuli teki taivahan kovaxi,	The wind made the sky hard,
Samacko veden viluxi,	The frog made the water cold,
Vis[i] raudan karkiaxi.	The water made the iron hard,
Juovus viinaan vihansi,	Drink away your *viha* in alcohol,
Olunna omat pahansi,	Your own evil in beer,
Metenä muuna muojuvesi...	Your color in other nectar...

(SKVR XII₁:4203. Paltamo. 1824 or earlier).

...Moa kiven kovaksi loati,	...The earth hardened the stone,
Vesi rauan karkieksi,	The water hardened the iron,
Tuuli taivosen viluksi.	The wind made cold the sky.

(SKVR I₄:206. Uhut. 1836).

Hardness and Softness

An exploration into the dynamistic dimensions of corporeality reveals a key duality in Finnish-Karelian folk concepts, namely that between "hardness" and "softness". We have already seen in the discussion of *nenä* how a soft or weak *luonto* enabled dynamistic infection while a hard or strong *luonto* prevented it. In fact, not only *luonto* but also dynamistic *väki*-agents in the environment could be described as "soft" or "hard". For example, in some variants of the "Birth of Iron" incantation type, the term *kova* ("hard") replaces the term *vihainen* ("full of *viha*", "angry") when describing iron in some variants. This supports the idea that "hardness" here referred namely to dynamistic hardness:[107]

...Ei rauta kova olisi	...Iron would not be hard
Ilman kyittä, keärmehittä,	Without the viper, without the snake,
Mavon mussitta verittä...	Without the worm's black blood...

(SKVR I₄:185. Ponkalaksi. 1877. – Huotari Lukkani).

The dynamistic hardness of elements in the environment did not necessarily correspond to their physical rigidity or resistance: those elements mentioned in folk healing incantations as dynamistically "hardest" were iron, fire and water. As we have already seen, these same elements were also prototypical sources of *vihat*:

Kolm on kovoa miestä (yl. veljestä),	There are three hard men (or brothers)
Rauta, tuli ja vesi;	Iron, fire and water;
Ves on vanhin veljeksistä.	Water is the eldest of brothers.

(SKVR VI₁:3267. Savo. 1888. J. Hotinen p. 13).

But while dynamistic hardness did not necessarily require physical hardness, the two types of hardness could be translated or converted into each other. Dynamistic hardness of the body (obtained through magic, for example) could translate into physical hardness (protection from bullets or stinging wasps, see below). Conversely, physical hardness/sharpness (teeth possessed by a *tietäjä*, for example) could translate into dynamistic hardness (the ability to defeat the *väki* of illness-agents by penetrating their dynamistic boundaries and resisting penetration of one's own boundaries). "Physically" hard or sharp things which penetrated the *material* body (e.g. bullets, wasp stings) could also be conceived in the traditional world view in dynamistic terms: that is, as *dynamistically* hard or sharp and thus capable of penetrating the *luonto* boundary of another person or entity. Penetration by such dynamistically hard entities was thus thought preventable through reinforcement of one's own dynamistic *luonto* boundaries:

> A wasp will not sting if one spits, thus making one's own *luonto* harder (*karkaisee luontonsa*), and recites the following...
> (SKVR VI₁:3699. Kangasniemi. 1889. E. Lång 103. – Topias Hokkanen, 25 years).

> This Nuasman, or by his army nickname Perki (Berg), had been a soldier during the last Finnish war and according to Seppänen's story he had, using this incantation, made himself "hard" so that no bullets were able to penetrate him, and every time he went to battle on the war front he recited this:
>
> | | |
> |---|---|
> | Veijjon ukko, kultahelma, | Water's master, golden skirt, |
> | Vettä vänkillä vetäse, | Draw water with all your might, |
> | Ett'ei ruuvvit rupsahaisi, | So the gunpowder would not boom, |
> | Pahat jauhot paukahaisi, | The evil dust explode, |
> | Ett'ei lyijy miestä löisi, | So the man would not be struck by lead, |
> | Tinapalli paiskoisi! | Or the ball of tin be smashed! |
>
> (SKVR XII2:7929. Suomussalmi. 1892. – Juho Seppänen, farm master, 58 years. Heard from his mother's father, the late Sakari Nuasmanen).

Conversely, *tietäjä*s who had lost their teeth through old age were no longer considered to have hard or effective *luonto*. Placing an (iron) object in one's mouth while performing magic, however, could compensate for this lack:

> When a person who has become toothless begins to recite incantations, he must put an iron cross (for example made from needles) in his mouth, otherwise his *luonto* is ineffective.
> (Paltamo. 1909–1910. L. Merikallio 167. – Maria Luttunen).

> When a person has lost their teeth, their magic doesn't work anymore. But if they hold a needle in their mouth, then it will work, even if they don't have teeth.
> (Uusikirkko. 1903. Samuli Paulaharju 917).

A bullet which had already penetrated a human body (suggesting its superiority in terms of both physical and dynamistic hardness) could also be used in place of teeth to perform magic:

The most effective weapon is to put a bullet in one's mouth which has been shot through a human body – then one doesn't need to have any teeth. (Sotkamo. 1909–1910. L. Merikallio 198. – Heikki Meriläinen).

The fact that keeping such a bullet in one's mouth explicitly made one's body both dynamistically and physically hard can be seen from the following example:

...If one enters the battlefield and puts in one's mouth a bullet which has been shot through a forest animal and one recites the "Words of War" (which the narrator no longer remembered), then he need not fear the enemy, their bullets will be sure to go around him, or if they go toward him, then they won't penetrate his jacket, they will drop to the ground or collect on his bosom, if he is wearing a sash or some kind of fastened overcoat, they won't slip down to the ground...These are called "bewitched bullets". And if one puts these bewitched bullets in his gun and uses them to shoot back at the enemy troops who first fired the bullets, then they can't be bewitched again, they do the job they were sent to do, they go back containing their own *viha*. And if nine men have these bewitched bullets and shoot three bullets apiece, then the enemy troops are defeated, nothing can stand up against the bullets. (SKVR I$_4$:2084. Kellovaara. 1889. – Poavila Ontroppaine, heard as a boy).

A similar notion may underlie one informant's mention of certain *tietäjä*s who had become immune to sorcery during wartime by "going through fire and water" (cf. Siikala 1992:212). Such *tietäjä*s were described as "rock-hard" (*kivekkäät*).[108]

Numerous incantations to cure various types of *vihat* also include passages in which the *tietäjä* argues that the true, fundamental essence of the offending *viha*-agent is not hardness but *softness*, thereby cajoling the *viha*-agent into submitting to the *tietäjä*'s authority and removing its dynamistic force from the suffering victim. The attribute of *softness* was applied to nearly all *viha*-agents, regardless of whether they were animate or inanimate, or physically soft or hard. *Viha*-agents described as made of "silk" or "wool" included the snake, wasp, bear, dog, wolf, lizard, "toothworm", iron, stone and even the female vagina. Often all body parts of the *viha*-agent involved in the transfer of *vihat* to its human victim (head, mouth, teeth), even the *vihat* itself, were defined as "woolly": *"Your mouth is wool / your head is wool / your five teeth are wool / your vihat are woolly / you yourself are woolly"*,[109] or *"May your vihat, too, be woolly!"*.[110] These qualities were also attributed to the *viha*-agent's ancestors: *"Your mother is silk / your father is silk / you yourself are silk"*.[111] Healing incantations also redefined the true, secret essence of stones or rocks using additional images of 'softness'– the offending stone could be said to be actually a dumpling or made of feathers, for instance:[112]

One applies a stone taken from the edge of the field to a wound caused by a stone and recites:

...Maan munaksi mainitsevat,	...They call you puffball,[113]
Minä villakuontaloksi,	I call you mop of wool,
Höyhenyiseksi höpäjän...	a feathery fool...

(SKVR XII$_1$:3840. Sotkamo. 1888. – Jaakko Mytty, heard from Antti Pikkarainen in Sotkamo).

Birth of the Snake

...Villa suusi, villa pääsi,	Your mouth is wool, your head is wool,
Villa viisi hammastansa,	Your five teeth are wool,
Villanen otus iteckin;	You yourself are a woolly creature;
Villa myttylä isänsi,	Your father is a bundle of wool,
Villa myttylä emänsi,	Your mother is a bundle of wool,
Villanen otus iteckin.	You yourself are a woolly creature.

(SKVR VI₁:3798. Etelä-Savo? 1828?).

Anger and Fear

Earlier in this paper I raised the issue of a possible connection between dynamistic forces and human agency. I now probe this question further by looking at the association between dynamistic forces and emotion, an association already suggested by the connection between "taking fright" and having a "weak" or "soft" *luonto*. According to information extrapolated from the folklore texts, two emotions had important implications for dynamistic strength and weakness: anger and fear. From a dynamistic point of view, these emotions were opposed to each other. As we have already seen, the emotion of fear was linked directly to "weakness" or "softness" of one's *luonto*: according to one informant, having a strong *luonto* was seen to be the opposite of being a "coward".[114] The same idea can be seen in the following description of a rite performed to "harden" one's *luonto*: "If one killed a snake before the first cuckoo called in spring and ate a bit of its meat, then one's *luonto* remained hard (*karkea*) so that one feared nothing."[115]

Anger, on the other hand, as a manifestation of heightened agency, went hand in hand with "raised" or "hard" *luonto*. Having a "hard" *luonto* and being angry ensured that a *tietäjä* could effectively staunch blood,[116] and having a raised *luonto* and at the same time being in a fit of fury (*vihan vimmassa*) gave the *tietäjä* the ability to release a patient from a curse.[117] "When one becomes angry, the magic is more "*luonto*-filled" (*luonto-sampi*)".[118] In at least one *luonto*-raising incantation, vehemence (*kiivaus*) was used as a parallel term for *luonto*:

Nouse, *luonto*ni, loasta,	Rise, my *luonto*, from the *loka*,
Kiven alta kiivauteni...	From beneath the stone my vehemence...

(SKVR XII₁:3515. Piippola. 1909).

Moreover, when a battered wife wished to subdue her husband's violent or angry (*vihainen*) nature through magic, she did so by "lowering" his *luonto*:

A woman can subjugate her husband's *luonto*, so that he won't be angry (*vihani*), when she cuts hairs from her husband's forehead and puts them under her left heel, steps on them and says:
Thus is your *luonto* pressed down as these hairs!
(SKVR I₄:1907. Akonlahti. 1912. N. Lesojeff 94. – Hilipän Otti).

91

In one description from South Karelia, a woman whose husband "has murder towards her on his mind" could be taken to the forest by a healer to perform a ritual (involving a tree felled by a storm) in which the following formula was uttered:

masentukoon *luontosi*	may your *luonto* be brought down
kun tämä puu on masentunut	as this tree was brought down by
tuulen alla.	wind.

According to the informant, "when this has been done many times, the husband becomes good like before..."[119]

It would appear from the foregoing examples that anger made one's own personal dynamistic force stronger and "harder", while conversely, the lowering of one's *luonto* made one less "angry". What is interesting here is that the emotion of anger is not only linked to *luonto*, but is also a fundamental part of concepts surrounding *nenä* and *vihat* illnesses as well. Both terms are linked etymologically to the notion of anger (see Manninen 1922; Åstedt 1960; Jokinen 1960), and *nenä-* and *vihat-*agents could also be described as hostile or angry (*vihainen*) in the context of incantations:

Words for Staunching Blood

Ei rauta vihanen ok	Iron would not be angry
Ilman kärmeen kähytä,	Without the hissings of the snake,
Kusiaisen kutkelmoita....	Without the itchings of the ant...

(SKVR VII$_3$:770. Leppälahti. 1865).

One set of instructions for removing iron's *vihat* stated that if a person had repeatedly been injured accidentally when using an iron blade such as a knife, then the blade possessed hostility or anger (*viha*) towards that person.[120] In many incantations, the *vihat-*agent was reprimanded and reminded that in former times it had not been "angry" (*Et silloin vihanen ollut*).

The most interesting etymological associations connected to *vihat*, however, are those of sharpness, biting and burning (SKES:1732–1733), for they suggest that the *väki-*force in *vihat* was able to injure because it was hard enough (and sharp enough) to penetrate not only the physical boundary of the body but also the dynamistic or *luonto* boundary of the self. And this "hardness" was the result of anger. This can be seen in the following description of so-called "human *vihat*" (*ihmisen vihat*). Because anger was what made persons dynamistically hard, two persons who wounded each other in anger *not* capable of infecting each other with their *vihat*, since their *luonto-*forces had been protectively hardened by their own anger. Their *vihat*, however, could enter (through biting, for example) a *third* person *who was not angry* and was therefore was not dynamistically "hardened":

A human's vihat
When two men fight, then their *vihat* oppose each other – they are not infected by *vihat*. But if someone who is not angry goes in to separate them, then he will receive *vihat* if bitten by the fighters. For that, one must know the "Birth of the Human": "you are earth, I am earth".
(SKVR VII$_3$:136. Soanlahti. 1890. – Taaria Tuttavainen, 68 years, learned from her relatives).

This same notion can be inferred from the description presented earlier in this paper, in which anger made it possible for one person's *luonto* to enter another person, particularly if the second person took fright: "When an (ordinary) person becomes angry and lets out a curse, and the other person is startled, then the *luonto* of the one who utters the curse enters the [startled] person immediately."[121]

Conclusion

To summarize, Finnish-Karelian beliefs and practices linked to folk healing and the supernatural distinguish four prototypical concepts related to dynamistic body cosmology:

Väki: dynamistic force existing in the environment (e.g. in water, fire, earth, rock, cemeteries).
Luonto: dynamistic force *emanating from the self* and interacting with the environment.
Vihat: *väki* force which has entered the body *through wounds, breaches or breaks in the skin*, i.e., the boundary separating the "physical" body from the environment. The bodily penetration of a dynamistic force originating from outside the body always results in bodily illness or pain.
Nenä: *väki* force which has entered the body *through the weakened outer boundaries of a person's luonto-force* rather than physical wounds. As with *vihat*, the penetration of this dynamistic force into the self always results in illness.

I suggest that the concepts of *hardness*, *softness*, *anger* and *fear* are the key concepts needed to access meaning in beliefs and practices linked to dynamistic forces and the human body. In the older Finnish-Karelian dynamistic world view, hardness and anger were linked both to each other and to human agency (the power to exert one's will over one's surroundings), while softness and fear were linked to a lack of agency or active subjecthood.

According to Finnish-Karelian dynamistic thought, in order for *väki* in the outside world to penetrate the body/self, one of two things (or both) had to occur: either the human *luonto*-boundary had to be "opened" through loss or lapse of agency (fright, shock, fear, falling down, thinking of the possibility of infection), or the infecting *väki* had to be made, *through anger*, sharper and harder than the *luonto*-boundary it penetrated. Anger was seen to harden dynamistic force, and this either allowed the hardened (sharpened) alien *väki* to penetrate the human body, or, if a person's *luonto* were made harder through anger, allowed the body to resist penetration from outside forces. The very term *vihat* (linked etymologically to anger, wrath, hostility) concurs with the idea that the intruding entity, through its anger, was made hard enough to break the surface boundaries of the body.

Both *nenä*-illnesses and *vihat*-illnesses were manifestations of *väki* force in the human body, and both were linked to anger – only their prototypical mechanisms of penetration differed. *Nenä* illness followed both of the infection *schemata* mentioned above: in some cases it entered the breached *luonto* boundary of the body/self which had been opened through fright, thinking or falling. In other cases, anger was seen to make the force resulting in *nenä* illness dynamistically sharp or hard: the *väki* agent was seen to be 'angry' and thus capable of penetrating the victim's *luonto* boundaries even if the victim did not experience shock, fright, or other types of loss of agency. In the case of *vihat*, on the other hand, the penetrating *väki* was again made hard or sharp by anger, but at issue was its penetration of the *physical* boundary of the body (through wounds, lesions in skin), rather than the *luonto*-boundary.

According to the dynamistic sub-model of causation, sharp and damaging entities affected the body not only through their physical properties but also through their *väki* force or *vihat*, which remained in the burn or wound and was responsible for the ensuing infection and pain. The body was not thought to necessarily heal itself, instead, when the *väki* or *vihat* force was removed, then the harmful effects also disappeared.

Conversely, a hard *luonto* made what we would call the *physical body* harder, more impermeable to bullets, for example, thus preventing *väki* force or *vihat* from entering the body in the first place. It may be impossible to reconstruct the precise distinction between the physical boundary of the skin and the dynamistic boundary, based on the few available references to traditional dynamistic thought, but we can nevertheless posit that this dynamistic boundary was an important interface between the body/self and the threatening Other in the outside world.

Finnish scholars have long been interested in ethnomedicine and folk models of illness. This paper has attempted to supplement this research by approaching body concepts and illness concepts as closely interconnected, two sides of the same coin. If the infection of illness was perceived to be dynamistic in nature, then we must pay attention to corresponding dynamistic aspects of the body, since illness, as an "undesirable condition" in the person or self, always carries implications for the nature of that person or self. In this article I have attempted to sketch out the hypothetical dimensions of the body from a dynamistic perspective, but a holistically reconstructed model or image *schema* of the body based on Finnish-Karelian folk categories of illness has yet to be written.[122] Such a reconstructed model would be the methodologically appropriate blueprint from which our investigations into mind, body, self and illness in traditional Finnish-Karelian thought could proceed. In other words, it is essential to avoid the assumption that Western body concepts are 'universals', thereby using them uncritically as starting points for our investigations. We must be cautious, for example, not to attribute the modern Western body/mind dichotomy to the traditional Finnish-Karelian world view. As early as 1842, Elias Lönnrot pointed out the problem of the Cartesian divide between body and mind existing in the scientific biomedicine of his time, and observed that traditional folk medicine was better at recognizing the interrelationship between mind and body (Laaksonen 1983:14).

On the other hand, we must also be careful *not* to reconstruct past "embodied minds" or "mindful bodies"[123] on the basis of the familiar, everyday categories of our own culture. What things might fall under the category of 'body' in a premodern, face-to-face community? And what might be subsumed under the category of 'mind'? How might the body have been situated with regard to agency, self and environment, normal and supranormal, subjectivity and objectivity? These are the questions which must be answered if we wish to reconstruct, from the ground up, an emic model of the body as it might have been conceived within the Finnish-Karelian rural populace prior to the rapid and sweeping changes brought by widespread industrialization and modernization.

NOTES

* This article is part of a larger forthcoming study funded by the the Academy of Finland and by the research project *Changing Models of Girls' Culture* (HY, led by Prof. Satu Apo). My thanks go to Seppo Knuuttila for his comments to an earlier draft of this article.

1 According to Emily Martin (1994), popular images of the body as a fortress against disease, a machine or factory whose component parts can break down, or containing an internal 'army' of antibodies are all products of the latter part of the 20th century.

2 For example: Sault 1994; Briggs 1994; Lock – Scheper-Hughes 1987; Laqueur 1990.

3 See Apo 1993, 1995, 1998; Kurki 1995; Keinänen 1996; Korhonen 1996; Löfström 1998, 1999; Stark-Arola 1998a.

4 See: Harva 1916; Kuusi 1955; Apo 1998; Stark-Arola 1998a, 1998b.

5 The materials used as a basis for this study include ethnomedical descriptions, folk beliefs and Kalevala-meter incantations recorded in Finland and Russian Karelia between the 1830s and the 1950s and are housed in the Finnish Literature Society Folklore Archives in Helsinki.

6 Knuuttila 1989:167. According to Ronald W. Casson (1983:430), a *schema* (plural: *schemata*) is a conceptual abstraction which, in the context of human information processing, aids in reconstructing stimuli received through perception, systematically organizing how experience is understood. F.C. Bartlett (1932) is usually credited with being the first to use the term *schema* in its contemporary sense.

7 Knuuttila 1989:170; Siikala 1992: 28, 51–53, 77; Kurki 1995:103–104.

8 The model of magical harm due to the 'evil eye' (*paha silmä*) or 'mouthings' (*suutelus*) (see Vuorela 1960), should not, in my view, be considered an example of dynamistic *väki*-force, since the two types of supernatural harm operated according to different principles and mechanisms. For example, women were at higher risk from *väki* forces in the environment solely due to their gender, but not from the evil eye (Apo 1998:81–82; Stark-Arola 1998a:234–238), and there is no evidence that persons who were dynamistically more powerful (possessed stronger *luonto*) were thereby more capable than other persons of exerting the evil eye. However, being part of the same magico-mythical world view, the two models could in some cases be seen to interact with each other (for example, the use of female *väki* to ward off 'eyeings' or 'mouthings', see Stark-Arola 1998a).

9 See: Harva (Holmberg) 1916:7–16; Manninen 1922:122; Haavio 1942:51; Kuusi 1955:240; Vilkuna 1956; Hautala 1960:13; Honko 1960:58, 88–89; Apo 1993, 1995, 1998, Stark-Arola 1998a, 1998b

10 The first Finnish folklore scholar in recent decades to explicitly bring the question of dynamistic forces back into the scholarly limelight was Satu Apo (1993, 1995, 1998).

11 "Finally, the thing given is not inactive. Invested with life, often possessing individuality, it seeks to return to what Hertz called its 'place of origin' or to produce, on behalf of the clan and the native soil from which it sprang, an equivalent to replace it" (Mauss 1990:12–13).
12 Holy – Stuchlik 1981:23; Siikala 1992:51.
13 Holy – Stuchlik 1981:18; Shore 1996:209.
14 For arguments against traditional generative and structuralist "checklists", see e.g. Coleman – Kay (1981).
15 Christfrid Ganander uses the following terms to define the word *väki*: "strength, force, might, powerful essence, vigour (*styrka, kraft, magt, väldesaft, robur, succus*)" (Ganander 1787 III: 228, in Siikala 1992: 172–3).
16 See also Stark-Arola 1998:119–122.
17 See: Suomussalmi. 1915. Paulaharju 7655; Hyrynsalmi. 1915. Paulaharju 7657. – Eeva Aikarinen, 84 years.
18 See: Kajaani. 1916. Paulaharju 7654. – Kaisa Reeta Torulainen; Himola: 1884. Krohn 6698.
19 Kuhmo. 1916. Paulaharju 7652. – Old man of Kiviniekki farm.
20 SKVR I$_4$:24. Suopassalmi. 1889. Meriläinen 1283. – Simana Riikone, heard in his home district.
21 SKVR I$_4$:1499. Pontselensuu. 1889. – Vasselie Ratskoff; SKVR I$_4$:1501. Luusalmi. 1889. – Hotatta Karppane, heard from his father.
22 See also: Pistojärvi. 1889. Meriläinen II 1116. – Mihhei Wassiljef.
23 SKVR I$_4$:1079. Vaarakylä. 1888. – Vasselie Ontroppaine.
24 SKVR XII$_1$:3706. Puolanka. 1888. – Lassi Heikkinen, castrator, 60 years; SKVR XIII$_1$: 3709. Kestilä. 1888. – Jaakko Kolehmainen, 80 years.
25 SKVR I$_4$:1079. Vaarakylä. 1888. – Vasselie Ontroppaine.
26 SKVR I$_4$:1490. Tuhkala. 1888. – Samppa Riiko.
27 SKVR XII$_1$: 3721. Northern Ostrobothnia. 1880.
28 SKVR XII$_1$:4382. 1880.
29 See: Kivijärvi. 1911. I. Marttini b) 1042. – Maura Marttini.
30 Kuusamo. 1938. Maija Juvas 490.
31 Kuusamo. 1938. Maija Juvas 488.
32 See: Kuusamo. 1938. Maija Juvas 488.
33 Kangasniemi. 1935. Oskari Kuitunen b) 2650b). – Vilppu Laitinen, crofter, 68 years; see also Karttula. 1937. Juho Oksman 1433. – Taavit Tolonen, b. 1877, carpenter; Vuonninen. 1933. Samuli Paulaharju 22417. – Anni Lehtonen, b. 1868.
34 SKVR XII$_2$. 5443. Northern Ostrobothnia. 1880.
35 Lapinjärvi. 1929. Maija Juvas (SS).
36 Säkkijärvi. 1937. Ulla Mannonen 3613a. – H. Suni, 81 years.
39 SKVR XII$_2$:4930. Kittilä. 1920. – Koskaman Jänssi, 82 years.
40 Vuonninen. 1933. Samuli Paulaharju 22417. – Anni Lehtonen, b. 1868.
41 Salmi. 1932–38. Maija Juvas 175. – Mistress of Lutjonen farm.
42 See: Pihtipudas. 1893. Pihtiputaan kirjall. seura, Niilo Huttunen 830. – Man, 55 years; Muhos. 1894. H. Meriläinen II 2189. – Jaakko Saunakangas, 65 years, heard from Juho Mällinen.
43 See: Pihtipudas. 1893. Pihtiputaan kirjall. seura 707. – Married woman, 38 years.
44 See also: SKVR I$_4$:2059a). Suopassalmi. 1889. Meriläinen 1287. – Siimana Riikone; Vuonninen. 1933. Samuli Paulaharju 22417. – Anni Lehtonen, b. 1868.
45 Kuusamo. 1883. G. Laitinen b)24. – Paavo Pringen, approx. 60 years.
46 Kangasniemi. 1889. E. Lång 92. – Topias Hokkanen, 25 years. Heard from Heikki Paju in his own parish.
47 Kuhmo. 1916. Samuli Paulaharju 7652.
48 Sotkamo. 1909–1910. Lauri Merikallio b) 205. – Heikki Meriläinen.
49 Paltamo. 1909–1910. L. Merikallio b) 180. – Maria Luttunen.
50 Haukivuori. 1937. Oskari Kuitunen b) 3264. – Ruusa Laitinen, 55 years, farm mistress.
51 Kangasniemi. 1865. Henrik Laitinen b4) 103; Haukivuori. 1937. Oskari Kuitunen b) 3264. – Ruusa Laitinen, 55 years, farm mistress.

[52] Tulomajärvi. 1943. Helmi Helminen 2312. – Anni Jogorov, b. 1894. See also: Salmi. 1934–36. Martta Pelkonen 665. – Fodossu Stopanovna Homa; Tulemajärvi. 1943. Helmi Helminen 2318. – Olga Fomin, b. 1905; Säämäjärvi. 1928–9. E. V. Ahtia. KKTK-KKA; Suistamo. 1935. Eino Toiviainen KRK 154:193. – Julia Särkkälä; Tulomajärvi. 1943. Helmi Helminen 2312. –Solomanida Petrov, b. 1862; Kontokki. 1936. Vasili Jyrinoja E 132, pages 10–11.

[53] See also: SKVR VII₂:5063. Suistamo. 1900. – Iivana Härkönen, 75 years, heard from his wife Palaga Saharjevna and her grandfather Ondrei Lytsy; SKVR VII₅:5064. Suistamo. 1906. Konstantin Kuokka; SKVR VII₅:5065. Suistamo. 1884–5. – Helena Levantjovna, widow, 65 years; SKVR VII₅:5074. Ilomantsi. 1885. – wife of Räty; SKVR VII₅:5075. Ilomantsi. 1885. – Juhana Puhakka; SKVR I₄:1972. Latvajärvi. 1886. – Miihkali Arhippaini; SKVR I₄:1973. Vuonninen. 1911. – Anni Lehtonen; SKVR VII₅:5066. Suistamo. 1884–5; Salmi. 1936. Eino Toiviainen 30. – Jaakko Kämäläinen, 62 years.

[54] See also: Pentikäinen 1971:237; Sortavala. 1941. J. Hyvärinen 2353. – Maria Jokitalo, b. 1888; Salmi. 1934. Martti Haavio 937. – Oksenja Petrovna Karhu, 81 years.

[55] Kitee. 1894. O. A. F. Lönnbohm 1390.

[56] Tohmajärvi. 1891. J.H. Hakulinen 246.

[57] Porajärvi. 1943. Helmi Helminen 1482. – Ivan Hermonen, 75 years.

[58] See also: Tulomajärvi. 1944. H. Helminen 2293. – Solomanida Petrov. b. 1862; Archangel Karelia. 1932. Samuli Paulaharju 18566. – Anni Lehtonen, b. 1868.

[59] The Karelian term here, *kalman väki*, can refer either to 1) the actual cemetery residents, to the "dead" supernatural beings often believed to dwell in the cemetery *en masse*, or to 2) the impersonal, dynamistic force associated with cemeteries and the dead.

[60] The permeability of the boundaries between oneself and the natural world in the premodern magical world view, and the "open body" and "fluid body image" of premodern and non-Western societies, in which the boundaries of the "self" did not necessarily follow the boundaries of the body but extended beyond them, have been discussed by a number of scholars in the fields of history, anthropology, and sociology (Taylor 1989:192; Roper 1994; Sault 1994; Falk 1994:12, 42 note 14). The existence of "open" versus "closed" body images and the importance of body image for the social behavior of individuals have also been recognized by psychologists and psychoanalysts in studies of "high barrier" versus "low barrier" body boundaries (Tiemersma 1989:60). Pasi Falk attributes the "open body" to the fact that in traditional societies, the subject is constituted within a framework of a rigid cultural Order and strong community bonds wherein the "self" identifies with the collectivity, particularly the "eating community" to which it belongs. This fits well with the Finnish-Karelian situation in the 19th century, in which the most basic eating community was the farm household. This was not only the fundamental unit of production, consumption and reproduction in rural society, it was also the group-self with which the individual most closely identified. Accusations and suspicions of sorcery also followed this basic division between "self" (individual or farm household) and "other" (neighboring farm households), as magical harm against the self was seen to come from other farms, but not from within one's own household (see Stark-Arola 1998a).

[61] See: Harva 1948:255–256; Siikala 1992:214–215.

[62] Koivisto. 1935. Erkki Kansanen 155. – Gunilla Hoikkala.

[63] Porajärvi. 1943. H. Helminen 1486. – Ivan Hermonen, 75 years.

[64] Pistojärvi. 1889. H. Meriläinen II 1102. – Mihhei Wasiljef, 68 years. Heard from a "Lapp" in the area of Oulanka about 45 years prior.

[65] SKVR XII₂:5176. Kuhmoniemi. 1885. – Jaakko Pääkkönen, castrator.

[66] Paltamo. 1909–1910. L. Merikallio 163. – Maria Luttunen. Parentheses in original.

[67] These entities may have been conceived of in dynamistic cosmology as animate. In discussing incantations for the "Birth of the Stone", Tuulikki Kurki (1996:53) states: "the concept of a stone which rises and 'grows' out of the earth gives it features indicative of an animate being". According to Kaarle Krohn (1917:73), in both Ostrobothnian variants of the "Birth of the Stone" and Olonets Karelian variants of

the "Words to Staunch Blood", the stone was said to have had the capacity to grow until the time of Christ's death.

68 Same-theme variants given by the same informant are counted as a single variant.

69 SKVR VII$_3$:132, 134, 139, 140, 141, 142; SKVR XII$_1$:3839, 3841, 3846; 3858, 3861, 3862, 3879, 3886, 3887, 3888, SKVR XIII3:8538, 8539, 8540, 8541, SKVR II:617, SKVR I$_4$:51, 53, 54, 59, SKVR VI$_1$:3500, 3501, 3503, 3518, 3522.

70 SKVR VII$_3$:134, 233, 235, 245, 247, 248, 256, 263; SKVR XII$_1$:3979, 3983, 3991, 3993, 4004, 4005, 4007, 4011, 4017, 4028, 4030, 4032, 4043, 4035, 4042, 4044, 4045, 4046, 4047, 4054, 4055, 4056, 4059, 4063, SKVR II:632b, 635, 638a, 723, SKVR I$_4$:87, 94, 95, 102, 103, 104, 109, 111, 223, SKVR VI$_1$:3530, 3531, 3532, 3533, 3534.

71 SKVR VII$_3$:770; SKVR VII4:1339, SKVR XII$_1$:4087, 4123, 4199, 4202, 4203, 4227, 4230, 4267, 4277, 4280, 4308, 4312, 4333a, 4335, 4336, 4350, 4353, 4358, 4362, 4363, 4364, 4365, 4371, 4375, 4382, 4384, SKVR XII$_2$: 6356, SKVR II:644, 646, 661a, 665a, 668, 668b, 669, 728, SKVR I$_4$:130, 132, 133, 151, 153, 153a, 156, 158, 161, 162, 163, 172, 193, 194a, 215, 221, 225, 230, SKVR VI$_1$:3286, 3297.

72 There exist numerous examples in the FLS Folklore Archives' Ethnomedical Index under the heading "kynnen vihat".

73 SKVR XII$_2$:5167, 5171, 5182, 5184, 5186, 5210, 5227, 5231, SKVR VI$_1$:4004, 4006, 4008; SKVR I$_4$:456, 457, 460, 460a, 460b, 463. See also: Archangel Karjala. 1915. Samuli Paulaharju 6024. – Varvana Huotari, approx. 40 years; Archangel Karjala. 1931. Iivari Ievala 505; Kiiminki. 1917. Samuli Paulaharju 6594. – Heikki Kaakinen, 80 years.

74 SKVR XII$_2$:5139, 5141, 5149, 5152, 5158, SKVR I$_4$:450a, 452.

75 SKVR VII$_3$:977, SKVR VI$_1$:3722, 3762, 3789. See also: Pyhäjärvi. 1884. Kaarle Krohn 1963. – Eenokki Vehkalahti, 47 years; Impilahti. 1884. Kaarle Krohn 5471. – Irina Hilipovna, over 30 years; Rantsila. 1935. J. Simojoki KRK 223:1229.

76 SKVR VII$_3$:999, 1000, 1001; SKVR I4: 1490. See also: Kelloniemi. 1911. Nasto Lesojeff 26. – Muarie Okahvanen; Pudasjärvi. 1932. Samuli Paulaharju 19856. – Hilja Kuopus, 30 years; Russian Karelia. 1888. H. Meriläinen II:236. – Iivana Malinen, 55 years.

77 SKVR VII$_3$:999, 1000, 1001; SKVR I$_4$: 1490.

78 SKVR VII$_3$:999, 1000, 1001; SKVR I$_4$: 1490. See also: Kuhmo. 1932 (1916). Samuli Paulaharju 19860–19861. – Matti Kyllönen, 78 years; Sortavala. 1936. Juho Hyvärinen 822. – Heikki Saikkonen, b. 1904; Vuonninen. 1911. Samuli Paulaharju 4311. – Anni Lehtonen, 43 years; Karjala. 1866. H. Laitinen 3, 178; Metsäpirtti. 1934. Lauri Laiho 731. – Matti Jantunen, 70 years.

79 SKVR XIII$_3$:8960, 8961a, 8963, 8965. See also: Sääksmäki. 1887. K. K. Aalto VK 1:111; Jääski. 1938. Ida Utriainen KT 162:52; Joutseno. 1890. Vihtori Alava V:942. – Kaisa Ravattinen, 58 years, heard from Mari Rosti; Viipuri parish. 1890. Vihtori Alava V:331. – Liisa Sipilä, 55 years.

80 There exist 3 examples in the FLS Folklore Archives' Ethnomedical Index under the heading "kärpän purema".

81 SKVR VII$_4$:1002, 1006, 1006a, 1030, 1033, 1033a, 1034, 1035, 1035a 1035c, 1067, SKVR XIII$_3$: 8816, 8818, 8823, 8825, 8861, 8864, 8885, 8886, 8887, 8888, 88908892, 8893, 8894, 8895, 8896, 8904, 8905, 8906, 8908, 8909, 8914, 8917, 8918, 8919, 8924, 8925, 8926, SKVR XII2: 4970, 4973, 4984, 5000, 5008, 5073, 5109, 5113, 5114, SKVR II:743a, 744, 746, 760, 762, 770, SKVR VI$_1$: 5025, 5027, 5038, SKVR VI$_1$:3798, 3800, 3802, 3807, 3810, 3815, 3817, 3818, 3822, 3831, 3872, 3909, 3922, 3939, SKVR I$_4$:371, 419, 425, 425a, 442, 443, 446, 449.

82 In Finnish-Karelian tradition, toothache was often seen to be caused by a "toothworm" (hammasmato). The toothworm was described as "biter" and "digger" of bone (see Kurki 1996:59), so that it, too, was seen to penetrate physical boundaries of the human body.

83 SKVR VII$_3$:604, 744a, SKVR XIII$_3$:8730, 8732, 8734, 8736, 8737, 8738, 8744, 8745, 8746, 8747, 8749, 8750, 8751, 8758, 8759, 8762, 8764, 8765, 8766, 8768, 8772,

8779, 8780, 8781, 8782, 8786, 8788, 8790, SKVR XII$_1$: 4495, 4555, 4556, 4557, 4561, 4587, 4592, 4600, 4601, 4630, 4640, 4641, 4642, 4643, 4656, 4657, 4662, 4664, 4668, 4670, 4671, 4676, 4677, 4680, 4681, SKVR XII$_2$:6275, SKVR II:672, 674, 692, 692b, 698, 698a, 698b, 701a, 743a, SKVR VI$_1$:3178, 3230, 3236, 3243, SKVR I$_4$:266, 271, 273, 277, 330.

[84] SKVR XII$_1$:3907, 3962, 3964, SKVR II:621, 627, SKVR I$_4$:65, 66, 68, SKVR VI$_1$:3575, 3582.

[85] SKVR VII$_4$:2357, 2362, SKVR XIII$_3$:9213, 9232, SKVR XII$_1$:4384, XII$_2$:5317, 6347, 6351, SKVR VI$_1$:3474, 3475, 3484, 3485, 3488) see also SKVR XII$_2$:5320, 5340, 5341.

[86] SKVR XII$_2$:5318, 5362, 6313, 6315, SKVR II:932, 938, 941, SKVR I$_4$:223.

[87] SKVR VII$_4$:1959,1962,1963,1964,1965,1966,1967,1968,1970,2197,2203, 2207, 2208, 2388; SKVR XII$_2$:6212; SKVR XIII$_3$:9241; SKVR XV:656, 657, 658, 659.

[88] SKVR VII$_3$:134.

[89] See also: (snake) SKVR VII$_4$:1035a. Suistamo. 1914. – Konstantin Kuokka, (water) SKVR I$_4$:223. Katoslampi. 1888. – Mikko Vasiljus, heard from his grandmother, (stone) SKVR XII$_1$:3839, 3875, 3885, 3888, (tree) SKVR XII$_1$:4032, 4055, 4059, 4063, (fire) SKVR XIII$_3$:8780, SKVR XII$_1$:4656, SKVR VI$_1$:3244, 3245, (iron) SKVR XII$_1$:4350, 4353, 4371, 4375, (bear) Suomussalmi. 1888. H. Meriläinen II:399. – Aaprami Juntunen, 56 years.

[90] Kianta. 1932. Samuli Paulaharju 19626. – Anna-Pieta Lohilahti, old woman of Kemivaara farm, 79 years.

[91] Pihtipudas. 1885. Kaarle Krohn 15404. – Heikki Arenberg, 50 years.

[92] See also: Harva (Holmberg) 1916:15; Honko 1960:89; Siikala 1992:164, 173, 216.

[93] SKVR VII$_4$:49. Kesälahti. 1828. – Juhana Kainulainen; SKVR VII$_4$:56. Ilomantsi?. 1846; Ylikiiminki. 1909–1910. L. Merikallio 121. – M. Meriläinen, 83 years.

[94] SKVR VII$_4$:48. Tohmajärvi. 1889. – Pekka Eronen, 73 years.

[95] SKVR XII$_1$:3523. Kuusamo. 1883. – Paavo Pringer, approx. 60 years.

[96] SKVR VII$_4$:54. Tohmajärvi. 1891. – Seppä Juh. Riikonen, 85 years; SKVR VII$_4$:55. Tohmajärvi. 1889. – Pekka Eronen, 73 years; SKVR I$_4$:10. Kivijärvi. 1903. – Maura Marttini, heard from her mother; SKVR I$_4$:17. Katoslampi. 1889. Mihhei Vasiljeff, heard from a "Lapp" about 45 years ago.

[97] SKVR XII$_1$:3514. Kärsämäki. 1883. – Olli Keränen, 70 years.

[98] SKVR XII$_1$:3529. Kärsämäki. 1883. – Aapo Paakinaho; SKVR I$_4$:8. Mihheilä. 1889. Toarie Ohvolasjovna, heard from her father; SKVR XII$_1$:3719. Puolanka. 1888. – Lassi Heikkinen, 80 years. Heard as a boy from Lassi Tervo; SKVR I4$_1$: 2. Kiimaisjärvi. 1888. Risto Nikitin.

[99] SKVR I$_4$:15. Uhut. 1889. Jehkimä Ohvonasjeff.

[100] SKVR I$_4$:130. Miinoa. 1839.

[101] SKVR I$_4$:230. Kurki. 1872. – Miikkula Juakkoni.

[102] SKVR XII$_2$:5845. Ruija. 1931. – Erkki Kelottijärvi, fisherman, 72 years. See also: Kuopio. 1935. Reino Raatikainen KRK 114:26. – Aaro Sepponen, 59 years.

[103] The Latin name for the puffball plant is *Lycoperdaceae.*

[104] See also: SKVR XIII$_3$:8784. Karjala. 1847.

[105] SKVR XII$_1$:4365. Kittilä. 1920. – Tuomas Lomajärvi, "Loma-Tuokko", male *tietäjä*, 79 years.

[106] SKVR VI$_1$:4004. Pielavesi. 1917. A. Kokkonen 51. – Juho Kokkonen, 70 years.

[107] See also: SKVR XII$_2$:5395. Kuhmoniemi.

[108] SKVR II:662. Repola. 1846.

[109] See also: SKVR I$_4$:175. Tsena. 1821. – Jyrki Kettune.

[110] SKVR XII$_1$:4620. Suomussalmi. 1909. – Jeremias Seppänen, Kovan Jeru, 68 years.

[111] In an incantation entitled "After a bear-bite". SKVR VII$_4$:1001. Kesälahti. 1828.

[112] In an incantation to heal snake-bite. SKVR XIII$_3$:8925. Jääski. 1879.

[113] In an incantation to heal lizard-bite. Säräisniemi. 1936. J. Kaakinen 235.

[114] See also: (bear) SKVR VII$_4$:1000, 1001, Vuonninen. 1911. Samuli Paulaharju 4310. – Anni Lehtonen, 43 years; (dog) Metsäpirtti. 1934. Lauri Laiho 731. – Matti Juntunen,

99

70 years; Vuonninen. 1911. Samuli Paulaharju 4311. – Anni Lehtonen, 43 years; (wolf) SKVR XIII$_3$:8964; (lizard) Ii. 1917. Samuli Paulaharju 6596. – Matti Jokela, 76 years; Taivalkoski. 1939. Matti Tienari 945a. – Eeva Latvalehto, elderly farm mistress, 78 years; (stone) SKVR VI$_1$:3510, 3511, 3524; SKVR VII$_4$:147–150, 152, 153, SKVR XII$_1$:3853, SKVR XIII$_3$:8540; (wasp) SKVR VI$_1$:3722, 3762; Ilomantsi. 1884. Kaarle Krohn 7081. – Olli Tarvainen, 75 years; Isojoki. 1889. N.N. Möykky, 87 years. – Jaakko Korpi, 35 years; (snake) SKVR I$_4$: 373, 441, 449, SKVR VI$_1$:3802, 3804, 3806, 3814, 3826, 3831, 3872, 3917, 3939; SKVR VII$_4$:1035,1035a, SKVR XIII$_3$:8817, 8859, 8885, 8904, 8910, 8925; (iron) SKVR II:643. Kannila. 1884. – Ondrei Johorjov and Stefan Vasiljov; (vagina) SKVR VII$_4$:2203. Salmi. 1909. – Stepan Jänöi; SKVR XV:433. Savo. 1816. – Hans Laitin; SKVR VII$_4$:1965. Tohmajärvi. 1891. – Juhana Riikonen, 85 years, smith; SKVR XV:659. Liperi. 1837; SKVR VII$_4$:1964. Tohmajärvi. 1889. – Pekka Eronen, 73 years, heard from agricultural day laborer Matti Martikainen.

Kaarle Krohn (1917:73) interpreted formulas which described the 'softness' of stone (*"Ei kivi kovasta tehty/kivi tehtynä munasta,/vaha vaahen kokkaresta"*) as referring to myths of the beginning of the world according to which the stone was physically soft in primeval times.

[115] The Latin name for the puffball plant is *Lycoperdaceae*.

[116] SKVR XII$_1$:3518. Simo. 1891. – Anna Pahnila, 40 years.

[117] Virrat. 1936. Eino Mäkinen 1510. – Heikki Joutsenjärvi, farm master, b. 1861.

[118] SKVR XII$_1$:4399. Länsipohja. 1933. – Aappo Niemelä, old man of the farm, 84 years.

[119] SKVR XII$_2$:5443. Pohjois-Pohjanmaa. 1880.

[120] SKVR I$_4$:681. Kivijärvi. 1911. – Muaria, widow of Iivana, son of Juakko.

[121] Muolaa. 1936. Juho Toijonen KT 120: 78.

[122] Pori. 1893–97. V. Andersén. 221.

[123] Paltamo. 1909–1910. L. Merikallio 163. – Maria Luttunen.

[124] Satu Apo's writings on female *väki* (1993, 1995, 1998), which led the way to the current inquiry into cultural models of dynamistic forces, and Tuulikki Kurki's (1995) Master's thesis on models of healing rituals represent important steps in this endeavor.

[125] E.g. Lock – Scheper-Hughes 1987; Strathern 1996; Davis 1997; Young 1994.

Abbreviations for Archival Source Materials

KKTK-KKA = *Kotimaisten Kielten Tutkimuskeskus, Karjalan Kielen Arkisto* (*Karelian Lexical Archives of the Research Institute for the Languages of Finland*).

KRK = *Kalevalan riemuvuoden kilpakeräys* (*Collection contest in honor of the100th anniversary of the Kalevala*). 1935–6. Finnish Literature Society. Helsinki.

KT = *Kansantieto-lehti kysely* (*Answers to the questionnaire in the journal 'Folk Knowledge'*). 1936-present. Finnish Literature Society. Helsinki.

SKVR = *Suomen Kansan Vanhat Runot* (*Ancient Poems of the Finnish People*). 1908–1948. Finnish Literature Society. Helsinki

VK =*Vähäisiä keräelmiä* (*Minor collections*). 1900–1930s. Finnish Literature Society. Helsinki.

BIBLIOGRAPHY

Alles, Gregory D. 1987: Dynamism. M. Eliade (ed.) The Encyclopedia of Religion, 4:527–532.

Apo, Satu 1993: "'Ex cunno väki tulevi". Naistutkimus 3:4–14.

– 1995: "'Ex cunno väki tulee'. Fyysiseen naiseuteen liittyvä ajattelu suomalais-karjalaisessa perinteessä". Naisen väki: tutkimuksia suomalaisten kansan-omaisesta kulttuurista ja ajattelusta. Hanki ja Jää, pp. 11–49. Helsinki.

- 1998: "'Ex cunno come the folk and force: concepts of women's dynamistic power in Finnish-Karelian tradition". S. Apo – A. Nenola – L. Stark-Arola (eds) Gender and Folklore: Perspectives on Finnish and Karelian Culture. Studia Fennica Folkloristica 4. Finnish Literature Society, pp. 63–91. Helsinki.

Bartlett, F. C.1932: Remembering: A Study in Experimental and Social Psychology. Cambridge University Press. Cambridge.

Berking, Helmuth 1999: The Sociology of Giving. Sage. London.

Briggs, Charles 1994: The Sting of the Ray: Bodies, Agency and Grammar in Warao Curing. Journal of American Folklore 107(423): 139–166.

Casson, Ronald W. 1983: Schemata in Cognitive Anthropology. Annual Review of Anthropology 12:429–462.

Coleman, L. – Kay, Paul 1981: Prototype semantics. Language 57:26–44.

Davis, Kathy (ed.) 1997: Embodied Practices: Feminist Perspectives on the Body. Sage Publications. London.

Falk, Pasi 1994: The Consuming Body. Sage Publications. London.

Haavio, Martti 1942: Suomalaiset kodinhaltiat. Werner Söderström. Porvoo.

Hahn, Robert A. 1995: Sickness and Healing: An Anthropological Perspective. Yale University Press. New Haven and London.

Haraway, Donna J. 1991: Simians, Cyborgs and Women: The Reinvention of Nature. Free Association Books. London.

Harva (Holmberg), Uno 1916: Jumalauskon alkuperä. Otava. Helsinki.

- 1948: Suomalaisten muinaisusko. WSOY. Porvoo.

Hastrup, Kirsten 1995: A Passage to Anthropology: Between Experience and Theory. Routledge. London and New York.

Hautala, Jouko 1960: "Sanan mahti". J. Hautala (ed.) Jumin keko: tutkielmia kansanrunoustieteen alalta. Finnish Literature Society, pp. 7–42. Helsinki.

Holy, Ladislav – Stuchlik, Milan 1981: The Structure of Folk Models. Academic Press. London.

Honko, Lauri 1960: Varhaiskantaiset taudinselitykset ja parantamisnäytelmä. J. Hautala (ed.) Jumin keko: tutkielmia kansanrunoustieteen alalta. Finnish Literature Society, pp. 43–111. Helsinki.

Jokinen, Laura 1960: Suomen kielen maaginen viha. Sananjalka vol. 2:78–95.

Keinänen, Marja-Liisa 1996: The ritual transformation of a newborn in Savo-Karelia. H. Leskinen – R. Raittila – T. Seilenthal (eds) Ethnologia & Folkloristica. Congressus Octavus Internationalis Fenno-Ugristarum Pars VI. Moderatores. Jyväskylä.

Korhonen, Teppo 1996: Anasyrma in the Finnish Tradition. Ethnologia Fennica 24:13–30.

Knuuttila, Seppo 1989: Kansanomainen maailmankuva. J. Manninen – M. Envall –S. Knuuttila (eds) Maailman Kulttuurin Kokonaisuudessa: Aate- ja oppihistoiran, kirjallisuustieteen ja kulttuuriantropologian näkökulmia. Pohjoinen. Oulu.

Krohn, Kaarle 1917: Suomalaiset syntyloitsut: vertaileva tutkimus. Finnish Literature Society. Helsinki.

Kurki, Tuulikki 1995: Tautikäsitykset parantamista ohjaavina tiedollisina rakenteina: tutkielma suomalaisesta kansanlääkinnästä. Unpublished Master's Thesis, University of Joensuu.

- 1996: Kansanparantamisen mallintamisesta. K. Kortelainen – S. Vakimo (eds) Tradition edessä: kirjoituksia perinteestä ja kulttuurista. Suomen Kansantietouden Tutkijain Seura. Helsinki.

Kuusi, Matti 1955: Pohjoispohjalaista taikuutta kahden vuosisadan takaa. Kalevalaseuran Vuosikirja 35: 221–246.

Laaksonen, Pekka 1983: Kansanlääkinnän tutkimuksen vaiheita. Kansa Parantaa. Yearbook of the Kalevala Society 63. Finnish Literature Society, pp. 11–24. Helsinki.

Laqueur, Thomas 1990: Making Sex: Body and Gender from the Greeks to Freud. Harvard University Press. Cambridge and London.

Laughlin, Charles D. 1993: Fuzziness and Phenomenology in Ethnological Research: Insights from Fuzzy Set Theory. Journal of Anthropological Research 49:17–37.

Lintinen, Jaakko 1959: Säikähtäminen. Proseminaarityö. S 84. Department of Folklore Studies, University of Helsinki.

Lock, Margaret – Scheper-Hughes, Nancy 1987: The Mindful Body. Medical Anthropology Quarterly 1(1): 6–41.

Löfström, Jan 1998: Changing conceptions of gender polarity in Finland: from rural to urban culture. S. Apo – A. Nenola – L. Stark-Arola (eds) Gender and Folklore: Perspectives on Finnish and Karelian Culture. Studia Fennica Folkloristica 4. Finnish Literature Society, pp. 239–259. Helsinki.

– 1999: The hermaphrodite figure in Finnish rural folklore and oral tradition presentation given at Nordic researcher workshop "Representations and practices of gender in Nordic cultures"April 22.–24. 1999, Jyväskylä, Finland.

Manninen, Ilmari 1922: Die Dämonistichen Krankheiten in Finnischen Volksaberglauben. Folklore Fellows Communications (no. 45). Suomalainen Tiedeakatemia. Loviisa.

Marett, R.R. 1914/1909: The Threshold of Religion. Methuen. London.

Martin, Emily 1994: Flexible Bodies: Tracking Immunity in American Culture-From the Days of Polio to the Age of Aids. Beacon Press. Boston.

Mauss, Marcel. 1974/1904: A General Theory of Magic (translated by Robert Brain). Routledge and Kegan Paul. London and Boston.

– 1990/1950: The Gift: The Form and Functions of Exchange in Archaic Societies. Routledge. London.

Preuss, Konrad T. 1904: Der Ursprung der Religion und Kunst. Globus 86.

Prins, Baukje 1993: The Ethics of Hybrid Subjects: Feminist Constructivism According to Donna Haraway. Paper for the EASST/PICT workshop on Feminism, Constructivism and Utility, at Brunel, the University of West London, United Kingdom.

Roper, Lyndal 1994: Oedipus and the Devil: Witchcraft, Sexuality and Religion in Early Modern Europe. Routledge. London and New York.

Sault, Nicole (ed.) 1994: Many Mirrors: Body Image and Social Relations. Rutgers University Press. New Brunswick.

Shore, Bradd 1996: Culture in Mind: Cognition, Culture and the Problem of Meaning. Oxford University Press. New York.

Siikala, Anna-Leena 1992: Suomalainen šamanismi. Finnish Literature Society. Helsinki.

SKES = Suomen Kielen Etymologinen Sanakirja. 1955–1978. Y. H. Toivonen – E. Itkonen – A.J. Joki – R. Peltola (eds) Suomalais-Ugrilainen Seura. Helsinki.

Stark-Arola, Laura 1998a: Magic, Body and Social order: the Construction of Gender Through Women's Private Rituals in Traditional Finland. Studia Fennica Folkloristica 5. Finnish Literature Society. Helsinki.

– 1998b: Lempi, tuli ja naisten väki – Dynamistisista suhteista suomalais-karjalaisessa taikuudessa ja kansanuskossa. J. Pöysä – A.-L. Siikala (eds) Amor, Genus ja Familia: Kirjoituksia kansanperinteestä. Tietolipas 158. Finnish Literature Society, pp. 117–135. Helsinki.

– 1998c: Sacred beings and 'mirror' communities: from bodily ailment to collective self-image. Orthodox Karelian folk ritual. Temenos 34:195:220.

– Forthcoming: Peasants, Pilgrims and Sacred Promises: Ritual and the Supernatural in Orthodox Karelian Folk Religion. Finnish Literature Society. Helsinki.

Strathern, Andrew 1996: Body Thoughts. University of Michigan Press. Ann Arbour, MI.

Strathern, Marilyn 1988: The Gender of the Gift: Problems with Women and Problems with Society in Melanesia. University of California Press. Berkeley.

Sweetser, Eve 1987: The definition of lie: an examination of the folk models underlying a semantic prototype. N. Quinn – D. Holland (eds) Cultural Models in Language and Thought. Cambridge University Press, pp. 43–66. Cambridge.

Taylor, Charles 1989: Sources of the Self. The Making of the Modern Identity. Cambridge University Press. Cambridge.

Tiemersma, Douwe 1989: Body Schema and Body Image: An Interdisciplinary and Philosophical Study. Swets & Zeitlinger. Amsterdam.

Tilvis, Riitta 1989: Jiäksiminen kriisiriittinä. Pyhän lupauksen antaminen ja toteuttaminen Salmin pitäjässä 1890–1939. Department of Comparative Religion, unpublished pro-gradu thesis. University of Helsinki.

Van Baal, J. 1971: Symbols for Communication: an Introduction to the Anthropological Study of Religion. Assen: Van Gorcum & Comp. N.V.-Dr. H.J. Prakke & H.M.G. Prakke.

Vilkuna, Asko 1956: Das Verhalten der Finnen in "Heiligen" (Pyhä) Situationen. FF Communications N:o 164. Suomalainen Tiedeakatemia. Helsinki.

Vuorela, Toivo 1960: Paha silmä suomalaisen perinteen valossa. Finnish Literature Society. Helsinki.

Young, Katharine 1994: Whose Body: An Introduction to Bodylore. Journal of American Folklore 107(423):2–8.

Åstedt, Kaarina 1960: Mytologisista Nenä-Yhdynnäisistä. Kalevalaseura Vuosikirja 40, pp. 307–322.

Witches and Devils

ÉVA PÓCS

World View, Witch Legend, Witch Confession

This paper explores the various mental models of witchcraft formulated from confessions made in Hungarian witchcraft trials from the 16th to 18th centuries. These models offer a glimpse of changes in the peasant world view during the early modern period. The different types of witch-legends recounted in court and their alterations reflect the variants of and changes in the Central European concept of witchcraft.

My survey was produced thanks to my work with a research team involving historians and folklorists seeking to explore the social and ideological background of witch-hunts, its conditions both within the legal system and the institution of popular witchcraft. Part of my research is based on the analysis of the narratives included in witch-trial confessions.[1]

The concept of witchcraft is used here in a social anthropological sense,[2] i.e., as an institution to explain misfortune and regulate social conflicts – an institution found in most early modern European rural societies with or without the presence of witch-hunts and the persecuting elite's demonology. According to the world view inferable from the mechanism of the institution, misfortunes are caused by humans, enemies within the society purportedly able to bring about harm – *maleficium* – to people and property by using their supernatural powers. Since witchcraft was the most important belief-system to prevail in early modern European rural societies, or at least in the Central Eastern European region to which Hungary belongs, these narratives, in a larger context, illustrate the transformation of the popular world view taking place during that period. At least in this part of Europe the human-centered explanations for misfortunes were preceded by ideologies of superhuman causes, i.e., demonic beings – illness demons, fairies, ghosts and revenants – who belonged to folk belief-systems.

Injuries perpetrated by humans could be forestalled by both the actual and alleged practice of benevolent, "white" magic, and maleficent, "black", magic. The ability to bewitch people and its presumed practice were not "peculiar" in terms of this system; their consequences could be eliminated within the system itself. As Keith Thomas writes:[3] "It was accepted in the Middle Ages that there were individuals capable of performing acts of *maleficium* by occult means, just as there were others who used their magic for beneficent purposes". White magic as an actual practice, black magic as

Myth and Mentality
Studia Fennica
Folkloristica 8, 2002

a practice very often just *ascribed* to the witch and counter black magic as an activity to prevent or retrieve the witch's *maleficium*: these balanced each other, and they were part of the traditional blow-preventing and conflict-settling routine of "village witchcraft".

The fact that misfortunes were ascribed to human agents may be explained by the growing prevalence of the institution of witchcraft. In fact, witchcraft soon eclipsed *supernatural* explanations: demonic creatures from the super-natural world were supplanted by the "village witch". Now the specialists of magic, rather than working to prevent supernatural forces, had to turn their attention to identifying witches and finding compensation for the injuries they caused. Thus the establishment of the institution of "village witchcraft" brought about the collapse of the archaic "pre-witchcraft" world view. This process was brought to a halt by the witch-hunts, which, in addition to inter-fering with the local institutions of popular witchcraft, also muddled up the ideologies of the peasant world view whereby misfortunes were explained in human terms; witch persecution confused these views with its Satanic doctrines. Nevertheless, the institution of popular witchcraft and the figure of the "village witch" had already existed before witch-hunting started, at least in Central and Western Europe. During the era of witch-persecution, that is between the 15th and 18th centuries in Europe, official persecution and its ideology and the popular system were organically linked and even determined one another. Regarding the latter, we have practically one single source, the trial records written down by the representatives of the elite culture.

The following is an account of some details of my research on the narratives of the witch-trial records. I have attempted to draw conclusions about the various mental models of witchcraft from the characteristics of the court narratives told by the witnesses, accusers and accused. The *narratives* show that the harm purportedly caused by witches reflect the operation of the rural institution of witchcraft – to use Macfarlane's term[4] – "the sociology of accusation", the conflicts underlying accusations, the system of relations, and the related practice for solving conflicts. I could complete the examination of the narratives with contextual information on the accused witches, with data referring – directly, although incompletely – to the social background of the witches, and to the beliefs and magical practice ascribed to them.

The analysis I made in Sopron was first and foremost based on the testimonies concerning *maleficium*. Witnesses were called upon to testify against witches and provide evidence of *maleficium*. Their narratives describe both the antecedents and consequences of the damage. Before the *maleficium* is committed, the witch and the victim have interacted several times. According to the narratives, these encounters are inextricably linked to the damage. My analysis of certain types and combinations of (inductive) interactions preceding the *maleficium* allowed me to distinguish between the various types of witches on the basis of their regularity and difference. The analysis of the narratives was based on a system we had set up for our collective computer research.[5] We had established the possible patterns of *maleficium* narratives on the basis of the combination of textually recurring elements in several sample-texts.

These text-elements constitute different sequences with characteristic orders and omissions. These are the possible text elements in the order of their frequency:

C = Conflict;
T = Threat curse;
R = Real appearance;
S = Supernatural appearance;
M = Maleficium;
I = Identification;
H = Healing.

The different types of witches are distinguished according to the encounters ("conflicts") which bring about the *maleficium*, and can be characterized by different sequence-types. The type of encounter chosen to express the real conflict symbolically in the unit *conflict* of the narrative sequence is far from random. The symbolic expression of the conflict is a key distinguishing feature of the "witchcraft" types.

I was able to distinguish three simple and two compound sequence-types in the 397 narratives from Sopron County. A single witch is rarely associated with one single narrative-type. In fact, in the testimonies several different narrative-types tend to appear in the identification of the accused person, that is, here we have several coexisting aspects of witchcraft instead of independent witch-types.

Let us now look at the established narrative-types:

Type A) is the *defrauded witch*: these are the cases of *maleficia* based on neighborhood conflicts. This type has been well-known since the Essex analysis by Macfarlane.[6] The structural pattern of their narratives is as follows:

C - T - M - I - H

The C-element of the narratives ("conflict") indicates the violation of a social norm. In other words, this means a denial of any form of *giving* and thus defrauding the other. The witch restores the balance lost by defrauding the other party to excess. To restore the balance, she may bewitch the victim so that both the first offence, that is, refusing a request, and the second offence, that is, the magical retaliation, produce an inadequacy in the same area of everyday life. For example, the victim who has broken his promise to wed the witch is rendered impotent.[7]

Another important characteristic of this narrative-type is the T-element (threat, curse) as a communicative reinforcement predicting the *maleficium*: the witch threatens and curses – and the fulfillment of this is the *maleficium*. This is, when the witch makes the victim aware of the bewitching, the event that inevitably follows the conflict, thus the witch informs the victim that, due to the conflict, he/she is going to bewitch the victim. This is in fact a "declaration of war" to the actual enemy. The declaration is conveyed through the channels of the community's everyday communication.

The two-sided defect is followed by the conflict-solving steps taken by both of the opposing parties in order to restore the original status quo: the victim repairs – in fact or symbolically – the material or moral injury suffered by the witch and this is the condition of the witch's curing the harm done in a magic way. Often the victim makes up for the injury by eliminating the cause of the conflict. In other words, he/she gives the formerly denied loan or food to the witch. Thereafter the witch repairs the damage by breaking the spell. Consider the following example of a witch and victim conflict. The witch's landlord gave the witch an eviction notice and allowed the victim to move into the house. Due to the bewitching, the victim's entire family experienced poor health until they finally moved to another dwelling.[8]

In a case of this type, within the belief-system the only prerequisite for *maleficium* – and in general the functioning of the whole witchcraft-system – is the belief in the fulfillment of the *curse*. According to these narratives, the most important role of witchcraft as a rural institution is to relieve social tensions within the community and to confirm its social and moral standards. The conflict in the narratives indicates that the *social balance* has been upset. Balance is restored by repairing the damage caused by the *maleficium*. Based on social conflict, this form of witchcraft complies with a world view in which destructive human agents bring misfortunes upon fellow members of their community. A witch of this type can be anyone who takes part in the economic and moral exchange-system and communicative-system of a smaller community. Any community member was capable of violating the norms. Supernatural attributes or special expertise in magic were not required. Besides, the *curse* as type of word-magic was an *everyday device* accessible to all.

Type B) is the "*learned witch*" and has the following structural pattern:

R - M - I - H

The most important structural unit is R (= real appearance), which means that the witch practices magic or his/her appearance arouses suspicion of such activity (for example, he/she enters the byre at the first milking of the cow on Good Friday night or places a magic object somewhere[9]). As a consequence, *maleficium* is brought about, without an intermediary step which is in our case the bewitching of the domestic animals: e.g. "taking away" the yield in milk and eggs.

In this case, conflict is caused by 1) magical activity against others to increase one's *own* fortune, or 2) the ambivalent magic/healing action of sorcerers and healers which can be interpreted as *maleficia*, or 3) the competitive actions of healers and midwives by which they symbolically destroy each other; as opposed to the *social* conflict of type A. This shall be called *magical* conflict. A failed attempt at healing, that is, when the negative side of ambivalent magic dominates, overturns the balance of the positive-negative magic for the patient or the rival. According to the story, the *real appearance* renders *identification* unnecessary, and the *healing* is usually the magical practice of the witch. Therefore she is persuaded through requests or threats – but never by the "balancing" presents so characteristic of the "defrauded witch". Thus here negative magic, attributed to the opponent, causes the original imbalance and is then restored by positive magic. The witchcraft models, based on "magic conflict" reflect the changes in the popular worldview. White magic and black magic are no longer complementary. Practitioners of magic are now considered "devilish persons" and "permanent witches" in the actual *maleficium* cases. Furthermore, their bad reputation is based on a fear of malefic spells. The witches featured in these cases usually have livestock and are often successful peasants or herdsmen. They are often accused of practicing the everyday household magic practiced by all: setting a Christmas table, St. George Day milk-magic, among others.

The bad reputation of the "established" witch is itself enough – even without a social conflict – to arouse suspicion of bewitching. This is why the conflict remains unmentioned in many of the narratives regarding "learned witches". These people are under suspicion *because* of their "witch-reputation" based on former bewitchings. Naturally, the *maleficia* involving this type of narrative are often attributed to sorcerers, midwives and healers, that is, all kinds of magical specialists in the community: that is the sorcerer-"ancestors" who were integrated into the system of witchcraft because of the ambivalence of healing and magic, of the breaking of the "magic universe" of the medieval rural communities, and because of the disintegration of rural magic systems.

The third simple type is C, and the two compound types are A+C and B+C. Their most important element is S (supernatural appearance): this text-motif of the *maleficium* narratives is about the supernatural agents of destruction. The structural pattern of type C is as follows:

S - M - I - H

The A+C type contains the C-element of type A and the S-element of type C. It has the following structural pattern:

C - T - S - M - I - H

B+C type contains the R-element of type B and the S-element of type C. Its structural pattern is:

R - S - M - I - H

The key structural unit of this type of narrative is the unit S (supernatural appearance) which appears in all three sequence-types. It describes the witch as a human able to assume the form of a supernatural being. This can "only" be a legendary motif, but more often it is a text-element mirroring a direct experience, namely a dream or vision or another altered state of mind. In the S-element of the narratives all kinds of supernatural apparitions are present: the three fates who appear upon the birth of a child, the group of merrily dancing fairies who enter the house, etc.

To illustrate this point, consider some of the data characteristic of the "fairy-witches" described in the trial against Kata Fúró Csallóköznyék, in 1725: "...although the witches are dirty during the daytime, at night they put on clothes as white as snow, and at Karcsák they dance on top of the stove...". In the same trial, they were described like this: "...four of them opened the door and entered the room, three of them were dancing, and the witness folded her hands and was staring at their dance and there were many of them on the porch too...".[10] Naturally, the supernatural apparition is invariably assumed to be the one accused of being a witch; and, according to the narratives she is usually already recognized in the vision. These narratives are records of clashes between the human and the supernatural worlds. They involve a "supernatural conflict", a loss of equilibrium between the "two worlds". Comparing these cases with the sequences of other types, it appears that this supernatural appearance is in the position of the menace in the first type. This indicates that the two motifs play a similar role in the narrative sequence. The supernatural appearance also has a communicative function as it forecasts the *maleficium* to come. This message does not travel through the community's informative network, however, instead it is conveyed from the supernatural world. This occurrence proves that witchcraft as a system of norms and sanctions preserves the remains of a supernatural norm and sanction system.

The factor inducing the *maleficium* corresponding to the conflict, declaring itself in the elements C and R of the first two types, is a fear of the supernatural, that is, the supernatural metamorphosis of the individual "reputed to be a witch". In the actualization of the *maleficium*, the supernatural conflict brought about thanks to the witch's reputation may have a role equal to the social conflict of the "defrauded witch" and the magic conflicts of the "learned witch". In this way, the compound-type narratives refer to a dual conflict, the simultaneous presence of an everyday (social and/or magic) conflict and a supernatural conflict.

The person reputed to be a witch represents a new type; D) the type of the *accused witch*. These narratives show how the village communities of the period under investigation were divided into two factions: the witches and those who opposed them. Tension would mount between the two groups thanks to the fear of being bewitched. The established witch can bewitch anyone, even without personal motivation: already not that one *is* the witch, with whom we have the conflict, but we have the conflict with *that* one, *who* is the witch. The unit *conflict* starting *one type of* the accused witch narratives refers to a previous bewitching, or it tells about the conflict caused by the suspicion of the witch's bewitchings.

The *other type* does not contain the unit *conflict*, as the tension between the two opposing parties is not necessarily expressed symbolically by the interaction of two persons.

Likewise, we have a similar situation when the tension between the two parties erupts into an attack on the court. Thus the witches being persecuted bewitch the legal authorities, the people who have brought them to trial. The unit *conflict* is missing from the narratives of these cases, not because of an absence of conflict, but because the conflict situation cannot be described on the level of everyday clashes within the village's personal communication system. The pattern is simply:

M

where the object of bewitching is the court. For example, after her many bewitching cases, Ilona Faragó's finally tries to stop the authorities from entering the village by making their horses ataxic.[11] By analyzing the contextual factors of the trial narratives we can also learn about the institutionalization of village witchcraft. If the same case of *maleficium* is linked to various injured parties or if a stereotypical conflict situation is mentioned in varying accused – accuser contexts, the *maleficium* no longer appears as a traditional practice for solving conflicts. Because witch-hunts have already disrupted the community, the role of the witch has become constant.

The above types of *maleficium* narratives apply to seventy-three estimable witch cases brought to trial in Sopron County. The quantity of the data enables us to draw certain conclusions from the proportion of the narrative types, its changes in time and from their stratification, concerning the development of different aspects of witchcraft. The diversity of the narrative types suggests that in Sopron County witchcraft was – even when the witch-hunts began – an established institution in village communities. The first records from Sopron County containing a large number of *maleficium* narratives date back to the late 16th and early 17th centuries; the C (= supernatural witch) type is predominant in these narratives. The A and B types appear after rare precedents towards the end of the 17th century, but the prevailing types of these decades are C, B+C and A+C. The largest number of *maleficia* was reported between 1730 and 1745; this period coincides with the first wave of persecution in Sopron County. This 15-year-period was the heyday of the A type. Our statistics suggest that the A type, the "neighborhood"' based on social conflicts, was reinforced, if not actually spread by the persecution. Regarding Sopron County, we may even assume that the persecution itself introduced and established this type over the more archaic B and C types. According to our statistics, at least in Sopron County, the prevailing C type and the less wide-spread B type – the aspects of witchcraft based on "supernatural" and "magical" conflicts – are "older": they preceded the A and A+C types, which represented witchcraft based on "social" conflicts. The A type of narrative reflects par excellence the witchcraft-conflicts and offers an adequate human-centered explanation for misfortunes. This pattern of conflict emergence and resolution exists only as witchcraft, and only within a given economic and social formation – in this part of Central Europe among the interdependent communities of self-sufficient serfs' villages. This was the classical form of witchcraft; the B and C types of conflict-solving systems (based on the ambivalence of magic on the one hand and on the opposition of the human and the supernatural worlds on the other) became integrated into this type's social boundaries. In this process of integration the supernatural conflict-explaining principles lost their function; hostile demons from the supernatural world gave way to human witches. The text-elements of the A, A+B and A+C narrative-types showing traces of earlier stages indicate these tendencies: they denote their own "history" the double conflicts of the mixed types (A+C and A+B) also illustrate how supernatural and magical conflicts "turn" into social ones.

An important goal of my research was to find out which factors of the narrating situations influenced the sequences of the narratives. All the recorded narratives were recounted in court. Structurally, they may be identical to a record describing a particular witch's activities told in the storyteller's original community. The exceptional telling situation must have produced some alterations in the text. In court the narrative is told in favor of or against the witch indicted; the question is whether the person charged with witchcraft meets the established criteria for a witch, and whether her activity suits the mental model for the system of rural witchcraft or not. These narratives concentrate on the criteria of witchcraft, the meaning of which is always changed in the interaction between the speaker and the listener – the accusers, the witnesses and the judges. As a contextual factor, it changes the meaning as well as the structure of the text. This can be easily seen if we consider whether the same story is told by a disinterested witness, or by one who speaks in favor of or against the witch. The best way to illustrate the influence of these kinds of contextual factors is to examine the confessions of the witch. Unlike the accusers and witnesses, who, though slightly influenced by the narrating situations of the court, recited the popular criteria of traditional witchcraft in their communities, the witch confessions mainly reflect the demonological views of the elite persecutors, whereas popular witchcraft models appear in them in a more or less modified form, depending on the expectations of the judges.

In the view of witch-hunters the rural institution of witchcraft is transformed into a Satanist sect. Witch-persecution, which began amid the movements against heretics, converted the anti-heretic doctrines into a witch-ideology with two basic elements: the *alliance with the devil* and the *witches' Sabbath*. Witches were supposed to have acquired their bewitching capacity as a result of such an alliance; in fact, according to canon law, performing any sort of magic was only possible with the help of Satan. Witches also belong to a secret sect led by Satan – as the stereotype of witch-persecution was defined by Norman Cohn.[12] The Devil grants power to witches at the customary meeting of the sect, the witches' Sabbath. According to the 15th to 18th century demonological literature, the main elements of the Sabbath are the following: flying to the meeting, initiating new members, defying of Christian faith, making an alliance with the Devil, worshipping the Devil, the Devil's mass, a feast with music and dancing, sexual intercourse with the Devil – "an inversion of approved social life".[13] The witches' Sabbath as a regularly held collective meeting was an important constructive element of witchcraft-trials: when someone confessed to having participated in such a meeting, the witch persecutors were better able to discover the identities of the other witches who had taken part in them, and thus reveal the presumed conspiracy.

In addition to witchcraft trials, official demonology had other ways of influencing the popular world view : the most important of these means was the sermon. However, the most important channel of its influence was constituted by the preconceptions, the prompting questions of the trials which could be intensified by torturing those accused of witchcraft. By imposing demonological doctrines on them, a new type of "heretic witchcraft" was produced. This was not a coherent system formed by a consistent ideology: the expectations could vary from region to region, and from court to court. Unlike the Western-European witchcraft trials in Hungary (and also in Croatia and Slovenia) alliance with the Devil did not play a key role in tortures. In fact, several trials were based only on the charge of *maleficium*. As a result of the effects of different intensity, witch confessions show varying degrees of the diabolization of traditional witch concepts. These degrees also reflect the process by which the demonological doctrines of the witch-hunting elite were adjusted to suit the local system of folk beliefs – the adaptation was mutual. The exchanges initiated by the judges are usually directed towards the witch who is confessing at the trial, and their aim is to make her plead guilty. The judges wanted to hear about the "Satanic" witchcraft in keeping with demonological doctrines, and they expected the accused to admit to a kind of witchcraft often unfamiliar to her. The witch and the judges appeared to be engaged in dialogues of the deaf characterized by an initial display of differing but parallel meanings, and subsequent attempts to make them converge. At the same time, the narratives are transformed to such an extent that both parties should be able to interpret them almost in the same way. What Larner wrote about witchcraft trials in Scotland generally holds true: "Witch confessions represent an agreed story between witch and inquisitor in which the witch drew, through hallucination or imagination, on a common store of myth, fantasy, and nightmare, to respond to the Inquisitor's questions".[14] Witch and judges eventually accept the story – not, however, as *the same* one, but only as one *having the same meaning*. Only after this can the time for confession come. Having studied hundreds of confessions, I am quite convinced that witches never admitted to anything they were completely unfamiliar with, even when tortured. According to Kieckhefer, "...virtually all suspects seem to have confessed... as they could imagine themselves as having committed...".[15] Yes, but the question is *what* they could imagine: only what they *were familiar with*. It is clear that they adjusted their new knowledge to what they already knew. As Siikala has put it: "The basic elements of cognition, by which an individual organizes the knowledge he has noticed, and applies this knowledge to the interpretation of his new experiences, are based on his earlier experiences in a certain culture...".[16]

Torture proved an effective method for accelerating the exchanges and rapidly bringing the representatives of "popular witchcraft" and "elite demonology" to a state of mutual understanding.[17] The questions posed to elicit confessions and the responses of the accused witches represent different levels of the degrees of diabolism mentioned before. This is not always merely a theoretical series; sometimes it applies to the same witch's confessions made at different stages, ranging from voluntary confessions to those made under varying degrees of torture. The three elements of narrative patterns of the witch-stereotype prompted by the judges are the following: the abandonment of Christian faith and the pact with the Devil; the Sabbath, that is, the meeting of witches with the events listed above; and finally *maleficium* with the help of the power acquired from the Devil. These three elements constitute oppositions (as it was observed by Rowland in his comparative analysis of the Sabbath[18]), which make up the fixed structure of the dialogue in court. Through the asymmetric connections of these oppositions, the content elements of these dialogues are arranged into sequences where the "popular" models of witches – sometimes even "pre-witchcraft" concepts – and the "elite" witch-interpretation of the judges approach each other.

During the first stage the accused witch rarely confesses to the unfamiliar abstraction of alliance with the Devil or participation at Sabbaths, but the questions – as prompts – recall some mental or experimental model somewhat corresponding to elite interpretations. Therefore it is regarded as synonymous, and, in the narratives, is referred to as "sabbath" and "alliance". This common element is usually "collectivity" and the motive of "initiation" or "calling": the defendant answers the question concerning the Sabbath by narrating a collective experience or event (e.g. the appearance of demons or an actual gathering in the village), and when asked about the alliance, she speaks about an event which can be interpreted as a calling or initiation (e.g. a shamanistic initiation into the other world, or an actual initiation rite). The model thus recalled is in most cases based on the opposition of *this world – the other world*, the opposition of the demonic "ancestors" of the witch and the human world; the witch's mediators or ancestors, who are initiated in the other world. The following stage of interactions sees the replacement of the opposition of *the human world – other world, or the living – the dead* with those of *the human world – the non-human world – moral community – the negation of moral community* (a reversed world); *divine – diabolical*. Mediation between the living and the dead is reinterpreted as initiation into the Devil's world: the archaic, demonic witch-ancestors become *human* witches, the scene of "pre-Sabbaths" in the other world is transferred to the *quasi-other-world* of our earthly existence; the journey of the soul is not into the ethereal world now but into the "diabolical other world" of the earth.

Let us examine two confessions made by the same witch at a Sopron County trial. The first confession is made voluntarily while the second is elicited through torture shortly after the first one:

"And this delinquent, Kata Szabó, confessed that on Saint George's Day twelve years ago, when she had gone out to her stable at night, she found there Mrs. Gyuri Lôrincz, also known as Orsik, and Mrs. Gyuri Tóth, both of them the inhabitants of Röjtök, who immediately asked her to be their companion. Then she replied that she could not do their craft but they encouraged her to have herself signed up with them, and she would be able to bewitch and heal right away. As they were saying these words they told her to give them her hand. She did so, and they said: 'Well, now you are our companion.' Then they left, but came back early the next morning and took her to the forest. The two women were shaking down wild pears from the trees and she picked up the fruit and put it into the aprons of the other two. They took them all, saying: 'These pears are not for you, because you have just joined us. But for the next St.George's Day you will know better.' Then they left her."[19]

"And Kata Varga, referred to above, under second degree torture confessed that she had been allied with the Devil, with whom she had also copulated under a pear tree on the edge of the forest when she was picking pears on St. George's Day. Her companions were then and ever Mrs. Görög i.e., Kata Szabó, Mrs. György Lôrincz and Mrs. Gerencsér."[20]

The confessor tries to adjust the model the witch had recalled on the former level to the new one, thus more closely emulating the elite witch-stereotype – he/she, so to say, makes his/her story more intelligible to the judges. The most important element of this process is the concretization of the persons taking part in the Sabbath by, for example, identifying witch-companions, but there are plenty of examples for the rationalizing explanation of the "experiences of the other world" regarded as the Sabbath on this level.

As I have already stated, the answer to the question regarding the Devil's pact at the first stage was usually an admission of some sort of initiation, or joining a company, but the defendant almost never confessed to actually being allied to the Devil in demonological terms, at least under repeated torture. Even then the confession was not made in an entirely abstract form: one or two elements, or at least a thread remains, linking the confession to some experimental model. In the following text, the thread is the blue coat worn by the Devil, who appears as a country lad:

> *"Fassion Catharinae Szabo Andreae Takacs vidua sub examine torturae elicita.*
> Are you allied to the Devil? And if you are, for how long? What sort of mark do you have as proof of this? Who else is in your company of witches besides you?
> Yes, she has been allied to the Devil for four years. She saw a man dressed in a blue dolman, who had hit his nose and was writing his name into an almanac-like small book in his own blood, in the long bush between Börzsöny and Röjtök. She had no mark as she was to get one on Whitsunday but she did not, because by that time she had already been caught. Her companions, who forced her to be a witch were Mrs. Gyuri Tóth and Mrs Gyuri Lőrincz, the late Mrs. Gerencsér from Börzsöny and Mrs Major (first name Örzse), who had been in the service of the late Mrs. Balog. They told her that if she stayed with them for a year they would let her leave them whenever she wanted to."[21]

At the first stage, the confessor – having adopted the judges' abstract witch-model, and standing on the Devil's side in the *God – Devil* opposition usually admits the *maleficium* as well. At this stage, the *maleficium* is not at one end of the ambivalent magic in the popular system but a truly diabolical art, the absolute evil – as a consequence of the above-mentioned doctrines of canon law concerning magic. As Muchembled writes, the "myth of Satanism" "transposes" traditional beliefs "into realm of diabolism".[22] The defendants who reached this stage in several cases admitted to being "agents" of the Devil and treated as equals by him. In fact, the Hungarian trial records depict witches admitting to *maleficium* and alliance with the Devil with a certain haughtiness, as though they were proud of their deeds. The answer to the court's question, "Who did you turn into your horse?" often resembles that of the witch from Arad county in 1756: "Nobody. For my horse was, in the mask of a black dog, the Devil himself, and I rode on him".[23]

As for the "other-wordliness" of witchcraft, its most characteristic symbolic expression is the flight to the Sabbath. The court dialogues about flying contain particularly suggestive examples of the phenomenon of the cultural context modifying the meaning, to the parallel existence of different semantic levels and to the shifts between the concrete and the symbolic meaning. The archaic interpretation of "flying" – the "flight of the soul into the other world" – had no place in the world view of the persecutors. Flying was either a deceitful illusion inspired by the Devil, or reality – a "physical" reality, in which flesh-and-blood people flew with the Devil's help. Witches journey to the symbolic/earthly other-world, a world unequivocally regarded by the court as earthly. Being human, witches can only fly with the aid of the Devil. Thus, if one confesses to flying, he/she confesses to witchcraft as well, and, on the other hand, he/she indirectly acknowledges his/her participation in a Sabbath. The discussions of demonology concerning the nature of flying – whether it is real or a dream, illusion or the Devil's trickery – are actually concerned with the reality of the Sabbath: the "earthly" flight, deprived of its "other-worldly" nature, can easily become the central issue of the court's examination, the most important proof of witchcraft. To the above-mentioned change in paradigm – the mythical "antecedents" of witchcraft and the human witch's duality – we can now add a new paradigm, specifically characteristic of witches: the "attributed experience", that is, the experience of flying expressed in witchcraft accusations, in pleas or in confessions. Arguments about the degree of reality in flying – and more generally in the Sabbath as a whole – play an important role here: it must be explained, proved or denied that the accused person did actually fly. The examiners who accused the witches of flying knew only about real, physical/ earthly flying with the assistance of the Devil. The accused and the witnesses, however, who were villagers, were acquainted with the concept of "the flight of the soul"; some of the villagers had, on one or more occasions, experienced it themselves. The courtroom exchanges lay bare the confusion between the "shamanistic" journey of the soul and "physical flying". In the dialogues the two meanings – the symbolic and the real, the flight of the body and the flight of the soul – frequently alternate. Presumably the different levels of symbolic-metaphorical modes of expression, the duality of heavenly and earthly "other worlds" and "spiritual" and physical flights already coexisted in the original environment of witchcraft, in its "pre-persecution" state. The judges' questions and the witches' confessions are often reminiscent of a dialogue of the deaf: neither party understands the meaning of the other's questions and explanations. Both parties seem to move along different levels of meaning, searching for a fixed point in their former knowledge – their models of experience – that might correspond with the new meaning. They progress towards a "common story" – one that would be accepted and shared by both parties – in asymmetrical oppositions. Concrete symbols are taken as concrete reality by the court: ignoring the symbolic meaning, the judges pursue the concrete threads. The other party appears to "understand" the court's approach, because they can interpret it symbolically. In court the proportion of the "original" levels of meaning apparently tends to shift towards concretizatlon and demythologization: thanks to the exchanges in court, the meaning of flying is supplemented by rational explanations brought forth by the judges. In a witch trial at Megyaszó the accused claims that they held Sabbath on the Ingvár-peak, but "only her mind was here, nor her body": they left their homes through the keyhole. After the court has given a different, more concrete interpretation of these symbols of "soul-flight", the witch explains how they went through the keyhole: they stretched themselves out, like a rope[24] – that is, she too reaches a different semantic level. The fluctuation between levels of meaning, the understanding of a different level, the "cross-talks" between two levels are typical when several witnesses are narrating the same event.

Data of this kind – and they can be found in great numbers – suggest that the general patterns of narrating an otherworldly experience (the parallel presence of different levels of meaning, the concrete and the abstract, the real and the symbolic) made it easier for the accused to adapt their views to the court's demands: they could confess the "earthly" aspect of their "heavenly/earthly" adventures without having to plead guilty to things that were unintelligible and thus untrue for them: in light of the "heavenly level" these were also "true" in a sense. Even when someone was subjected to torture, he/she was not forced to confess things untrue or strange to him/her, but only something that was acceptable to both parties. This mutually acceptable version was the work of several authors, *a story of common consent*, which was pieced together in court.[25] It was momentarily dominated by the earthly/concrete/demythologized element, and the narrated events are often hardly more than illustrations of the doctrines of demonology about witches' Sabbaths; yet it potentially contains all the experiences and cultural patterns accumulated in the past, and all the "older", no longer valid levels of meaning (it also contains an additional, new one: this is "flight with the Devil's help").

In a different situation, after leaving the court, reentering the usual environment of folklore narratives, all these temporarily eclipsed meanings can easily become valid again. Numerous examples of this phenomenon could be taken from the data on witchcraft *after* the persecution, from 20th century witch-folklore. These, however, would constitute yet another story.

Translated by David Olah.

NOTES

[1] The sources of the records of witch-trials analyzed are: Schram 1970 II.7–302; Schram 1982, 253–265. Klaniczay – Kristóf – Pócs (eds) 1989:630–665.

[2] For more about this concept of witchcraft, see: Thomas 1975:599–637.

[3] Thomas 1971:540.

[4] Macfarlane 1970:226–239 on the social context that gave rise to witch-accusations. His book is the first to analyze the sociology of Early Modern European witchcraft. He describes the functioning of "rural witchcraft" in Essex in the Tudor and Stuart periods in a network of relationships between accuser-accused-identifier-healer.

[5] Participants in the elaboration were István Bacsa, Katalin Benedek, Anna Imre, Gábor Klaniczay, Éva Pócs .

[6] Macfarlane 1970.

[7] 1755, Kapuvár, Sopron County, Schram 1970:II. 289.

[8] 1742, Csorna, Sopron County, Schram 1970:II.173.

[9] 1745, Kapuvár, Sopron County, Schram 1970:II. 209.

[10] Koncsol 1992:66, 65.

[11] 1740–41 Tótkeresztúr, Sopron County, Schram 1970:II. 119.

[12] Cohn 1975:97–98, 252.

[13] Larner 1981:90.

[14] Larner 1981:136.

[15] Kieckhefer 1976:92.

[16] Siikala 1985:221.

[17] "...peasant and lawyer combined to produce an agreed statement which had meaning for both" (Larner 1981:145); "...the mechanisms of repressive interrogation, and the use of torture in particular, forced suspects to make sense of their actions or maleficence in terms satisfactory to the questioners..." (Rowland 1990:180)

[18] Rowland 1990:164–168.

[19] Röjtök, Sopron County 1746, Schram 1970:II. 256.

[20] Röjtök, Sopron County 1746, Schram 1970:II. 256.

[21] Keresztúr, Sopron County 1746; Schram 1970:II. 227–28.

[22] Muchembled 1990:149.

[23] Komáromy 1910:593.

[24] 1731. Megyaszó, Zemplén County, Kazinczy 1885:373–374.

[25] See Carlo Ginzburg's opinion (1984:40): "... the witches sabbath was neither a learned myth (as Cohn argued) nor a popular myth, but a compromise formation..."

BIBLIOGRAPHY

Cohn, Norman 1975: Europe's Inner Demons: An Enquiry Inspired by the Great Witch-hunt. London.

Eliade, Mircea 1956: Symbolisme du "vol magique". Numen 3. Pp. 7–13.

Firth, Raymond 1973: Symbols. Public and Private. Ithaca, New York.

Ginzburg, Carlo 1984: The Witches' Sabbat: Popular Cult or Inquisitional Stereotype? L. Kaplan (ed.) Understanding Popular Culture. Europe from the Middle Ages to the Nineteenth Century. Berlin & New York & Amsterdam. Pp. 39–51.

Harmening, Dieter 1988: Hexenbilder des späten Mittelalters. P. Segl (ed.) Der Hexen-hammer. Entstehung und Umfeld des Malleus maleficarum von 1487. Köln. Pp. 177–194.

Kazinczy, Gábor 1885: Megyaszói boszorkányok 1731–ben. [Witches in Megyaszó in 1731] Hazánk, Történelmi Közlöny III. Pp. 372–375.

Kieckhefer, Richard 1976: European Witch Trials. Their Foundation in Popular and Learned Culture, 1300–1500. London – Henley.

Klaniczay, Gábor – Kristóf, Ildiko – Pócs, Éva (eds) 1989: Magyarországi boszorkányperek. Kisebb forráskiadványok gyujteménye. 1–2. [Hungarian witch trials. Smaller documents] Budapest.

Komáromy, Andor 1910: Magyarországi boszorkányperek oklevéltára. [Hungarian witch-trial records] Budapest.

Koncsol, László 1992: Kacsa, Kacsa. boszorkány vagy! Régi csallóközi bunügyek. [Kacsa, Kacsa, you are a witch! Criminal cases from ancient Csallóköz] Pozsony.

Larner, Christina 1981: Enemies of God. The Witch-Hunt in Scotland. Baltimore. Maryland.

Macfarlane, Alan 1970: Witchcraft in Tudor and Stuart England. London.

Muchembled, Robert 1990: Satanic Myth and Cultural Reality. B. Ankarloo – G. Hen-ningsen (eds) Early Modern European Witchcraft: Centres and Peripheries. Oxford. Pp. 139–160.

Rowland, Robert 1990: Fantasticall and Devilishe Persons: European Witch-beliefs in Comparative Perspective. B. Ankarloo – G. Henningsen (eds) Early Modern European Witcharaft: Centres and Peripheries. Oxford. Pp. 167–168.

Schram, Ferenc 1970: Magyarországi boszorkányperek 1529–1768, I–II. [Witch trials

in Hungary] Budapest.
- 1982: Magyarországi boszorkányperek 1529–1768, III. [Witch trials in Hungary] Budapest.
Siikala, Anna-Leena 1985: Interpretation in Oral Narration. In: Papers IV. The 8th Congress for the International Society for Folk Narrative research. Bergen, June l2th-17th 1984. Bergen. Pp. 221–227.
- 1989: Changing Interpretation of Oral Narrative. An Example from the Cook Islands. A.-L. Siikala (ed.) Studies in Oral Narrative. Studia Fennica 33. Pp. 189–199.
Thomas, Keith 1971: Religion and the Decline of Magic. Studies in Popular Belief in Sixteenth and Seventeenth Century England. London.

ÜLO VALK

The Devil's Identity

On the Problem of His Pre-Christian Prototype in Estonian Mythology

Supernatural Beings as Creators of Identity

In this paper* I apply the concept of identity to mythological beings who are interpreted as the collective creations of group consciousness. Belief in supernatural beings has been an essential factor in shaping a shared sense of identity in various communities and social groups. In Europe it has been significant in the traditional peasant societies, in medieval and early modern Christian culture.

Lauri Honko has pointed out that social roles may be associated with supernatural traditions and beliefs about mythological beings: "The tradition of a fisherman is different from that of a cattle breeder, in learning a profession or role, people also learn the supernatural tradition connected with it."[1] One could even say that traditions, centered around supernatural beings, help to construct the identity of both large and small social groups. The collective belief in a guardian spirit of the farmhouse (Est. *majahaldjas*) who protects both family and farm property unites the people living together. Likewise, the ship spirit klabautermann (Est. *kotermann*) of sailor folklore has helped to shape the identity of their social group. The legends about threshing-barn demons (Est. *rehetont*) were an integral part of the repertoire of the heaters of the barn ovens (*rehepapp*). They had their specific supernatural traditions and experiences – a kind of "esoteric" knowledge of their own.

Both classical and folk mythology can be interpreted as reflections of society with its different layers and subgroups. In Germanic mythology *aesir* were the battle gods of Vikings, Odin being the god of chiefs, Thor the god of warriors. *Vaniir* (Frey, Freya) were fertility gods, worshiped mainly by farmers. In Vedic Indian religion the abstract deities *Ādityas* (later the supreme deity Brahman) were mainly worshiped by the educated and theologically-minded Brahmins. Indra, Maruts and the Rudras were the gods of warriors, *kshatriyas*, who turned their supernatural physical strength against the enemies of Aryans. Aśvins and Vasus gave prosperity and were most important for wealth-producing *vaishyas*.[2] According to Georges Dumézil, the basic functions of the gods of different Indo-European traditions correspond to the threefold division of their societies: the priests, the warriors and the farmers/cattle-breeders.

Myth and Mentality
Studia Fennica
Folkloristica 8, 2002

In Catholic tradition the belief in patron saints of different professions, congregations, ethnic and social groups has sustained their shared identity and distinguished them from others. St. Martin is the patron saint of France and of tavern-keepers, beggars, wine-growers and drunkards. St. George is the patron saint of England, Aragon, Portugal and the Slovenes; he was especially revered by warriors returning from the Crusades. St. Nicholas is the patron saint of Russia and of sailors, thieves, children and virgins.[3] Even in the 20th century, Catholics have appealed to their common saints and guardians for aid in bolstering group identity. Gabriel is an archangel, a divine messenger, who, in the New Testament, announced the future birth of John the Baptist and appeared to the Virgin Mary. In 1921, by papal decree, he was declared the heavenly patron of postmen and telephone operators. Quite recently Clare of Assisi was named the patron saint of television.[4]

Supernatural beings at the top of the mythological hierarchy have traditionally served to construct the identity of large social groups, transcending ethnic and geographical boundaries. The belief in God, the heavenly father, unites all the Christians of the world. *Credo in unum Deum...* is the first precept in the Christian confession of faith. Throughout the history of Christianity the creed has led to serious conflicts with the representatives of other religions who determine their identity differently.

Christians also have a common enemy – Satan, the former archangel who was banished from heaven after his rebellion. He is the Evil One; he is opposed to the Christian church and to every single Christian, trying to entice them into a sinful life and consequently draw them into his power. Popular Christianity has a multitude of devils. The shared and perpetual struggle against these devils serves to establish a sense of solidarity among fellow Christians. However, the Devil also has his allies – witches, wizards and pagans who serve the Evil One or have even consciously made a pact with him. They are the enemies of Christians who through the sacrament of baptism have entered into a pact with God. According to the medieval and early modern view, the people who have gathered either around God or Satan form the antagonistic armies of two warring kingdoms. Even the early Christians called themselves soldiers of Christ (*militia Christi*). Later, accusations leveled against an individual for his/her dealings with the Devil would lead to trials and eventual excommunication. Heretical movements and medieval witches both received similar treatment. We can see that both the idea of God and the Devil have worked to construct the identity of social subgroups either in a negative or a positive way (attachment to God and hostility to the Devil or vice versa).

Identity of Supernatural Beings

Thus, supernatural beings help in shaping the group identity of believers, but at the same time one may also speak about the identity of supernatural beings themselves. As folkloric characters, they are subject to changes as folklore itself undergoes changes over time. Although some may disappear from the living tradition and be forgotten, new supernatural beings may be introduced. In contemporary Estonian folk beliefs, the popularity of extraterrestrial humanoids from flying saucers has eclipsed interest in other beings of traditional folk religion, including the Devil. One may ask just what are the main components going into the creation of a supernatural being's identity? The three main elements appear to be the following: 1) appellation, 2) beliefs – the appearance, function, attitude towards people, etc.; 3) plots – typical activities of the mythological being in folk narratives.

The appellation of a mythological being at first seems to be the basic component to create the being's identity. However, it proves to be dubious. Demonic beings have plenty of euphemisms, different dialects often have their own words for the same or closely related beings. Moreover, appellations usually do not cross language borders, even though mythological beings tend to be internationally known. Even if a mythological term is known in more than one language the meaning may be totally different. (The name of the Baltic thunder god *Perkons/Perkūnas* has turned into an euphemism for the devil in the Balto-Finnic languages: Est. *pärgel*, Finn. *perkele*). Many folk legends and memorates also describe supernatural encounters, but the mythological being remains undefined. Sometimes the appellation and the corresponding interpretation are lacking, because the experience is too extraordinary to be classified according to the traditional pattern. In many cases, however, such legends can be easily classified since the plots and motifs have been ascribed to a certain mythological being in the folk tradition.

Beliefs are actualized in folk norms and prohibitions, in customs, and ritual behavior; they are also reflected in folk legends. Plots, attached to a given mythological being, occur in folk narratives. However, sometimes they may be actualized in reality if personal supernatural experiences are interpreted according to traditional belief legends. One may thus assert that a supernatural being's identity is basically determined as a combination of the three: the appellation, traditional beliefs and typical plots.

The Pre-Christian Devil in Estonian Folklore

Oskar Loorits and several other researchers of Estonian folk religion have adhered to the view that the Devil is a late figure, a representative of Christian mythology adopted during the Middle Ages. However, this statement can be contested. It has become clear that "the opposition between the Supreme God (god of heavens) and his mighty adversary (the evil god of the underworld) is successively traced in all separate Finno-Ugric mythologies, just as in the Samoyed ones, so it can be safely assumed to have Proto-Finno-Ugric and Proto-Uralic origin".[5] I am of the opinion that the Christian Devil of Estonian folklore had a prototype in pagan mythology. In principle, it is possible to make a distinction between three basic layers of Estonian folk traditions about the Devil: pre-Christian, Catholic, and Lutheran. Together they form the popular image of the Estonian Devil, a combination of these three characters. Undoubtedly, the former supernatural being of pagan mythology has been substantially reinterpreted to conform with the concept of the Christian Devil. Nevertheless, pre-Christian traits and plots still contributed to the core of the Estonian popular image of the Devil and formed part of the corpus of beliefs. Due to these elements, the identity of the former pre-Christian character has remained intact. The Christian Devil of 19th and 20th century folklore can be regarded as the descendant and successor of the pagan Devil. Even the appellation (*kurat*), the most changeable component, has stayed the same.

How does one find the pagan Devil from the later layers? One can leave out the Christian legends and beliefs which undoubtedly have their origins in medieval European traditions. The Devil as a Christian moralist and as a satyr-like being should be excluded.[6] The devil as a dominant figure of Christian folk religion has also eclipsed the former fairies and diverse spirits. These late substitutions and interfusions should also be found and set aside.[7] When the Christian legends and secondary roles of the Devil have been eliminated, a considerable amount of plots and beliefs that probably are based on pagan tradition still remain. In this paper I only briefly discuss a few of them.

The appellation of the Devil *kurat* refers to his connection with the left side.[8] This is probably a very archaic trait. In many cultures, the opposition between the right and the left side is related to concepts of good and evil. In the Estonian language this opposition is explicit: *parem* (literally "better") denoting the right and *pahem* (lit. "worse") the left. Estonian folk legends and beliefs about the Devil are loaded with symbols of the left.

To make a contract with Satan one has to give blood from the ring finger of one's left hand. The Evil One appears from the forest from the left side and later disappears in the same direction.[9] The Devil steals a boy and drags him along, grasping the child by his left hand.[10] The devil is said to follow people invisibly on the left side. Good angels keep to the right.[11] The Evil One appears as a young man, but he has a horse's hoof instead of a left foot.[12] To fend off the Devil one has to make a cross with the left heel.[13] Estonian folk legends about the Devil are rich in such details. The abundance of left-hand symbolism suggests that it is more than coincidental.

The same connection between the Devil, evil and the left can be traced in European Christian traditions. One of the medieval religious tales describes a sinner repenting on his deathbed. On his left, he sees devils; on his right he sees Christ showing his wounds and cleansing him with a drop of His blood.[14] In medieval artistic interpretations of Judgement Day, the Devil and the powers of Hell have traditionally been depicted on the left-hand side of Christ. Crucifixion scenes have the unrepentant criminal on the left side of the Savior.

Parallel appellations of demonic beings, semantically close to the Estonian *kurat*, can be found in other traditions. *Levyi* ("left-hand being") is one of the Russian euphemisms for the Devil.[15] In Judaic legends Samael was the demon who tempted Eve in the guise of a serpent. He was also the mate of Lilith. According to rabbinical lore, the meaning of his name is "the left". He has also been regarded as the lord of the sinister left.[16]

Thus, in the Estonian tradition, *kurat* is apparently a pre-Christian appellation of a demonic being. Among the hundreds of euphemisms for the

Christian Evil One are also other words that probably have denoted his pagan prototype. Even *pergel/pärgel* (Finn. *perkele*, Lp. *Pärkel*), etymologically connected with the Baltic *Perkons/Perkūnas*, can be regarded as one of them. It is a typical feature of several Finno-Ugric traditions that the demiurge's evil adversary has a borrowed name and he is endowed with positive functions in the source mythology.[17] In some Estonian runo-songs the Devil bears a rather honorable and archaic title *altmaa/altilma isand* ('lord of the underworld'). It is noteworthy that this corresponds exactly to the name of the Ob-Ugric lord of the Nether World *Kul'- ōtər (Xul'- ōtər)*.

Just as the Devil's association with the left side seems pre-Christian, the same can be said about his connection with water in Estonian folklore. Water is his home element where he hides himself from Thunder. He often appears in saunas because they were usually situated near bodies of water. Also, some of the Devil's fears cannot be sufficiently explained according to Christian beliefs. As a demon of darkness he dreads the cockcrow that heralds the morning. In Estonian folklore, he has to flee from the wolves that kill different kinds of demonic beings. He also must escape Thunder.[18] Several devices for repelling the Devil – e.g. a rowan branch and metal, preferably silver, – are apparently pre-Christian as well.

In Estonian folklore, the Devil is firmly associated with the dead. There are several types of folk legends where *kurat* and *kodukäija* (revenant) substitute for each other in different variants. O. Loorits has suggested that the replacement of the dead with the Christian Devil is a relatively recent phenomenon.[19] However, the interfusion of the Devil and the dead, who are both chthonic beings, seems to be much older. The pre-Christian Devil has apparently been closely related to the inhabitants of the realm of the dead. In Christian folk religion, his connection with the evil demonic dead (deceased sinners, witches etc.) survived, whereas his affinity with the dead in general became more concealed.

In Estonian folklore recorded during the 19th and 20th centuries the Devil maintained his close link to death by hanging. Although people generally blamed the demonic water spirit *näkki* for drowning deaths,[20] legends told that it was the Devil who incited people to hang themselves. Disguised as a hare, he would appear when boys were playing the game of hangman; during the course of the game, one of the players would die. In Germanic religion, the practice of sacred hangings was associated with the cult of Odin. According to *Ynglingasaga* 7, Odin "was called the lord of ghosts or the king of the hanged".[21] The Old Prussian gods of the underworld and of the dead Patollus and Pecullus and their Lithuanian parallel figure Velnias ('devil') were also the lords of hanging.[22] There seems to be an affinity between Estonian and Indo-European beliefs which probably gives evidence of pre-Christian cultural contacts.

The image of the probable pagan Devil (*Äijö*) can be found in Setu archaic folk songs that describe the nether world. *Äijö* is used as a parallel name for *Tooni* and *Mana*, both denoting the lord of the dead. Folk songs reveal how the chthonic realm and its inhabitants, dangerous to the living, are opposed to heaven and its divine beings:

- - -

Tahtse iks kõik mano Taivalise,	The divine ones wanted to come near,
püvve mano Pühälise,–	the holy ones strove to approach,
taiju es mano Taivalise,	the divine ones could not come,
püvvü es mano Pühälise,	the holy ones could not approach,
lätsi ütsi Äijolane,	one demon (*äijolane*) went there,
lätsi mano Manalane.[23]	a dead one (*manalane*) approached.

In the last two verses *äijolane* (a demon, 'one of the kin of *Äijo*) is used as a synonym for *manalane* (an inhabitant of the realm of the dead). Parallel verses containing similar identifications can also be found elsewhere.

- - -

Saa es vell'o maale veerdü,	The [deceased] brother could not roll to the earth,
saa es osi maale oidu,	the straight one could not reach the earth,
olli iks kõik man Manalise,	the dead (*manalise*) were all standing by,
olli ümbre Äijolase.[24]	the demons (*äijolase*) were surrounding him.

Tooni and *Äijo* substitute for each other in the passages of folk songs that describe the nether world as a community of the dead:

- - -

Ülä om iks sääl Tooni nurme pääl,	The husband is there in the field of *Tooni*,
manalaste iks maie pääl,	at the lands of the dead,
künd iks sääl Tooni nurmi pääl,	plowing there in the fields of *Tooni*,
ülä iks kaitsi Tooni karja,	the husband was guarding the cattle of *Tooni*,
hoit iks Tooni hobesida.[25]	herding the horses of *Tooni*.

- - -

Imä iks hoije Äijo hobesit,	Mother was herding the horses of *Äijo*,
mamma kaitsi Äijo karja, –	mamma was guarding the cattle of *Äijo*,
senni iks hoije hobesit,	she was herding the horses,
konni poiga pä[h]itseh,	until the son [of *Äijo*?] was at her head,
senni tütär jalotseh, –	until the daughter [of *Äijo*?] was at her legs,
senni kaitsi Äijo karja...[26]	so long was guarding the cattle of *Äijo*...

We need not assume that the second passage is a later one, because the pagan *Tooni* has been replaced by *Äijo*, the euphemism for the Devil. Both words probably refer to the lord of the dead, though *äijo* later also started to mean the Christian Evil One, while *Tooni* preserved its old meaning in Estonian folklore. The song motifs of the cattle of *Tooni/Äijo* and his fields and pastures have been used in South Estonian tradition. Similar ideas about the Nether World can be traced in Baltic folklore and in the ancient Indo-European tradition.[27]

Although the lord of the dead and the Nether World seems to be the precursor of the Christian Devil in Estonian folklore, the whole problem is far from being solved. In fact, it is more probable that there were a group of mythological beings, more or less related, rather than a single prototype. It seems that such appellations of the Evil One as *juudas, kurat, tikõ, vanahalv, äio* conceal a whole family of demonic beings of pagan origin that were later combined to form the figure of the Christian Devil.

Norbertas Vėlius has thoroughly studied the image of the *velnias* (devil) of Lithuanian folklore. According to him, "the *velnias* is a typical chthonic being representing the left-hand members of such oppositions as *low – high, underworld – sky, water – fire, left – right, black – white, night – day* among others".[28] The same holds true for the Estonian Devil. Also, oppositions such as *death – life, dirty – pure, dangerous – harmless* could be added. It should be noted that not one of these essential oppositions could be explained as a consequence of late Christian influences.

We can still recognize the features of the pagan Devil of ancient Estonian mythology even though the entire demonic family of pre-Christian religion has, to a large extent, been colored by Christianity.

NOTES

*   The article is based on the paper delivered at the symposium "Tradition and Identity" at Mekrijärvi, Finland on Dec. 13. 1994. I am grateful to the Estonian Science Foundation for its support (grant no 4450).

[1]   Honko 1989:105.

[2]   Puhvel 1987:47.

[3]   Leach 1972:682; 966–967.

[4]   Farmer 1992:101; 193.

[5]   Ajkhenvald – Helimski – Petrukhin 1989:156–157.

[6]   V. lvanov and V. Toporov have interpreted the satyr-like features (horns, hoofs, tail) of the Slavic and Baltic Devil as the traits of the former cattle-god of these traditions (1974:66). In Estonian folklore this guise rather seems to be of foreign origin: it usually occurs in Christian legends where the Devil appears as a moralist who punishes sinners.

[7]   See Valk 1993.

[8]   Cf. *kurakäsi* 'left hand'.

[9]   ERA II 63, 175/9 (2) < Põlva. A reference to the collections of the Estonian Folklore Archives at the Estonian Literature Museum in Tartu.

[10]   E 33216/20 < Halliste.

[11]   H II 73, 548/53 (28) < Vastseliina. Cf. spitting over the left shoulder three times to repel the Devil. A strong link between the Evil One and the left side has been preserved in the folklore of the Orthodox Setus in South Eastern Estonia. See Västrik 1996:171–172.

[12]   H I 4, 394 (7b) < Saaremaa.

[13]   ERA II 7, 315 (11) < Märjamaa.

[14]   Tubach 1969: no. 4405. See also Matth. 25:31–33; 41.

[15]   Maksimov 1991:151.

[16]   Conway 1879:95; 131. Cf. also the meaning of *sinister, laevus* in Latin. On the symbolism of the opposition between right and the left see also Ivanov – Toporov 1974:259–305: Tolstyie 1974.

[17]   Ajkhenvald – Helimski – Petrukhin 1989:157.

[18]   See Valk 1996.

[19] Loorits 1949:§ 37.
[20] Valk 1999.
[21] Ward 1970.24.
[22] Puhvel 1987:227–228
[23] Hurt 1904:669.
[24] Hurt 1904:673.
[25] Hurt 1904:668.
[26] Hurt 1904:141.
[27] See Puhvel 1969; Vėlius 1987.
[28] Vėlius 1987:292.

BIBLIOGRAPHY

Ajkhenvald, Aleksandra – Helimski, Eugene – Petrukhin, Vladimir 1989: On Earliest Finno-Ugrian Mythologic Beliefs: Comparative and Historical Considerations for Reconstruction. M. Hoppál – J. Pentikäinen (eds) Uralic Mythology and Folklore. Ethnologica Uralica 1. Budapest. Helsinki. Pp. 155–159.

Conway, M.D.1879: Demonology and Devil-Lore I. New York, London.

Farmer, David Hugh 1992: The Oxford Dictionary of Saints. Oxford, New York.

Funk & Wagnalls Standard 1972: Dictionary of Folklore, Mythology and Legend. M. Leach – J. Fried (eds). New York.

Honko, Lauri 1989: Memorates and the Study of Folk Beliefs. Nordic Folklore. Recent Studies. R. Kvideland – H. K. Sehmsdorf (eds) Indiana University Press. Bloomington & Indianapolis. Pp. 100–109.

Hurt, Jakob 1904: Setukeste laulud. Pihkva-eestlaste vanad rahvalaulud ühes Räpina ja Vastseliina lauludega. Välja annud Dr. Jakob Hurt. Esimene köide. Helsinki.

Ivanov, V.V. – Toporov, V.N. 1974: Issledovanija v oblasti slavjanskih drevnostej. Leksičeskie i frazeologičeskie voprosy rekonstrukcij tekstov. Moskva.

Loorits, Oskar 1949: Grundzüge des estnischen Volksglaubens I. Lund.

Maksimov, Sergej 1991: Krestnaja sila. Nečistaja sila. Nevedomaja sila. Kemerovo.

Puhvel, Jaan 1969: "Meadow of the Otherworld" in Indo-European tradition. Zeitschrift für vergleichende Sprachforschung. 1969, B. 83. H. 1. S. 64 – 69.

– 1987: Comparative Mythology. The John Hopkins University Press. Baltimore & London.

Tolstoj, N.I. – Tolstaja, S.M. 1974: K semantike pravoj i levoj storony v svjazi s drugimi simvoličeskimi èlementami. Materialy vsesojuznogo simpoziuma po vtoričnym modelirujuščim sistemam I (5). Tartu. S. 42–45.

Tubach, Frederic C. 1969: Index Exemplorum. A Handbook of Medieval Religious Tales. FF Communications No. 204. Helsinki.

Valk, Ülo 1993: About the Origin of the Estonian Devil. Specimina Sibirica Vl. Savariae, Szombathely. Pp. 179–186.

– 1996: Thunder Chasing the Devil An Estonian Folk Belief in the Indo-European Context. Professor August Robert Niemi and comparative Folklore Investigations of the Balts and Baltic Finns. Papers of the International Conference held on 1–2 December, 1994, Vilnius, Lithuania. Vilnius. Pp. 16–21.

– 1999: The Guises of Estonian Water Spirits in Relation to the Plot and Function of Legend. P. Lysaght – S.Ó. Cathain – D. hÓgain (eds) Islanders and Water-Dwellers. Dublin. Pp. 337–348.

Vėlius, Norbertas 1987: Chtoniškasis lietuvi mitologijos pasaulis. Folklorinio velnio analizė. Summary: The Chthonic World in Lithuanian Mythology. An Analysis of velnias (Devil) in Folklore. Vilnius.

Västrik, Ergo-Hart 1996: Vanahalvast. Palve, vanapatt ja pihlakas. Setomaa 1994. a. Kogumisretke tulemusi. Vanavarvedaja 4. Tartu. Pp. 165–188.

Ward, Donald 1970: The Threefold Death: An Indo-European Trifunctional Sacrifice? J. Puhvel (ed.) Myth and Law Among the Indo-Europeans. Studies in Indo-European Comparative Mythology. University of California Press. Berkeley & Los Angeles, London. Pp. 123–142.

PASI KLEMETTINEN

Many Faces of Evil

This article explores various manifestations of the Devil within the context of Christian concepts of demons, witches and traditional beliefs in unruly poltergeists.[1] The article is based on the writer's doctoral dissertation, *Rioting Devils – Devils and Witchcraft in the Folk Beliefs of the Karelian Isthmus and the Lake Ladoga Area*. The most notorious cases of poltergeist activity originate in turn-of-the-century agrarian communities. The folklore inspired by these cases, however, is in the written record thanks to a number of collections spanning the 1930s and the 1950s.[2] The devils of Hörkkö, Heinjoki, Maironiemi and Kuokkaniemi caused a great stir, and the trouble-makers were widely discussed.

The Classical Devil Figure

In *The God of the Witches,* Margaret Murray asserts that, over time, the pre-Christian horned god supplanted the devil of Christianity: "The God of the old religion becomes the Devil of the new". According to Murray, the horned figure was once the fertility goddess worshipped by witches during the 1600s, notably in Anglo-Saxon cultures. The Romans of antiquity were also familiar with a similar two-faced god named Dianus or Janus (Murray 1970:23–45). Later historical studies have been unable to trace the existence of actual witch communities, however, since horned figures have had scores of meanings tied to the time, place and ethnic belief systems from which they had sprung (Cohn 1975:108–110; Ginzburg 1991:89–110). The horned being that surfaces in many pre-Christian visual arts or other types of artistic expression may be a shaman in ritual dress, a sorcerer, a chief or even a divine being (for example, stone carvings, cave paintings and the illustrations on shamanistic drums). Clearly, notions of demons and gods from both pagan beliefs and world religions have contributed to the syncretic figure of the Christian devil.

In Christian mythology, God banishes Lucifer from Heaven for his sin of pride, and thus the Devil emerges as the fallen archangel sent to plague the lives of sinful human beings. The Devil with his ethereal spiritual essence, is believed to have retained his divine skill of flight; and this he does with

Myth and Mentality
Studia Fennica
Folkloristica 8, 2002

supernatural alacrity (Cohn 1975:66). According to Jeffrey Russell, Pan, the mythological figure in Greek mythology, has had a profound icono-graphical influence on the Devil's image as a winged goat figure (Russell 1988:254). Moreover, a divine goat figure emerges as an object of worship in the ancient religions of India, Assyria and Egypt (Rudwin 1973:39). For example, the Etruscan god of death, Kharu, has been depicted as a beaked, furry, unkempt, long-eared creature with wings (Russell 1988:157). Many mythologies identify winged and horned creatures with otherness and the afterlife; growths or appendages serve as symbols of the superhuman and the divine (Siikala 1992:140–144).

The pagan gods demonized by Christianity are ubiquitous in medieval religious art throughout Europe. The demons portrayed in religious art are characterized by dark colors, horns, tails, horse or goat hooves, long hair, furry bodies and dog or donkey ears (Danielsson 1932:10; Oinas 1985:98). Representations of the Devil as a furry creature with horns and hooves recall those of the mythical figures of fauns and satyrs: the Devil's carnal nature was underlined in the process of converting people to Christianity (Rudwin 1973:48). In the Western world, black, which is generally associated with the demonic, symbolizes death, darkness, coldness, the unknown, the hidden and the unclean (Cohn 1975:69; Russell 1988:253; 1991:40). As part of the historical binary opposition, the black devil exposes the racist attitudes of white European Christians, and their demonization of the enemy during the Crusades.[3] The association of the color red with the Devil is linked to Christian mythical images of the horrors of hell, eternal purgatory, sin and wanton sexuality. In major Oriental religions the color red is customarily identified with demons (Wall 1968:44–61).

Archetypal devil images are fused with the notion that evil and physical imperfection are inextricably linked; thus, the Devil appears to us as an ugly, black, filthy creature with asymmetrical body parts (Parkin 1985:6–9). The following belief legends describing evil spirits were collected on the Karelian Isthmus:

> My late aunt always used to say that she and my late uncle had seen the Devil flying through the air on the way to Revo Island. He had hooves like a black horse and a long tail.
> (Koivisto. Ulla Mannonen 5887. 1938)

> In Kuolemajärvi parish there was an old bachelor who lived all alone in his house. Nobody wanted to sleep in one of the rooms because demons would always turn up and dance across the floor. Around bedtime they would swing a cat's tail about and wave the fluffy tail in front of the guest. The Devil would always have a nasty leer on his face...
> (Kuolemajärvi. Nelma Strömberg 170. 1936)

In the belief legends that I studied, the devil rarely shows up as the Devil of Christianity. For example, in the Maironiemi material the archetypal devil figure appears only once as an uninvited guest and is depicted as a "tailed" being (Sääminki. J. Hautala 151. 1938). We must keep in mind, however, that accounts of the devil's physical appearance would have been superfluous to both the tellers of such tales and their audience. During the course of the narrative, the cultural frame of reference renders such descriptions immaterial; in other words, "all parties are vividly aware of the subject being discussed" (Wolf-Knuts 1991:132).

Physical Transformations

The concept of metamorphosis – of a person, animal, or supernatural being – into another form looms large in myths from around the world. To some degree it reflects the human belief in the existence of a soul or spirit – an entity capable of moving independent of the body and abandoning the body after death.[4] The notion of a many-faced devil stems from some Christian notions about the Devil: a being able to transform itself into a myriad of shapes in order to harass human beings and then change that form as the need arises. This notion of the Devil's ability to metamorphose may be regarded as an expression of the human fear of chaos and formlessness (Cavendish 1975:5–6).

According to church dogma, the Devil can metamorphose into a man, a woman, an animal or a monster. Earlier written accounts of the devil's metamorphoses can be found in Jewish legends. (Russell 1984:49; 1991:29). The transformations were not necessarily taken literally. Some interpreted them according to a notion of the devil as a maker of illusions to fool the human eye (Levack 1987:31). Rudwin's historical perspective suggests that the devil initially appeared as an animal, then as a human and animal hybrid (monster) and finally as a human figure (Rudwin 1973:38). This cultural evolutionary view parallels the theory describing the historical development of godly figures: the belief in animistic spirits gradually evolved into the pantheon of gods of Antiquity, and then culminated in the apotheosis of Christ. From this perspective, the figure of Christ emerges as the iconographical denouement of Western religious development.

Oral tradition tells us that a key supernormal criterion for a devil is the ability to change form; after all, people going about their day-to-day business only identify a seemingly ordinary person or animal as an evil spirit once this person or creature has undergone a supernormal metamorphosis (cf. Ivanits 1989:39–40). Unruly devils are capable of turning themselves into men, boys, dogs, cats, hares, balls of straw or fire – and even bottles. According to narrative tradition, people see the devil in ordinary human or animal figures that suddenly disappear or become invisible: "As a man was walking down the road he saw a tall black man. The man offered the devil a cigarette and the stranger suddenly disappeared" (Jaakkima. Nenonen, Martti KRK 131:302, 1935–36). The following belief legends describe how the devil of Maironiemi, to the astonishment of the farmer, changes his shape into a human being, an animal, an invisible spirit and then back again:

> ... When the man began his journey, the dog ran after him and when he reached the spot where he usually fed his horse, the dog turned into a man and when they left, the man helped him harness the horse. When they arrived at home,

the man helped him unharness the horse just like any ordinary coachman would do ...
(Kerimäki. Siren, Signe. 31. 1891)

Then the farmer took his new horse to fetch some hay from the barn in the meadow. On his way to the meadow he saw a dog running after him along the road. When he reached the barn he was shocked to see that the same dog that had followed him had suddenly turned into a cat which climbed up into the hayloft. From the hayloft the cat pushed a pile of hay down in front of the horse, which the horse started to munch greedily. Once the farmer had his hay load ready, he drove home, unharnessed the horse and put it into the stable. As he was leaving the stable, he heard the horse tossing its mane. Going back in to take a look, he was once again shocked to see that an invisible being was brushing the horse so its coat shone and that its mane was combed into place...
(Punkaharju. KT 76. Makkonen, Veikko 126–127. 1936)

Sorcerers can also conjure up various forms of the devil to act as spirit helpers: "The devil of Maironiemi has been summoned to the Kuopio market. The old hag of Pohjanmaa conjured up the devil as a dog to follow the man from Maironiemi" (Punkaharju. Vallaskangas, Ida. KRK 88:4. 1935–1936). The spirit helpers of sorcerers found in tales seem to have an affinity to the otherworldly spirit helpers used by shamans. Shamans call upon these spirits and turn them into animals to take vengeance upon either his personal enemies or the evildoers in the community. The sorcerer's helpers surfacing in Finnish spells and incantations are generally hawks, horses, dogs, burbot or pike, bulls, rams, bears, black or golden cocks and snakes. (Siikala 1992:192–205). The following paragraphs offer a closer examination of manifestations of the devil and demons as distinct types of incarnations.

Zoomorphism

Christian thought closely associates animalism, sexuality and Satanic evil; in fact, the three seem to form an inversion of the Holy Trinity (Russell 1988:126). Within the Christian frame of reference, the carnal essence of the Devil could be manifested in a wild and impetuous force of nature out to destroy human civilization and the order brought about by culture (Wolf-Knuts 1992:109–114). The animals especially identified with the Devil in the Judeo-Christian tradition are the horse, pig, dog, snake, cat and toad (Cohn 1975:70; Russell 1988:254). In Finnish folk belief the snake is generally regarded as the Devil's creation (Simonsuuri 1950:103).[5] None of the archival data, however, describes the rioting devil appearing as a snake, or magically causing harm through a snake.

In medieval folklore the most common incarnations of the devil are lambs, dogs, cocks, pigs and various other farm animals (Russell 1984:49). Poltergeist narratives often depict the devil taking the form of an animal such as a dog, cat, hare or horse. Paul Danielsson states that the animals most often identified with demons are large, of a certain color, fiery-eyed or one-eyed creatures (1930:96–97). Similar traits are associated with trolls, guardian spirits, giants and elves in Scandinavian folk belief.

According to Finnish folk belief, an animal's demonic behavior is brought about by a spiritual possession – that is, the devil's invisible invasion of the animal's body. Practically speaking, it is relatively easy to determine whether a game animal such as a squirrel or a black grouse has been demonically possessed: the animal is invulnerable to bullets; the hunter's gun refuses to fire, or despite his sure aim and many attempts, the bullet never hits the animal. In the following example, the hunter is advised to use a silver bullet to kill the animal that is "housing" the devil:

> If a man shoots a squirrel and the squirrel lives, it is time to load the gun with a silver bullet – then the squirrel is sure to fall. One hunter loaded the gun with a silver bullet and then fired: "You're shooting at my palm," cried the devil. The devil's palm was inside the squirrel.
> (Salmi. M. Haavio 1426. 1934)

According to Danielsson, a bird that is hard to kill or hard to hunt is called a "hard bird" (1930:112–113). The idea of the animal's hardness lies in the belief that magical measures – such as using a silver bullet – are the only means to kill or drive away demons (Kvideland – Sehmsdorf 1988:102–103). In addition to demonic features and signs, the supernatural criteria for pets and farm animals include mysterious appearances, disappearances and flying about the property.

Flying Demons

Both the ancient Roman and Germanic peoples believed in the existence of a demonic, nocturnal owl-like creature which lived off of human flesh and blood. (Lat. *strix* and Germ. *striga*). During the witch hunts in medieval Europe, people began to associate this flying demon with beliefs about the female witch's capacity to metamorphose, her nocturnal flights and the Witches Sabbath. Beginning in the 15th century, people believed that flying female witches brought harm to them, and sucked the blood of children, in particular, during their nightly excursions (Cohn 1975:206–210; Cavendish 1978:43–44; Ginzburg 1992:99–101). The formidable Saami witches of Finnish folklore were thought to transform themselves into birds to lure game birds to Lapland (Simonsuuri 1963:482–483).

The flying demon figures of the Christian tradition are comparable to an earlier belief in a soul bird; this creature would either convey the soul of the deceased to the kingdom of the dead or appear as the spirit of a dead person (Haavio 1950:13–45). In Arctic Shamanism the soul bird allows people to communicate with the inhabitants of that far-off world of the dead, and can also release the soul from the body during healing rituals (Siikala 1992:187–205). Although soul birds are not necessarily demonic creatures, they can be read as bad signs or omens depending on the context. According to folk belief, birds associated with darkness and night, such as the owl, hawk, cock and woodpecker, foretell bad luck and even death (Danielsson 1930:106–107; Haavio 1950:28–29). The notes taken on the following *memorate* describes a woodsman shooting in vain at a bird-like figure with gleaming eyes and a baleful laugh. The creature is suspected to be a forest spirit or even the devil himself:

> One man from Kaukola said that he'd seen a bird in the forest that wouldn't die, no matter how many times he shot at it. He fired about ten times but the bird didn't even move from the branch of the little tree, and just cawed as though it was laughing. The bird's eyes gleamed like flames, and the man said that after he had fired about ten times with no luck, he left without looking back. He said that it wasn't a bird after all; it was either a forest spirit in the form of a bird, or the devil himself.
> (Hiitola. Ulla Mannonen 5928. 1938)

In Karelian folk beliefs that deal specifically with materializations of the devil, the devil often appears as a bird or an unidentifiable demonic figure in flight. With their peculiar looks, sounds, demeanor, and their habit of hovering about treetops out of human reach, these creatures harass travellers going through the woods or along roads. The devil is often said to laugh raucously or caw like a jay or a magpie.

> In a Heinjoki parish in the village of Koprala the devil had come to haunt a certain household. Night and day, he moved about in various forms, laughed like a magpie and was always up to no good. He made himself invisible and opened doors and wandered from room to room.
> (Vuoksela. Eino Hakala KT 249:119. 1948)

In Finnish folklore an unanticipated or unwanted encounter with the devil is generally conveyed by the individual as a traumatic or unhappy experience. According to a second-hand memorate from Uusikirkko, a hair-raising nocturnal meeting with the devil left such a profound impression on two men trying to locate some horses, that it soon formed part of an orally-transmitted personal history:

> Our father said that when he was a young man, they were in Kiimasuo, a forest between Vanha Saha and Neuvola, he was with another man on an autumn night trying to find some lost horses in the forest. There, they saw the devil. He said it was dark as it could be and they could hardly see in front of them, and then something like a bird or a ball spun around their legs and turned about and uttered a cawing laugh; the other man had a gun and he tried to shoot at it, and he fired many times, but didn't hit it. The thing just cawed and laughed. They both said that it was the Devil, and both of them had their hair standing on end when they came back to the village – and even when they were old he said that it was the Devil and that even a bullet couldn't hurt it, or maybe there were even more of them...
> (Uusikirkko. Ulla Mannonen 8337. 1938)

Narratives about flying demons harassing travellers in the forest can be compared to earlier accounts of restive spirits of children in folk belief (Pentikäinen 1968). According to Ganander, the *liekkiö* was a ghost that dwelt in the forest where unwanted children had been left to die, and that frightened travellers with its screams (1984:49). Harva also writes that a *liekkiö* is a "bird that haunts the forest after dark by following travellers and using its unusual voice to imitate human sounds" (Harva 1948:453–455). More generally, the sounds uttered by the *liekkiö* are said to be reminiscent of screeches, caws and screams. In Scandinavian narrative tradition the soul bird of the murdered child can materialize in the form of a tawny owl, a great grey owl or an eagle owl.

The Mutt of the Underworld

In Greek, Indo-Germanic and Scandinavian mythology, the dog functions as a demonic gatekeeper to the kingdom of the dead and is thus also related to the Christian notion of the satanic assistant (Greek, Cerberus) (Krohn 1914:278; Kemppinen 1956:80; Siikala 1992:95). In Scandinavian folklore this dog surfaces from the land of the dead to collect the dying person's soul, and vanishes upon the person's death. In some situations, as when a lone traveller encounters a dog in the forest, the animal is seen as a prophecy of misfortune or even death (cf. Danielsson 1930:87–91; Woods 1959:33). In a Finnish competitive courtship song/poem studied by Krohn, the large and savage dog barks thus in front of the castle of Hell (Krohn 1914:278):

> The doors look dark,
> The Devil's houses are visible,
> The Devil's dog is barking.
>
> Loudly barked the big dog
> The savage hound prowled
> The Devil's splendid castle.

Also, when there is an evil agent to be expelled in spells, and especially curses, the target is often identified as a demon dog, mongrel, hound, or mutt of the Underworld (Krohn 1914:278). In the following spell collected in Nurmes, the bloody hound of hell emerges as the cause of a painful and fatal death (the disease originates in the land of the dead):

> Oh you bloody hound of hell,
> When you came to dine, to gnaw
> Bloody jaw bones,
> Bring pains to corners,
> To take the forehead bone,
> Snatch away the jawbone.
> Now the time of the Church has come,
> A public celebration for the Lord,
> Shame on you, the Devil's own,
> For eating and gnawing!
> (SKVR VII 2008)

A big black dog also plays a key role in Finnish incantations. The dog acts as the sorcerer's mythical helper spirit, a beast whose owner is allegedly "fattening it up in the castle by allowing the beast to gnaw upon the village witches" (Siikala 1992:94–95). Ideas about actual scavenging animals feeding on dead bodies add to the dog's special status as a diabolical creature in the world of the dead (Cavendish 1975:61–62). The memorate below depicts a dog entering a sauna through the wall; the narrator's interpretation points to the devil, a standard model of explanation that is also directed at the younger generation listening:

> I was with my late mother and my brother Risto in the sauna (we were little). Mother was already sitting up there on the bench and we were still on the floor. All of a sudden, a huge dog came right through the wall. It looked just like any other big dog. It looked just like Pamppunen's dog, and Risto started to say, "Ah, Veka's joining us for a sauna," and we didn't even have the good sense to be afraid. Mother started screaming and then uttered a blessing "Oh, bless us Jesus!" and hollered to us "don't touch it and open the door right away!" I opened the door and the dog went straight out without even giving us a glance. Then mother started getting dressed and so our bathing was finished. When we were in the house she said that it was an evil spirit. (Uusikirkko. Terijoen yhteislyseo. Irjo Kokko 703. 1936)

Poltergeist legends also describe dogs capable of assuming other shapes. Initially, the dog appears as a supernormal traveling companion or friend who insinuates himself into the home of a community member who has violated a norm. As time passes, however, the beast turns into an invisible and malevolent spirit, and takes to disrupting the lives of the inhabitants of the house. According to some field notes from Saari, a red dog, acting as the helper spirit of an offended sorcerer, pursues a Maironiemi farmer all the way home from the market place (Saari. Helvi Paakkonen TK 80:5. 1961). Analogous European material depicts a demon dog following travelers, and then arriving at the scene of a poltergeist occurrence, or as the poltergeist itself – as in some Danish folk belief narratives (Woods 1959:22–33). In the following example, the Western Finnish devil from Kylmänoja is said to have interrupted the trip of a farmer's daughter to Sunday school by turning up as a hungry dog:

> Once again it was time for the daughter to go to Sunday school and so she went. But the devil, as we already know, was already on his way. Miina was the daughter's name. No one noticed that the devil tricked Miina by appearing as a dog, trotting along by her side and begging for food as dogs are apt to do as they run alongside a traveller. Miina opened her bag, which was full of food, and started to give the dog some bits of food... and the dog refused to let her take even one step forward. And so Miina gave away all of her food without even knowing that this was the devil. Even when her rucksack was empty, the dog kept on begging. But Miina had nothing left to give. Then the girl was surrounded by a mist and couldn't see a thing and the dog was nowhere to be seen. What to do? Then the fog lifted, and she could find her way home once again, and she found all of the food that she had given the dog and put it back inside her rucksack. When she got home, the girl told her family about how the dog had demanded the food. As she spoke, the devil began to laugh

as hard as he could on the stove and said: "I can turn myself into anything I want."
(Loppi. Eelin Ketonen KRK 59:11)

The popular devil (Finn. *piru*) appears to materialize as a dog primarily in the folklore of Savo and Western Finland. This is probably due to the Scandinavian-Christian tradition which left a lasting impact on the cultural heritage of these regions.

The Black Cat

Literary sources for European Christian beliefs dealing with the devil and witchcraft usually identify the cat as a faithful ally of the witch (Rudwin 1973:41). We must remember, however, to make a distinction between animals given to witches by the devil, and demonic creatures in which the devil materializes (Robbins 1965:190–193). Danielsson's research shows us that in Scandinavian folklore, horses and dogs are more commonly associated with the devil than are cats (1930:99).

In Finnish folk belief, the cat is deemed an unclean animal. Thus, the appearance of a black cat, an especially heinous creature, generally foretells unhappiness and warns of imminent danger (Danielsson 1930:101). Lencqvist refers to an incantation in which the sorcerer summons a demon cat to his aid. The animal, by causing pain, impels the thief to return stolen goods: "Mistress of Pain, demon cat, give the legs a splendid claw, pain will make him hurry" (1982:58). In the minds of many, the demon dog and cat are virtually interchangeable as images associated with the kingdom of the dead.[6] Archival materials related to folk beliefs also reveal accounts of the devil himself assuming the form of a black cat. Likewise, one of the most frequent incarnations of the devil in Russian folklore is a black dog or cat (Oinas 1985:99).

> There was a haunted house in Impilahti. At night something would rattle objects indoors and during the day it would cause a ruckus in the attic and even in the hayloft. The people of that household soon had no peace of mind and were growing more and more desperate by the day. Finally, one Sunday after church, the owner of the house went to talk to the priest. The priest went to the house with his holy water and wine and held a sermon, and then walked around the house sprinkling holy water on the walls. They then noticed a huge black cat leave the house and head for the woods. After this the house was no longer haunted, and the people believed that the devil himself – as a black cat – had abandoned the house and stopped haunting it and troubling the inhabitants.
> (Salmi. KRK 151. Pohjanvalo, Pekka 172. 1935–1936)

In the following description of a Viena (Karelian) ritual curse, the participants are convinced that a demon has invaded the body of a cat. Thus, the devil is driven from the household by killing the creature and using its corpse. Field notes describing spirit possessions place great emphasis on whipping the dead cat and burying it in the churchyard; this serves as an explicit warning to the devil to remain where he belongs – that is, in the mythical land of the dead:

> If the devil has taken over a house, you can get rid of him by killing a cat and smearing its blood on the outer corners of the house. You must also hack off its tail and put it on the threshold and cover it with dirt. Then you take three young trees and tie them together to make a whip. Then use it to whip the corpse of the cat in the middle of the floor. One person asks, "What are you whipping?" The other responds: "The inhabitants of this house." Then place the whip underneath the house and make a coffin out of alder. Place the cat inside the coffin and bury it in the northern corner of the churchyard and say: "That's the place I'll throw you, and you'll get an even harder whipping if you come back." Then walk away without looking back. Upon reaching the house, enter through the window and say: "Old dwellers be gone and make room for the new!" Then build a fire by rubbing two sticks together to warm the house and do not put out the fire for three days – and then the devils will be gone.
> (SKVR I, 4 1971)

An unruly devil can invade a home by turning up as a black cat. In the belief legends I studied, the cat appeared to symbolize a chaotic outside force disrupting the life of an individual who has violated a norm. Acting as a demonic punisher sent by a sorcerer, the devilish cat makes a mess, and spoils or soils the food of the wayward individual. The metaphors of disorder and impurity are consciously elicited to defy the conventions of cleanliness, and thereby shame the victim – that is, the person who has broken a norm.

The Devil's Horse

As with dogs, people also believed that horses possessed extraordinary abilities and physical traits, according to Scandinavian, Germanic and Finno-Ugric mythology. In Scandinavian folk belief, a sacrificial horse buried with a deceased person is believed to convey the rider to the land of the dead or Valhalla (Odin's horse Sleipnir: Siikala 1992:126). Associated with the theme of death, the horse was also thought to possess the human potential to rise from the grave and haunt the living. (Danielsson 1930:68–71, 76–78, 99). A corresponding Biblical image of a devil on horseback in our midst, or rounding up people on horseback, is a widespread motif in Scandinavia (Thompson 1934:238). The image of four horsemen also turns up in Christian mythology: in the Book of Revelation, as they come to collect the sinful, they herald the end of the world and the arrival of Death (Lehner 1971:53–56).

In many belief systems the mythical horse figure symbolizes the supernatural shift from a certain condition, place or form to an other. In the mythology that comprises the Kalevala epic and incantation traditions, the horse emerges as one of the Devil's creations or a creature from hell. The craftsman can appeal to the creature to help rid a person, animal or place of evil (Krohn 1914:270–279):

Stallion the son of Hell's maiden
Mare the daughter of the maiden of Hell

Horse the devil's bastard son
Judas the steady branch
rested on the mountain for a week
A long time in Hell
A long time on the rock.

Take a horse from hell,
another horse from hell,
a foal chosen from the mountain
a bony hoof from the rock!

In belief legends, the supernatural horse motifs connected with a poltergeist's rowdy behavior are manifested in the sound of thundering hooves and horse heads appearing in windows. The fact that the horse noises are magically produced is alluded to subtly with the mention of horse hair and fur kept within a magical bag (principle of *pars pro toto*). Thus, individual parts of a phenomenon or living being serve to represent the whole – that is, metonymy. Likewise, a horse can convey an evil force in the human world to the graveyard and then back to its rightful home in the realm of the dead.

Anthropomorphism

Throughout history, the Christian Devil and its human incarnations have nearly always been depicted as masculine. For example, the Devil found in legends and literature appears as a young gentleman-like figure who is also a sly and clever con artist (Rudwin 1973:50–51). The fact that he is male stems from the dualistic Christian concept of the lords of Heaven and Hell.[7] In Christian tradition, the distinguishing features of a devil who appears as a human include missing body parts, and imperfections and extraordinary size and weight (compare to ghosts, monsters and giants) (Danielsson 1932:9–13; Russell 1984:49). Visible markings of the devil on the human body point to the physical examinations of those suspected of witchcraft during witch hunts, but have no direct correlation to the devil folklore I am examining (Robbins 1965:135–137). To a certain extent, the historical development of the Christian Devil figure has been influenced by the demonization of various ethnic and religious groups, and the association of physical characteristics with the concept of the devil (e.g. The Maoris and the Jews: Cohn 1975:70; Russell 1984:191–193). In the following cautionary legend, the devil appears as a hairy man before a man heading to the Koprala poltergeist house in search of female company:

> It was a Saturday night and Yllö Heikkilä was making his way to the notorious Koprala to meet young women. As he walked along the Pilkanpää heath, he saw someone walking towards him and wondered who else would be out at this time of night. As the figure drew closer and closer, Yllö could see that it was a human being covered with hair, and that this person was offering his

hand to be shaken. Yllö refused to shake the outstretched hand. Then the stranger said: "It's no use for you to go to Koprala, your future bride isn't there". Yllö began to ponder the stranger's words, changed his mind about going to Koprala, and turned back home and ended up heading to Ristiseppälä in his search for female company. There, he soon found one to his liking, and didn't waste any more time, and so the devil admonished him no longer. Many a time, Yllö earnestly recounted the night that the devil gave him warning on Pilkanpää heath.
(Heinjoki. Lempi Vanhanen TK 114:158. 1961)

Some of the field notes on unruly spirits describe a devil sent by a sorcerer to wreak vengeance against a household. This devil mingles with the group of people just like any ordinary man (a boy, a traveller, a beggar); in other words he seems to have no unusual or obvious demonic features. Although the devil generally adopts a masculine form, there is a feminine variant: to the dismay of the farmer's wife, the devil takes the form of a girl clad in red who has returned with the farmer from the market. (Uukuniemi. Arvi Räty TK 89:4. 1961). In the following western Finnish legend, the Ylöjärvi devil leaves the house as a distinguished traveller with two other companions, who all supernaturally disappear during the course of the journey:

Once a well-to-do traveller visited the Martins of Ylöjärvi. At the same time, there were also two other travellers. When they left, the third, a stranger, left with them. The men were very surprised when, after only a short distance, the stranger, the fine gentleman, suddenly vanished into thin air. They realized that they had been keeping company with the devil.
(Taivalkunta. Pohjois-Pirkkala)

Usually, however, supernatural appearances made by the devil in belief tales are of a demonic persuasion; in other words, the devil materializes as a fiendish figure who inspires fear and loathing in the hearts of those who set eyes on him. His sole function seems to be frightening people who are busy tending to their daily duties:

Two women were busy braking linen in the sauna. They heard a knock on the door, and in strolled the devil, and his fingers reached the hinges. The women began to scream and then ran away.
(Jaakkima. Martti Nenonen KRK 131:355)

One day in Mämmölä the devil made a visit to the manor. Elli was sitting on the steps sewing a shirt, and the shepherdess was on the lawn when it had arrived. The shepherdess was shocked, but Elli had said: "Don't be afraid, it can't hurt you". It had long hair with strands as thick as snakes. It tore at its hair and writhed around on the ground before returning to the forest.
(Kirvu. Pietari Munukka KRK 130:46)

The anthropomorphic devil that figures in belief tales can be identified as supernatural by its extraordinary color, build and clothing (comp. Scandinavian ghostly beings: Kvideland – Sehmsdorf 1988:122–125). Features associated with the devil are a black figure, a long body/great height, hairy body, a long nose, long hair, long fingers, a big nose and a big head (cf. Thompson 1934:234). Keeping an eye out for non-human features, and being able to recognize and label demons also seems to be a feature of Finnish folklore.

Magical Spheres

Features of the wealth-increasing *para*, which emerges in Scandinavian folk belief as a flying or rolling ball, are often associated with the figure of the unruly devil and his activities, particularly in Western Finland (Harva 1948:94–110, 440–441). Besides the physical appearance of the *para*, the devil and the *para* overlap in folk belief, as the *para* functions as an agent of the devil and a helping spirit of a witch (Harva 1928:7–8). Paradoxically, the riotous devil also emerges in belief tales as a supernatural helper and source of information to the people of a household (Klemettinen 1997:144–147). On the Karelian Isthmus, the devil has occasionally also been known to turn up as a hayrick. This form, which is closely associated with an agrarian milieu, alludes to the hay *para* which steals hay and gets tossed about by the wind (Harva 1948:448).

> In Ingria in the village of Termala, farmer Jokora Kokko, in the evening after bathing, went to sit down on the grass near the cellar. From a nearby bush he heard the sounds of pigs running about. He went to fetch his shotgun and then took aim, thinking that they were wild boar piglets. As he moved closer, the sounds grew fainter. He followed the sound. He then reached the fence and a pussy willow tree. On the other side of the fence was a vast forest. Whatever Jokora Kokko had been chasing had risen high into a tree, and it was like a hayrick with its cackling laugh. Jokora Kokko tried to shoot it, but his gun wouldn't fire.
> (Kivennapa. Pelkonen, E. KRK 134;137)

In Scandinavian folk belief, a magic ball lightly rolling along the ground symbolizes a witch's helper animal on a mission from its mistress. These magic spheres were made of animal fur, human hair and finger nails, as well as twigs, straw and wood chips. Following the logic of imitative magic, one could also add stick legs. People believed that allowing a few drops of blood to drip onto the enchanted sphere turned the lifeless ball into a witch's animal helper. In Scandinavian folk belief, this helper usually takes the form of a cat or a hare (Harva 1948:426–450; Kvideland – Sehmsdorf 1988:175–179). These hoarders of wealth were used in densely populated agrarian communities to steal milk and butter from other households. The following fragment from a Southern Karelian belief legend recounts how an overnight guest with magical powers drives away unruly devils by finding a fur ball and burning it:

> ... Kalle had once again lit the fire, and examined all the corners of the house. He finally noticed a single bit of kindling at the edge of the "cat's bench". He lifted it up and underneath it was a fur ball, like a ball made out of cow fur. Kalle took the ball outside and set fire to it with some kindling. "And, oh, the sound of steps which came out of it when the fur ball was burning, when they

left," Kalle would marvel even as an old man. "But in the morning when I went to show the farmer where I burnt the fur ball, there were no traces that something was burnt in that place, even though I snuffed the kindling many times while I was burning them. And I still wonder what happened to the coal because it was nowhere to be seen in the yard."
(Viipuri (?). Jukka Savolainen TK 94:82. 1961)

The witch's round, flying projectile, which people believed witches used to injure humans and animals, is representative of an earlier Scandinavian folk belief. The witch herself was thought to move in the form of a magical object called a *gandri* (Harva 1948:449–450; Honko 1959:92–100).[8] According to Lencqvist, a lumbago (*noidannuoli* literally means witch's arrow in Finnish) tears at the insides of the victim until the person dies (1982:95). Witches, gods, spirits and nasty neighbors would send similar projectiles of disease such as arrows, bullets, bone fragments, needles, pig's bristles, horse hair, pebbles and even small animals (Honko 1959:92–97; 1960:75).

The devil's assumption of the form of a sphere is hardly confined to Finnish folklore: Ivanits writes that the devil also appears as a ball of yarn in Russian folk belief (Ivanits 1989:40). In Lithuania, a ball of fire was believed to symbolize the devil (Harva 1948:448). According to Harva, the belief in a fanciful being turning up as a ball of fire can be explained by the natural, if unusual, occurrence of a lightning ball wreaking havoc on a building. The rational scientific interpretation partially explains the phenomena of round, fiery flying objects traveling through the house and entering and exiting through the chimney (Harva 1928:105; 1948:43).

> Sometimes it (the devil) would start by hanging from the lamp shade and then it would be like some fire ball in the lamp and then it would tumble to the floor and roll out, and of course, we were all terrified...
> (Koivisto. Ulla Mannonen 7740. 1938)

The belief legends making up my data bring forth a devil capable of metamorphosis; the devil can both arrive at, and depart from a house in the form of a spinning ball. Viewed from the perspective of Scandinavian folk belief, the personification of evil as a spinning ball can be interpreted as the conscious action of a magical object which has been animated by a witch or a sorcerer. In the following account from Sortavala, an angry woman asks the devil to assume the form of a ball and take vengeance on the house of Koipää:

> The farmer – whose house became possessed by the devil – had once been involved in a horse trading deal with a woman. The deal turned out to his advantage, and the woman then requested that they cancel their agreement. The farmer refused. Then the woman said to him: "Well, you'll come to regret this one!" The devil entered the house like this: one evening, after the sale, there was a sound from the porch. Since whoever was responsible for the sound did not enter the house, they opened the door and a ball of fire rolled in along the floor. It rolled right into the inglenook, and ever since that evening, the devil has occupied the house. And later, the devil played all sorts of tricks,

especially on the man of the house. And those have been told earlier ...
(Sortavala. Matti Moilanen 2555. 1937)

Not only does the devil assume the form of a ball when he arrives on the
human scene, he also wreaks havoc wherever he turns up. For example,
Western Finnish devil lore tells of the Kylmänoja *paara*, a round and agile
creature able to "stir up a great deal of harm as he moves" and a "round
black creature which rolls like a ball from corner to corner" (Janakkala.
HAKS. Irja Wartianen 6200. 1937). Likewise, Eastern Finnish devils appear
as balls of straw and fire to household members undergoing punishment:

> They say that the devil wouldn't appear to all the guests who spent the night
> in the haunted room, but those that did see him had some strange stories to
> tell: when he had just fallen asleep, he heard a strange humming sound from
> under the bed, and then the bed began to shake, and something grabbed the
> blanket and pulled it to the floor. This incident prompted the frightened guest
> to get up and light the lamp. As he did so, he noticed a strange ball of straw by
> the beam, it moved and nearly fell on his head, and then was nowhere to be
> seen. Then the pipes, matches, and cigarettes were hurled to the floor...
> (Parikkala. KT 32. Vieno Tiainen 15. 1938)

The aforementioned Maironiemi devil that arrives as a ball of straw is a bit of
an oddity since other similar motifs are not part of the data collected on that
particular poltergeist. It is true, however, that in the Parikkala narrative, the
northern farmer – after the agreement about the horse dispute – advises the
Maironiemi farmer to take a ball of yarn from underneath the threshold stone
and to burn it to stop the devil's rampage (Parikkala. Otto Harju 2797. 1938).

An Invisible Unruly Spirit

Rampaging devils generally turn up in belief legends as invisible spirits
which only make their presence known by speaking or taking action in certain
situations. Conventional interpretative models tend to suggest the presence
of the devil. The personification of Evil's unseen presence in a horse carriage
can be discerned by the carriage's extreme weight and the exhaustion of the
sweating horse. The heaviness of the invisible spirit recalls the Christian
concept of the Devil as an angel fallen from heaven; his sinful burden and
his evil spirit weigh him down to hell. Finnish folk belief defines invisibility
as a supernormal quality associated with spirits and gnomes (cf. Kvideland
– Sehmsdorf 1988:244).

   Eye-witness accounts of devil-related incidents demonstrate a firm belief
in the actual ugliness of the invisible demon responsible for mischief.
According to the Kuokkaniemi material, in particular, the poltergeist's motive
for becoming invisible is his bizarre and disturbing appearance. In the
following accounts, the devil dares not show his ugly appearance to a human
being, and thus, makes himself invisible. Likewise, in the variant from Uukuniemi, the devil is paradoxically called "the unseen ugliness" (Uukuniemi.
Eino Toivianen 470. 1939. 166).

The devil had been chatting away with the farmer just like any ordinary person would do, but he just didn't become visible. When the farmer had asked the devil to show himself, the devil refused and said that his ugliness would most likely give the farmer a severe shock...
(Sortavala. Juho Hyvärinen KRK 141:52)

The Koipää farmer was shoveling manure in the cow shed and said: "If I could see the devil just once." Then the devil replied from behind the pillar: "Here I am, but you can't see me. And I don't dare let you see me because I'm so ugly".
(Jaakkima. Tyyne Räty KRK 137:67)

The attachment of both human and animal traits to phenomena regarded as supernatural is one part of this problem-solving process; thus a seemingly irrational chain of events is analyzed through a dynamic belief system that encompasses evil spirits. A vital feature of the beliefs in demons and devils is that evil never shows its true face, but always assumes a disguise or a mystical veil of invisibility. Nonetheless, if the need arises, people – by relying on classifying signs – can always identify the personification of evil, and link it to supernormal or demonic phenomena.

Translated by Leila Virtanen.

NOTES

[1] In folklore studies, a poltergeist is an unruly supernatural being or spirit. Poltergeists typically toss household objects or stones about, and are often responsible for various knocking sounds.

[2] The primary research data is drawn from the Finnish Literature Society folklore archive's folk belief category E 601 – The devil causes a ruckus in the house (Simonsuuri 1961; Jauhiainen 1972). Although my work deals mostly with Karelian folklore, I have used archival material dealing with the Western Finnish devils of Ylöjärvi and Kylmäoja for purposes of comparison.

[3] According to Rudwin, the Bible contains no references to the devil being black. At a later stage, however, the church fathers began to compare the appearance of the devil to Maoris and Ethiopians. (Rudwin 1973:45).

[4] People and divine beings with the power to change from one form to another is a central concept in Greek mythology (Forbes 1990).

[5] The Biblical serpent that entices man and woman to sin appears in Kalevala epic poems and incantations as the "black worm", a viper (Krohn 1914, 246–257).

[6] As a pre-Christian concept, "hiisi" alludes to the mythical North and the land of the dead. It is also, however, a name for a being especially worshipped in the Karelian region as a guardian spirit of the forest and its game animals (Krohn 1914:278; Siikala 1992:139–140).

[7] According to the original Christian interpretation, the devil as a fallen angel is neither male nor female. The devil can, however, assume the shape of an alluring woman as a means of leading men astray (Russell 1984:149).

[8] Uno Harva refers to information on "gandri" by Fritzner (Fritzner, Hist. Tidskrift 4/1877:164).

BIBLIOGRAPHY

Cavendish, Richard 1975: The Powers of Evil in Western Religion, Magic, and Folk Belief. London.
– 1978 (1977): A History of Magic. London.
Cohn, Norman 1975: Europe's Inner Demons. An Enquiry Inspired by the Great Witch-hunt. London.
Danielsson, Paul 1930: Djävulsgestalten i finlands svenska folktro I. Djävulen i djurgestalt. Bidrag till kännedom af Finlands natur och folk H. 83, N:o 5. Helsingfors.
– 1932: Djävulsgestalten i Finlands svenska folktro II. Djävulen i människogestalt. Bidrag till kännedom af Finlands natur och folk H. 84, N:o 2. Helsingfors.
Forbes , Irving, P.M.C. 1990: Metamorphosis in Greek Myths. Oxford.
Ganander, Christfrid 1984 (1789): Mythologia Fennica. Helsinki.
Ginzburg, Carlo 1991: Ecstasies. Deciphering the witches' Sabbath. New York.
– 1992 (1966): The Night battles. Witchcraft & Agrarian Cults in the Sixteenth & Seventeenth Centuries. Baltimore.
Haavio, Martti 1950: Sielulintu. Kalevalaseuran vuosikirja 30. Helsinki.
Harva, Uno 1928: Para. Vertaileva tutkimus. Turun yliopiston julkaisuja B 7. Turku.
– 1948: Suomalaisten muinaisusko. Porvoo.
Honko, Lauri 1959: Krankheitsprojektile. Folklore Fellows Communications 178. Helsinki.
– 1960: Varhaiskantaiset taudinselitykset ja parantamisnäytelmä. J. Hautala (ed.) Jumin keko. Tietolipas 17. Forssa.
Ivanits, Linda 1989: Russian Folk Belief. New York.
Jauhiainen, Marjatta (ed.) 1972: Täydennyksiä uskomustarinoiden tyyppiluetteloon. Suomalaisen Kirjallisuuden Seuran kansanrunousarkisto. Helsinki.
Kemppinen, Iivar 1956: Suomalaisten muinaisrunojen Pohjola. Helsinki.
Klemettinen, Pasi 1997: Mellastavat pirut. Tutkimus kansanomaisista paholais- ja noituus-käsityksistä Karjalan kannaksen ja Laatokan Karjalan tarinaperinteessä. Suomalaisen Kirjallisuuden Seuran Toimituksia 687. Helsinki.
Krohn, Kaarle 1914: Suomen suvun uskonnot. Suomalaisten runojen uskonto. Suoma-laisen Kirjallisuuden Seuran Toimituksia 137. Porvoo.
Kvideland, Reimund – Sehmsdorf, Henning K. (eds) 1988: Scandinavian Folk Belief and Legend. Minneapolis.
Lehner, Ernst – Lehner, Johanna 1971: Picture Book of Devils, Demons and Witchcraft. Dover Pictorial Archive series. New York.
Lencqvist, Christian Erici 1982 (1782): Vanhojen suomalaisten teoreettisesta ja käytän-nöllisestä taikauskosta. Henrik Gabriel Porthan. Valitut teokset. Kääntänyt, esipuheen ja johdannot kirjoittanut Iiro Kajanto. Suomalaisen Kirjallisuuden Seuran Toimituksia 373. Jyväskylä.
Levack, Brian P. 1987: The Witch-hunt in Early Modern Europe. London and New York.
Murray, Margaret A. 1970 (1931): The God of the Witches. New York.
Oinas, Felix J. 1985: The Devil in Russian Folklore. Essays on Russian Folklore and Mythology. Ohio.
Parkin, David (ed.) 1985: The Anthropology of Evil. Southampton.
Pentikäinen, Juha 1968: Nordic Dead-Child Tradition. Nordic Dead-Child Beings. A Study in Comparative Religion. FF Communications 202. Helsinki.
Robbins, Rossell Hope 1965 (1959): The Encyclopedia of Witchcraft and Demonology. London.
Rudwin, Maximilian 1973: The Devil in Legend and Literature. Illinois.
Russell, Jeffrey Burton 1984: Lucifer. The Devil in the Middle Ages. Ithaca and London.
– 1988 (1977): The Devil. Perceptions of Evil from Antiquity to Primitive Christianity. Ithaca and London.
– 1991 (1981): Satan. The Early Christian Tradition. Ithaca and London.
Siikala, Anna-Leena 1992: Suomalainen šamanismi. Mielikuvien historiaa. Suomalaisen Kirjallisuuden Seuran Toimituksia 565. Hämeenlinna.
Simonsuuri, Lauri 1950: Kansa tarinoi. Porvoo.

- 1961: Typen- und Motivverzeichnis der finnischen mytischen Sagen. FF Communications 182. Helsinki.
- 1963: Uskomustarinat. M. Kuusi (ed.) Kirjoittamaton kirjallisuus. Suomen kirjallisuus I. Helsinki.

SKVR 1908–1948: Suomen Kansan Vanhat Runot I–XIV. Helsinki.

Thompson, Stith 1934: Motif-index of Folk-literature. Vol. 3 (f–h). FF Communications No. 108. Helsinki.

Wall, J. Charles 1968 (1904): Devils. London.

Wolf-Knuts, Ulrika 1991: Människan och djävulen. En studie kring form, motiv och funktion i folklig tradition. Åbo.
- 1992: The Devil between Nature and Culture. Ethnologia Europaea 22. Copenhagen.

Woods, Barbara Allen 1959: The Devil in Dog Form. A Partial Type-Index of Devil Legends. University of California publications. Folklore studies:11. Berkeley and Los Angeles.

UNPUBLISHED

Finnish Literature Society's Folklore Archive. Helsinki.

ULRIKA WOLF-KNUTS

Two Discourses about the Devil

Introductory Remarks

Narratives about the Devil belong both to the Church and to folklore. Church doctrine has given the Devil a certain eminence: he is the opposite of God, the main representative of evil. In folklore the image of the Devil is less clear-cut. Thus there are two different discourses on this mythical figure. One has official approval, as it is upheld by Christian theological experts on supernatural beings and described in the normative books of the Christian faith. The other one is unofficial and belongs to the people. The latter is orally transmitted in an unsystematic and contradictory way by lay people. Although they have adopted some features of the Church's image of the Devil, it has not proven entirely satisfactory.

The theological discourse is conveyed by the Bible, hymn books, catechisms, devotional manuals or collections of sermons. The discourse of folklore is oral, formed in various kinds of genres, not only in the longer narratives such as epics, legends or tales, but also in concise genres such as proverbs, wellerisms, spells, curses or swear-words. It is tempting to regard these two categories of texts as though they were contrary to each other, with "folklore" as the opposite of "elite culture". Church teachings on God and the Devil, on good and evil should, therefore, be quite different from popular Devil lore. This may influence scholarly approaches to concepts of the Devil. The official theological perspectives ought to be explored by the experts on Christian theology. The folklore points of view, however, should be described by folklorists using different methods to analyze different categories of texts.

This way of studying ideas about supernatural beings does not necessarily take the belief situation as it exists in a community into consideration in as broad a manner as possible. In a society where not only official Christian doctrine is taught, but where there is also a knowledge of religious topics apart from Church teachings, the people are forced to combine these two streams of belief to form a whole; otherwise it would be impossible to maintain a functional world view. This does not have to be logical, neither does it have to be consistent, and it does not have to avoid contradictions. However, it must be considered useful in certain recurring situations.

Myth and Mentality
Studia Fennica
Folkloristica 8, 2002

In practice, each society contains several discourses on one and the same topic, because of the coexistence of several mental strata (cf. Le Goff 1978:256). People constantly have to choose between different possibilities in order to build a functional model for their lives by using elements found in both official and unofficial sources. Indeed, everybody tries to build a meaningful model for his life with all the rules and norms that he has to follow, but this does not mean that everybody has the same model, or that one model only is accepted in a specific region. The official Christian tradition offers ingredients for a general model, but folklore reveals that there are many different ways of combining these and other elements of tradition. Folklore fulfills immediate needs by providing techniques for combining motifs, elements, and ways of thinking required to make different situations meaningful, functional or sustainable.

It is, however, problematic that this intimate connection with the situation in which tradition is actualized, shaped and reshaped for specific ends, is extremely difficult to document. This problem is accentuated even more if one is working with archival material from earlier centuries. Hence, a certain amount of interpretation is necessary in order to find out the ways of thinking, the norms, attitudes, dreams and ideals that have steered the narratives. This kind of interpretation demands extensive knowledge about the cultural context, that is, the environment of the recordings.

This is no easy task. For instance, in the Nordic countries a Christian phenomenon like the Devil has a very long and complicated history, reaching back to Protestant ideas and folklore issues of the 19th century, over several medieval ways of thinking, and combining with Norse topics stretching far back into Oriental and Near Eastern philosophies. Not only religious thoughts are evident, but also many kinds of concepts of how a society should be ruled can be traced in texts of this kind (cf. Russell 1977, 1982, 1986a–b).

The scholar interested in mentality or mental attitudes, does not "objectively" study a phenomenon (Le Goff 1978:254). Rather, he concentrates on how the phenomenon is described. What kind of wording is used in a recording, for example? What implicit hints can be found in a text? What deeper meanings are embedded in the concrete texts? These questions need to be addressed if we want to find out what norms and attitudes folklore communicates. They are best answered with an awareness of the cultural context.

Folk belief recordings, like all kinds of folklore, can be regarded as sources from which we can glean knowledge about very old strata of ideas about "supernatural reality" and world view. The fact that even today in a highly rational and scientific world we still believe in supranormal powers, be it God or magnetism, is evidence of the inertia of the belief in something beyond man's physical realm. These ideas are not necessarily apparent when hearing or reading the record. Every human being is free to assign meaning to a text according to his own needs. Not even the tradition bearer needs to be aware of those basic ideas. In the telling situation, he, too, imbues the text with his own meaning. The scholar, however, conscious as he must be of the rules of folklore, of how elements of folklore are understood and misunderstood, veiled and unveiled, that is, changed over time, space and according to recent needs, can interpret the texts and unfold those basic ideas (Lecouteux 1996:195).

By examining empirical records from a limited geographical region, Vörå in Finland, and over a limited period of time, 1860–1930, I shall address these questions: in what kind of society and in what normative system are discourses on the Devil maintained and, moreover, made compatible? A central question is: What kind of mental attitudes have enabled the survival of discourses on the Devil? By delimiting place and time I hope to limit the range of possible interpretations. By taking into consideration religious, historical, economic and educational facts in this region and regions that have influenced Vörå, I hope to decipher ideas and discover at least some possible interpretations when I look for what the texts tell *expressis verbis* and also what they tell implicitly. By analyzing the formulations and choice of words of the informants, it should be possible to discover how and what they thought about the Devil.

Located on central Finland's west coast, Vörå is undeniably a circumscribed place. Still, it is a cultural construct that has changed over time due to administrative causes. Sometimes it has been a more or less independent parish, while at other times the name has covered a larger geographical area. Culture, world view and folklore are not geographically limited entities, however; they are disseminated according to different rules than those decreed by official authorities. Therefore, a folklorist can find parallels and explanations for a folklore phenomenon of one particular region by looking at traditions in another one, for instance, in a neighboring parish or even in a neighboring country or wider geographical region, provided contacts have been upheld. Thus, the cultural context of a folklore phenomenon can, in a way, be vast.

The environment of the recordings, however, is not necessarily identical to the cultural context of the tradition. The context of the recordings is the moment when the folklorist happens to note down a text, often even as an answer to a query of his own. That context should be analyzed by means of performance theories. The cultural context is connected to different historical periods, cultural and economic history, and the history of ideas: in other words, to many levels of meaning that have changed over time. It is extremely important to consider carefully what a text means and has meant in different cultural circumstances if we want to understand the attitudes that produced it. "The history of mentalities cannot be of any use unless it is firmly tied to the history of cultural systems, belief systems, value systems and intellectual resources in which the mentalities have been shaped, where they have lived, and where they have been developed" (Le Goff 1978:257, my translation).

The Region: Economic, Social and Religious Environment

The region that I want to study is Vörå, an Ostrobothnian community on the western coast of Finland. The inhabitants' main language is Swedish. This region has had a typical multifaceted economic system. The people earned their living as peasants, complementing agriculture with other kinds of professions, like commerce, sailing or even preaching.

Vörå was open to several revival movements which arose and were kept within the official Church, like Pietism, the Evangelical movement *Svenska Lutherska Evangeli-Föreningen*, underlining the Word and mercy of God, to some extent, the protest movement *Kyrkans Ungdom* accentuating a personal relationship with God, not to mention several non-Lutheran movements like the Baptist movement, Pentecostalism or Methodism outside the Church. A Christian world view is, without doubt, the foundation of religiosity in Vörå (Åkerblom 1937; Åkerblom 1963; Näsman 1979).

The Material

The material examined here is divided into two categories. The first one consists of some books which are known to have been used and read in Vörå during the period studied here (Dahlbacka 1987:287f). These books, which I will call prayer-books, are collections of sermons by Martin Luther (Luther 1860a-c, 1867), Anders Björkqwist (*Trons öfning till Saligheten*, 1877), Johann Arndt (*Fyra Anderika Böcker om En Sann Christendom*, 1891) and Anders Nohrborg (*Den Fallna Menniskans Salighets-Ordning*, 1899). Furthermore, I have also studied the hymn-books of 1695 (still in use at the end of the 19th century), and 1886 (*Psalmboken* 1802, 1928), two song-books, namely *Sionsharpan* (1893) and *Sions Sånger* (1840), and Olaus Svebilius's catechism *Enfaldig Förklaring öfver D:r Martin Lutheri Lilla Cateches* (1878). Most of these works were first published long before the period under examination in this paper, but they were still in use and much appreciated in later times.

The second category of texts studied here is made up of folklore recordings in the classical 19th century sense of the word. The texts were collected from the middle of the 19th century to the 1930s and are now preserved in the archives of the Swedish Literary Society in Helsinki (SLS). Some of the texts are also published in *Finlands svenska folkdiktning* 1919–1952.

Many of the recordings are anonymous. In some cases, though, it was possible to check the informant's background; apparently they all had had formal schooling and were confirmed, which means that they had a basic knowledge of Church teachings. The community was also literate to some extent (Wolf-Knuts 1991:65ff.). Important centers where learned discourse was popularized were all represented in Vörå, i.e., Church, school, market-places, smithies, inns and other places where people met (cf. Le Goff 1978:255).

The folklore corpus examined consists of several genres. Due to the manner of collecting folklore at that time the genres documented are probably more or less those requested by the collectors (Förhandlingar 1888:101). This means that if there was more information about the Devil in genres left unmentioned by the collectors, it did not reach the written record. This process of selection also applies to the printed collections. Only those texts conforming to a model of good, decent, and respectable folklore were published. In the collection discussed here, there are stories told about the Devil as an actor on his own or together with one or more human beings.

The collection also includes pithy genres in which the Devil appears only as a swear word.

The examined material is extensive and varied enough to illustrate ideas and attitudes about the Devil under different circumstances. It includes a variety of Devil-related telling situations. Because it is limited to Vörå during a certain period, however, we can interpret the texts as products of a certain culturally-limited historical background (cf., however, Lecouteux 1996:194).

The Name of the Devil

In the collections of sermons and hymns the Devil is usually simply called the Devil, but other names also exist, like Lucifer, Leviathan, Beelzebub, Satan, the Evil One, the Big Dragon and so on. Folklore has a wealth of euphemistic names. *Fan* is the most common one. Not only is it a *nomen proprium* for the active, personified Devil, but it is also a swear-word. Also, the names *djävulen*, the 'Devil', and Satan crop up rather often in the recordings. This is the case as well with several adjectives, such as *den onde*, the Evil One, *den lede,* The Nasty One, *den gamle*, the Old One. Folklore also knows some solemn words, like Lucifer or the Prince of the World.

As a matter of fact, only a few names are common to both categories of examined texts. Vörå has had an abundance of names for the Devil. The inhabitants obviously knew which names were appropriate in a given circumstance. For instance, the name *fan* never occurs in the prayer-books. The people of Vörå have clearly developed a nomenclature for the Devil suitable for different occasions.

Names for the Devil reveal traces of several cultural layers, beginning with names from the Old Testament which include those inherited from even earlier cultural eras. Medieval and Norse traces are also evident. 'Leviathan', for instance, is probably a Phoenician name; Beelzebub derives from 'Baal', a non-Israel heathen god, Satan is derived from Hebraic and changed to Satanas in Gothic whereas Fan appears to stem from Anglo-Saxon *fandian*, a word that was absorbed by Old Norse *fændin* (Hellquist 1989:198). Just by analyzing the names applied to the Devil several cultural horizons open up. It is important to state, however, that none of these names is the "real" one. All of them are euphemisms, paraphrases or metaphors coined in different times in different cultures. These terms reveal an ever-present fear of the Devil, a perpetual fear that has compelled people throughout the ages to avoid calling him by name: "Speak of the Devil and he will appear!"

The Figure of the Devil

The prayer-books describe the Devil in different ways. He is said to be anthropomorphic, i.e., he appears as a man, or theriomorphic, i.e., he appears as a dog, a wolf, a lion or a snake. He is also thought of as a mythical figure, and is, therefore, imagined as a dragon, an angel or a ghost. His voice can be heard in a thunderstorm. In folklore accounts the Devil is more likely to take part in people's everyday lives. Here, too, he appears anthropomorphically, for instance, as an old man, a gentleman, a priest or as the director of a *gymnasium* (for a synopsis of the various motifs in Irish Devil lore, cf., for instance, Ó hEochaidh – Ó Laoire 1989).

Rural societies of the past attached little significance to the aged. They were either respected or regarded with fear and disgust. Respect for one's elders is a basic precept in classical tradition and in both the Old and New Testament; it was taught in Finland with the help of the Fourth Commandment and educational literature (Topelius 1906:110f). Fear and loathing of the aged may stem from a purely economic perspective; those unable to work and contribute to the household could be deemed worthless: "You shall gain your bread by the sweat of your brow" (Gen. 3:19). Therefore, old people in the past (and present) often led isolated lives from the productive generations; consequently, they were considered inferior, and were disregarded and marginalized (Schenda 1977:373ff.; Åkesson 1991:65f; cf. Sehmsdorf 1988:36). Shunning the old, however, can be a result of two opposing ideas. The sight of an old man was considered a good omen when one started a new endeavor. However, an old man was potentially dangerous, and therefore commanded respect. His presence is regarded as numinous (Naumann 1927a:345f). For instance, the supernatural quality ascribed to an old man is evident in the name of the mountain spirit in German folklore: he is called *Altvater,* "old father" (Naumann 1927b:351). Although marginalizing certain people may be a pragmatic solution to a given communal problem, it can lead to increased suspicion of those marginalized. "The power of the weak," an expression coined by Victor Turner, is useful to keep in mind here. In other words, such people are accorded special respect, or as Lynn Åkesson in her study of Swedish popular characters puts it: "Marginal man ... is not only inferior. He can also represent an alternative order, alternative social relations and above all his mere existence is a constant reminder of basic values between human beings and of the fragility of power" (1991:67). Thus, the marginalized individual is never regarded with indifference.

With the above-mentioned folklore in mind, it is possible to argue that the Devil appearing as an old man is numinous in one way or another. One must either fear or revere him; he is never simply dismissed – and this is not just because he is the Devil.

The same can be said for the Devil when he takes the form of a gentleman. These records are easy to regard as examples of cautionary folklore. A gentleman in Vörå is either a stranger and, therefore, dangerous, or he is allied with the authorities, as a priest or a bailiff. Simply the fact that he comes from the town already renders him untrustworthy and even menacing. We must also remember the rural people's suspicion of presumptuous "urbanites" who think they can teach rural, that is, backward people how to arrange their lives (Wolf-Knuts 1992:113; cf. Valk 1994:325ff., where the Estonian gentleman Devil is connected with the demonized German landlord). Here the texts express both fear and a superior smile.

That the Devil can even appear as a priest is further proof of his cunning and guile. The texts show the people's belief in his powers. He can even assume the most unexpected and far-fetched role; he can disguise himself as a priest, that is, take on a core role in the Church. Folklore describes the great lengths the Devil will go to lure man away from God.

As the director of a *gymnasium* he is the administrator of knowledge, a circumstance that is neither neutral nor meaningless, as will be shown below.

Like a human being the Devil has feelings; he is happy, he cries, he is afraid, he is cunning and he is loyal to his followers. Sometimes he appears as a child. It is not quite clear whether he also can appear as a woman. In folklore, on the other hand, the Devil is said to assume the form of an animal, especially a domestic animal such as a dog, but also a horse or a pig. The snake, a form which clearly suggests the Devil, mainly crops up in spells and charms. The folklore texts also combine human and animal traits in the Devil, perhaps to indicate his demonic nature.

Folklore accounts place the Devil in the realm of day-to-day human affairs; in the tradition of the Church, however, older continental cultural traits, and even pre-Christian ideas are combined (cf., for instance, Forsyth 1987). Interpretations of Church tradition tend to be symbolic and universal, whereas those of folklore tend to be more literal. Just how the individual inhabitant of Vörå imagined the Devil is hard to say. The material cannot even tell us whether the folk believed that he consistently appeared in the same form, especially because assuming various forms is a well-known characteristic of the Devil (and other supernatural beings) in both types of discourse. This means that he is always unpredictable, which, in turn corresponds well with what the Church teaches: the Devil is always present and ready to strike.

The Devil Meets Man

The Dwelling Place of the Devil

In the prayer-books the Devil appears in both the mythical and non-mythical world. Although he resides in Hell, he is said to long for Heaven. He can travel through the air or on the ground; the world is his realm. Here "the world" does not simply refer to the surface of the earth but instead works as a metaphor for the life of sin. Water is yet another dwelling place for the Devil. Indeed, the Devil always stays close to man. Sometimes he even takes a seat in man's heart.

In folklore, too, the Devil appears in a mythical and a non-mythical world. He is said to live in Hell, but he also visits the human realm; for instance, the Devil will materialize in a family's house, their yard, in the fields or on the road. Folklore most often places the Devil in a human being's most immediate environment, i.e., in everyday life. The Devil also meets human beings at crossroads, in the sauna and in the church. In terms of the supernatural, all these places are significant; for example, many magic rites are conducted at crossroads (Thompson 1965:D 1786. Magic power at crossroads; Finlands 1930:LXXVIII). The sauna also has a central role to play in Finnish folk medicine.

If a person meets the Devil in the church, the encounter usually takes place on the pulpit or inside the railings of the altar. We see, therefore, that the Devil can appear anywhere; consequently, human beings are never safe. The church building is, in this case, to be seen as a point of intersection between the two poles of religion, namely the sacred and the non-sacred, as Rudolf Otto puts it. On the non-sacred pole stands the human being, and on the sacred pole stand God and the Devil. Although God and the Devil make an incongruous pair, they occupy the same sacred class. After all, the sacred is made up of two complementary aspects, the *fascinosum* and the *tremendum* (Otto 1923:38, 49ff.). In many cultures, especially pre-Zoroastrian ones, these two aspects were combined in one and the same god. It was not until the division into good and evil gods in the Sassanide period that these dual aspects turned into absolute opposites (Forsyth 1987:109). In the texts where the Devil appears in the church and even in the holiest place in the church, he can be interpreted as God's "other half", the *tremendum*. When the Devil invades the house of God, he poses a real threat to man. If the man or woman firmly resists the Devil's temptations, however, this is a victory over the Devil.

Another plausible explanation for why the Devil is placed on the altar is simply that folk narrators are fully aware that they are no longer telling sacred stories in a "sacred" context. They, therefore, try to shock the listener by including blasphemous motifs where norms collide very effectively. This technique of constructing texts is well known from jokes (see, for example, Röhrich 1988:372).

The Devil's Actions

According to the prayer-books, the Devil is ever-present among humans in search of easy prey, i.e., he has a keen eye for human weakness, and human beings, therefore, are never secure. The Devil never sleeps nor rests. By deafening people's ears to God's Word, he tempts them into sin and makes it hard for them to concentrate on God's will. He pursues man in order to sabotage his good relationship with God, his Redeemer. The Devil is sly and false, he is fawning, he threatens man and disturbs him, he lies, cheats and makes man blind to the will of God. He resembles God so much that man can be mistaken as to his true identity. He causes damage, he pours water over the fire of faith, he tears Zion to pieces. Thus Zion emerges as a herd of sheep tended by Jesus, whereas the Devil is the wolf. The Devil rages like a tyrant or a roaring lion. He makes man anxious, he wants to take his soul; he either murders man or makes man a murderer. He damages the whole world. Man has to prevent the Devil from overcoming Christ. The Devil is full of rage and hatred, and he cannot endure love.

All these negative characteristics are the result of the envy that the Devil felt when he rebelled against God. Once an angel in charge of watching over life on earth, the Devil turned against God because he wanted to be equal to Him or, at least, superior to man. His downfall was due to vanity and pride (Rudwin 1973:6f). All uncleanliness, wickedness, sin and vice in man come from the Devil; everything he does is, according to the prayer-books, to cause man evil. In short, human beings should not expect anything good from the Devil.

According to this discourse, the human being has no advantage or happiness to gain from contact with the Devil. On the contrary, individuals should stay as far away from the Devil as possible. This, however, is impossible, because long ago, in a mythical time, contact was already established between man and the Devil. Man is forever in the Devil's clutches. The Devil and God are engaged in an eternal struggle over man. The Devil tries to destroy man's life, but God can help man against the Devil.

The portrayal of the Devil's deeds in the prayer-books can, of course, be interpreted literally. In the Lutheran tradition, however, sermons and other forms of religious education use the motifs found in these books in order to explain and describe different aspects of the human condition. Thus, people reading the prayer-book texts can understand them symbolically, according to their actual needs in various situations. Further details about how the individual might understand these texts are not available.

Most of the folklore texts describe interaction between human beings and the Devil. Unlike the Church discourse, folklore does not necessarily advise men and women to avoid all contact with the Devil. In fact, many texts describe how human beings and the Devil meet, talk and act together. Contact with the Devil can even be advantageous. Thus, the Devil of folklore emerges as an ambiguous figure; he is not the unequivocally evil being depicted by the Church.

Dealings with the Devil may be either planned or coincidental. People may seek out the Devil's aid in order to solve their worldly problems. They can also meet the Devil by chance and then take advantage of the situation. In both cases the result of the contact is positive from the human perspective. But it can also be disastrous to the human being: the Devil may cause him/her injury or even take his/her life. Unlike the prayer book texts, the folklore texts are not consistent in this respect.

We may ask how the individual in a community like Vörå, equipped with all the knowledge of Christian doctrine provided by school and Church, would even consider deliberately seeking out the Devil. On the one hand, this kind of logic in the narratives may be explained by the narrator's desire to shock, causing norms to collide. According to church discourse, man ought to be careful and avoid everything that makes him vulnerable to the Devil's attacks. By ignoring this norm and contrasting it with an individual seeking to establish the type of contact that Church discourse forbids, folklore efficiently shows who is the mightiest. The shrewd individual need not fear the Devil, especially if he reckons to get help from God.

There is another possible explanation for the texts about human beings who seek contact with the Devil. Church discourse says that it is impossible to get rid of the Devil. The Devil does not appear only in situations when man has done something wrong, but also when man leaves off doing the right things according to God's will or the community's rules. The Devil is always at hand in these situations. He is generally "always" and "everywhere" about trying to cause harm. Individuals are liable to sin on purpose and, therefore are perpetually getting closer to the Devil. In response to the fact that human beings can never escape the Devil, folklore offers an alternative to the hopeless message of the prayer-books: folklore tells about those who have gained from the inevitable fact of the Devil's constant presence. In this way the folklore texts are not only amusing, playing with fire as it were, they are also encouraging.

The Devil is apt to meet human beings at night, the time, according to folklore, when most dangerous supernatural figures are active. He can also appear in the morning or in the evening, and, thus, he is, like so many supernatural beings, a transgressor of borders (Stattin 1984:52f; Eskeröd 1947:85ff.). If an individual breaks the third commandment, for example, the Devil is bound to appear on Sunday morning. Wednesdays and Thursdays are also mentioned as days when encounters with the Devil were possible. Both of these days were connected with old Norse gods, Odin and Thor, respectively (Christiansen 1911:184; Piø 1973:214ff.). Hence, it is possible to see a trace of the process of Satanization in these texts. Furthermore, the Devil of course, shows up around the yearly festivals which, like morning and evening, can be regarded as times of intersection – in this case the intersection between different calendar periods and therefore filled with supernatural phenomena (Nilsson 1915:38ff.).

To protect oneself from the Devil one can use the Bible, a hymnbook or almanac. Because of their Christian power these books are generally regarded as effective guards against supernatural forces. Although the Devil himself belongs to the Christian sphere and is mentioned in these very books, they still work to deter him. Here we see that the Devil in folklore has been adapted to other folklore figures who are afraid of and, therefore, frightened by the Christian word. Other items from the Christian sphere that keep the Devil away are a lighted candle and blessings. Many texts tell how a priest rescues an individual from the Devil. Although help is sought within the Church, the church building is not, as we have seen, a safe place, as regards protection from the Devil. This is significant because church buildings, in different genres of folklore (Thompson 1965: R 325), as well as in today's society, are places of refuge against human enemies. The Christian realm provides help against a supernatural enemy, the Devil, only to some extent, namely, by the same techniques that are usually applied in genres about supernatural beings or in folk medicine. In this way folkloric ideas on protection from supernatural beings have had an impact on Devil lore.

Metal objects generally referred to in supernatural connections as a means of averting evil are also a form of protection against the Devil (cf., for instance, Ambrosiani 1922:52ff.). Correctly-answered questions put by the Devil to man compel him to disappear. He cunningly thinks he would snare man for lacking knowledge, but man turns out to be more cunning than the Devil. Hence, he gives in when he meets his superior.

The Devil in the Human Life Cycle

Individuals meet the Devil at different stages of their lives. By frightening away her sweetheart, the Devil helps a man to win the love of the girl of his desires. The moral of the story is that a man who fears the Devil is not

157

strong enough to get a woman for his whole life. The Devil also meddles in people's marriages; for instance, he causes a couple who have never quarreled before to quarrel. Actually, he is not skillful enough for this task, but needs help from an old woman who is even more wicked than himself. The Devil also turns out to be somebody's spouse. One tale describes how a girl who lacks humility in choosing a husband finds herself married to the Devil.

The Devil also has a role to play in pregnancy and childbirth. Either the pregnant woman is afraid of pain and, therefore, accepts the Devil's help; or she is pregnant and unwed and, consequently, wants to kill the child. In the first case pain is the crucial point. According to the Bible, a woman is made to give birth in pain (Gen. 3:16, cf. the Swedish translation where *smärta*, meaning pain is used for "labor"). If she escapes this fate, the only explanation seems to be that she has made a deal with the Devil. In the second case a social rule has been violated, namely, that children should be born within marriage, otherwise they will be a disgrace to the family and the community (Tillhagen 1983:24). Out of shame the mother-to-be wants to hide her pregnancy and asks the Devil for help. Furthermore, a pregnant woman should exercise extreme caution and avoid taking risks. If she is careless, many dangers, among them the Devil, are likely to bother her (Skjelbred 1972:76–98). This idea is illustrated in texts depicting the Devil asking a woman, who may not yet even know she is pregnant, for what she carries under her apron, namely, a male child. According to the texts, she can keep her son for ten years provided she does not teach him how to read.

Here we encounter the notion of the cunning Devil is always a threat to unsuspecting individuals. To the Devil literacy is loathsome. Reading brings knowledge, not only secular but also sacred knowledge, especially in rural Finland where most books were religious. This means that the Devil, in fact, feared that the child would be so knowledgeable of Christian dogma and doctrine that he would be able to force the Devil to disappear. He would be as capable as a priest, who, in some of the recordings is the rescuer of man. One recording indirectly supports this idea. The child, a boy, is clever enough to get rid of the Devil by correctly answering three questions. The text then claims that he later became the author of a hymn in the old Swedish hymn book (IF R II 151). He, in other words, was a master of sacred language. Bearing in mind the power of words and language, we can clearly see just why the Devil dislikes reading (Segerstedt 1968:102ff., 171f).

There is also, however, a complementary explanation. Reading means combining letters, reading means the use of the alphabet. This has, in itself, magic-apotropaic functions: "Was die Geister vertreibt, ist nicht nur das christliche Element, sondern auch die lang erprobte Magie, die zu Hilfe gezogen wird, da man doch nie sicher ist, dass die zitierten Heiligen und Gott die Geister in die Flucht zu schlagen vermögen" (Lecouteux 1996:209). Indeed, the combination of letters from the alphabet, reading and Christian literature, is a very strong combination. If we accept such an interpretation, it is clear that the Devil is handled like other supernatural beings who can be driven away by spells, charms, or other forms of verbal expression.

Fathers, too, offer their children to the Devil. They want to rescue themselves from danger, and thus, the children are sacrificed. The texts containing this motif often conclude with the children outwitting the parents and the Devil by appealing to the priest for help; they also may be rescued by some other means provided by the Church.

The Devil and Earthly Welfare

The Devil is also connected with earthly welfare in agricultural Vörå. He increases an individual's wealth, either directly by collecting money, or indirectly by collecting manure to be used as fertilizer; he may show a man how to sharpen his axe, one of the most important tools in forestry and the tar industry. In these cases the Devil is an active partner cooperating with man.

Other recordings demonstrate how even the Devil's name can be used in order to ensure wealth and success. It is told, for instance, that a woman churning butter has to turn her naked behind to the churn, break wind and swear by mentioning the Devil's name, if the butter seems not to come. This certainly has to do with the economic system in Vörå where butter was either a way of preserving cream or a product for sale. Moreover, it shows how the Devil is combined with the realm of magic, where nakedness and passing wind are often mentioned as apotropaic measures (Eckstein 1934–35:834f, 842, 907f). Interestingly, breaking wind appears somewhat inconsistent here because it is often regarded as a way to summon the Devil to appear (Bächtold-Stäubli 1930–31:223f). There is, however, also the idea that breaking wind is healthy. Consequently, it might have been regarded as having a positive effect on the churn and the butter as a means of driving bad powers away. Breaking wind, however, also emerges in popular thought as a way to express contempt. Thus, the text can be interpreted as a narrative telling just how little the Devil really means (Daxelmüller 1985:594, 597). It is obvious, therefore, that the Devil has been handled as other supernatural beings of folklore.

The Devil in folklore has a (silver) treasure, and hence he brings to mind dragons and other treasure watchers in Nordic folklore. He is associated with money, he acts as a banker, although not very successfully. The recordings describe how he lends money to a man in a barrel with full measure but demands only to get the level measure back, and, thus, the man gains the surplus of money. In this group of texts the Devil is ridiculed for his stupidity. Moreover, the Devil gives away money, but of course, under the condition that the recipient will eventually belong to him. Money is a great enticement and even the priest can be convinced to cooperate with the Devil for economic gain. Markets and business are other devilish domains. If a shopkeeper is dissatisfied with his business, the Devil will help him as long as the shopkeeper agrees that he will one day belong to the Devil. Time passes, his business flourishes and the shopkeeper is a wealthy man. When he must turn himself over to the Devil, however, he seeks the aid of an old woman. Thanks to her, the shopkeeper gets his fortune without losing anything. These texts are probably to be interpreted as expressions of the idea about Mammon as one of God's opposites. As a man of God, the priest should be indifferent to money, the realm of Mammon. Business should be conducted decently, honestly and by hard work; honesty and reliability are Christian ideals. On the other hand, there is an alternative ideal of gain, even if it means cheating other people (cf., for instance, Darnton 1987). Some of the texts show how human beings violate these norms without having to suffer. Again, the texts, which show how norms collide, can be seen as narratives of entertainment. On the other hand, we should keep in mind the idea of limited good, indicating that there is only a specific amount of wealth available; in other words, if one person takes too much, another person will inevitably have less or even become impoverished (Foster 1965, cf. Sehmsdorf 1988).

The Devil and the Life of Pleasure
Human beings are bound to meet the Devil whenever they are having fun. Dancing is dangerous: the partner may be the Devil himself. One text describes how the Devil danced only with the boys. This, however, need not be regarded as a violation of a norm against homosexuality. Apparently, homosexuality did not pose a serious threat in Finnish rural society, and there are several accounts for people of the same gender dancing together (Löfström 1995. I thank Gunnel Biskop for her comments on this topic). The main point of the text is something else: the girls, in fact, are eager to dance with the Devil. When finally taken as a partner, she turns out to be so proud that the Devil dances with her until her feet bleed. Thus, this text is a warning against pride.

Humility is another ideal in this kind of society. Card playing is also another pastime enjoyed by the Devil; the deck of cards is even regarded as the prayer-book of the Devil (Wünsche 1905:11; Herold 1931–32:1015). The Devil is also associated with smoking has a pipe of his own. If three persons succeed in lighting their tobacco with one and the same match, the Devil weeps. Playing cards and smoking are linked with idleness, yet another human failing to be censured. A good human being ought to be industrious.

Drinking alcohol also summons the Devil. This applies both to lay people and to priests. Not only is drinking associated with idleness, excessive drinking also leads to reckless and even destructive behavior. As a matter of fact many of the revival movements in Vörå opposed the use of alcohol completely. Texts depicting drunkards show how the Devil appears to man, but such narratives do not overtly condemn alcohol consumption. Instead, the recordings add several more facts that turn the texts into uncanny stories. The drunkards meet the Devil in the middle of the night, in a church yard, i.e., in combination with other breaches of norms than just drinking. Besides consuming alcohol, the sinners may indulge in gossip or boasting.

Every person who takes unnecessary risks, such as succumbing to – strong emotions, or feelings of delight, is likely to meet the Devil, especially, since human beings can be regarded as proud, boastful, chatty and naive in gossiping situations. By referring to the realm of the Church, i.e., a priest, a prayer-book, or blessing, man is helped. Also a ready wit, and stubbornness, often in combination with stupidity and naivete, can help. Maybe we see here some kind of paraphrase of the Christian idea of blessed childishness: "Whoever does not accept the kingdom of God like a child will never enter it" (Mark.10:15).

The study of the prevailing moral ideals in Vörå show that alcohol consumption, dancing, swearing, fornication, fighting and card playing were unacceptable because they were regarded as sinful activities (Wolf-Knuts 1991:55–65). But also fripperies, stubbornness and foolhardiness could be sins, as could be cruelty, anxiety and idleness. Ideally, each person should aim to be content, grateful and moderate in every respect. Thus one showed trust in God (Wolf-Knuts 1991:216ff.; cf. Scharfe 1980). Ideals, however, are usually beyond the reach of ordinary mortals; in other words, people always fail to meet the requirements for a good Christian life. Many of the texts can be interpreted as reports of people who did not surrender to this boring way of life.

The Devil, the Shoemaker, the Smith and the Judge

In Vörå, agriculture was practiced along with other kinds of economic endeavors to guarantee the livelihood of the inhabitants. Handicraft is often mentioned in the folklore recordings concerning the Devil: a shoemaker stays in church at night and witnesses Devils carrying away the skin of a thief. The shoemaker takes the skin and demands money for its return. In this way the shoemaker gains in the confrontation with the Devil. The Devil and the shoemaker are, perhaps, to be traced back to legends of Ahasverus and medieval traditions of the saints of the shoemakers, Saint Crispins and Saint Crispinianus. However, it is also likely that the texts should be interpreted in the light of the fact that in the Nordic countries shoemaking was regarded as a low status occupation because it was a journeyman trade (Jäfvert 1938:98; Hasan-Rokem 1986:122).

The hide of the thief motif can be regarded as a survival from a medieval legal tradition of skinning somebody as a punishment for crimes. Valentin Merkelbach, using general European folklore, combines the motif with the pre-Christian belief in the skin as a *pars pro toto*, ensuring that the Devil will also control the dead man's soul, with belief in vampires and with the custom of making death-masks out of human skin. The Devil would need the skin to change into a ghost, and in this way Merkelbach interprets the motif as a demonization of the concept of specters and haunting (Merkelbach 1964). This interpretation has no support in the Finnish-Swedish recordings, and the ideas about the Devil which they contain should also be viewed in terms of the fact that people handling skin and dead bodies were despised. Thus the Devil is placed side by side with the executioner and the horse flayer (Egardt 1962:218ff., 230f). His nocturnal visit to the church can be explained in terms of the shoemaker's violation of a norm: work should not be done at night, let alone in the church.

Another belief about the Devil is that when the Devil still resided on earth, a smith promised himself to the Devil if he failed to answer correctly twelve questions posed by the Devil. The smith succeeded, and the Devil was cheated.

The smith in Vörå folklore is a fairly respectable person, not only because he provides the inhabitants with weapons, but probably also because of his connection to classical mythology – to Hephaistos and the Cyclopes – and his role in old Norse mythology connected to Mimer and the dwarfs (cf. Valk 1994:319f; Hammarstedt 1921:188ff.). It is, therefore, not surprising that the contact between Devil and smith occurs in mythical time and this may give us a hint as to why they meet. In Nordic folklore the smith is said to have learned his supernatural skills from the dwarfs, namely skills to force metal (make metal flexible) and endure heat (Tillhagen 1981:197f; Christiansen 1982:263f). It is, of course, also possible to make associations with Hell, another hot place. In Vör folklore the smith is associated with mythical time, the beginning of civilization; in fact, one of the recordings depicts the Devil teaching a smith how to sharpen his axe. Indeed, this is how the axe was invented.

The Devil is also linked to the judicature. He helps people find lost or stolen objects. To achieve this end, however, the person who needs the Devil's help must coerce the Devil by threatening to squeeze his testicles, for instance. On the other hand, the Devil often may torture a *länsman*, a *tolvman* or another member of court for giving false testimony. Ferd Ohrt has suggested that this motif goes back to the New Testament theme of Pontius Pilate (Ohrt 1918:287ff., 300ff.). It is, however, possible to interpret this theme in a more pragmatic way: because perjury and bearing false witness are so wrong, they must be linked with the Devil. We should consider yet another idea, namely that these persons have authority and standing in the community. We have already seen that the Devil can appear as a learned man, a gentleman, or the rector of a *gymnasium*, and that the texts mock the priests, and that education is looked upon with scepticism. All these roles of the Devil differ from that of the "normal" peasant. Their difference thus renders them dangerous. Also, figures related to the judicature represent the authorities and, thus, a sound scepticism of them is considered appropriate.

The Devil, magicians and witches are described in several recordings. Folklore tells us that one can become a magician by cooking a tomcat until the flesh leaves the bones. At that moment the Devil will appear, stick a hole in the person's finger and note down his name in his book. We do not know, however, whether anyone has ever conducted this ritual. It is, indeed, possible to link this motif with the idea of the contract with the Devil, but the motif of the Book of Heaven has also to be considered as a complementary and opposite motif.

Those who could cure illnesses were also believed to have sold their souls to the Devil. Likewise, people with magic skills had acquired them from the Devil. The Faust legend has been modified and reshaped to fit into the Vörå world-view, as has the Wittenberg-legend type (cf. Edsman 1963:66). Students from the Nordic countries visited the university in the 17th century to study theology, and there they had access to the teachings of Martin Luther and the Reformation, i.e., in a counter-reformation way of thinking, with the Devil himself. Moreover, these texts have to be interpreted in light of the notion that education is dangerous. The texts on the Devil have very little to say about witches; the evidence is fragmentary.

Conclusions

From the above discussion it is evident that the Devil in the Church discourse is unequivocally evil. Only with God's help can human beings avoid the Devil. (A sophisticated theology might see the Devil as God's tool when He puts man to the test, but there is no clear evidence of this in the texts.) In folklore, on the other hand – and it is absolutely necessary to take into consideration both these discourses as one whole – because that was popular reality, this evilness is not so self-evident. Certainly, in this information protection is seen to be afforded by the Church against the Devil, but the Devil is often regarded as stupid and hence man can outwit him. Man can even take advantage of his great strength and naivete.

Technically, there are two contrary discourses, but in fact the borderline between them does not lie between Church tradition and folklore, as one might expect. To a great extent the two traditions coincide, but folklore often has a much more varied and nuanced picture of the Devil than does the Church tradition. The Devil of folklore is more vivid, more personal, more concrete and less symbolic than the Devil of the Church.

Both traditions are to be explained in the light of the complicated background of combined and intertwined cultural layers. Both discourses emanate from a reservoir of thoughts and ideas about the Devil collected and intermingled over thousands of years, from several cultural spheres, some of which can be at least approximately dated, while others are diffuse and belong to the imprecise era of folk belief. Certainly, we have to do with *la longue durée*.

The fundamental questions, therefore, are: what kind of normative system maintains in the discourses of the Devil? The norms of Vörå society, which did not differ in any special way from most Lutheran rural societies during the 1860–1930s, were those of self-discipline, self-restraint, and moderation. According to motif analysis, human beings are bound to meet the Devil when they are ungrateful for their existence, immoderate in their behavior, proud, indecent and selfish. The Devil is also present when the individual desires more than he/she should have, for example, more wealth; or when a woman craves an easy childbirth; or when someone wants beautiful clothing; or they indulge in excessive drinking or idleness. In short, whenever individuals are egoistic and conceited about themselves, the Devil appears.

On the other hand, this ideal of self-discipline and moderation is impossible to reach. Man is, and will always be egoistic; this probably is a condition for survival. Egoism and pride were the reasons why Adam and Eve where banished from paradise. Since then the Devil has been man's primary and constant enemy. One of the mental attitudes discovered in the Vörå material is, therefore, fear. There is fear in connection with the Devil's names, with his omnipresence and his aim to destroy man.

This perspective has to be deepened. Fear of the Devil means not only that man is afraid of eternal damnation. It also means that man himself regards the Devil as a wrong master, i.e., God is his right master. In a Christian society like Vörå human beings belong to God by means of baptism. Thus, it can be expected that the Devil is envious. He can be regarded as having "an unacceptable desire for something [man] that rightfully belongs to someone else [to God]" (Sehmsdorf 1988:41). In other words, the Devil envies God for his possession of man. This way of interpreting the texts is supported by the idea of the Devil's omnipresence. Of course this can be regarded as a parallel to God's omnipresence, but it can also be seen in connection with envy and the idea of a free soul, concepts well known in Nordic folklore. The free soul can be called *hug* and means that a person using it "by intense thinking can affect a person nearby ... so that this person feels ill" (Strömbäck 1989:17). The *hug* is connected with envy, and was regarded as a dangerous power (Strömbäck 1989). Everywhere it was possible for man to meet with another person's envy, and envy was a "real" entity to be feared because it caused much trouble, even death (Sehmsdorf 1988).

The Devil in Vörå was omnipresent; he looks for people to devour and appears if discussed. In other words, he wants to have man. Envy as a quality of the Devil is well known, and, was the cause of expulsion from Heaven.

The discourse of fear, is, thus, to be interpreted on the basis that the Devil is full of envy of God. Because the Devil has been anthropomorphized, he also has a free soul. This notion of free soul, however, should not be confused with the Christian concept of soul. The free soul allows "him" to be omnipresent and, thus, a danger to man. This is more than simply a Judeo-Christian idea of a struggle between God and the Devil over man; there is also another, perhaps older notion of a more or less uncontrollable free soul combined with the fear of the Devil, or, more precisely, fear of the Devil's envy.

However, another kind of attitude is also present. Mentally sound individuals cannot always be conscious of their failures, that is, their sin. It is also extremely difficult for any human being to curb his/her ambition. As we all know, Adam and Eve defied the rules of Paradise, but their transgression betrays an enterprising spirit. According to the myth, the consequence of their desire for knowledge is human life on earth. Indeed, if Eve had not given the apple to Adam, they would still be living a childless life in Paradise.

In Vörå this "enterprising" attitude, which I would like to call the "mental attitude of defiance" is rather obvious. In this discourse the Devil appears ridiculous. He is disguised as an animal. Norms collide in these humorous texts and the Devil invariably ends up the loser. Man does not fear the devil, rather, man takes advantage of his wealth, power and stupidity. In this respect the Devil recalls the supernatural beings of Scandinavian and Finnish folk belief; they too can be made to serve human ends, as long as the human agents know how to manage these beings, for instance, the *tomte*. We can see evidence of this enterprising attitude in man's apparent lack of fear of the Devil, his success in using the Devil's strength and skills to his own advantage, his more developed cunning, and his courage to tell these stories. Sometimes fear even leads to defiance. In this discourse neither the Devil nor God is the master. Man himself emerges as the strongest: he triumphs over the Devil.

Do these texts actually contain two "mental" attitudes? Perhaps these two ideas can be unified on another level of abstraction. Personal gain is an overriding concern in all of the texts. They show what man is prepared to do to improve his lot, either here on earth or in Heaven. Fear of the Devil results, or should result, in a better life on earth and a celestial life after death. Although fear works as a tool for salvation, a defiant attitude – and an entrepreneurial spirit – often enables human success in the earthly realm.

The discourses about the Devil in the tradition of Vörå cannot, as a matter of fact, be divided into opposite discourses, one derived from the Church and the other from folklore. Rather, they represent attitudes of fear and defiance. The discourse of fear is about the struggle between good and evil. The discourse of defiance is about success in this world and the need for endurance and cunning to get it.

BIBLIOGRAPHY

Ambrosiani, Sune 1922: Om 'stål' som makt- och skyddsmedel. Folkloristiska och etnografiska studier 3. Skrifter utgivna av Svenska litteratursällskapet i Finland 165. Helsingfors.

Arndt, Johan 1891: Johan Arndts Fyra Anderika Böcker om En Sann Christendom, hwartill kommit, under namn af Femte och Sjette Boken, åtskilliga smärre Anderika Traktater. Utgifwet af Samfundet Pro Fide et Christianismo 4. Stockholm.

Bächtold-Stäubli, Hanns 1930–31: Furz. HDA 3. Berlin & Leipzig.

Björkqwist, Anders 1877: Trons öfning till Saligheten. Helsingfors.

Christiansen, Reidar Th.1911: Litt om torsdagen i nordisk folketro. Festskrift fra nordiske sprog- og folkemindeforskere på 80 års dagen den 6. August 1911. Stockholm.

Christiansen, Inger 1982: Smed. Kulturhistoriskt lexikon för nordisk medeltid 16. [København.]

Dahlbacka, Ingvar 1987: Den evangeliska rörelsen i svenska Österbotten 1845–1910. Åbo.

Darnton, Robert 1987: Stora kattmassakern och andra kulturhistoriska bilder från fransk upplysningstid. Stockholm.

Daxelmüller, Christoph 1985: Furz. Enzyklopädie des Märchens 5. Berlin & New York.

Eckstein, F. 1934–35: Nackt, Nacktheit. HDA 6. Berlin & Leipzig.

Edsman, Carl-Martin 1963: Sjätte och sjunde Mosebok. Saga och sed 1962. Uppsala & København.

Egardt, Brita 1962: Hästslakt och rackarskam. Nordiska museets handlingar 57. Stockholm.

Eskeröd, Albert 1947: Årets äring. Nordiska museets handlingar 26. Stockholm.

Finlands 1930: Finlands svenska folkdiktning 7,5. Register. Skrifter utgivna av Svenska litteratursällskapet i Finland 195. Helsingfors.

Forsyth, Neil 1987: The old enemy. Princeton, New Jersey.

Foster, George M. 1965: Peasant society and the image of limited good. American anthropologist 67.

Förhandlingar 1888: Förhandlingar och uppsatser 3 (1887–88). Skrifter utgifna af Svenska litteratursällskapet i Finland 9. Helsingfors.

Hammarstedt, N. E. 1921: Smedens anseende hos skilda folk. En bergsbok. Stockholm.

Hasan-Rokem, Galit 1986: The cobbler of Jerusalem in Finnish folklore. The wandering Jew. Bloomington.

Hellquist, Elof 1989: Svensk etymologisk ordbok. Lund.

Herold, Ludwig 1931–32: Kartenspiel. HDA 4. Berlin & Leipzig.

Jäfvert, Ernfrid 1938: Skomod och skotillverkning från medeltiden till våra dagar. Nordiska museets handlingar 10. Stockholm.

Le Goff, Jaques 1978: Mentaliteterna, en tvetydig historia. Att skriva historia. Stockholm.

Lecouteux, Claude 1996: Die Volkserzählung als Bewahrerin früherer Glaubensvorstellungen. Fabula 37.

Löfström, Jan 1995: Homoseksuaalisuus suomalaisessa suullisessa perinteessä ja muistitiedossa. Elektroloristi 2.

Luther, Martin 1860a: Doct. Martin Luthers Kyrko-Postilla 1. Winter-Afdelningen. Stockholm.

– 1860b: Doct. Martin Luthers Kyrko-Postilla 1. Sommar-Afdelningen. Stockholm.

– 1860c: Doct. Martin Luthers Kyrko-Postilla 2. Stockholm.

– 1867: Doct. Martin Luthers Hus-Postilla. Jönköping.

Merkelbach, Valentin 1964: Der Grabhügel. Mainz.

Näsman, Nils 1979: Det religiösa livet. Svenska Österbottens historia 2. Vasa.

Nilsson, Martin P:n 1915: Årets folkliga fester. Stockholm.

Naumann, H. 1927a: Alter Mann. HDA 1. Berlin & Leipzig.

– 1927b: Altvater. HDA 1. Berlin & Leipzig.

Nohrborg 1899: Den Fallna Menniskans Salighets-Ordning, föreställd uti Betraktelser öfwer de årliga Sön- och Högtidsdagars Evangelier. Lund.

Ó hEochaidh, Seán – Ó Laoire, Liam 1989: An diabhal i seanchas thír chonaill. Béaloideas 57.

Ohrt, Ferd. 1918: Manden som vidste ret. Edda 9.

Otto, Rudolf 1923: Das Heilige. Stuttgart & Gotha.

Piø, Iørn 1973: Den lille overtro. København.

Psalmboken 1802: Den Swenska Psalm-Boken, Med de Stycken, som därtill höra ... år 1695 öfwersedd och nödtorfteligen förbättrad. Örebro.

– 1928: Swensk Psalmbok för de Ewangelisk-Lutherska församlingarna i Finland. Antagen aw kyrkomötet 1886. Tammerfors.

Röhrich, Lutz 1988: Erzählforschung. Grundriß der Volkskunde. Berlin.

Rudwin, Maximilian 1973: The Devil in legend and literature. La Salle, Ill.

Russell, Jeffrey Burton 1977: The Devil. Ithaca & London.

– 1982 (1981): Satan. Ithaca & London.

– 1986a: Lucifer. Ithaca & London.

– 1986b: Mephistopheles. Ithaca & London.

Scharfe, Martin 1980: Die Religion des Volkes. Gütersloh.

Schenda, Rudolf 1977: Alte Leute. Enzyklopädie des Märchens 1. Berlin & New York.

Segerstedt, Torgny T. 1968: Ordens makt. Uppsala.

Sehmsdorf, Henning K. 1988: Envy and fear in Scandinavian folk tradition. Ethnologia Scandinavica.

Sions Sånger 1840: Sions sånger. Bägge samlingarne. Wasa.

Sionsharpan 1893: Sionsharpan. Helsingfors.

Skjelbred, Ann Helene Bolstad 1972: Uren og hedning. Bergen.

Stattin, Jochum 1984: Näcken. Stockholm. (Skrifter utgivna av Etnologiska sällskapet i Lund 14.)

Strömbäck, Dag 1989: Den osynliga närvaron. Hedemora.

Svebilius, Olaus 1878: Enfaldig Förklaring öfver Doct. Martin Lutheri Lilla Cateches, ställd genom spörsmål och swar. Helsingfors.

Thompson, Stith 1965: Motif-index of folk literature 2. Copenhagen

Tillhagen, Carl-Herman 1981: Järnet och människorna. Stockholm.

– 1983: Barnet i folktron. Stockholm.

Topelius, Zacharias 1906: Läsning för barn 3. Helsingfors. (Samlade skrifter 28.)

Valk, Ülo 1994: On the descent of demonic beings. Mitteilungen für Anthropologie und Religionsgeschichte 9. Münster.

Wolf-Knuts, Ulrika 1991: Människan och djävulen. Åbo.

– 1992: The Devil between nature and culture. Etnologia Europaea 22.

Wünsche, Aug. 1905: Der Sagenkreis vom geprellten Teufel. Leipzig & Wien.

Åkerblom, Bror K. 1937: Vörå sockens historia 1. Åbo.

Åkerblom, Bror 1963: Vörå sockens historia 2. Vörå.

Åkesson, Lynn 1991: De ovanligas betydelse. Stockholm.

UNPRINTED

Helsingfors
Svenska litteratursällskapet i Finland, Folkkultursarkivet
SLS 28, 33, 37, 51, 134, 152, 163, 180, 213, 220, 231, 267, 275, 276, 280, 313, 322, 324, 333, 338, 346, 369, 398, 569, 865, 1103
Åbo
Åbo Akademi, Folkloristiska arkivet
IF RI-II J.O.I. Ranckens handskriftssamlingar I–II

ABBREVIATIONS

HDA Handwörterbuch des deutschen Aberglaubens
IF Åbo Akademi, Folkloristiska arkivet
SLS Svenska litteratursällskapet i Finland

I thank Dr. Virginie Amilien, Oslo, and Prof. Patricia Lysaght, Dublin, for many valuable comments and an inspiring correspondence on the Devil.

Values and Collective Emotions

SATU APO

Alcohol and Cultural Emotions

Using a number of different source materials, I have examined the agrarian popular thought associated with alcohol during the period 1840–1968.[1] The broad scope of this time period may come as a surprise to some readers, since such a lengthy timespan encompasses numerous transitions in both the socio-cultural milieu and customs concerning the use of alcohol. On the basis of Finnish folklore materials (which are valuable from an international standpoint as well), we can nonetheless endorse one of the earliest maxims in the study of mentalities: that folk or popular thought contains both rapidly shifting elements and long-term structures. In the present paper[2] I trace out the latter; according to available records, these sorts of alcohol-related mental models have existed for decades and even centuries.

I have asked numerous questions of the folklore texts and older ethno-graphic descriptions. The most tantalizing of these questions is: why has alcohol been so highly emphasized in Finnish culture? One can easily get sidetracked in the profusion of alcohol-related folklore in the Finnish Literature Society Folklore Archives alone. Even the oldest myths sung in Kalevala meter, as well as aetiological legends which express fundamental concepts of worldview contain valuable information about beer and spirits.

Basic Premises of alcohol-related Thought among rural Finns

In the speech, narratives, songs and writings of the Finnish rural populace, an extremely lush flora of meanings is associated with alcoholic beverages, intoxication and alcoholism. I was able to generalize these meanings into models, basic beliefs at a higher level of abstraction, only after years of working with numerous bodies of data and finally reaching the point of saturation in which themes and semantic structures began to repeat themselves, and new texts no longer added anything substantial to the material analyzed so far (cf. Glaser – Strauss 1967).

The basic beliefs of alcohol-related thought within the traditional Finnish-Karelian agrarian culture include, at the very least, the following:

Myth and Mentality
Studia Fennica
Folkloristica 8, 2002

* Alcoholic beverages were entities which possessed *väki*, a supranormal, dynamistic force.
* Alcoholic beverages and intoxication were highly valued in both a social and an economic sense.
* The right to consume alcohol and become intoxicated was earned through one's own labour contribution or the wealth one possessed.
* Intoxication was a physical and mental state actualized within the framework of a sacred ritual or other celebration in which it was either allowed or expected for persons to behave differently than in everyday life.
* Social rules and sanctions guided the use of alcohol.
* Visible intoxication was interpreted as amusing in most situations.
* One became an alcoholic for reasons over which the individual had little or no control.
* It was difficult or impossible to rid oneself of an alcohol problem.
* The strict controls on alcohol consumption demanded by the state, local government or ideological leaders were often seen to be neither just nor sensible.

I have crystallized these basic beliefs into linguistic propositions; their denotative meaning is nonetheless only part of the constellation of semantic associations and mental images which are linked to the proposition in the mind of the thinker, speaker, writer or listener.[3] Some of the most interesting associations are unverbalized emotional reactions which are evoked within the processing mind (cf. Honko 1986).

How can one access the powerful emotions intertwined with alcohol-related beliefs by analyzing the texts which present them? I am assuming here that it is precisely this network of emotion-laden attitudes which has kept old, even archaic, alcohol beliefs and practices alive from generation to generation.

In clarifying cultural emotions linked to alcohol I therefore do not consider it useful to make a distinction between emotion and cognition (structure of information or knowledge).[4] Both are concerned with meaning, and for this reason treating "emotion" and "meaning" as separate issues is likewise unfruitful.[5] Emotion can be considered a specific part of knowledge structure; the nature of this component is qualitative.[6] Which affective attributes are associated with various cognitions and how powerful these attributes are vary across individuals, groups and cultures.[7] The emotions linked to the *schema* of hard liquor were most likely very different for a church social worker living in Helsinki, the capital of the country, in the 1950s than they were for a lumberjack living in the backwoods of Eastern Finland during the same period. Variation is also produced by the context or background of the phenomenon: different emotions are aroused when a public figure imbibes than if one's own parent drinks.

If emotional variation is so complex, then how is it possible to define concept- or model-specific emotional overtones which are assumed to be collective and analyzed at a higher level of abstraction? I have constructed these concepts not by observing or interviewing living actors, speakers or writers, but by interpreting a wide range of texts.

A researcher working with textual materials can, nonetheless, use two paths to a greater understanding of the data. The first is textual analysis, and the second, a reliance on the researcher's own understanding of the world, culture, language and his/her hermeneutic and linguistic competence.

Textual analysis which maps out collective emotions is facilitated by the fact that what folklorists deal with are densely recurring structures of signification.[8] Similar meanings recur across narratives and songs as well as in brief verbal expressions, in sayings and proverbs, for instance. The theme, subject matter, or belief thus appears in multiple textual variants, while the same meaning structure or its generalization can also be expressed through numerous folklore genres.[9] In such a corpus, the texts soon begin to explain each other.[10] Repetition and variation also facilitate the interpretation of the meaning structure's emotional overtones: the researcher can add to his/her abstracted model those emotions which are represented in several textual versions.

In addition to the intertextual analysis I have outlined, the researcher can use a close reading of key texts. He or she can identify the emotions expressed by the speaker or writer in the same way as in everyday communication, that is, intuitively, by relying on one's own comprehension of language and the world. For as long as humans have constructed, with the aid of language, representations of real or fictive worlds, these representations have aroused emotional reactions in those who receive and interpret them. The researcher can also consciously and systematically sensitize his/her affective responses by learning to use models and techniques of analysis which have been developed by linguistics and psychology for the study of verbal expression.[11]

Using these as my points of departure, I strive to clarify with what matrix of emotional attitudes alcohol was bound up in traditional Finnish folk thought. I use a four-step methodological process in the reconstruction and interpretation of cultural models associated with alcohol and its use (cf. Holland – Quinn 1987). In this process, we begin with the expressions contained in the texts. First, homologous structures of meaning are mapped out. Next, these structures are generalized into a collective cultural belief about alcohol (1). I have intuitively identified the emotions and emotional overtones anchored in the cognitive units (concepts, models), relying on my own cultural and linguistic competence (2) and subsequently I have, using a close, reflexive reading, analyzed the expressions contained in individual texts (3). The final phase is the comprehension of the belief content and its associated emotions through contextualization (4). The contextual framework I provide for alcohol-related models of thought is an intertextual framework made up of all the alcohol-related folklore texts with which I am familiar, as well as the contexts of folk worldview, the social and economical structures of Finnish culture, and lastly, the history of Finnish alcohol practices.[12]

In the following, I discuss Finnish traditional alcohol beliefs, illustrating them with examples from my source materials. I also trace out the hypothetical consequences, for both the individual and the community, of the most important of these basic beliefs.

Ale as a Sacred Drink

The most archaic layer of alcohol beliefs and images includes concepts of alcohol's supranormal force or power. Ale and beer contained the same sort of *väki*, or dynamistic force, as other entities which required special handling: fire, women, iron, sacred religious objects and places, and the force known as *kalma* which was associated with death and manifested itself in corpses, burial clothes, cemeteries, cemetery bones and soil. *Väki*-filled entities were capable of transforming or altering other entities: fire transformed flammable objects to ash, the vagina sapped the phallus of its potency, iron broke through surface boundaries, leaving the object "open", *kalma* caused decay, ale transformed the person who drank it both inwardly in terms of perception and outwardly in terms of behavior.[13] According to the old proverbs, the person under the influence of alcohol no longer felt his poverty or pain; even losses appeared as gains.[14] According to one of the earliest recorded proverbs in Finland, he who imbibed was no longer himself in the eyes of those around him: "No man is his mother's son when drunk" (recordings from 1655 to1800).[15] The person who was drunk behaved like a clown "Two caps on the jolly drunkard's head, and neither of them are his", (from 1770 to 1920) or a fool, "Something always happens to the drinker: either the dog eats his shoes or his mittens catch fire" (1765–1950).

Beer and its influence on human beings were perceived through metaphor: beer was a living thing, forcing its way inside the human body like a disease demon or some other spirit being (Apo 1994:213–215). The drink moved inside the drinker ("rose" and "fell" in Finnish vernacular) and made him act differently than he normally would in everyday life. This "different" sort of behavior included excessive self-exposure, the relinquishing of self-protection: "What is in the mind when sober, is on the tongue when drunk" (1720–1930; cf. "*In vino veritas*").

In an old folk poem recorded in the 1700s which depicts the origin of ale, the components of the drink – barley, hops and water – tell what they will bring about in the person who consumes them once they are united:

Sitte me miehet juotelem	"Then we'll make the men drunk
hurscat iloitelem	the pious merry
hullut tappeluttelem."	and the fools fight.
(Kuusi 1963:140).	

Beer was sacred in the sense that it was a vital component of the most important rituals within the agrarian community. Beer drinking promoted the growth of grain in the pre-Christian "Ukko's Bushel" celebration held each spring; Ukko was the god of thunder. Beer and intoxication ensured the following harvest at drinking fests held on All Hallows' Eve (*kekri*) and Christmas; at weddings it increased the young couple's fertility. During birth, funerals and bear-killing feasts, ale (and later home-distilled spirits) facilitated the transfer from one world to the next of both humans and that animal held to be most similar to man, the bear.

The idea that alcoholic drinks were seen to be sacred and possess *väki* made them objects of respect and caution in the sphere of emotion and valuation. As a cultural entity, alcohol was special and "marked". As such, it was linked to a highly restrictive set of behavioral rules: not just anybody was allowed to do just anything with alcohol. *Väki*-filled entities endangered particularly the well-being of the weaker members of the community, that is, women and children.[16] Rules for alcohol-related behavior which functioned according to age and gender distinctions are age-old, at least as old as the use of alcohol itself, that is to say, approximately 2000–3000 years old in Finland.[17]

Notions of alcohol's power and ability to manipulate the drinker in various ways have long been everyday, overlooked metaphors in the Finnish language or then part of the tradition of folk humour. Many lines from popular songs ("fifteen litres of the oppressed masses' power in an old milk jug"), sayings ("the liquor made him do it"), and humorous anecdotes have nonetheless been created through the application of archaic models of alcohol-related thought.

The Social Value of Intoxication

Alcoholic beverages, beer and cheap spirits, were portrayed as "marked" in another way as well. The northern agrarian culture was a culture of scarcity. In the 19th century, before the first wave of industrialization at the beginning of the 1870s, many landowning peasants, crofters, and landless persons suffered from a low standard of living. For example, during the famine years of the late 1860s, the majority of the rural populace was forced to eat grain substitutes such as ground pine bark (Soininen 1974:394; 1980:386-387). Even in so-called good years, the food culture of agrarian Finland was highly ascetic. At the core of Finnish cuisine were grain-based foods (bread, porridge, gruel), vegetables such as rutabagas, cabbages, turnips, peas and potatoes after the 1740s, as well as salted fish, and more rarely, meat. Butter was rarely seen on the dining table even at the end of the 19th century (Talve 1997:122–129).

The most common everyday beverage was buttermilk mixed with water, and in the winter, when the cows were not milking, home-made non-alcoholic beer and water. Warm liquid refreshments such as coffee and tea are relative latecomers to Finnish folk foodways; they became part of daily life only slightly over a century ago, at the end of the 1870s (Talve 1997:132).

Ale and spirits, grain-based drinks which require a multi-stage preparation process, were seen in a culture of scarcity to be delicacies, even luxuries. In many, if not most households, beer and liquor were not for the daily consumption of all adults. The economic and thus social value of cheap spirits becomes understandable if we recall that one criteria of wealth in the mid-19th century was the household's ability to eat "pure bread" year round, without having to resort to cheaper grain substitutes such as chaff, pea-stems, pine bark and calla (*Calla palustris*).[18]

175

Alcoholic beverages have also naturally always been drugs, producing psycho-physiological pleasure or alleviating pain. The pleasurable effects of alcohol were both strong and easy to induce, nearly automatic; they could be achieved by a man who was tense, exhausted, ill, or elderly, in so far as he was able to get hold of this valued substance.

Essentially, the right to imbibe alcohol and to become intoxicated was in most cases earned through doing work in sufficient quantities and sufficiently well. Only those farm masters who managed their farms with such successful results that there remained a surplus of grain after the household's immediate needs were met, including the payment of taxes and necessary purchases, were able to buy alcoholic drink or brew ale and distill liquor (until 1866) without risking the viability of his farm. Agricultural labourers also had to obtain their liquor through work. Farmhands and serving maids could receive part of their pay in the form of either grain or liquor, and with one's wages it was also possible to purchase spirits from the farm master, from local vendors, or from places licensed to serve alcohol. Even the most wealthy members of the community (large-scale landowners, inheritors of fortunes) had to scale their drinking according to their economic carrying-capacity.[19]

The linking of alcohol consumption to productive work is one basis for the norms which defined the community members' rights to receive, procure and consume valued substances such as ale and spirits. The negative, prohibitive version of this basic principle can be summed in Biblical form as "he who does not work, neither will he imbibe". The positive version of this same principle would be: "the man who has done his work deserves his liquor."

The fact that the right to consume alcohol was earned through labour was so self-evident that it is not directly expressed, for instance, in proverbs or other sayings. In my own corpora of source materials, the sacred link between work and alcohol shows up more clearly in responses to the alcohol-related questionnaire which I distributed to the network of informants of the Folklore Archives of the Finnish Literature Society in 1989. When 60- and 70-year-old writers evaluated our modern-day alcohol culture, what irritated, even angered them the most is that nowadays even those who do not work (early-retiring pensioners and the unemployed) can drink; in the good old days "a person lived by his work, not just by drinking" (SKS. Alkoholi 1989). A farmer born in 1920 writes: "Now ... the professional loafers are given unemployment benefits and the money goes straight into liquor and beer." In a third commentary, a woman born in 1913 summed up as follows: "At least in former times one had to earn one's beer money, but now we taxpayers pay for the drunken revels of these unemployed and early retirees!"

The precious prize of liquor, however, was not within the reach of all, even if they did work. Certain ethnographic descriptions from the early 19th century[20] as well as older Finnish proverbs indicate the alcohol boundaries which divided village communities and households: "Those who shovel manure are one group, and those who drink ale are another" (1780–1800; the most recent example is from the 1910s; Kuusi 1953:134, 501–502). Beer and spirits were not accessible to the very poor. Even members of a family or household producing surplus grain were divided into the "haves" and the "have nots" with regards to alcohol; according to Elias Raussi (1966:157) who described life in the Karelian Isthmus in the 1840s and 1850s, women and their underage children "were the worst grumblers and with squinty eyes and dry mouths looked most bitterly upon those who drank" and "always raised a hue and cry about the bottles, so that the men were not able to drink openly and in peace in their own homes".

To be able to consume spirits meant that one belonged to the "better half" of the hierarchically-ordered household and village community, a half which consisted of men who were adult, able-bodied and self-supporting (as well as the male hired hands who sat at their tables). Social tensions, even aggression seem to have surrounded alcohol in the folk culture during the age of home brewing and distillation (Apo 2001:105–106). The patriarchal wielding of power restricted the use of this prestige beverage by women, young persons, the elderly and hired servants. Alcohol boundaries were demarcated through, for example, proverbs: "Young men unwed, spirits yet untested"; "Women drink beer like oxen drink water"; "An old man/woman drinks beer, a rotten tree draws water" (Kuusi 1953:389, 134).[21]

All of this greatly enhanced the social prestige value of alcoholic drinks and intoxication. By consuming spirits and becoming inebriated, the male drinker communicated to himself and those around him that he was one of the privileged (or had momentarily attained their level) and was qualified to join the ranks of other adult, able-bodied men. Masculine honor and the right to alcohol were closely intertwined. An over-emphasis on the merits of alcohol was nonetheless avoided. The boundary line between a rational and irrational appreciation of spirits (and earlier, beer) could be drawn with the help of humorous discourse, most often proverbs and anecdotes.

The two anecdotal "true stories" given below deal with the socio-economic value of intoxication and associated emotions. The first takes up a position from outside and above the drinker:

> In the village of Kiikala, the master of Seppä farm, Vihervä by name, was visiting the manor house of his relative Pertteli Haali in the 1930s.
>
> As they were standing on the manor grounds and looking together at the manor's handsome buildings and lands, one of the manor's labourers came into the yard, extremely drunk, and started to shout abuse and complaints at the manor's owner. The master of Haali manor merely snorted, and didn't seem to take offense at his workman's rebuke.
>
> When the workman had staggered away, Vihervä asked Haali in amazement why he had not become furious and fired the man on the spot. The master of Haali only laughed and explained to the master of Seppä farm:
>
> – If that sort of fellow ever actually has enough money to buy a bottle of spirits once in a while, then he should be allowed to act like a man!
> (Hakokorpi-Jumppanen – Virtanen 1977:225).

In the second anecdote, the drunkard's own interpretation and evaluation of intoxication is presented:

> Once, in the summer, I left home in the morning and walked along Market Street, intending to go to the banks of Kymijoki River and fish. There, on the steps of Hämäläinen's shop, lay a man stone cold drunk. I said to him:

– Wouldn't it be better to go to a park bench along the river banks and sleep? The police will be along soon to haul you off to jail.

The man looked about him and said:

– There are handsome houses around here. There are wooden houses and houses of stone. And somebody owns them. And the people who own them are rich. But they'll never be able to get drunker than I am right now, no matter how rich they are. And he remained sprawled out on the steps.

(Hakokorpi-Jumppanen – Virtanen 1977:149).

Being able to achieve intoxication put one in the same class as the privileged members of society: through alcohol the attempt was made to equalize – momentarily – the disparities in social and communal life.

Alcohol as an Instrument of Social Communication and Exchange

It is possible to derive the principles associated with the consumption of alcohol *a priori* from ontological and evaluative beliefs concerning alcoholic beverages and intoxication. Because alcohol was an entity containing *väki*, it induced changes in the person who consumed it. In such circumstances it was natural that the person under the influence of alcohol behaved differently than when sober. Because intoxication was precious and represented the passport to the category of fully authorized and self-sufficient men, its possession had to be displayed in front of others. There was no reason to hide one's own drunken state: to get good and drunk was the Rolex of the old folk culture.

Folklore texts indicate that the display of one's own intoxication was an important part of the cultural model of drinking. Humorous sayings lend irony to this norm: "What a waste to have been drunk when there was no one there to see it", "If only there were enough spirits so that it could be smelled on the breath, the rest could be faked." Young boys are described as having been particularly eager to display their drunkenness. One's first intoxication took on the significance of an initiatory rite: by being drunk, the young man announced his passage to the ranks of adult men.[22]

Because being heavily inebriated was highly valued and the sign of being a man who could handle his own affairs, there was no need to be ashamed of the bodily reactions that accompanied intoxication. Passing out during officially sanctioned drinking carried little stigma in the texts I have surveyed. However, it was not appropriate to admire loutish behavior. Such exaggeration could be laughed at, as in the following anecdote:

It is told how, during a "brother-in-arms" evening at the Military Academy, the director Father Pulkkinen concluded his welcoming address with the words:

– We have many kinds of foods and a whole litter of bottles. They're likely to produce a handsome vomit.

(Hakokorpi-Jumppanen – Virtanen 1977:177).

Because alcoholic drink was a luxury good, it was used in numerous types of social exchange. Spirits symbolized positive emotional states and social attitudes: respect, affection, gratitude, and kindness, and these could also be bought with alcohol. Prior to the use of coffee and tea, home-brewed spirits were the most important refreshment to have on hand for guests; they were on the one hand intended for distinguished visitors, particularly those of a superior social rank, and on the other hand for close and welcome friends. The bundling visits (or night courting) that led to the formation of couples included the girl offering a drink to the young man she desired. Through alcohol, the upper-classes also demonstrated politeness, which can be interpreted as kindness, to their subordinates. Before the spread of the temperance ideology in the latter half of the 19th century, a man with business at the local parsonage might be offered a drink or even two.

Peasants are also described as having used alcohol to show their respect for village specialists doing work on the farm, for visiting "masters". Those artisans held in highest regard were the smiths and masons, while less esteemed, but still respected, visitors included fiddlers, castrators, cuppers and healers. With the gift of spirits, master craftsmen were distinguished from other members of the village community and from lower-ranking craftsmen and -women. Persons could demand this mark of rank not by asking directly, but through non-verbal hints. Countless anecdotes tell of chimneys which drew badly but whose flues opened as if by magic when the master chimney-builder finally received the bottle that was overlooked the first time. Folklore collector Samuli Paulaharju describes the self-respect of the smiths from two Ostrobothnian parishes, Kauhava and Härmä, as follows:

> The smith was a great master craftsman, and thus he was to be treated according to his skill. ... One had to offer the smith a good shot of liquor. It was a show of respect to the master, who otherwise would have been unwilling to make the visit. The former smith of Kauhava, by the name of Kuuroo, was so set on spirits that he wouldn't even start forging without them, and Riivi-Juha demanded a lot of alcohol. If the villagers complained that the scythes forged by Juha were not sharp enough, Juha would say: "Why didn't you bring more water for tempering the metal?"
> (Paulaharju 1932:238–239).

Through alcohol it was also possible to persuade the other to give something that ego wanted or needed. The transfer of ownership was ritually facilitated with spirits. The person making the request preserved social "face" if asking and giving were masked as an exchange occurring between two equal parties. At weddings, funds were raised for the young couple with the aid of a so-called "one-time" drinks (or "morning-tankard"): the wedding guest enjoyed a drink offered by the bride and gave money or the promise of a gift in return.[23] The promise was binding, since the consumption of the alcohol – the concrete internalization of the promise before witnesses – sealed the bargain.

The same ritual scheme was used in the transfer of other objects as well: the reciprocal relationship between giver and receiver was constructed with the aid of alcohol. The giver was in possession of something valuable, for example, grain, cattle feed, fish, other objects which could be sold or were needed to pay taxes, or a daughter of marriageable age. At this point the petitioner, offering spirits or beer, asked whether the giver would be willing to give him the desired object. If the giver accepted the "gift" offered by the petitioner, then he, without a word having been spoken, committed himself to giving the "return gift".

In the mid-1800s, one form of ritualized request for neighborly aid, "driving around with spirits", was known in the Karelian Isthmus.[24] If the driver, the person in need, managed to persuade the possessor of the desired item to take a drink, then he had the right to ask for something in exchange, which he named while offering the drink. Elias Raussi defined the custom of "driving around with spirits" practised by the poor as nothing more than a request for charity which circumvented the law against begging by able-bodied persons. Offering alcohol both put a respectable face on the matter and bolstered the petitioner's self-esteem; the roles of beggar and gift-giver were transformed into the more equal roles of parties engaged in barter. Even government officials, who received the greater part of their salary in the form of agricultural products straight from the peasant farmers, sent spirits in exchange for the "return gifts" of hay, turnips, straw and charcoal which were really the wages due them (Raussi 1966:118).

Ritualistic imbibing of alcohol softened the more difficult transfers of objects, those which contained the risk that the other party might harbor resentment, be humiliated or lose "face". Spirits were seen to lubricate social exchange in an ethical or Christian sense as well. According to Raussi, alcohol "went to work" on the drinker in such situations: it made him a kinder and perhaps more generous giver:

> In these situations alcohol effectively reveals its power to soften hearts which are calculating and hard to the extent that it causes people to perform acts of charity.
> (Raussi 1966:117).

Intoxication as Transgressing Social Boundaries

Intoxication-oriented drinking behavior and intoxication display can be inductively inferred from the folklore texts, which contain references to the inevitability or at least desirability of drunkenness. Drunkenness and major festivals and celebrations (such as weddings, funerals, All Hallows' Eve, and Christmas) belonged together. This is summed up in a proverb: "One should drink on Christmas and eat meat on Shrove Tuesday" (1744–1985; Kuusi 1953:78). In important rituals it was required that at least some of the ritual participants were in a "sacred" mental state,[25] and the easiest way to enter an altered state of consciousness was to succumb to the influence of alcohol.

It is worth keeping in mind, however, that seeking intoxication was not the only way to enjoy alcohol. According to written descriptions of folk life, in the 19th and early 20th centuries the agrarian forefathers of today's Finns had already mastered all of the so-called "civilized" or "European" forms of alcoholic enjoyment as well, ranging from the controlled behavior at the dinner table to the social sipping of one or two drinks.[26] This rich alcohol culture among the folk thus included both drinking which breached the boundaries of everyday activity as well as the *Geselligkeit* type of alcoholic enjoyment and associated behavior (see Falk 1983:197–237 and Partanen 1991:217–230).

Ritual drinking at festivals and celebrations did not mean unbridled excess or chaotic behavior. Intoxication occurred under the watchful eye of the community, and it was permitted to only some of the celebrants, most often to adult men. Drinking was kept within reasonable bounds also by the fact that the consumption of beer and liquour were closely integrated with other activities, with the sub-rituals of the celebration. If these were not carried out honorably, one could expect not only social sanctions but also supernatural misfortune.

Even the sober participants at the celebration were able to transgress everyday norms and deepen their experience of togetherness, of *communitas* (Turner 1969:129–138; Falk 1983:214–220). They monitored the unpredictable behavior of the intoxicated participants and entertained themselves by observing the violation of social boundaries and the contravening of norms. At weddings, for example, it was expected that drunken scenes would take place among the men – the altercations were either verbal or physical. The drama of the drunken brawls were in fact relived and enjoyed numerous times: first in actuality, later through narration. Guests returning home from a wedding found waiting for them a household thirsty for tales of excitement:

> The household eagerly displayed their curiosity and inquired from the returning wedding guests the quality of the wedding and various details such as how much clothing the bride had brought in her dowry and how fine it was. And they always remembered to ask: "Were there any fights?" And mistakenly, in my opinion, they say that it's not a good wedding without a fight. (Raussi 1966:308).

In addition to the drama of a fight, another titillating aspect of intoxication was that it facilitated social voyeurism: drinkers often revealed things about themselves which were merely hinted at or kept hidden in daily life. In addition to everything else, the person under the influence of alcohol was "amusing": he was physically clumsy and mentally suited to the role of clown or fool.

The surveillance practiced by village, kin group and household did not extend to the drinking societies popular with young unmarried men. The works of novelist and playwright Aleksis Kivi (1834–72) for example, contain depictions of drunken behavior in this unrestrained context; the *locus classicus* in Finnish literature being the drinking engaged in by the Seven Brothers at their forest home in Impivaara.

Finnish ethnographic writers[27] (Eljas Raussi, Aleksis Kivi, Johannes Häyhä, and Samuli Paulaharju, among others) have portrayed in their works the Finnish drinking behavior which was considered typical for ordinary situations.[28] These depictions contain so many recurrent, features that it is not difficult to discern from them two primary cultural scripts for alcohol-influenced behavior: vying for superiority and male bonding. In the former, virile males sort out their hierarchical ranking through contests and fights, while in the latter they approach each other with demonstrations of trust and express their enjoyment of each other's company and intimacy. These models are not mutually exclusive: a good-natured tussle can alternate with bonding behavior.[29]

According to 19th and early 20th century ethnographers, the drinking society was not the place for sorting out the group's socio-economic hierarchy, since in a small community this hierarchy was already self-evident. Men knew whether they were landowners or landless, large-scale or small-scale farmers, adults or youth, of working age or elderly, married or unmarried, members of large, well-to-do kin groups or small, less influential ones, Pietists or "sinners". Vying for superiority was only relevant for a man's standing when he was among equals or part of a closely-matched pair ("which is better, a cobbler of wooden shoes (= carpenter) or leather shoes?"; "Who is stronger, Juhani or Tuomas Jukola?"). Additionally, two equally-ranked groups might fight each other, for example the "wild boys", or *häjy*s (the equivalent of village gangsters) and the other young men of the parish.

Forms of male competition ranged from conversation to knife-fights. Through speech it was possible to gauge intelligence and expertise, for example through question-and-answer games, riddles, trick questions and claims concerning matters of religion;[30] and the drinking society might also evaluate the narration, joking and singing skills of its members. More physical forms of friendly competition were games and contests.

Forms of male bonding behavior, according to the aforementioned ethnographic writers, were companionable conversation, singing in unison and hugging, and sometimes dancing together.

Drink as the Measure of a Man

In depicting the "ordinary" drinking practices in the context of the rye harvesting bee, Johannes Häyhä (1982:345–346) describes a scene in which supper has been eaten and the men have spent time together in the sauna. In the farmhouse, the adult (i.e., married) men have made *norri*, a mixture of coffee and hard liquor, from the spirits provided by the farm master. "When the liquor had risen to their eyebrows, then the men tested their strength through competitions, by pulling the stick and finger-pulling". The challenge to measure one's own strength against that of others was presented in the form of an insult. Pietu Savo went before "Little Pentti" and said to him in a threatening tone of voice: "There your father cooks a ruff-fish / boils a toad's head."

The poetic lines contain two traditional defamatory images: first of all, the preparation and consumption of cheap or polluted substances was a highly degrading image; additionally, a person could be effectively insulted by indicating that he or she was from a group, a family, kin group or local community which behaved disgracefully. Following the challenge, the men engaged in a finger-pulling contest; Pentti wins this "fierce battle". Gradually the drinkers grow weary, "some from the influence of spirits, others from overexertion." They sleep on straw beds on the floor of the farmhouse until morning.

The most famous description of males jockeying for supremacy in the context of drinking is found in the sixth chapter of Kivi's novel *Seven Brothers* (1870). The Jukola brothers have spent Christmas at Impivaara following the peasant holiday tradition, eating and drinking well. For Christmas Eve supper, they have enjoyed "steaming bear meat", flat rye bread and strong ale.

On the basis of seniority, Juhani Jukola is the official leader of the male group. Once under the influence, he wants to clarify the group's hierarchy based on the brute physical strength of the virile males:

> "A word with you, Tuomas. Aapo once claimed that you were stronger and tougher than me, but I just don't like to believe that. What about a go at it? Let's try our strength!".
> (1991:119, trans. Richard A. Impola).

Juhani and Tuomas test each others strength twice, first through wrestling and then by engaging in a tug-of-war. Tuomas wins both matches. After this Juhani beats both Aapo and Timo in wrestling matches. Simeoni acceeds at the outset that Juhani is stronger; and all know that neither Lauri nor Eero are any match for their older brother. Juhani then announces the final results of the tests and the inferences to be drawn from them, that is, the ranking within the group:

> "As far as strength goes, I'm the second best of the Jukola bunch /literally 'herd'/. Of course, Lauri and Eero are still untested, but they'll hear bees buzzing in their ears if they try. And Simeoni has already admitted that he's weaker than I am."
> (1991:126, trans. Richard A. Impola).

The rank of alpha male is an enviable reward, it gives the leader the right to enforce his will and others the obligation to submit to his leadership. Being relegated to second place arouses within Juhani annoyance and suspicion. As he becomes more thoroughly drunk, he expresses his negative emotions openly. When Tuomas forbids the wasting of beer to make ale steam in the sauna, a proposal suggested by Juhani and seconded by Eero, Juhani remarks: "Tuomas is pretty cocky after winning at wrestling just now and thinks he can rule the roost as he pleases." (1991:132, trans. Richard A. Impola). The confusion over ranking leads the brothers into a free-for-all during which a burning ember drops onto the straw-covered floor. The cottage burns to the ground and the brothers flee on bare feet through the frozen wilderness to the village and their former home, Jukola farm.

Kivi also describes alcohol-driven jockeying for supremacy in his play *Nummisuutarit* (The Heath Cobblers, 1864). In the second act, the young cobbler Esko has arrived at his sweetheart's wedding and tries to put Teemu the fiddler in his place by judging first of all, who is the better fiddle player, Teemu or Joseph Oinasmäki and second, who is able to carry the heavier sack of grain, Esko or Teemu as well as finally, which of them wins at wrestling. The conflict climaxes in a fight in Teemu's cottage, where the fiddler and his father join forces to give Esko a good thrashing.

The most notorious of young men's gang brawling in Finnish folk culture took place in Ostrobothnia in the first half of the 1800s. In one of his most highly acclaimed works, *Härmän aukeilta* (1932), Samuli Paulaharju describes the Ostrobothnian village culture from the point of view of its own members. His observations are based on interviews with older informants who still remembered the tales and songs depicting famous local fighters and criminals. According to Paulaharju, the ordering of the unofficial male hierarchy in the parish of Härmä was not dependent on socio-economic factors, but was organized instead on the basis of "honor". In practice, this meant contests to determine who had the most courage in aggressive situations among males: "true Härmä honor meant that one feared nothing, ran away from no one, never asked for mercy even in situations of life or death" (Paulaharju 1932:304). The cult of honor, manifested in forms approaching the pathological, inspired men to compete over who was the most *häjy*: wild, mean, and ready for violence.

This constant gauging of oneself against others was further encouraged by drink. Weddings, which demanded of men that they be ritually intoxicated, were a highly suitable context for this sort of behavior. Candidates for challenges and witnesses to a man's bid for honor were plentiful, as were the most desired prize: the admiration of young women. Verbal duels were just the warm-up; after this the participants got down to the main business at hand: fights involving wrestling or knives. The most exciting brawls were those involving gangs of young men fighting together: the challengers were the "wild ones" or *häjys*, and the challenged were the men who did not belong to their ranks.

Among the *häjys* themselves there could also arise situations in which groups of men vied with each other for superiority. Paulaharju (1932:306) tells of the Laituri family wedding, in which the two leaders of the *häjys*, Antti Isotalo and Antti Rannanjärvi "started to argue over which were more *häjy*, the men from Upper-Härmä or those from Lower-Härmä." This led to a melee on a grand scale, although without knives. The men of Lower-Härmä lost the fight, "and many left for home completely bald, while others had only a few tufts of hair left on the sides of their heads."

According to Heikki Ylikangas, the winner of these highly aggressive showdowns received as his reward a "reputation" which raised his value in the eyes of young women – and caused competing suitors to step aside. Having "honor" or a "reputation" could compensate for a lack of those socio-economic resources usually necessary for marriage; an overall decrease in young men's ability to meet the social criteria for marriage was a result of the growth of population in Ostrobothnia at the beginning of the 19th century (Ylikangas 1976:89–90, 310).

Men's Intimate Merry-Making

Much less is known about the other behavioral pattern for "traditional Finnish drinking", the expression of solidarity among men. Male bonding-type behavior in which contests for superiority are not apparent either at the level of speech or other activity do however appear in the works of ethnographic writers.

Groups of males drinking in like-minded solidarity are described as small, involving 2–3 men. The men have a previous acquaintance and are usually friends or colleagues.

Johannes Häyhä describes the secret drinking of the parish clerk and the schoolmaster at a parish catechismal meeting while the deacon and others are asleep. The drinkers express their aggression in this context as well, but it is directed at outsiders. Finding a common grudge brings the drinkers closer together. The antipathies of the clerk and schoolmaster are directed at the deacon who disapproves of alcohol, as well as at the "mean old man of Holttola farm", the other potentate and moralizer of the parish. The subject turns to the upper-class members of the community more generally, those who tax the ordinary peasant farmers. Together the drinkers sing the "Song of the Flea" in which a flea is fed as the holiday meal to thirteen officials entitled to collect taxes; each receives the part of the flea which best applies to him.[31]

In the last chapter of his *Seven Brothers*, Kivi included a description of an autumn harvest bacchanal attended by the brother Timo, now the master of a wealthy croft. Timo's comrades are two farm masters, Kyösti Tammisto and Aapeli Karkkula; the "merry binge" takes place in Tammisto's home. The drinking in question is "lawful" according to the norms of the community, it is merry-making associated with the end of the harvest and All Hallows' Eve. Thus Timo continues to indulge in it each year, even though his wife disapproves.

In this drinking situation, the male members of the fictitious group "spoke to each other earnestly, sang, and hugged each other like dearest friends" (1991:333). Elsewhere as well, Kivi presents singing and dancing (men either together or alone) as an indicator of euphoric experiences or as part of the pursuit of it. Singing in the out-of-doors, swinging, and the clatter of dancing correspond to a joyous state of mind. The harvest drinkers cast bleary-eyed glances at the autumn landscape: "carefree, they looked out with dim goat's eyes, singing away and tossing their heads to and fro, heads which buzzed and popped merrily. Far away were the sorrows and griefs of ordinary, suffering mortals." (1991:333, trans. Richard A. Impola).

Paulaharju's (1932:129–130) description of a Michaelmas celebration among farm masters in Härmä corresponds to Kivi's fictitious harvest spree; Michaelmas was likewise a day for celebrating the end of an agrarian cycle:

Michaelmas was a real drinking day for the men, when even the men of the remotest cottage also had a feast and drank themselves into a stupor ... Then there soon came from the masters' chambers and grandfathers' cottages alike the sound of a full-throated racket and a song well-known in Härmä. The men who had feasted on rye then attempted to wet their throats with barley juice and sang:

...

Ensin kallistethan,	First you tilt the bottle,
sitten pullistethan,	Then you shake the bottle,
sitten vasta oikeen ryypätähän.	Only then begins the real drinking.

On the basis of ethnographic descriptions it is tempting to assume that drinking situations which stressed male bonding and harmony constructed and upheld male friendships in the tension-riddled communities of village and parish.[32] The ties which existed automatically within households and kin groups, among neighbors and according to religious affiliation were not enough: men wanted comrades of their own choosing as well. The emotions of solidarity, intimacy and warmth were expressed in drinking situations both verbally and physically, by "singing with arms around each others' necks." Intoxication made it permissible for men to engage in same sex intimacy (Löfström 1994:3–8).

The Popular Comedy of Drunkenness

The bumblings and blunderings of an intoxicated person – whether that person is oneself or someone else – has for centuries been the most popular comic theme in Finland. Humorous drunks can be found from our oldest proverbs: "Two caps on a jolly drunk's head, neither are his own" (1770s; Kuusi 1953:180, 501). Only a couple of decades ago, the mere appearance of a bottle, the pop of a cork and the tinkle of glasses was enough to evoke an atmosphere of mirth in the minds of those present. Drinking and intoxication were an institution in Finland's cultural humour just as circus clowns, vaudeville or stand-up comedians have been in other cultures.

The comical aspects of drinking were enjoyed several times: first in the drinking situation itself as either a participant or observer, and afterwards as a narrator or listener. In humorous "true stories" and fictions, the drinker of alcohol appears in one of three roles: as a clown, a fool/simpleton, or a trickster.

Clowning arises when adult persons no longer have control over their perceptions and motor skills but rather fall into wells or canals, drive straight into telephone poles, eat the dishrag that fell into the salad, etc.[33]

Drunken fools make mental and cognitive blunders. They look for a match that has fallen on the floor by lighting a boxful of matches, think they are in a pub when they are really in a church, etc.

The drunkard of the story may also appear as a trickster; here he makes another person, preferably one in authority, appear more ridiculous than himself, as in the following anecdote:

We boarded the train. Taavetti smiled contentedly and held one bottle in his hand, opened another bottle and took a swig, revelling in pure enjoyment ...

Across from us sat a portly gentleman, who followed Taavetti's doings with a sour gaze. When Taavetti took another swig, the man could no longer keep silent and began his reproachful sermonizing:

– Look here, I'm already an old man and I have never in my life taken a single drink.

Taavetti took another swig, listened to the gentleman's reproof, swallowed his drink, put the cork back in the bottle and slammed the cork with his palm as if to lend weight to his words and said:

– Nor will you be taking one now!

(Hakokorpi-Jumppanen – Virtanen 1977:237–238).

The overwhelming popularity of alcohol humour is easy to understand. The humour derived from watching someone under the influence is simple and demands little intellectual effort of the audience. Humour associated with the clown or simpleton is moreover "innocent", devoid of malice, since the reason for the blundering is not the drinker's chronic lack of intelligence but rather a passing mental state. The laughing observer knows him/herself also to be capable of such idiocy after a certain number of drinks.

The link between alcohol and amusement in Finland is so strong and self-evident that it has given rise to ironic forms of metahumour: the popular aphorism "Fun without alcohol is pretence" has been in use at least since the 1930s. The strong connection between intoxication and merriment is nonetheless culture-specific; for example in Spain and France, public drunkenness and the physical and mental stumbling it gives rise to are not considered "fun" but rather a state of indisposition and a lack of finesse (Pyörälä 1991:83, 86–88, 103–104; Keryell 1997:174).

Alcohol, Fear and Fatalism

Traditional folk thought in Finland also included concepts of alcohol's darker side, as well as instructions for minimizing these negative influences. Alcohol-related fears have been expressed most visibly in women's lyric poems in the Kalevala-meter, the majority of which were recorded at the end of the 19th century in Eastern Finland and Ingria. In them, the idea that a girl would end up marrying a heavy drinker is presented as a horrifying scenario. Because divorce among the landowning classes was a practical impossibility, and difficult even in landless families, a wife had no way to rid herself of an alcoholic husband.

This fear was expressed by women of all ages: by girls at or approaching marriageable age, wives, and mothers of adult children. Mothers warned their daughters against marrying a drunkard (Timonen 1989:114–115; Knuuttila 1985); the same theme was repeated in the ritual insults directed at the bridegroom and performed at weddings:

Voi mun silkkinen sisoini,	Oh my silken sister,
kuin olit kauan karvapäänä /avohiuksin/,	You were long bare-headed,
viivyit villahartiana.	Your shoulders covered by your tresses.
Sait viimein vihasen miehen	Finally you got a hostile husband

lihan syöjän, luun purian	An eater of flesh, a biter of bone
veren pellolle vetäjän	Who scatters your blood on the field,
tukan tuulelle jakajan.	Who scatters your hair to the wind.

Kuin tuo kirkosta tulevi,	When he comes from church,
tuo käy joka kapakan,	he visits every tavern,
sekä juo joka kopekan.	and drinks every kopeck.
Tuop kulakat /nyrkit/ kupehillein	He brings the fists to strike your sides
pärehalot hartioille.	A wooden log for your shoulders.
(SKVR XIII:3859, v. 1847).	

According to Seppo Knuuttila, the most horrible situation imaginable was that a farm without a son and heir would end up with a son-in-law who turned out to be a drunkard: that a strange man would ruin not only the daughter's life but the farm's prosperity as well.

The laments of the drunkard's wife are impressive in terms of both sheer numbers and content. The traditional rules of discourse permitted plain talk regarding painful and shameful issues in the context of poetry and song. For example, the physical repugnance of the heavy drinker was described in powerful images:

Usein humalahurjan	Often he is wild for drink
useammin viinavillin	even more often lusting for liquor
oksennus olille jääpi,	he leaves his vomit on the bed-straw,
vaahti vaipalle valuu	His slobber on the bed covers,
korjata vihaisen vaimon	to be cleaned by the furious wife,
sekä tyynen työnnytellä.	to be scrubbed by the stoic spouse.
(SKVR VII:4418, v. 1838).	

Lyric poetry had a clearly therapeutic function. The language of the songs was an "alternative" language in which it was permitted to express and deal with matters which had to be hushed up in normal everyday conversational situations (cf. Abu-Lughod 1986:24–35, 255–259; Virtanen 1987:180–185). The collective, established expressions of fear and pain, the poetic lines and images which were handed down from woman to woman and generation to generation, supported the individual woman in her crisis. The songs defined the themes of her pain and showed her that she was not alone in her suffering – others before her had been compelled to endure the same experiences.

The songs sung by men also contain themes related to alcoholism. The singers complain of having "become a drunkard" and of the associated loss of their reputations:

Akat saatanat sanovat,	Those accursed old women say
pakanat panettelevat	those evil ones call me
syömäriksi, juomariksi,	a glutton, a drunkard,
kylän kaiken koinuriksi.	a chaser of every skirt.
(SKVR VII:2169).	

In the images presented in men's lyric songs, the curse of alcohol implies a certain fatalism: the helpless person is at its mercy. The idea of alcoholism as one's fate or destiny, and the powerlessness of the individual within its grasp also appears in the responses to a questionnaire sent in 1989 to the respondents' network of the Finnish Literature Society Folklore Archives. The respondents, who were 60–90 years of age, described the agrarian alcohol culture of the 1920s and 30s. The most common explanatory model for alcoholism was a "weak nature". The weaker (or softer) a person was, the more easily alcohol took hold of him, "infected" him or penetrated him. This infection was facilitated by the victim living in a den of alcoholic iniquity: in an alcoholic family or household, in a household where spirits were sold illegally, or in a lumberjack camp.

Because alcoholism was the result of causes beyond a person's control, it was considered difficult to cure.[34] "Getting religion" or becoming a born-again Christian, in other words, continuous contact with supernatural aid, was seen to be the most effective road to recovery. Pressure from his wife could also push a man to quit drinking, as could a personal crisis such as a serious illness, an accident, or the death of someone close.

In this type of thinking, alcoholism was seen as destiny and the alcoholic as powerless and helpless; he could do little more than continue toward his bitter end. The village community, for its part, shielded itself by stigmatizing hotbeds of alcoholic vice: drunkards, households where alcohol was sold, and families with a history of alcohol abuse. Such persons were segregated from "decent" folk by, for example, the prevention of possible marriages between the two groups (see Apo 2001:269–271).

Alcohol Control as Social Power

Following Finnish independence, Finns had to live over half a century (1917–1968), meaning nearly two generations, under alcohol legislation so strict that there have surely been few parallels in the history of Western nations. The countryside, in which the majority of the population lived until the 1960s, was stripped of liquor stores as well as licensed pubs and restaurants. If persons wished to imbibe alcohol in the privacy of their own homes, they might have had to drive tens of kilometres to buy it. Even though the overall consumption of alcohol was one of the lowest in Western Europe until the 1970s, the famous Finnish "lust for liquor" was curbed not only through the infrequency of suppliers but also through strict controls on business hours and the surveillance of customers. The potential buyer of alcohol had to have proof of the right to purchase it in the form of a "liquor card"; a record was also kept of all purchases and alcohol abusers. The law requiring buyers to show their identification to the State Alcohol Supplier (ALKO) was repealed only in 1971 (Hakokorpi-Jumppanen – Virtanen 1977:273–284). Pubs and taverns (and their assumed clientele) were divided into three hierarchical categories, and the activities taking place within these establishments were strictly regulated. ALKO inspectors monitored the morality of drinking habits, and alcohol use was closely supervised by county police, as well as municipal temperance supervisors and temperance committees.

This seemingly irrational control over the public's use of alcohol has numerous historical roots. In Western Europe, anti-alcohol campaigns got their start and received the most support from areas of reformed religious movements, in sub-cultures already taking great pains to minimize economic and social risks. These risks were minimized through industriousness and hard work, through rationality, thrift, and long-term planning. Sensuality and enjoyment represented irresponsibility and waste. The risks associated with alcohol were controlled through strict self-discipline, but after the 19th century, also through government activities and popular movements. In Europe, the total prohibition of alcohol was instituted only in the northernmost Protestant countries: in Finland (1914/1919–1932) and in Norway from 1916–1927.

Protestant austerity and purity, which intensified as the middle class rose to become the leading social class in 19th century Scandinavia, nonetheless fail to suffice as explanations for the extremity of Finnish alcohol policy. I posit two important additional factors here, the first of which was the class divisions and social problems inherent in the Finnish rural communities. The rapid population growth which began already at the end of the 1700s had produced a significant class of impoverished rural proletariat for which there was neither sufficient agricultural land nor year-round wage labour. Industry was able to employ only part of this excess population, nor did emigration (to America for example) eliminate poverty. The problem was alleviated only gradually in the 20th century as numerous land reforms were instituted and industrialization increased. Not until the "Great Migration" from rural to urban areas in the 1960s and 1970s did the rural impoverished class become history in Finland (Valkonen et al. 1980).

Most contemporaries did not see poverty as a structural problem which required structural changes to the society, such as land redistribution or new wage policies. It was easier to blame the rural poor and male workers in the cities: their problems were self-inflicted, stemming from laziness and lack of know-how, from wastefulness, irresponsible procreation and drinking. Prying the lower classes away from drink reduced the risk that poor families would need to be supported by the wealthier members of society. "A worker can't afford to drink", proclaimed A.A. Granfelt, a pillar of the temperance movement, in 1898 (Sulkunen 1986:214).

Landowners, that is, farm masters, lost some of their traditional patriarchal power over the landless when the first wave of industrialization (e.g. railway construction, logging) began to transform the countryside in the 1870s, while the remainder was diminished in the wake of the reform of the municipal government (1865, 1919) as well as land reforms in the 1920s and 1930s. The lumber industry and the growing public transport infrastructure offered new jobs; popular movements and the party system gave the disempowered (youth, women, landless) at least some degree of control over their own lives independent of the master's will. The prohibition against home-distilling enacted in 1866 removed the production and distribution of alcohol from the hands of the landowners; but landowners did not want to relinquish these rights to outsiders, that is, shopkeepers and innkeepers. The consumption of alcohol in the new public spaces of the rural community (the general store, railway station, clubhouse) was "disorderly", in other words, drinking taking place outside the supervision of the patriarchal household. Thus rural districts where landowners occupied key positions in the government remained alcohol-free for over a century (1866–1968).[35]

The second reason behind the strict control over alcohol in Finland is associated with the tensions which arose in the national elite's attitude toward the "folk", in other words, the rural majority, the "ordinary" or "common Finns". Many factors were involved in shaping these tensions during the construction of the Finnish nation between 1830 and 1918, not the least of which was Finland's precarious position as part of the Russian empire.

Complaints concerning the crudity of the common folk by representatives of the upper-classes became more common as the population increased throughout Western Europe after the 18th century, and as even the lowest classes began to demand political power and improvements in their economic conditions. Particularly those suffering from a lack of land and employment, referred to as "excess population" or the "rabble" were seen to be both a burden and a threat to society (Thompson 1996:181). The urban proletariat spent their leisure time beyond reach of patriarchal supervision (Peltonen 1997:45), a problem which could be dealt with either by making the older patriarchal discipline more efficient or by using the milder methods offered by popular education and enlightenment. The diverse branches of enlightenment thought arose in large part from the sphere of the bourgeoisie and intelligentsia. The underlying assumptions of this ideological tendency included the belief in the possibility and desirability of social and individual change: reason and rational thought indicated the 'natural' direction for development and methods for bringing it about.

In 19th century Scandinavia, the evolutionary idealism of the middle class and their belief in progress became an absolute requirement: every member of society was expected to improve him or herself and his or her surroundings; the great ideologies of the 19th century defined the interim goals of this development. It would be possible to achieve a better world and future when humanity had sufficiently refined and elevated itself; this self-ennoblement required that one distanced oneself from ignorance (backwardness, superstition), and restrained oneself from fulfilling selfish and impulsive desires ("bestiality" or "brutishness"). Most sub-ideologies of this belief in progress, such as those found in the women's movement, temperance movement and labour movement, included the endeavor to control human sensuality and place the body under stricter discipline. In these processes it was particularly those popular customs and practices connected to alcohol, sex, hygiene, childcare and housekeeping which came under fire from the progressive idealists (cf. Frykman – Löfgren 1987).[36] This evolutionary idealism (which was also the macro-ideology of the labour movement) lured people with the carrot of emancipation first into the straitjacket of self-discipline (cf. Mäkelä 1998:102) and then, in the 1920s and 1930s, toward the construction of a brave new man, the "hero", through physical or spiritual struggle (cf. Härmänmaa – Mattila 1998).[37]

All of these international ideologies adopted by the Finnish elite which affected the ordinary people were influenced by cultural and geopolitical factors unique to 19th and 20th century Finland. The most significant of these was the balancing act carried out with the Russian Empire and Soviet

Union on the one hand, and the small size of the Finnish middle class as compared to the rural populace, on the other (Alapuro 1997:13–24; 142–144).

From the perspective of the 19th century urban middle class and public officials, the "typical Finns" were the Other in four senses: they belonged to a different social class (the "folk"), represented a different type of culture (agrarian culture), spoke an unfamiliar language (Finnish) and belonged to a different race.[38] In this sort of conceptualization, the image of fellow countrymen remained hazy, and this facilitated the attribution of unrealistic features to the folk, either hyper-positive or -negative. The most visible idealizers of Finland's Finnish-speaking populace were the authors J.L. Runeberg (1804–1877) and Z. Topelius (1818–1898), both raised in towns on the western Swedish-speaking coast. Much easier was the negative, racist portrayal of the Other. This can be seen in the numerous cases in which the common people, particularly the poor, were labelled as ignorant and backward, lazy and "brutish", in other words immoral and lusting after alcohol.[39] Already in the 1800s the agrarian population could be divided, if need be, into two groups: the enlightened and development-worthy landowning farmers on the one hand, and ordinary rank and file, that is, agricultural labourers, on the other.

Nonetheless, a nationalist-minded elite desperately needed a "good folk". The macro-level strategy against the security threat posed by Russia and later the Soviet Union had been, ever since the period of Russification (1899–1917), to forge the nation to be as homogeneous and as like-minded (at least in terms of its goals) as possible. The aim was to bring all of society's different classes and residents from all parts of the country in line with the nationalist agenda. The achievement of this goal required the constant effort of everyone, even the common people. A dirt-poor, backward and irresponsible (particularly drunken) citizenry was poor security for the motherland in terms of both economics and defense; the populace had to be improved and it had to learn to improve itself, assisted by grand ideals and popular movements. In matters of alcohol use, both rural and urban workers, that is, the Finnish poor, were assumed to be stupid and helpless. Since they were not able to regulate their own drinking, they had to be protected from strong liquor through the efforts of society at large.

The middle class and prosperous farmers nonetheless ended up deeply disappointed by the common people at the turn of the century. Socialist ideologies had spread throughout Finland and the working class had begun to organize themselves. The Great Strike of 1905 and the triumph of the Socialists in the first Parliamentary election in 1906 were interpreted as alarming signs of the rupture of national unity.[40] In the Finnish Civil War (1917–1918), the worst nightmares of the bourgeoisie power holders were realized.

After 1918, in independent Finland, it was difficult if not impossible to change the macro-strategies associated with foreign affairs and security. On the other side of the eastern border there now lay a socialist empire. The elite had to continue to rely on the common folk even though it now had proof that they were not as pious and humble as their portrayals in Runeberg's poems and Topelius' tales. Thus the common people were again divided into two: of the rural populace only those landowning farmers and crofters who had sided with the Whites, the winners in the Civil War, were accepted as "true citizens" (Alapuro 1997:142–145).

Yet it was necessary to somehow get along with the "wrong" type of folk, and in a constructive manner. Negative viewpoints were thus expressed in a roundabout way: as "enlightenment" and education, through humour and in private speech and writings.

The alcohol issue provided both a suitable branding iron and rod of discipline. I would argue that the infamous "Finnish boozer mentality" has been blamed, partly unconsciously, for more than merely Finns' supposed inability to handle their drink. By using the image of the Finnish boozer mentality it was possible to conceptualize the lack of culture and self-discipline, the unpleasantness, and ultimately the Otherness associated with the Finnish-speaking labourer in town and countryside. The existence of the Finnish boozer mentality was demonstrated through reference to violent crime: the majority of murders and assaults in Finland were committed under the influence of alcohol. The fact that this was the case in many other countries, too, was overlooked (Peltonen 1997:67, 87).

The concept of the Finnish boozer mentality originated in connection with the first crisis facing the image of the folk in 1900–1917; in the 1920s, after the Civil War, it was taken up even more visibly by criminologist Veli Verkko (Peltonen 1988:15–36). This "boozer mentality" was often conceived of as a biological and hereditary feature of Finns. Notions which had already arisen in the 1850s in the context of language controversies concerning the racial inferiority of Finnish speakers as compared with Western Germanic groups resurfaced in the 20th century, resuscitated by a new "scientific" race ideology.[41] From the perspective of the upper class, originally Swedish-speaking elite, tight alcohol controls can be interpreted as symbolic control over the less civilized folk. At the same time, the enlightened citizenry (including the leaders of the labour movement) could project the images and fears evoked by alcohol (and the bestiality it unleashed) outside themselves, onto the "boozer mentality" possessed by the "typical" Finn. The "hard liquor" question also had a socio-political dimension: by "liberating" the Finn of meagre means from his liquor, society was supposed to protect him from the wretchedness of utter impoverishment. Idealist Finns from across the political spectrum bore the vexation incurred by alcohol control as their national duty, in a sincere desire to save their unwise fellow citizens from themselves.

Experiences of Alcohol Control

Beliefs about the Finns' inability to hold their liquor became the folklore of the entire nation. The "hard liquor" question was seen to be a burning dilemma requiring drastic social measures, even though the overall consumption in Finland between 1871 and 1968 was one of the lowest in Europe, between 1.1 and 2.9 litres of 100% alcohol per person per year (Alkoholikysymys 1976). Belief in the existence of an alcohol problem was reinforced by the living examples known to all, that is, persons who caused harm by excessive drinking. The fact that during the first half of the 20th century alcohol was in most cases drunk for its intoxicating effects cannot be disputed.[42] Of the older, popular alcohol culture, all that remained was the intoxication-oriented drinking at celebrations and marketplaces as well as the wild imbibing of male groups. Other traditional modes of drinking had already withered away. The use of alcohol for nourishment and refreshment had already been supplanted by the new hot drinks, coffee and tea, which also functioned as the refreshments served when socializing and entertaining guests. The circumscription of the Finnish traditional alcohol culture was responsible for the notion that Finns have never known how to use strong drink in the same manner as other Western European peoples.

The strict policy concerning alcohol provoked a counterreaction. Even the traditional rules and regulations developed by the rural populace themselves ("ethnocontrol") had given rise to grumblings and methods for their circumvention among the community's thirstier members (Apo 2001:105–106). Although popular methods of control could at times seem unpleasant, they nonetheless enjoyed a broad base of support, as they were in harmony with the social structure and basic processes of agrarian culture. The right to material goods (especially alcoholic beverages) came through hard work and diligence; additional restrictions were linked to those "natural" differences of status and power that prevailed between men and women, adults and non-adults, parents and children, masters and servants, rich and poor. After 1866, however, the restrictions on alcohol use came from outside the local community: from the central and regional governments, as well as ideological opinion leaders. Compared to the earlier regulations stipulated by the Swedish Crown in the 18th century, the new restrictions were both more severe and of longer duration.

The part of the populace that had supported the traditional rules of the game reacted to the stricter system in predictable ways such as illicit distilling ("moonshine culture"), smuggling, engaging in illegal "middleman" activities, the use of substitutes, as well as alcohol humour. It should be kept in mind that the rebels' ancestors, whether rich or poor, had managed to regulate autonomously their drinking for centuries, even millenia, without drifting into a large scale alcohol catastrophe, not even during the era of home distillation.[43]

The folklore material and recollected narratives from the 20th century provide insights into how the ordinary person felt himself/herself to be the object of oppressive alcohol regulation. Experiences and emotions come through loud and clear in the following memoir, in which the narrator and heroine is a rural woman from Häme:

> In the 1940s I was visiting my relatives in Lahti. I came by boat from Jyväskylä and thought I would go and buy one bottle of spirits as a present for my father.
>   I went into the liquor store and had received the bottle, paid for it, put it in my bag and was just at the door, when the director of the shop grabbed me by my neck and took my bag and said, "let's go into my office".

I received such a shock that I nearly wet my pants. Then the director started calling me a boozing bootlegger and said that I, a female creature, should be ashamed for buying hard liquor and not something milder.

But then I felt my temper start to rise. I took my alcohol card, threw it on the desk in front of the director and began to swear: what the bloody hell is this card then given to women for, if they can't use it even once? I said, "drink your liquor and keep your card, I'm not such a boozer that I can't get along on bread". I took the bottle from my bag and kicked it under the director's table so that it clattered. I said, there's that drop, drink that too and eat the card.

I stormed out of the shop. It was full of people and I could hear the roar of the men's laughter.

I entered the street and managed to walk a short distance before Mr. Director was running behind me with the bottle of spirits, handed the bottle to me and the card, but I was still so furious that I had decided not to bother with it anymore.

Finally I took the bottle and put it in my bag, and the director kept on nagging, "alright, now go with your bottle and behave decently". I said that a bottle like this of such dishwater isn't likely to go to my head nor my ass, and since I'm going a hundred kilometres with this bottle to a place where the nearest neighbor is three kilometres away, then nobody's going to hear the singing, you needn't worry. Then he bowed and asked forgiveness for the scene. I said, it would be better if the director would rake those city bootleggers over the coals, so they wouldn't sell people blended brandy which was really bottles of piss.
(Hakokorpi-Jumppanen – Virtanen 1977:27-28).

It is of secondary importance whether or not the confrontation described in the narrative actually took place and exactly in the manner presented by the narrator. The shop director's memories of the event may have differed from his customer's perceptions, but a memoir like this has other criteria of significance such as: can this description and the narrator's interpretation (for example the emotions she expresses) be plausibly situated in Finland of the 1930s–1940s? In the context of the information concerning this period, I propose that it can.

Recollected narratives, like many stories, are a sort of "thick description" (Geertz 1973:27–28), that is, rich in semantic texture. One can read "into" them or "out of" them not only the narrator's intended and "conscious" meanings but also others (cf. Peltonen 1997:81). From the perspective of culture and social history, it is interesting that the upper-class actor, the shop director, apparently saw it as his right to treat the other party, a lower class woman, with a lack of consideration, even brutally. The mere conjecture of the other person's social classification appears to have been enough to motivate the degradation: the Other belonged to the ordinary populace, in other words, to the group of suspect persons.

It was thus not necessary for the representative of the stigmatized category to have actually done anything, to break even a single rule; he or she could be humiliated, in other words, become the object of preventative intervention for the sole reason that he/she appeared to be a member of the "common folk" rather than of the refined and educated class.

The cultural degradation carried out by the elites aroused within the ordinary Finn an entire scale of negative emotions as this rural woman's memoir reveals. The narrator is startled, feels herself humiliated, is offended, becomes angry and rebels, defending herself and fighting back to the best of her capabilities. The experience was so powerful that the narrator still wished to recount it in writing thirty years after the fact.

In defending herself and fighting back, the woman relied on the rules of the game played from time immemorial. The purpose of aggressive and humiliating behavior is to cause the threatening person to become unsure and embarrassed. At this time his *luonto* (= personal supranormal force) and *väki* would weaken, rendering him incapable of harming his opponent. The female narrator succeeded in her objective, but only partly – the shop director was apparently still convinced that alcohol and the Finnish "folk" do not mix.

The Power of Alcohol in Finnish Thought

In the folklore materials reflecting the traditional agrarian Finnish culture, alcohol appears as a cultural product enmeshed in an exceptionally dense web of mixed emotions and attitudes. In terms of methodology, the reconstruction and interpretation of this web or matrix requires a multi-layered analysis: the identification and selection of meaningful linguistic expressions, the defining of the expression's cognitive content (their propositions, images, and schemata), the interpretation of its value content or emotional overtones, combined with understanding framed by intertextual and historical contexts.

In the following, I subjectively and critically evaluate the collective emotions associated with alcohol. My evaluation is based on the idea that alcohol continues to occupy a contradictory and emotionally-charged status in Finnish culture.

At the level of the individual (Ego + Alcohol) hard liquor – and prior to this, ale – was conceived of as an entity "more powerful than a man", it was thought of as an animate and sentient being. It could penetrate inside a person like a disease demon or infect him chronically, if he lived for an extended period in an alcohol-ridden environment. The models associated with this type of thought are analogous with Finnish folk models of illness. A mode of comprehension which emphasizes the *väki* and power of alcohol is intertwined with an emotional attitude which is overly reverent, mystifying and fatalistic. The result is a belief in the difficulty, if not impossibility, of "curing" the alcoholic.

At the level of the individual, alcohol was also naturally the basis for powerful feelings of a positive nature. In the experience of the majority of the rural populace, Finnish agrarian culture was a culture of poverty and scarcity until the 1960s. Many sensual pleasures were out of reach, available only to relatively few. The powerful and easily-produced pleasure of alcohol was a luxury and highly valued, its possession elevated the imbiber to the ranks of the privileged. In addition, it served as a sign of having joined, or of

196

belonging to, the group of fully authorized, autonomous and able-bodied men.

These beliefs gave drinking the added experience of social success and its accompanying emotions: feelings of heightened self-esteem, even pride. In men's cultures these sort of emotions are valued; a less desirable by-product was the exaggerated competitiveness produced by alcohol.

At the level of group (Ego + Alter + Alcohol), intoxication and the consumption of alcohol made it possible for virile males to jockey for position in the male social hierarchy. Gauging oneself against others, and contests for supremacy can be seen as a regressive form of behavior in the sense that in a more sober frame of mind it would not have been appropriate to dispute openly whether Ego was more powerful, the better fighter, or more knowledgeable than Alter. Judging from western forms of entertainment, it seems that many males experience contests for supremacy as engrossing and exciting, the dramatic spice of life.

In this way, alcohol is bound up with the possibility of being able to experience thrilling excitement and pleasurable aggression which arise when the man accepts a challenge and grapples with the Other. The emotional tempest culminates in either the flush of victory or the disgrace of defeat. Alcohol also opened the door to other sorts of positive social experiences. Under safe cover of intoxication it was possible to draw close to other men, both emotionally and physically. Jockeying for status and male bonding would seem to be deeply satisfying experiences. In so far as a given culture does not provide sufficient opportunities for jockeying and bonding when sober, men are likely to make use of the opportunity provided by intoxication.

Also at the level of society and culture (Ego as a representative of a social class or ethnic group + Alter as the representative of an opposing group + Alcohol) drinking was associated with powerful emotions. Among the lower classes, that is, the majority of the rural populace, the concept arose that the "lords and masters", that is, the power-wielding farm masters and government officials, wished to impede the alcohol consumption of the ordinary person. At the same time, the typical Finn was stigmatized as the bearer of the "Finnish boozer mentality", thought to lead to behavior which had to be reined in with a firm hand. After the elites became more Finnish during the first half of the 20th century, the belief in the "Finnish boozer mentality" was transformed into a sort of self-directed racism in which one's own ethnic group or at least a significant part of it was defined as uncivilized and pathological.[44] The roots of this phenomenon can be sought from the traumatic political events of 1905–1918 as well as from the nearly century-long struggle against rural poverty and cultural backwardness.

For the majority who had been defined negatively and became the target of tight controls, the situation was difficult. The fundamental assumption of an overstringent alcohol policy was distrust of the ability of less wealthy Finns to regulate their own drinking in a prudent manner. The assumption that if they were poor, they were also irrational consumers of alcohol, was insulting to not only industrial workers, but also to less wealthy farmers and agricultural labourers. The Finnish boozer mentality in fact stigmatized all Finnish-speaking Finns. Alcohol began to be associated with the humiliating stigma of social and cultural inferiority. This stigma was activated when comparing oneself to those better off, or comparing Finns to "persons from cultures more civilized than our own".

Not all Finns internalized the official Finnish alcohol policy and ideology, however: some expressed resistance, which ranged from quiet resentment to open defiance. Folklore materials and recollected narrative depict rebellious attitudes directed against all persons wielding power over the use of alcohol, including those who restricted the consumption of alcohol both officially and unofficially, from wives to customs officials, from shop clerks at ALKO to temperance activists. The third strategy was to accept, but externalize or project the negative features associated with ordinary Finns: others may have been uncivilized and unenlightened, but not ego.

At the level of cultural emotions, the most dangerous consequence of a strict regulatory policy containing aspects of humiliation is a widespread aversion to control. Many Finns who have lived in the restrictive alcohol culture which lasted until 1969 have experienced antipathy towards all sorts of restrictions. Hostility toward control may have been handed down as a family tradition from generation to generation and may appear, for example, in a family's unwillingness to interfere with the drinking of children and youth. If within a culture there exists a widely-supported notion that interference in another person's consumption of alcohol is a bad thing in itself, new, grass-roots norms for alcohol use within a society are slow to develop. Such norms are nonetheless usually necessary in order to minimize the drawbacks of alcohol use, no matter how strict or liberal the official alcohol policy might be.

Translated by Laura Stark-Arola.

NOTES

[1] My corpus of source materials includes alcohol-related Kalevala-meter mythic and ritual poems, lyric songs, proverbs from the period 1544–1985, descriptions of folk beliefs and practices from the Folklore Archives Folk Belief and Folk Medicine card catalogues, descriptions regarding 19th century folk culture by contemporary ethnographic writers, as well as the anthology of alcohol folklore and memoirs written by the informants during the 1970s entitled *Kippurahäntä* (Hakokorpi-Jumppanen – Virtanen 1971). A separate corpus is composed of responses to a thematic questionnaire drawn up by the author, to which 72 members of the Folklore Archives respondents' network replied in 1989.

[2] The present paper is a summary of research funded primarily by the Finnish Foundation for Alcohol Studies; funding has also come from the Finnish Literature Society. Seppo Knuuttila and Klaus Mäkelä have made comments to the manuscript, and in locating source materials I have received assistance from Senni Timonen. My sincere thanks go to all of them.

[3] Meaning-based knowledge is represented in the human mind in many forms. These include singular or typical actualizations of a category or class (instances and prototypes), as well as abstracted and more complex *schemata* and scripts (Anderson 2000:144–169). Mental images are linked to different human senses: in addition to visual and spatial imagery, one can experience auditory or tactile imagery as well (ibid:111).

Information concerning the typical features of concepts and categories ('alcohol', 'intoxication') is organized into *schemata. Schemata* represent categorical knowledge in a general fashion, by listing it, breaking it down into its component parts, and arranging it hierarchically. The *schema* of "hard liquor" contains, among other things, information concering the fact that the substance belongs to the macro-category of "intoxicating beverages", as well as information concerning the various characteristics and components of hard liquor: its attributes and their paradigms. Attributive variables are for example, the raw materials which go into making it (grain, potatoes, cellulose), sensory characteristics (color, taste, smell) as well as its effects, norms for usage, etc. (Anderson 2000:154–157).

The term "script" is used for *schemata* which represent recurring processual activities. The script for a wedding is cultural information which is familiar to most persons, likewise how to act in a restaurant (Anderson 2000:159–164).

Folklorists assume that the similarities apparent in the speech and other activities of multiple informants index shared, collective knowledge, in other words, cultural models (cf. Holland – Quinn 1987). These are processed both in social interaction and in the solitary thought processes of individuals. Cultural models can also be presented materially in various artefacts, for example writing, pictures, objects, food and drink, clothing and architecture. Following this assumption, I posit that the alcohol beliefs which I have condensed into abstract propositions refer to the schematic and script-like knowledge shared by many Finns concerning "spirits", "beer", "drinking", "intoxication", and "alcoholism" during the period 1840–1968.

[4]   In John R. Anderson's handbook *Cognitive Psychology and Its Implications* (2000) the "place" of emotion in the nervous system and function of emotion in cognitive processes is not defined. The intermeshing of cognition, emotion, and physical reactions has nonetheless been demonstrated in certain psychological theories (for social psychology see, for example, Scherer 1996 and for cognitive psychotherapy see, for example, Sewell 1995). In addition, some anthropologists interested in emotion research have taken this route as well (Leavitt 1996).

Here I define emotion as a three-part process: at the level of current activity it includes perception and the associated information content ("the cork of the champagne bottle popped open"), the emotional reaction arising from this ("how nice"), as well as a physical reaction, a feeling (smiling or laughing, a tintillating sense of expectation). The stages of this process occur in such rapid sequence that they are experienced as simultaneous. Representations of opening a champagne bottle – whether a memory or image, verbal or visual – may set in motion the same process.

[5]   The distinction between meaning and feeling has been dealt with by, for example, John Leavitt in his overview "Meaning and Feeling in the Anthropology of Emotions" (1996). Emotions associated with lingistic expression have been defined as either connotative or affective meanings (Karlsson 1994:218–219).

[6]   A cognitive-philosophical discussion of the way in which the human mind deals with qualities is presented by, for example, Joseph Levine (1997).

The majority of human knowledge seems to be "emotional knowledge", in which the cognitive content has received nuances to a greater or lesser degree from qualitative determinants, in other words, emotional overtones. For humans to function rationally in their environment, they must categorize this environment into a least three classes: positive phenomena (those perceived as objects of aspiration or providing safety), negative phenomena (those which are dangerous and should be avoided) and neutral phenomena (possessing little or no emotive force). Qualitative emotions which evaluate interpretations of the human universe are indispensible in the directing of individual and collective behavior; emotions appear for this reason to be a significant part of mnemonic processes, as Kirsti Määttänen (1996) has pointed out.

Cognitions (beliefs, concepts) can also be distinguished according to modality: the determination of whether the object of belief is possible, likely, certainly true, or (cf. Sperber 1997) desired or intended (cf. Strauss 1992).

[7]   It has been shown that emotional behavior is shaped by culture in many ways. The

conceptualization, categorization and verbalization of emotions vary from one language to another. For example the word *tunne* in Finnish corresponds to the English terms "emotion", "feeling" and "sentiment". Variation can also be seen in the association of emotions and emotional expressions with actual or imagined situations. A mother in India laughs derisively at a fretful toddler, the observing American anthropologist perceives this behavior as odd (Leavitt 1996:520). Cultural variation in emotional behavior does not preclude the fact that there is also a universal, species-wide dimension to emotion. The "fundamental" emotions posited by psychologists (e.g. hostility, fear, joy, sadness) can be identified in the behavior of culturally-distant persons as well.

[8] The repetitive nature of form and content in folklore has been explained as arising from an important requirement in the transmission of oral knowledge: the preservation of the message is bound up with its acceptance by the receiving party. Idiosyncratic constructions are more difficult to commit to memory than familiar-sounding ones; in addition, uniqueness can seem unpleasantly strange or peculiar (see Jakobson – Bogatyrev 1966).

[9] Oral-traditional genres are at the same time genres of expression. In addition to the contents of the tradition, they also contain genre-specific features as well as modalities, the customary attitudes taken towards the thing expressed (Jason 1977:17–26.) Genre-specific modalities largely determine which emotions are customary to express in the context of a given genre.

[10] The researcher engaged in intertextual analysis deals with the information contained in texts using the same methods that a language-user employs in handling verbal information in general. In the processing of verbal information, paradigmatic and syntagmatic relations of meaning are taken into account. The former encompass similarities (synonyms, homologies, analogies, and the metaphors constructed from them), hierarchical relations of subordination (hyponyms), *pars pro toto* relationships (meronyms, metonyms), attributives which define qualities and characteristics, and relations of opposition (Karlsson 1994:203–207, 215–218).

[11] The language-user (speaker, thinker, writer) expresses conscious and unconscious attitudes and stances (including emotional attitudes) by making semantic choices, for instance, in relation to modalities, the definition of the subject ("I", "us" or passive), verb tenses, conjunctions, adjectives and adverbs, etc. (cf. Karlsson 1994:211–212; Purra 1994); he or she can also use various rhetorical devices (dialectic opposition, repetition). These sorts of markers and indices are also conveyed to the interpreter of written materials or oral materials recorded in writing.

The listener strives to interpret from speech not only verbal meanings but also the unspoken peripheral communication accompanying it, above all gestures, facial expressions, eye contact and posture (see Karlsson 1994:10–11, Schiffrin 1994, Briggs 1988:233–252). Words, messages read "between the lines", and non-verbal communication all evoke emotional reactions in the listener which the listener can use to reach conclusions concerning which emotions the speaker is experiencing. If the listener monitors the silent monologue within his/her own mind, he or she notices that the images linked to voiceless word-expressions also arouse emotions (cf. Honko 1986:117–118).

[12] The success of this sort of analysis and interpretation can be gauged by allowing it to be read both by members of the culture in question and by experts on the historical material.

[13] On fire-*väki* and female *väki* see Apo (1998:81–82, 88) and Stark-Arola (1998). Pasi Falk (1983:167–173, 185) has discussed the ritual consumption of alcohol and alcohol as a substance which transforms its drinker.

[14] The earliest recording of the proverb *Humalass on huojis elää: ei ole köyhä eikä kipee* ("It is a relief to live intoxicated: one knows neither poverty nor pain") is from the years 1770–1800 (Kuusi 1953:271, 502). "When drunk, all debits appear as credits" was still in use in the 1980s (Kuusi 1988:179).

[15] The years given in parentheses indicate the date of the earliest and latest recordings,

usually only in terms of decades (see Kuusi 1953:271, 501). The proverbs are from Matti Kuusi's anthology *Vanhan kansan sananlaskuviisaus* (The Wisdom of the Old Folk in Proverbs, 1953).

[16] According to ethnographic descriptions from Eastern Finland, adult (married) women could imbibe cheap spirits and beer, but not to the same extent as adult men. Cheap spirits intended for women could also be diluted by mixing them with molasses (Apo 2001:103–104).

[17] It was possible to prepare an alcoholic beverage more archaic than beer from tree sap and honey: people possessed the knowledge to make the clay containers necessary for fermentation already in the Stone Age; these could also be made from wood and birchbark (cf. Huurre 1995:54–55). Agriculture – necessary for the preparation of beer – became a way of life in Finland by the Bronze Age at the latest (from 1500 B.C.; Huurre 1995:92, 99). Agriculture has been the most important livelihood of the population since the beginning of the Christian era.

[18] Haatanen 1968:1, 47–49; Raussi 1966:84, 134–135; Talve 1997:133.

[19] According to anecdotes, male heads of farming households were able to gauge how much drinking the farm could support: "the master of Kivelä farm had given his sons instructions, saying that this farm can survive one man's drinking, but there are seven of you, and if you start to drink, all is soon lost" (Finnish Literature Society = SKS. Alkoholi 1989. The informant was a farmer from Savo-Karelia born in 1914).

[20] These have been written by Elias Raussi (1800–1866) and Johannes Häyhä (1839–1913) as well as Antero Warelius (1821–1904), who described the parish of Tyrvää in Satakunta. The descriptions were written or published in 1854 (Warelius), in the 1860s (Raussi's manuscript, published 1966) as well as in the years 1893 and 1899 (Häyhä).

[21] The earliest recording of both of these proverbs is from the work published by Henrik Florinus (1633–1705) entitled *Wanhain Suomalaisten Tawalliset ja Suloiset Sananlascut* ("Common and Charming Sayings of the Ancient Finns"). The proverbs were collected during the period 1655–1702 (Kuusi 1953:455–461, 501).

[22] Finnish archives contain numerous photographs from the early decades of the last century depicting groups of young Finnish men drinking alcohol and striking impressive poses (Peltonen 1988:57, 71).

[23] The gentry interpreted this custom in cruder terms: at folk weddings alcohol was sold to guests (cf. Sarmela 1981:41–42).

[24] "Driving around with liquor" could function as a genuine barter or exchange, in which each party benefitted, but it could also be a request disguised as a symbolic exchange (Raussi 1966:116–120). The custom has also been discussed by Matti Peltonen (1988:43–47).

[25] Drinking at Christmas and the intoxication of the household's male members, particularly the head of the household, were considered important – they were seen to promote the success of the following year's harvest. When, during the reign of Swedish King Gustav III (1771–1792), the government wanted to reduce the use of grain in the distilling of cheap spirits by placing annual limits on how much alcohol could be distilled, peasant farmers sent anxious letters to Stockholm stressing the vital importance of distilling alcohol during the Christmas season (Mäntylä 1985:104, 121–122, 145).

[26] Depictions of 19th century Finns drinking in a "civilized" manner which were fictitious but nonetheless intended to portray reality can be found for Eastern Finland from, for example, the works of Johannes Häyhä and for Western Finland from Volter Kilpi's (1874–1939) *Saaristo* ("Archipelago") series, particularly his novel *Alastalon salissa* ("In the Hall of Alastalo Farm", 1933).

[27] An ethnographic writer can be considered one who has chosen as his or her theme a comprehensive description of the way of life of an actual group of people. Ethnographic writers can be a researchers (anthropologists, ethnologists), a novelists who creates fiction, a writers of memoirs, or a so-called archivist writers (Kaarina Sala's term) who send their manuscripts to a folklore or literature archive.

Ethnographic writers usually announce their thematic intentions clearly either in the text itself (most often at the beginning) or in other writings, for example, in letters or diaries.

28   Raussi and Häyhä describe the period of home distillation in Southeast Finland, and Kivi describes the same period for "Southern Häme" (Uusimaa). Paulaharju (1875–1944) has, using interviews, portrayed the agrarian society of 19th century Central Ostrobothnia in his book *Härmän aukeilta* ("From the Plains of Härmä", 1932).

29   Male competitiveness and bonding behavior do not belong exclusively to drinking situations, but under the influence of alcohol they are manifested more visibly and with more forceful expression of emotion.

30   Men's attempts to size each other up intellectually while drinking do not appear only in the context of the older folk culture. Particularly in the drinking sessions of the intelligentsia, the most popular (and often only) programme for the evening has been the ranking of the men present according to expertise and intelligence. During the period of my own university studies (1967–72), this took place through a never-ending discussion of Marxist theory, particularly the logic of capital.

31   At issue is once again a traditional formula for slander: a "disgraceful" catch (a flea) unfit for consumption is divided up and parts are given to the person to be ridiculed (Häyhä 1983:74–75).

32   Anthropologists have repeatedly discarded the myth of the harmonious small-scale community (i.e., village community) (see, for example, Pelto – Pelto 1978:34–37 as well as Suolinna – Sinikara 1986 on Finland).

33   These examples have been taken from the anthology of alcohol-related folklore entitled *Kippurahäntä* (1977) and edited by Maria Hakokorpi-Jumppanen and Matti Virtanen.

34   The traditional popular thought associated with alcohol did not include the concept of alcoholism as an illness, at least not a prototypical illness. Alcoholism was the result of a structural weakness in one's personality; this sort of person was unable to resist neither the "infection" by an alcoholic environment nor his own craving for drink (Apo 2001:261–263). According to descriptions in the Folklore Archives, a man could also be bewitched, "ruined" to become a drunkard; he was deliberately "infected" with a lust for drink by, for example, throwing the remnants of his drink into the fire (Apo 2001:148).

35   The rapid "drying out" of the countryside already before the impact of the temperance movement (1880s–1910s) has been studied by Matti Peltonen (1990; 1997:54–59).

36   The many changes in the lives of individuals, families and working communities inspired by popular education and enlightenment resulted in real improvements in their quality of life (emancipation). The decline in infant mortality, checks on the spread of infectious diseases and modern education whereby individuals are taught that they can influence society and their environment through science and political skills are all valuable achievements. In comparison, decreasing the already moderate consumption of alcohol has not significantly promoted the ordinary Finnish citizen's attainment of the "good life".

37   According to Irma Sulkunen (1986:260–278) the temperance movement also functioned for approx. three decades (1870–1905) as the "civil religion" of the working class in Finland.

38   Finland's Swedish-speaking and Finnish-speaking populations were seen to represent different races (Peltonen 1988:28–29).

39   The issue of the darker side of enlightenment and especially popular education, i.e., the stigmatizing of those who are to be enlightened and their subordination into the upper classes' standards of discipline and moral decency, has been raised most visibly by M. Foucault in his work from the 1960s. The uncensored opinions of the middle class elite concerning the Finnish rank and file, and the measures taken to produce a unified citizenry, have been discussed, for example, in Irma Sulkunen's study of the Finnish temperance movement (1986) and Panu Pulma's and Oiva Turpeinen's *Suomen lastensuojelun historia* ("The History of Child Welfare in Finland", 1987).

40   As reflected in Finnish literature, the collapse of the romantic view of the folk can be

seen in early 20th century depictions of the folk as primitive, even bestial (Molarius 1998:109–110). Darwinism had shown that humans were also part of the animal kingdom. For nearly a century, a threatening, civilization-swallowing bestiality was projected repeatedly onto ever newer "others". In global terms, these "others" were conceived of as peoples and cultures other than Europeans; while from the perspective of the Swedish-speaking elite in Finland, they were Finnish-speaking Finns, and among the Finnish-minded elite, they were the lower class, the rural folk and industrial workers. The most important power-holders in rural society, i.e., the wealthy landowning farmers of the late 19th and early 20th centuries, distanced themselves from not only the base inclinations of the landless but also from the decay and corruption bred by the cities.

[41] This older racial thinking is the topic of, for example, Gunnar Suolahti's essay *Vanhempi fennomania ja Suomen itsenäisyyden aate* (1921/1993:345–382). Racial concepts which were influential in the 20th century and their relation to the "Finnish boozer mentality" have been discussed by Matti Peltonen (1988; 1997).

[42] The existence of an intoxication-oriented mode of drinking does not in itself say anything about Finnish culture except that within it, this type of drinking is practiced. This cultural form only receives ideological significance through interpretation. This drinking custom can be seen as a relic which has disappeared in other cultures just as is Finnish sauna, the Finnish academic degree ceremony lasting several days, and the declaration of "Christmas Peace" to the nation on noon, December 24. In a stigmatizing interpretation, intoxication-oriented drinking is seen to reveal the primitiveness and backwardness of the "typical Finn", it is contrasted with the ideal of "civilized" or "European" consumption of alcoholic refreshment. In a positive interpretation, intoxication-oriented drinking can be seen as a "natural" or authentic mode of drinking, as straightforward enjoyment in which the drinker does not need to guard against intoxication nor hide from others his/her psychophysical state.

[43] According to Matti Peltonen, the traditional alcohol thought survived tenaciously despite pressures from temperance enlightenment, a fact which can be seen from a survey conducted in 1946. Nearly half of the respondents did not consider even frequent intoxication-oriented drinking to be "misuse of alcohol". The most permissive group proved to be farmers, those most familiar with the older alcohol culture; of them less than half (47%) considered frequent intoxication to be misuse of alcohol (Peltonen 1997:113–114.)

[44] According to Pasi Saukkonen (personal communication), Finns have thoroughly internalized the negative stereotypes concerning themselves; nonetheless in speech they set themselves above the stereotypes and do not consider themselves a "typical Finn".

BIBLIOGRAPHY

Abu-Lughod, Lila 1986: Veiled Sentiments: Honor and Poetry in a Bedouin Society. University of California Press. Berkeley & Los Angeles.
Alapuro, Risto 1997: Suomen älymystö Venäjän varjossa. Hanki ja Jää. Helsinki.
Alkoholikysymys 1976: Alkoholikysymys, in Spectrum tietokeskus. Osa 1. Werner Söderström Oy. Helsinki & Porvoo.
Anderson, John R. 2000: Cognitive Psychology and Its Implications. Fifth edition. Worth Publishers. New York.
Apo, Satu 1994: Ale, Spirits, and Patterns of Mythical Fantasy: The Origin of Alcoholic Beverages According to Finnish Folklore. A.-L. Siikala – S. Vakimo (eds) Songs Beyond the Kalevala: Transformations of Oral Poetry. Studia Fennica Folkloristica 2. The Finnish Literature Society. Helsinki.
– 1998: "Ex cunno Come the Folk and Force": Concepts of Women's Dynamistic Power in Finnish-Karelian Tradition (1993). S. Apo – A. Nenola – L. Stark-Arola (eds) Gender and Folklore: Perspectives on Finnish and Karelian Culture. Studia Fennica

Folkloristica 4. The Finnish Literature Society. Helsinki.
- 2001: Viinan voima. Näkökulmia suomalaisten kansanomaiseen alkoholiajatteluun ja -kulttuuriin. Suomalaisen Kirjallisuuden Seura. Helsinki.
Briggs, Charles L. 1988: Competence in Performance: The Creativity of Tradition in Mexicano Verbal Art. University of Pennsylvania Press. Philadelphia.
Falk, Pasi 1983: Humalan historia: Juomisen merkitysten historiallisuus. Unpublished licentiate thesis. University of Helsinki. Department of Sosiology.
Frykman, Jonas – Löfgren, Orvar 1987: Culture Builders: A Historical Anthropology of Middle-Class Life. Rutgers University Press. New Brunswick.
Geertz, Clifford 1973: Thick Description: Toward an Interpretative Theory of Culture. C. Geertz: The Interpretation of Cultures: Selected Essays. Basic Books. New York.
Glaser, B. – Strauss, Anselm 1967: The Discovery of Grounded Theory. Aldine. Chicago.
Haatanen, Pekka 1968: Suomen maalaisköyhälistö tutkimusten ja kaunokirjallisuuden valossa. Werner Söderström Oy. Porvoo & Helsinki.
Hakokorpi-Jumppanen, Maria – Virtanen, Matti 1977 (eds): Kippurahäntä. Alkoholiaiheisen perinnekilpailun satoa. Suomalaisen Kirjallisuuden Seura. Helsinki.
Holland, Nancy – Quinn, Dorothy (eds) 1987: Cultural Models in Language and Thought. Cambridge University Press. Cambridge.
Honko, Lauri 1986: Empty Texts, Full Meanings. On Transformal Meaning in Folklore. Arv: Scandinavian Yearbook of Folklore, Vol. 40 (1984):95–125.
Huurre, Matti 1995: 9000 vuotta Suomen esihistoriaa. Otava. Helsinki.
Härmänmaa, Marja – Mattila, Markku (eds) 1998: Uusi uljas ihminen eli modernin pimeä puoli. Atena Kustannus Oy. Jyväskylä.
Häyhä, Johannes 1982: Vuodenajat. Kuvaelmia itäsuomalaisten vanhoista tavoista. Suomalaisen Kirjallisuuden Seura. Helsinki.
- 1983: Perhe ja kylä. Kuvaelmia itäsuomalaisten vanhoista tavoista. Suomalaisen Kirjallisuuden Seura. Helsinki.
Jakobson, Roman – Bogatyrev, P. 1966: Folklore als eine besondere Form des Schaffens. (1929). R. Jakobson (ed.) Selected Writings IV. Slavic Epic Studies. Mouton. The Hague & Paris.
Jason, Heda 1977: Ethnopoetry: Form, Content, Function. Linguistica Biblica. Bonn.
Karlsson, Fred 1994: Yleinen kielitiede. Yliopistopaino. Helsinki.
Keryell, Gaela 1997: Suomalainen humala kansallisena instituutiona. Alkoholipolitiikka 62(3):167–185.
Kilpi, Volter 1933: Alastalon salissa. Kuvaus saaristosta. 1–2. Otava. Helsinki.
Kivi, Aleksis 1928: Nummisuutarit. Komedia viidessä näytöksessä. (1864). Suomalaisen Kirjallisuuden Seura. Helsinki.
- 1991: Seven brothers: a novel. (1870). Translated by Richard A. Impola. Finnish American Translators' Association. New Palz, New York.
Knuuttila, Seppo 1985: Osa joutuu juomarille. Kotiseutu 3/1985:144–147.
Kuusi, Matti 1953 (ed.): Vanhan kansan sananlaskuviisaus. Suomalaisia elämänohjeita, kansanaforismeja, lentäviä lauseita ja kokkapuheita vuosilta 1544–1826. Werner Söderström Oy. Porvoo & Helsinki.
- 1963: Suomen kirjallisuus I. Kirjoittamaton kirjallisuus. Suomalaisen Kirjallisuuden Seura & Otava. Helsinki.
- 1988 (ed.): Rapatessa roiskuu. Nykysuomen sananparsikirja. Suomalaisen Kirjallisuuden Seura. Helsinki.
Leavitt, John 1996: Meaning and feeling in the anthropology of emotions. American Ethnologist 23(3):514–539.
Levine, Joseph 1997: Are Qualia Just Representations? A Critical Notice of Michael Tye's *Ten Problems of Consciousness*. Mind & Language 12 (1):101–113.
Löfström, Jan 1994: The Social Construction of Homosexuality in Finnish society, from the Late Nineteenth Century to 1950's. Unpublished Ph.D. thesis. University of Essex: Department of Sociology.
Molarius, Päivi 1998: ”Veren äänen” velvoitteet – yksilö rodun, perimän ja ympäristön puristuksessa. M. Härmänmaa – M. Mattila (eds) Uusi uljas ihminen eli modernin

pimeä puoli. Atena Kustannus Oy. Jyväskylä.

Mäkelä, Klaus 1998: Suomalaisen alkoholipuheen pitkä kaari. Yhteiskuntapolitiikka 63(1):102–104.

Mäntylä, Ilkka 1985: Suomalaisen juoppouden juuret. Viinanpoltto vapaudenaikana. Suomalaisen Kirjallisuuden Seura. Helsinki.

Määttänen, Kirsti 1996: Muisti ja muistamisen tunnot. K. Määttänen – T. Nevanlinna (eds) Muistikirja. Jälkien jäljillä. Tutkijaliitto. Helsinki.

Partanen, Juha 1991: Sociability and Intoxication. Alcohol and Drinking in Kenya, Africa, and the Modern World. The Finnish Foundation for Alcohol Studies. Helsinki.

Paulaharju, Samuli 1932: Härmän aukeilta. Werner Söderström Oy. Porvoo & Helsinki.

Pelto, Pertti J. – Pelto, Gretel H. 1978: Anthropological Research: The Structure of Inquiry. 2nd edition. Cambridge University Press. London.

Peltonen, Matti 1988: Viinapäästä kolerakauhuun. Kirjoituksia sosiaalihistoriasta. Hanki ja Jää. Helsinki.

– 1990: Alkoholi ja uusi maalaisjulkisuus. Alkoholipolitiikka 55(1):2–12.

– 1997: Kerta kiellon päälle. Suomalainen kieltolakimentaliteetti. Hanki ja Jää. Helsinki.

Pulma, Panu 1987: Kerjuuluvasta perhekuntoutukseen. Lapsuuden yhteiskunnallistuminen ja lastensuojelun kehitys Suomessa. P. Pulma – O. Turpeinen: Suomen lastensuojelun historia. Lastensuojelun Keskusliitto. Helsinki

Purra, Pia 1994: Yksi avioliitto – kaksi tarinaa. Sukupuoli ja kieli erään avioparin oma-elämäkerroissa. J-P. Roos – E. Peltonen (eds) Miehen elämää. Suomalaisen Kirjallisuuden Seura. Helsinki.

Pyörälä, Eeva 1991: Nuorten aikuisten juomakulttuuri Suomessa ja Espanjassa. Alkoholipoliittisen tutkimuslaitoksen tutkimusseloste 183. Alkoholipoliittinen tutkimuslaitos. Helsinki.

Raussi, Eljas 1966: Virolahden kansanelämää 1840-luvulla. Suomalaisen Kirjallisuuden Seura. Helsinki.

Sarmela, Matti 1981: Suomalaiset häät. M. Sarmela (ed.) Pohjolan häät. Suomalaisen Kirjallisuuden Seura. Helsinki.

Scherer, Klaus R. 1996: Emotion. M. Hewstone – W. Stroebe – G. M. Stephenson (eds) Introduction to Social Psychology. A European Perspective. Second Edition. Blackwell Publishers.

Schiffrin, Deborah 1994: Approaches to Discourse. Oxford, UK and Cambridge, Blackwell Publishers. Oxford, UK & Cambridge, Ma. USA.

Sewell, Kenneth W. 1995: Personal Construct Therapy and the Relation Between Cognition and Affect. M. J. Mahoney (ed.) Cognitive and Constructive Psychoterapies: Theory, Research, and Practice. Springer Publishing Company. New York.

SKVR = Suomen Kansan Vanhat Runot. (The Ancient Poems of the Finnish People). Raja- ja Pohjois-Karjalan runot VII2. A.R. Niemi (ed.) (1931).

SKVR. Etelä-Karjalan runot XIII2. V. Salminen (ed.) (1937). Suomalaisen Kirjallisuuden Seura. Helsinki.

SKS. Alkoholi 1989: Thematic inquiry into the use of alcohol. The Folklore Archives of the Finnish Literature Society (= SKS).

Soininen, Arvo 1974: Vanha maataloutemme. Maatalous ja maatalousväestö Suomessa perinnäisen maatalouden loppukaudella 1720-luvulta 1870-luvulle. Suomen Historiallinen Seura. Helsinki.

– 1980: Maatalous. E. Jutikkala – Y. Kaukiainen – S-E. Åström (eds) Suomen taloushistoria I. Agraarinen Suomi. Tammi. Helsinki.

Sperber, Dan 1997: Intuitive and Reflective Beliefs. Mind & Language 12 (1): 67–83.

Stark-Arola, Laura 1998: Lempi, tuli ja naisen väki. Dynamistisista suhteista suomalais-karjalaisessa taikuudessa ja kansanuskossa. A.-L. Siikala – J. Pöysä (eds) Amor, genus, familia. Suomalaisen Kirjallisuuden Seura. Helsinki.

Strauss, Claudia 1992: Models and Motives. C. Strauss – R. D'Andrade (eds) Human Motives and Cultural Models. Cambridge University Press. New York.

Sulkunen, Irma 1986: Raittiusliike kansalaisuskontona. Raittiusliike ja järjestäytyminen 1870-luvulta suurlakon jälkeisiin vuosiin. Historiallisia Tutkimuksia 134. Suomen Historiallinen Seura. Helsinki.

Suolahti, Gunnar 1921 (1993): Vanhempi fennomania ja Suomen itsenäisyyden aate. M. Klinge (ed.) Vuosisatain takaa. Kulttuurihistoriallisia kuvauksia. Suomalaisen Kirjallisuuden Seura. Helsinki.

Suolinna, Kirsti – Sinikara, Kaisa 1986: Juhonkylä. Tutkimus pohjoissuomalaisesta lestadiolaiskylästä. Suomalaisen Kirjallisuuden Seura. Helsinki.

Talve, Ilmar 1997: Finnish Folk Culture. Studia Fennica Ethnologica 4. Finnish Literature Society. Helsinki.

Thompson, E. P. 1996: Herrojen valta ja rahvaan kulttuuri. Valta, kulttuuri ja perinnäistavat 1700–1800-luvun Englannissa. Gaudeamus. Helsinki.

Timonen, Senni 1989: Pohjois-Karjalan lyriikka. Kalevalaseuran vuosikirja 68: 108–135.

Turner, Victor 1969: The Ritual Process: Structure and Anti-Structure. Routledge & Kegan Paul. London.

Valkonen, Tapani – Alapuro, Risto – Alestalo, Matti – Jallinoja, Riitta – Sandlund, Tom 1980: Suomalaiset. Yhteiskunnan rakenne teollistumisen aikana. Werner Söderström Oy. Helsinki & Porvoo.

Virtanen, Leea 1987: Setukaiset kertovat lauluistaan. L. Virtanen (ed.) Viron veräjät. Näkökulmia folkloreen. Suomalaisen Kirjallisuuden Seura. Helsinki.

Warelius, Antero 1938: Kertomus Tyrvään pitäjästä 1853. (1854). Suomalaisen Kirjallisuuden Seura. Helsinki.

Ylikangas, Heikki 1976: Puukkojunkkareitten esiinmarssi. Väkivaltarikollisuus Etelä-Pohjanmaalla 1790–1825. Otava. Helsinki.

HENNI ILOMÄKI

Narratives of Ethnicity

Karelian War Legends

Notions about ethnic differences clearly emerge in some folklore genres.
Proverbs often express ethnic differences by using, for example, a
stereotypical "Russian" to represent the entire ethnic or national group. War
legends in particular tend to convey the Otherness of the enemy. As ethno-
historical constructions, these narrative portrayals of war, persecution,
plundering, and other expressions of inter-group conflict combine seemingly
plain facts with folk beliefs and assumptions. Although "war" is at issue,
the narratives are actually more often about violence against civilians and
they cope with such attacks. The examples below were collected from Kirvu
and Sortavala:

> During the Great Wrath the Cossacks went to Rätykylä, set the Puha house
> on fire and then disappeared. Meanwhile, the owners were hiding in a nearby
> forest. When they saw the Cossacks leave, they came out of hiding and put
> out the fire. As the Cossacks were making their way to the place where the
> school is today, they saw that there was no longer any smoke rising from the
> Puha house. So, they promptly returned and set the house on fire once again.
> This time, they didn't leave until the buildings had burned all the way to the
> ground. And this is how the Cossacks burned Puha. (139)[1]

> During the war, there were stories about Russians who came from the shore
> of the White Sea to the Finnish North to rob and burn people's homes. If the
> people didn't get away in time, they were usually killed. The Russians would
> spear women and children to death, and imprison the menfolk. Since the
> Russians were familiar neither with the area nor with the river and its rapids,
> they forced Laarikainen, a landowner they had captured, to steer the leading
> boat. As they proceeded along the river, Laarikainen said nothing about the
> waterfalls and simply urged them to keep rowing because of a supposed
> counter-current ahead. Just as they reached the waterfall, Laarikainen leaped
> to the rocky shore and the Russians went down the waterfall. Their boats
> were smashed to bits and the enemies drowned to death. People say that
> Russian spirits still lurk about the niches and crannies of the rocky riverbank.
> (140)

Myth and Mentality
Studia Fennica
Folkloristica 8, 2002
Do narratives of this kind reveal how their narrators regarded neighboring
ethnic groups? How is ethnicity or ethnic consciousness manifested in these
particular narratives?

207

Ethnic Consciousness

How is our membership in a given group determined? How is affinity or difference recognized? How is this expressed in narrative? Is ethnicity primordial or is it only invoked by an encounter with a supposed Other? Anthropological studies have shown that many ethnic groups have a word meaning "human" to describe their own group. The human tendency towards ethnocentricism generally causes each society to view its own culture and form of social organization as the best and most reasonable. Thus, all others are strangers or even non-human (animals). Value-laden binary oppositions, such as culture and nature, cleanliness and pollution, are then paralleled with notions of the familiar and the strange (Lotman 1975:87–97). The mere sound of a foreign tongue invokes suspicion and even contempt. In fact, the original Greek meaning of the word barbaric was "speaking incoherently". In Herderian terms, a feeling of solidarity with one's own people derives from the National Romantic assumption that each national group has an intuitive grasp of its own shared culture. Therefore, those belonging to the group feel convinced that their models of behavior and communal habits passed down from time immemorial have been chosen for a reason. Unfortunately, these building blocks of cultural identity have occasionally gained political currency and thus have been exploited for violent political purposes.

Thanks to increasing contacts between cultures and the growing visibility of minority groups in recent decades, more and more research has been devoted to ethnicity or ethnic identity (cf. Poutignat – Streiff-Fenart 1995:30–33, 59–69). Frederik Barth was one of the first to initiate scholarly discussion on ethnicity. Even today, Barth's ideas still hold a key place in the debates (Barth 1969). He defines ethnicity (ethnic identity) as one aspect of social organization; it is crucial to recognize just what makes "us" different from "them". A belief in the existence of a shared cultural background is one of the key requisites for group identification. However, commitment to the group and a sense of estrangement from others prove even more fundamental. Barth has claimed that the ethnicity debate has more to do with an attempt to define a familiar Other encountered in day-to-day life than with trying to understand truly unknown Others (Barth 1996:13). Rather than being an ongoing process, self-identification with a group takes place and becomes salient largely in the event of conflict. If day-to-day encounters fail to raise the issue of ethnic difference, the researcher must approach ethnicity from a new perspective.

Each and every member of a society cannot share the exact same cultural information. Thus an ethnic group's culture or knowledge is more accurately the observer's generalization, which effectively covers the various notions held by all the individuals within a community (Holy – Stuchlik 1983:48). The observer's perspective invariably distorts, but so does the tendency to conflate individual and collective perceptions of ethnic identity. Identity is not an external fact which first exists outside of time and space which is then simply manifested in custom or behavior (Bromberge – al 1989:145). A given community does not necessarily have a solid foundation for its members' ethnic consciousness. After all, upon finding oneself in a strange culture, one may feel a fleeting sense of being at "home" thanks to a familiar custom, etc. At the same time, however, one still lacks a firm grasp of the other culture's complexity. Only some facets of the culture are apparent, and these invoke a sense of the familiar (Andersson 1992:39). Thus, ethnic identity is by necessity situational and flexible.

An individual member of an ethnic group can only be partially aware of his/her ethnic identity. If culture is defined as an aggregate of an infinite number of elements with indicators forming a series of salient attributes, the familiarity of these attributes cannot, however, automatically produce a sense of cultural belonging. After all, ethnicity is merely one factor fostering a sense of group membership; it is a manifestation of the individual's observation and analysis. Ethnic awareness cannot invalidate individual identity, instead ethnic consciousness functions symbolically. Its basic form may emerge more clearly than its variations (Cohen 1996:61–62). Could war tales be symbolic expressions of this identification of the Self versus the Other?

The Elements of Ethnic Self-Consciousness

Can ethnic identity be objectively determined? How does one recognize one's own culture? Human beings tend to classify objects in the world and place these objects in relationship to each other to grasp the whole picture. This tendency enables community members to apprehend the bundle of qualities that attest to their groupness (e.g. Dwyer 1979:13). Both scholarly and folk categories are based on conceptual systems. According to one definition, the parts making up cultural consciousness are concepts guiding action such as beliefs and attitudes; they do not simply help the individual to recognize objects in the world, but also serve to constitute that world (Witherspoon 1971:110). People can easily perceive "reality" and its rules in an inconsistent manner. Not all factors are even linked to ethnicity. Cultural awareness is hardly predicated on the existence a fixed array of concepts; instead, it is more likely to be a system placing concepts in relation to each other – regardless of how consciously the community itself determines these concepts (Holy – Stuchlik 1983:47). Ethnic group identity provides a perspective on and filters the cognitive perception of self and group characterization, which, in turn, enables cultural continuity. Group members recognize this and accept it; ethnic identity binds the individual to the collective, guides actions, and is thus emotionally valued.

Kaija Heikkinen provides an alternative perspective on ethnicity. She is careful to distinguish between the individual and communal sphere. Heikkinen defines ethnic self-consciousness by underlining the fact that the existence of a given ethnic group is shaped and defined by external circumstances. Concrete ethnic or national ties determine one's membership in a group; the subjective commitment to an ethnic group's unique features is conscious. Evidence of ethnic identity thus emerges as personal awareness. Referring to Russian research on stereotypes, Heikkinen regards the phenomena (such as traditions, customs and rituals) making up ethnic uniqueness as signs. The essence of these signs is manifested in an individual's ethnic awareness. This emerges on the level of feeling, behavior, and orientation according to cultural values and other stereotypical notions of the Self and the Other (Heikkinen 1989:74–76). Although ethnic homogeneity is largely a fallacy, people still shape their sense of cultural identity in relation to other groups – and thus they construct cultural boundaries.

Despite the wealth of scholarship, we still lack an all-purpose definition for ethnic identity. So far, we have had to make do with external criteria such as common origins, customs and culture, religion, physiological characteristics and language (for a detailed description of ideal types, see Nygren 1988:91). In a given context, even a single characteristic can provide a basis for group identity (Hakamies 1993:36–41, 132). Thus, do war legends serve to reflect ethnic consciousness in times of conflict? Does the above-mentioned local narrative illustrate a sense of group-identification? Some scholars have asserted that each community's shared cultural concept is bound to be expressed orally, if only in the most oblique way (Holy – Stuchlik 1983:47). There appears to be evidence for this claim. Alan Dundes, for example, has registered a number of folklore items that help sustain ethnic identity (Dundes 1983:240–251). Such folklore conveys the unique nature of an ethnic group, that is, the prevailing power and continuity of its oral traditions. The oral tradition examined in this article is the war legend: accounts of violent inter-group conflicts.

Borderland Ethnicity

For centuries, Finland was a battleground for Russo-Swedish wars. Finland was part of the Kingdom of Sweden from the mid-1100s until 1809, after which it was ceded to Russia and achieved greater autonomy as the Grand Duchy of Finland until 1917, when Finland became an independent state. The peace treaty ratified by Russia and Sweden in Pähkinäsaari in 1323, according to early historical records, ceded vast tracts of land in Eastern and Northern Finland to Russia. This initiated the cultural divide between western and eastern Finland: thus the Roman Catholic Church – and later the Evangelical Lutheran Church – became established in the west and the Orthodox Church in the east. Thanks to the repeated battles between Sweden and Russia, Finland's eastern border was drawn a number of times. This lack of stability had far-reaching consequences for Karelians living near the border. The population surged back and forth across the border as a consequence of evacuations, forced settlements and occasional promises of tax relief. In addition to the state wars, the border populations were plagued by raids and sudden outbreaks of violence. The idea of a border in Karelia was not established until Finland's independence from Russia in 1917 (Klinge 1972:70). The power struggles between political forces held little meaning to the borderland populations. Nonetheless, their daily lives were disrupted. The national identity of the people across the border was uncertain and open to debate; their ethnic identity was constantly being called into question.

The ethnic identity of those living near the border was liable to change because of political and historical circumstances. Places on both sides of the border were home to ethnic groups seeking refuge from the respective victors of the war. The refugee population was made up of Finns and Karelians (Kirkinen 1970; Pöllä 1995). Attitudes to dialect and other expressions of folk culture would vary according to the proximity to the unstable border. Cross-border trade was practiced among the various ethnic groups up until the second half of the 19th century. Some of the merchants were Karelians, others Russians (Tarkianen 1986). Ethnic identity was easily malleable: the Karelians across the border could be easily regarded as Swedes or Russians depending on the speaker's locality (Hakamies 1993:133; Heikkinen 1989: 32–35).

The above discussion raises a key question: does the existence of a state border bring about a new perspective on inter-group relations? What kind of impact does a mutable border have on ethnic awareness? Rudolf von Thadden's work explores this very issue. His study of the inhabitants along the German – French border illustrates just how malleable – and thus complicated – a concept ethnicity actually is. von Thadden asserts that ethnicity is largely independent of geographical place, but is shaped by historical events (von Thadden 1991). Can an exploration of Finnish-Karelian folklore provide further support for von Thadden's research?

Ethnic Consciousness in War Legends

The folklore archives of the Finnish Literature Society contain a vast collection of war legends. I have chosen 142 variants which include the basic types and motifs. Although legendary accounts of battles, atrocities perpetrated by the enemy, and, of course the resourcefulness of the narrator's own group were told throughout the area now known as Finland, most of the material used for this paper was collected in Northern Ostrobothnia and Eastern Finland, that is, the regions closest to the unstable eastern border. Even though I draw largely on Karelian materials, my aim is not to discuss Karelian identity in particular, but rather to explore ethnic identity in general. Hence, there are no indications as to which side of the border the material was collected.

The motifs are often known internationally, whereas the narratives are almost invariably linked to a specific locality, house or individual person. These one-episode legends generally assume the following pattern: the enemy appears, steals property, burns houses, and/or kills the inhabitants. Since the narrative is told from the victim's point of view, it is no wonder that these are accounts of how the victims overcome their persecutors by relying on their wit, bravery and resourcefulness. In fact, there is an overwhelming number of variations on the triumphs of the victim, that is, the narrator's own people. Even when they are losers, by the close of the narrative, the "we" of the narrative are morally victorious.

A detailed portrait of the enemy is hardly vital to the war legend's plot. Nevertheless, a few basic features are always repeated. Are ethnically-laden notions characteristic of war legends?

Reference Group

If we assume that "we" are united by common origins, how do war legends define outsiders? This genre of folklore uses a range of "ethnonyms" to describe the enemy. Although legends collected on both sides of the Finnish-Russian border rarely spell out who "we" are, "Finns" are occasionally mentioned. The people with whom the narrator identifies may be the villagers or the village women, etc. Often, the narrator will refer to a particular individual, such as the example in which the narrator alludes to his grandfather's looting of a Russian supply truck (41). In some narratives the adversary is not specified at all, in which case the narrator simply refers to them as "they". One out of six narratives identify Russians as the enemy; in nearly one-third of the stories the attackers are Russians, but a derogatory term is used. Cossacks is another term referring to the same ethnic group. Other national groups mentioned are Finns, Swedes, and Kalmucks. The groups whose ethnicity remains obscure are the people across the border; terms such as "certain people", "guerrillas", usually refer to Finns as well as the parallel term, *Ruotsit*, which actually means Swedes.

Of the various terms, "Russian" is the most commonly mentioned among eastern Finns. *Ryssä* (a derogatory term for a Russian) is known throughout the country. A term used to express extreme otherness, *cynocephalos*, can be found all the way to the Western coast. It is associated with a number of parallel terms meaning soldiers or enemies, or Russians. The term *cynocephalos* is used to describe both the actual attackers and the shrewd spies who supposedly traveled with them. In the tales collected from Ladoga Karelia, Finns or *Ruotsit* appear as the enemy – but the characteristics attributed to them are no different from those attributed to Russian attackers. Borderland narrators had a wide range of terms at their disposal. In part, the wide array of enemy terms derived from the unstable border and the fact that people often had to resettle across it in the event of political changes.

Language and Religion

In order to gain a clearer understanding of ethnicity, scholars have also studied individual commitment to a group (Anttonen 1996:18). The basis for such a commitment lies in the individual's confidence in his/her group's moral superiority – regardless of how this superiority manifests itself. In border conflicts, the core of ethnic consciousness abides in the values signifying group identity. War legends underline the difference between the Self and Other. The difference is even audible: the enemy's speech is incomprehensible (3); or their dialect sounds comical (13, 20, 64). Moreover, the enemy's linguistic incompetence renders him an easy dupe (96).

Religion, like language, can also serve to distinguish "us" from "them". War legends clearly underline religious differences. Lutheran narrators may denounce the enemy for desecrating the church; but, even more common are depictions of "Finns" who burn the Greek Orthodox chapel with the congregation still inside (71) or destroy monasteries during Orthodox Easter celebrations. The narrator's point of view determines how the event is perceived – a heroic feat or wanton destruction.

> During the time of the Koljo battle, the Russians set up their main camp at the Iisalmi parish. They broke all the church windows, hacked away at all the doors, the floor boards, and used them, as well as the fence surrounding the church, as firewood. (77)

> During the time of the Great Wrath, the Russians made short work of the altar books with their sabers. (79)

> In Pielisjärvi, Uusikylä, there is a story about how the Äijänpäivä Lake received its name. During some skirmishes along the border, the Russians had come to the Finnish side and made camp in two adjacent houses with the doors facing each other. Some Finns came along and they saw that the Russians were celebrating Easter in the camp. The Finns blocked the doors and set the camps on fire, killing all the Russians inside. (97)

> ... when the Finnish army set off to destroy the Salovetskoi monastery, which was on an island in the sea, and when they were 30 *versts* from the monastery, the place where you can see domes of the church shining, they said: You won't be shining at this time tomorrow, instead, you'll be going up in smoke to the sky. (80)

Way of Life, Appearance, Region

Culture can dictate aesthetic sensibility. Therefore, the enemy's appearance, characterized by an unfamiliar style of dress and a long beard, may, in the eyes of the narrator, look downright odd. Rarely do the texts call attention to the appearance of the narrator's own group. When this occurs, it is usually only an oblique reference embedded in the plot. Such narratives call attention to physical features, such as hair color, that is, blond versus dark, to convey proof of the enemy's slowness of wit: the enemy believes that the swimming escapee is a water fowl (104, 105, 112). Thus, the enemy is implicitly identified as dark-haired and rather dense. The enemy cannot believe that such a light object could be human. Drawing upon only a few basic details, which are of course deemed inferior, the narrator can communicate the outsider's Otherness.

> People were so terrified of the Russian enemy when they were lurking about here, that, even during my childhood, parents would tell their children stories about Russians to get them to behave. They would say things like: "If you're noisy, the tall-hat will come". The stories said that the Russians wore tall hats. They were also called *cynocephalos*. Since the typical Russian had such a keen sense of smell, it was necessary to use fir twigs to disguise your own scent. (111)

> Russians wore dresses with a sash around the waist. They had long beards. Often, they would carry a hatchet and a spear. You could tell a Russian by his smell, as soon as he stepped in the door. The Russians stank because they ate rotten meat and drank flax oil and when they killed an animal they would drink its blood through a straw. (1)

Each human being has a distinctive scent; and this scent may reveal something about his/her diet, health, age, sex and cultural background. Sense of smell can function as a means of making social distinctions; and odors can be easily interpreted as markers of foreign cultures (Le Guérer 1992:24–33).

War legends even portray the enemy's everyday tools with contempt. Such a harsh assessment no doubt stems from the narrator's beliefs, which are in turn influenced by his own ethnic group. Moreover, the narratives also commonly underline the supposed inferiority of the enemy's diet and dwelling place. Narrative accounts of how the "sun shines through the chimney" (2) of the enemy's house attest to their technological backwardness. Countless references are made to their diet: the enemy is depicted as eating with his fingers (25), and mistaking soft soap for sour milk (12). Not only do the enemies have poor table manners, their attitude to food is also considered suspect. The legends also portray them as gluttons unable to curb their appetites. This character flaw also renders the enemy a poor warrior. Indeed, they are even inclined to gorge themselves before a battle and thus forgo all chance at victory (102). The enemy's obsession with food can even be fatal: some narratives describe them leaping from their hiding places in the trees out of a fear of starvation (106–109).

The Otherness of the foreign invaders is further underscored by the narrative portrayals of their bungling ineptitude: the enemy troops ski down a hill along one track and crash into each other (128); they begin a chase in a broken boat (129); they get tangled up in fishing nets while swimming (138); or, they simply display poor marksmanship (120). The narrator's party is familiar with the area whereas the enemies invariably get lost (27), because they are strangers to the region (26) and hence incapable of tracking down the escapees (19), or of finding the escape route known to all the locals (28). Having the survival skills needed in the local environment is a key criterion for belonging to given group. The possession of such skills strengthens group identification. The absence of such vital expertise further undermines the status of a foreign individual or group in the eyes of the local people.

The legends may also highlight the enemy's stupidity. This intellectual inferiority is conveyed in a number of ways. For example, one can easily fool the enemy (27) by wearing shoes the wrong way around. The resulting footprints cause the pursuer to draw the wrong conclusions and set forth in the opposite direction (120). The enemies make themselves an easy target by pushing their way one by one through a gorge (137). When their prisoners break free, they believe that their own men are just making noise (113). The invaders can even be enticed to ski to their doom after a torch tossed into a pit (125). They dive to their death into rapids upon seeing the sign of a shrewd local and cheer: "He made it: I caught a glimpse of the paddle!" (14, 15). As in the international motif[2] the enemy perceives the "forest getting closer". Thus, he is depicted as both foolish and cowardly:

> Both of them took a spruce from the forest and made their way to the Russian houses that stand facing each other. When the Russian guard heard a crackling sound in the woods, he asked his companion "Who do you think is making that noise?" The other replied, "There are many in the woods that crackle: the

elk, the reindeer, the rabbit." The Finns approached from behind the spruce trees and then one of the guards said, "What does it mean when the forest moves closer? The other said: "Don't be silly: the forest does not move." (131)

Not only is an area regionally defined, it is, perhaps even more so, a culturally defined concept. The land settled by an ethnic group is a domain of communication: it is based on the reciprocal contracts and personal experiences concentrated within the area, which creates a horizon of interests (Bausinger 1994:117).

Character and Morality

The enemy is often described as living in dread of the forest (25). Evidence of their cowardliness abounds. For example, in some legends ten men are terrified by a lone guerilla. At night the enemies on the island are struck with terror, they even take flight upon seeing a hardy-looking woman (85–88). They are puzzled by a strange and foreboding dream about headless men (100, 127), or a dream in which "a Swedish pig roots the foundation of a building" (130). According to the war legends, the enemy can easily be spooked and misled by the sight of extra ski tracks in the snow; he will invariably assume that there are as many men as there are ski tracks (81, 36).

Thanks to these narratives, the enemy, that is the Other, emerges as downright unscrupulous. A legend popular in Northeastern Finland further attests to their vile nature. In this example, the enemy seeks to escape the island by firing at his fleeing prisoner, who has managed to steal away with the only boat. He calls to the escapee, "Come back Laurikainen, let's cook some porridge, let's add a pat of butter, let's put a spoon in your hand". Among themselves, however, the enemies whispered: "Oh, if he returns we will pour molten tin into his eyes" (104).

All the qualities used to describe the enemy no doubt express the narrator's sense of superiority. Nevertheless, the narrators knew these people to be "cunning and deceitful" (45). The enemy was a "beast" (44), "more brutal than a Turk" (42). Women were particularly vulnerable. According to the narratives, women could face torture (39, 40), rape, being kidnapped and taken as a wife, or even being sold (69–71) or mutilated, that is, the enemy would chop off their breasts (74). The enemy did not think to spare children or the elderly. According to folklore, the enemy could even spear them to death (35, 36, 44, 45, 48, 57, 74) or subject them to castration (66, 67). Burning prisoners was yet another common practice (58, 72–75); and prisoners would be roasted in an oven (48, 60, 66) or over an open fire (57). They would poke out their prisoners' eyes (61), or nail a victim down by his tongue (63). According to a narrative from Kirvula, the only survivor of the village was a cat (73). Likewise, a Kurkijoki war legend describes the devastation wrought by the Swedes: only one villager and a cow survived (4).

Perhaps the most appalling accounts have to do with beings never encountered in real life: Kalmucks, *cynocephalos*, and the like. According to a narrative from Hiitola, a girl flees the *cynocephalos* by going up the chimney, causing her pursuers to think she has gone directly to heaven (141). A legend from Rantsila also conveys humorous delight in another's misfortune:

> A *cynocephalos* was chasing an old woman. She climbed up a tree right by the water's edge. Her image was reflected in the water. When her pursuer caught up with her, he said: "She came from this direction, went this way, and I can smell her scent right here." Upon seeing her reflection, the *cynocephalos* was convinced that she was (down there) in the water, so he charged in to grab her, but he drowned. And thus the old woman escaped the grasp of the *cynocephalos*. (142)

Among the folk, guerrillas, who were also known as the *kivekkäät*, appear to occupy a mythical reality:

> The *kivekkäät* are no longer with us today. They were savage creatures. And, although they looked human, that is, they had human faces, they were covered with hair. During the famine in Lapland, these beings roamed the entire area of Finland. They were wolf-like predators and if they came upon a solitary wanderer in the woods, they would kill and devour him. (34)

Some of the horrific elements also appear in other folklore genres: magic tales, incantations, and bylinas. A portrayal of a woman's breasts being hacked off is also found in a ballad sung in the Kalevala meter. The enemy who sucks the blood of his victim with a straw recalls the motif used in incantations; such a motif is also used to describe the groom in wedding poems. Personal *chronicates*, on the other hand, recall the tale about the sturdy men who have "flown with birch wings for fun, and sometimes even fallen into the river" (17). Nevertheless, the narratives were usually regarded as true, and even some written sources have negatively portrayed the enemy (Halén 1979; Tarkiainen 1986).

Despite the overwhelmingly negative portrayals of the enemy, some narratives cast the enemy in a more appealing light. The enemy may show kindness to a child; some may offer the woman with a child some bread (30, 31), pay for the slaughtered cow (68), be fair to the brave farmer's wife by giving up plans to rob (88), etc. Gun Herranen has observed similar features in legends about Russians told among the Swedish-speaking Finns (Herranen 1980).

Generally, in war legends the narrator's own reference group appears as morally victorious. The definition of this group, however, is far from comprehensive. In fact, "our" ethnic identity receives scant attention except for allusions to highly esteemed traits such as bravery, know-how and resourcefulness. Thus the identity of the narrator's group emerges in stark contrast to the representations of a strange Other. Although physical appearance commonly surfaces as a criterion of identity, the fundamental markers of identity seem to be cultural, that is, the enemies are unclean, their diet strange, their handiwork skills inferior; they have no respect for human life or religious symbols. Interestingly, however, the enemy is occasionally granted a human face, with positively valued qualities.

The Truth-Value of the Narratives

The war legends make no claims to objectivity – and this clearly emerges in some of the accounts:

> Before the Russians even arrived in this country, wild rumors were circulating about their evil deeds. By repeating these rumors people would frighten each other – even though they were already terrified to begin with. It was rumored that the Russians were on their way and would kill everyone, every living thing. Not even children would be spared, and if they were, that was just as horrible a fate, because then they would be raised by Russians. The Russians were thought to be capable of committing any number of atrocities and so people tried to find all kinds of hiding places, holes in the ground, caves, and the like. When the Russians finally made it here, there was no one to be found. (29)

The qualities ascribed to the antagonists could apply to any given enemy group. Nevertheless, occasionally the narrator does lace the legend with actual cultural details and express his/her misgivings about these foreign ways. The plot can even be hinged on ethnographic features such as the way that dwellings are built so that their doorways face each other, making it easy to block the gable doors, trap the Russian inhabitants inside, and burn them alive. This accurately describes a type of Russian village plan where the houses are located on either side of the main road. A double standard appears to be at work here: such deeds committed by the enemy only confirm existing notions of their cruelty, whereas the same deeds committed by the narrator's own group simply show bravery and shrewdness. Although the enemy is often described as Russian, essentially the same features are ascribed to the *ruotsit*, "robbers" or "warriors".

In light of the distribution of my materials, the Karelians who settled along the Swedish-Finnish and Russian border were the key narrators of war legends. It is important to recall, however, that the historical eras of the borderlands have blurred the inhabitants' consciousness of their ethnicity. Thus the role of war legends in the process of ethnic self-awareness must be approached with some reserve.

The 1930s – the period when the greater part of the material was collected – witnessed a burgeoning interest in Finnish national culture. No doubt, the political climate had an impact on the shades of meaning attached to the ethnonyms. This partially explains the positive/negative notions associated with the term "Finn" and "Russian", respectively. Furthermore, this drift is not only evident in actual accounts of battles, but also in raids and other conflicts. Ulla-Maija Peltonen has noted that in this material the enemy is invariably a Russian (or a Cossack) (Peltonen 1996:190). According to earlier variants collected in Russian Karelia, the enemies were defined as Swedes – or even Karelians. What constitutes a Karelian, however, has always been rather obscure. In other words, there is no absolute Karelian identity. The concept remains vague even among contemporary Finnish-Karelians. In World War II Finland ceded parts of Karelia to the Soviet Union, after which the inhabitants of Salmi parish, for instance, crossed the new border to live within the Finnish border. When interviewed by Kaija Heikkinen, they used the terms "Karelian", "Finn", "Russian" and "Swede" according to the context (Heikkinen 1989:354). Although the narrative milieu of war legends is more or less "Karelian", contrasting different ethnic groups is not their main function. Ethnonyms for the Other often describe active subjects, but their Otherness is ultimately determined by other factors.

War legends as such do not seem to make up the substance of ethnic awareness. What then could be their relationship to the process of ethnic consciousness? The relationship between the narratives and ethno-historical reality can provide a few clues. The term for the conflict described in the war legends can be neutral, such as the "time of persecution" or "war time", but just as well a historically documented confrontation such as Swedish/Finnish War, The Battle of Koljo or variations on the Great Wrath (1714–1721). "Border fight" or "Russian fire" may refer to an ethnic conflict, but the latter, as in the case of the "fire war", only refers to an inter-group conflict. Just as many terms are associated with spontaneous raids: robbery, banditry etc. The stories need not refer to actual state wars. Even if the narrated incidents have purportedly taken place at various times and in various places, they are thematically, particularly when it comes to horrific elements, exceptionally uniform. Locality is one of the central features of various types of war legends, and the members of the narrator's own group or neighboring groups can be named individuals. Nevertheless, these horror stories are seldom personal narratives.

This particular issue can be further illuminated by a study of the Finnish Civil War (1918) narratives collected in the 1960s: these texts share thematic similarities with Karelian war legends. According to Ulla-Maija Peltonen's findings, the Civil War narratives only add two new motifs to the 17 horrific motifs from those of previous wars (Peltonen 1996:198). Now, however, the opposing forces are identified from a social rather than an ethnic perspective. In spite of the fact that the proportion of Russian soldiers was not particularly significant, the working class "Reds" were associated with the Russians by the "White" upper class. Peltonen underscores the significance of group identity in recollected narration. According to her, a group-bound reality was constructed through narration. Narratives were made up of the narrators' collective assumptions, characteristic of the social group in question. In this conceptual material the folkloric themes were used and adapted to support the interpretation. The narration itself was formed to be a supporting factor to identity (Peltonen 1996:280–287). The traditional images of horror proved useful in verbalizing the differences between one's own group and the other. The aim was not so much to arrive at describing the qualities of the Other, but to describe the features not describing the Self. Oral tradition is thus a material paradigm, of which the motifs are to be picked up. Explanatory legends, beliefs, joking lore, as well as magic tales have been equally useful.

The process is hardly unique. Even contemporary newspaper articles about ethnic conflicts world-wide deal with similar issues. Viewed from a distance, the ethnic differences between various groups are unclear, but the media portrayal of the horrors of war undeniably recall the variations on Karelian ethno-historical themes.

A Mental Border, Placing the Other

The Finnish archival data has been gathered with a certain type of legend in mind. Free narration might have produced another kind of text. The opinions expressed in the legends are filtered through both the demands of narration and the narrator's later experiences. The archive materials, however, tell us nothing about the narrator's home environment, social status, or possible educational background (e.g. the influence of newspapers) and how these factors would have influenced the narratives. Thus, over time, many factors contribute to the development of the archived war legends. Of course, this material can tell us little about the real aims of the narrators. Evidently, the narrative purpose is hardly to delineate the actual characteristics of the enemy; instead, the aim is to verbally express general contempt. War legends conversely serve as cultural representations of the narrator's own ethnic group: by contrasting the "familiar" and the "strange", they serve as markers of engagement. More important than the content of a cultural motif would appear to be its significance as a distinguishing factor – and its emphasis during a time of crisis. The Other cannot make it in the local conditions, cannot function and behaves inappropriately. Because he does not share the same cultural heritage and knowledge, he is peculiar in every way: he is Other, not one of "Us".

Although the actual contents of war legends cannot be considered the verbalizations of group identity, their narration may be a means of acknowledging Otherness. War legends provide a possible answer to a fundamental question: who are we? Traditions are constructed to bind individuals to the collective (Anttonen 1996:20, Ilomäki 1993:51–52, 1994:105). Such an awareness does not arise from a clearly identifiable ethnic identity, but instead, a sense of belonging to one cultural group evolves from a sense of stark separation from another. In other words, it is a triggered response: thus, only when in contact with the Other, does one need to perceive differences. In a crisis situation, the legends negatively affirm group identity: the enemy is the negation of the self. When faced with another ethnic group, one's own ethnic identity emerges as the defining and supportive measure of group identity. Awareness of cultural belonging thus becomes not only a useful but also a necessary foundation for ethnicity. Barth rightly says that ethnicity appears as a communal structure of cultural difference (Barth 1996:13). Perhaps "ethnicity" is ultimately an umbrella concept, under which many levels of consciousness of the we-concept can fit.

The possible variations on traditional elements to describe the Other according to local details make war legends useful in strengthening identity. Ethnic identity is built into the texts through familiarity, in the realm of a shared language, religion and customs. Even today the relationship between ethnic commitments and political realities can potentially lead to tragedy.

Translated by Leila Virtanen.

NOTES

[1]   The texts are numbered to indicate the precise archive references at my disposal.
[2]   Also in Shakespeare's "Macbeth" and the Japanese film director Akira Kurosawa.

BIBLIOGRAPHY

Andersson, Vibeke 1992: Udvandrere, livsformer og kultur. In Kulturbegrebet. Nord Nytt 45.
Anttonen, Pertti 1996: Introduction: Tradition and Political Identity. P. Anttonen (ed.) Making Europe in Nordic Contexts. Nordic Institute of Folklore. NIF Publications 35. Turku.
Barth, Frederik 1969: Ethnic groups and boundaries. The social organization of culture difference. Universitetsforlaget. Oslo
–   1996: Enduring and emerging issues in the analysis of ethnicity. H. Vermeulen – C. Govers (eds) The anthropology of ethnicity: Beyond 'Ethnic groups and boundaries'. Het Spinhuis. Amsterdam.
Bausinger, Hermann 1994: Region – Kultur – Eg. In Österreische Zeitschrift für Volkskunde 97.
Bromberger, Christian – Centlivres, Pierre – Collombo, Gérard 1989: Entre le local et le global: les figures de l'identité. In L'autre et le sembable. Regards sur l'ethnographie des sociétés contemporaines. Presses du CNRS. Paris.
Cohen, Anthony P. 1996: Boundaries of consciousness, consciousness of boundaries'. Critical questions for anthropology. H. Vermeulen – C. Govers (eds) The anthropology of ethnicity: Beyond 'Ethnic groups and boundaries'. Het Spinhuis. Amsterdam.
Dundes, Alan 1983: Defining identity through folklore. A. Jakobson-Widding (ed.) Identity: personal and sociocultural. A symposium. Acta Universitatis Upsaliensis. Uppsala studies in cultural anthropology 5. Uppsala.
Dwyer, Peter D. 1979: Animal metaphors: An evolutionary model. In Mankind 12. Annick Le Guérer 1992, Scent. The mysterious and essential powers of smell. New York, Turtle Bay books.
Hakamies, Pekka 1993: Venäjän-Taipaleelta Viinijärvelle. Erään karjalaisryhmän identiteetistä ja assimilaatiosta. Suomalaisen Kirjallisuuden Seura (Suomi 168). Helsinki.
Halén, Harry 1979: Idän vierasheimoisten vierailuista Suomessa Venäjän sotaväen mukana. In Historiallinen aikakausikirja 77.
Heikkinen, Kaija 1989: Karjalaisuus ja etninen itsetajunta. Salmin siirtokarjalaisia koskeva tutkimus. University of Joensuu Joensuun yliopiston humanistisia julkaisuja 9. Joensuu.
Herranen, Gun 1980: Historical legends expressing nationalism in a minority culture. Folklore on two continents. N. Burlakoff – C. Lindahl (eds) Essays in honour of Linda Dégh. Trickster Press. Bloomington. Indiana.
Holy, Ladislaw – Stuchlik, Milan 1983: Actions, norms and representations. Foundations of anthropological inquiry. Cambridge University Press.
Ilomäki, Henni 1993: Oudot vieraat meidän mailla. In Kauas on pitkä matka. Kirjoituksia kahdesta kotiseudusta. Suomalaisen Kirjallisuuden Seura. Kalevalaseuran vuosikirja 72. Helsinki.
–   1994: The war between us and the other. U. Bratislawa (ed.) Folklore in the identification process of society. Ústav etnologie SAV. Etnologické stúdie 1.
Kirkinen, Heikki 1970: Karjala idän ja lännen välissä. Kirjayhtymä. Helsinki.
Klinge, Matti 1972: Ryssänviha. In Vihan veljistä valtiososialismiin. Yhteiskunnallisia ja kansallisia näkemyksiä 1910- ja 1920-luvuilla. WSOY. Porvoo & Helsinki.
Le Guérer, Annick 1992: Scent: the mysterious and essential powers of smell. Translated from French by Richard Miller. Turtle Bay Books. New York.

Lotman, Juri 1975: On the metalangue of a typological description of culture. Semiotica 14.

Mäntylä, Jyrki 1959: Paikannimisananparret impilahtelaisen aineiston valossa. Kalevala-seuran vuosikirja 39.

Nygren, Anja 1988: Etnisyys ryhmän ominaisuutena: konseptuaalinen analyysi. Kulttuuri-antropologian pro gradu -tutkielma. Helsingin yliopisto.

Peltonen, Ulla-Maija 1996: Punakapinan muistot. Tutkimus työväen muistelukerronnan muotoutumisesta vuoden 1918 jälkeen. Suomalaisen Kirjallisuuden Seuran Toimituksia 657. Helsinki.

Poutignat, Philippe – Streiff-Fenart, Jocelyne 1995: Théories de l'ethnicité. Paris, Presses Universitaires de France. Paris.

Pöllä, Matti 1995: Vienan Karjalan etnisen koostumuksen muutokset 1600–1800-luvulla. Suomalaisen Kirjallisuuden Seuran Toimituksia 635. Helsinki.

Sananlaskut 1978. Suomalaisen Kirjallisuuden Seuran Toimituksia 346. Helsinki.

Tarkiainen, Kari 1986: Se Wanha Wainooja. Käsitykset itäisestä naapurista Iivana Julmasta Pietari Suureen. Suomen Historiallinen Seuran Historiallisia tutkimuksia 132. Helsinki.

Thadden von, Rudolf 1991: Aufbau nationaler Identität. Deutschland und Frankreich im Verleich. B. Giesen (ed.) Nationale und kulturelle Identität: Studien zur Entwicklung des kollektiven Bewusstseins in der Neuzeit Suhrkamp. Frankfurt am Main.

Voionmaa, Väinö 1969 (1915): Suomen karjalaisen heimon historia. WSOY. Helsinki.

Witherspoon, G. J. 1971: Navajo categories of objects at rest. In American Anthropologist 73.

PEKKA HAKAMIES

Proverbs and Mentality

Paremiologists often emphasize the fact that proverbs reflect the attitudes of their users towards fundamental concerns of human life (Röhrich – Mieder 1977:3; Basgöz 1990:11). This inherent quality of proverbs has prompted paremiologists to try and understand "national character" or "national psychology" through proverbs. Often, however, the results of such studies have been unconvincing. Archer Taylor, for example, was rather skeptical about such an approach (Taylor 1931:164–168). Friedrich Seiler was also critical of some earlier studies (Seiler 1922:286–289). Mieder and Röhrich are also doubtful about the possibility of studying this field (Röhrich – Mieder 1977:71). Michal Wulff's book provides a survey of paremiological studies concerning "national character" (Wulff 1990:42–47).

One of the weaknesses of these studies is their lack of a clear definition for "national character". What kinds of things or entities are we dealing with when studying national traits? If we were to attempt to characterize in more detail or to devise more precise definitions for the rather indeterminate concepts of "national character" or "national psychology", we would soon perceive that we are working in a domain shared by those who study mentality. In other words, we are working with the unconscious or partially conscious collective and fundamental attitudes and ways of thinking that are resistant to change. If some additions or specifications were to be added to the definition, many studies concerning "national character" could be included under the above title Proverbs and Mentality. However, "mentality" may refer to a smaller cultural crosssection than "national character" or "national psychology". In general, "national character" appears to be a broader concept than mentality and research on the latter has focused more narrowly on some aspect of "national character".

So far, researchers of mentality have yet to provide an accurate definition of their research target. For example, in his empirical study on the "Swedish mentality", Åke Daun uses the term without a definition but to some extent synonymously with the concepts "world view", "national character" or "central attitudes" (Daun 1989). Mentality has perhaps been less defined than characterized, i.e., by itemizing some of the central properties of the concept. According to these characteristics, mentalities are long-term, unconscious or pre-conscious mental constructions. Mentality is a way of thin-

Myth and Mentality
Studia Fennica
Folkloristica 8, 2002

king and a way of judging phenomena that is shared by a large group which changes its way of thinking slowly or which remains unchanged over a long period of time. Mentalities are fundamental attitudes. Citing Anders Floren and Mats Persson, Juha Manninen lists the following properties of mentality: they are everyday phenomena such as norms, attitudes and manners; they are shared by large communities; they are resistant to change and they are unconscious or preconscious (Manninen 1989:67). Michel Vovelle characterizes mentality as an unconscious collective representation which is resistant to change (1990:7–9). Nevertheless, these are only a few explications of the concept, not shared by all mentality researchers, and in general the content of the concept is still vague (c.f. Peltonen 1992:14–15; Knuuttila 1994:54–56).

Presumably there are only a few examples of paremiological research on "mentality". In Franziska Baumgarten's article, *A Proverb Test for Attitude Measurement*, the concept of *mentality* refers to those personality traits which express moral tendency – the way of thinking, reasoning and evaluating (Baumgarten 1952). More recently, in his article about proverbs and social history, James Obelkevich has pointed out the possibility of studying mentality or mentalities "in the strong sense." Obelkevich does not regard the concept of mentality as synonymous with "national character," a term he considers to be in disrepute nowadays, but instead something connected with the ethos and world view of a nation, region or single village. (Obelkevich 1994:221.)

In recent years paremiologists have been less concerned with outlining a given national character, but more with the notions associated with some specific, restricted matter which presumably correspond more accurately with the idea of mentality. As a matter of fact, mentality has been studied using proverbs for a long time without actual reference to the term "mentality". In terms of content, analogous studies have been done, such as Matti Kuusi's article on the value of women in Finnish and Ovambo proverbs (Kuusi 1994b) and the article by Pavao Mikic: *Zum Auffassung vom Tod in den Sprichwörtern der serbokroatischen und der deutschen Sprache* (1989). It must be noted, however, scholars have often dealt with this topic without adequately problematizing the domain of research and their own approaches. One specific problem can be addressed by asking whether it is the proverbs or the mentality behind the proverbs that is the actual object of study and whether this issue is truly acknowledged in the first place. For instance, although Mikic's subject is death in proverbs, his starting point is the assumption that proverbs repeat the general idea of the majority of their users (1989:39). Mikic arrives at the conclusion that death proverbs are rather similar in German and Serbo-Croatian languages and that the speakers of both languages believe that death is predestined and inevitable (1989:53). Paremiologists' mentality research has often been somewhat superficial: proverbs are divided thematically into groups and the relations between the groups are then examined. At times this also involves some problematization of the research and the relating of proverbs more deeply to other information connected with the research target.

Paremiologists often begin by assuming that proverbs are the verbal expressions of experience accumulated over a long period of time and that has been passed from one generation to the next with little change. It is easy to find individual examples of proverbs having been in use for centuries or even millennia. On the other hand, however, we can notice changes in emphasis during the last few centuries (Kuusi 1994a). In his article, Obel-kevich tries to trace the arrival of new proverbs in England during past centuries and some tendencies of the change (1994:224–226). Mentality is often thought to be quite resistant (for the longue durée -view, see Vovelle 1990:126–153). Mentality researchers have blamed anthropologists and especially folklorists for having exaggerated the stability of the old death system (Vovelle 1990:68). This mistake could be avoided by making more comparisons between the proverb materials collected during different historical periods-an approach, which until now, has been fairly rare.

When discussing the use of proverbs in mentality research we must first decide whether proverbs actually reflect mentality and how. In principle, there are two ways of doing this. One possibility is based on the comparison of the results of various empirical studies. Firstly, the researcher explains the mentality expressed by the proverbs and then finds further evidence to support the assumption about the community's mentality. For example, in his study of Moroccan proverbs, Edward Westermarck states that it is necessary to understand the culture being researched and that one should not draw conclusions about a people's way of thinking only from their proverbs (1930:52). Friedrich Seiler also makes the same point (1922:294). In actual research this relates mainly to the study of individual proverbs and their meaning and significance for the speech community.

This approach has its problems. Even if proverbs can reveal an aspect of the user's way of thinking, this hardly means that proverbs are always the most reliable key to this knowledge. If the results gained from proverbs must be controlled using extensive comparative material, we may wonder whether proverbs are still relevant in mentality research. After all, there is always the possibility that the study of mentality based on proverb materials and supported by additional information is simply turned upsidedown to create a study of how the proverbs illustrate the already familiar mentality or culture-bound behavior. Something akin to this took place in A.A. Koskenjaakko's study of the law and court in Finnish proverbs (Koskenjaakko 1913). Indeed, some proverbs require so much additional information and explanation that the starting point turns into an explanation of why certain proverb exists.

Another alternative is more emic in its approach. Here, the starting point is the users' own ideas of the proverb's position in the culture in question and the users' idea of their probative force as a reflector of their disposition. For this purpose we need the users' ideas about and definitions of the proverbs. These ideas and definitions do exist and have been documented from a number of different ethnic groups. More evidence can, of course, be obtained from these definitions and characteristics than those put forward by researchers concerning proverbs on the basis of their perceptions. In fact, these properties, i.e., the communicative role of proverbs, offer a logical ground for the use of proverbs in mentality research. On the basis of the general characteristics of the proverb and its role in discourse we can assume that proverbs are indeed relevant material for mentality research. Why would a culture even have these concise and witty sayings regarded as the sum of collective experience and expressing key norms and attitudes if they wholly failed to fulfill these expectations?

Ilhan Basgöz has used proverbs themselves as proof of what the "people" think of proverbs. They, according to him, are *folk definitions of proverbs* (1990). According to Basgöz, proverbs are an inter-cultural phenomenon and many ethnic groups define them in the same way. They are regarded as truthful and valuable words of wisdom based on longterm experience. Accordingly, the Scots make the following claim: "In proverbs the conscience of the people sits in judgment" (Basgöz 1990:11). Although Basgöz is astonished by the similarities between scholarly and popular definitions, the explanation is quite simple: researchers base their characterizations upon users' descriptions and ideas from their own experience. Strictly speaking, proving the reliability of proverbs using proverbs themselves is a vicious circle and logically impossible: a sentence cannot state its own truth value.

In practice mentality research which is based on proverbs always involves a combination of the emic confidence in the properties of the proverbs as a genre of verbal tradition with the empirical validation of the proverbs by other materials. Proverbs must necessarily be related to other information concerning the culture or community in question; when doing ambitious studies of a strange culture, however, proverbs are in danger of remaining mere illustrations. In my opinion the significance of proverbs in mentality research lies in the fact that we can obtain compact material fairly easily for researching different ideas and attitudes. Nevertheless, we cannot rely too heavily upon their validity.

As previously mentioned we cannot make a direct correlation between proverbs and mentality. A study of proverbs may be of little use when trying to understand the actual behavior of a given group of people. Westermarck, for example, cites two examples from his Moroccan study. First of all, he found no Moroccan proverbs underlining the importance of affection between spouses. Secondly, he also notes the existence of the proverbial disapproval of lying. All the same, wives and husbands may love each other and express it, but in their culture public display of or reference to these emotions is forbidden. In general, Westermarck presents numerous examples of how the norms suggested in proverbs are not always followed in actual behavior (Westermarck 1930:52–53). Referring to Westermarck's research, Matti Kuusi voices similar doubts in his comparison of the place of women in Finnish and Ovambo proverbs (1994b). Here the limitations of the proverb material emerge and so does the need for additional information concerning the life of the society or culture in question.

In principle, the scholar attempting to study mentality on the basis of empirical data confronts the same kinds of dilemmas when trying to assess the limitations of the data. What conclusions can be drawn about what people really think on the basis of popular literature, testaments or examination records? (see Vovelle 1990:236).

The research on values and norms within proverbs requires an analysis of the content and meaning of the text; this analysis poses specific difficulties. The figurative or metaphorical nature of proverbs often can hide their real meaning (e.g. Westermarck 1930; Krikmann 1974). This is a central issue in proverb research which will not be discussed here. At times it is impossible without contextual information (examples of usage or explanations of their meaning) to understand the general meaning of proverbs to their users. Semantic problems can be avoided by accepting the analysis of the literal surface meaning of the text and by researching the metaphors and other linguistic devices that are used in proverbs and which may reveal something about their users' way of thinking (c.f. Rooth 1969:xxx–xxxiv).

Paremiologists often determine the representativeness of proverbs by how frequently they are used. Proverb scholars have, without exception, estimated that a proverb's frequency in literature or archive record files correlates fairly directly with its "popularity" amongst people and this, in turn, correlates with the phenomenal domain that we may regard as mentality (e.g. Seiler 1918:59–63; Westermarck 1930:48). Matti Sarmela in his article where he uses quantitative argumentation has commented on the differences between the cultural climates of Western and Eastern Finland: "Changes in the norms and values of knowledge transmitted by oral tradition could perhaps best be demonstrated by comparing proverbial sayings with their diffusion, age and popularity in different regions" (1974:98).

Accordingly, Pentti Leino has dealt with the representativeness of proverb material and, unlike many others, he has problematized the matter to some degree (1970:45). According to Leino, the amount of records generally indicates a proverb's rate of frequency, and, despite its shortcomings, this approach is extremely useful. Arvo Krikmann also considers the relation between archival records and the "ontological population", that is, the actual folklore tradition; problematic but in his opinion, too, statistical information can be used as grounds for making conclusions (Krikmann 1985:4).

In his work, Matti Kuusi strongly advocates the use frequency of proverbs suggested by the volume of archival records as a relatively reliable measure of their popularity. Kuusi states that "as exhibits of national psychology the well-known *Ei ole koiraa karvoihin katsomista* (literally: "You shouldn't look at a dog's fur") and the elsewhere well-known, though rare in Finland *Punatukkane ee piäse taevaasee* (literally: "Redheads can't get to heaven") belong to completely different classes" (1994a). Kuusi initially used this type of argumentation in his 1953 article on changes in popularity of proverbs (in English: Kuusi 1994a). In this article, however, he expresses some doubts about the correlation between a given proverb's actual popularity and the amount of records. Later (1981) he becomes even more doubtful about the evidence offered by an item's frequency. Although they are always relative and rough, they can provide important information. *Proverbia Septentrionalia,* which is a monumental report on the common proverbs of the Baltic-Finnish peoples, is specifically based upon the number of records (Kuusi 1985).

Nevertheless, the connection between the amount of records, "popularity" of proverbs and their mental representativeness is presumably more complex.

On the one hand, we can consider the reliability of the material edited by individual collectors; yet, on the other hand, we must also acknowledge those general features that have influenced the accumulation of data. Conclusions about the popularity of the proverbs and hence about their representativeness are especially difficult to make if only published, literary material is available. In that case the tendencies of individual editors and collectors can more greatly distort the mentality presented in the books by a sample of proverb texts. Also, it is difficult to draw any conclusions about the popularity of a proverb text cited in a book. A great number of similar texts may be a sign of its popularity and the true norm behind the proverbs, but it is also theoretically possible for a single proverb to represent a fundamental communal norm or value. In a proverb collection lacking mention of popularity or representativeness we are left without this information.

Many scholars have noted the similarities between proverbs from various nations, especially when the study concerns neighboring nations. On the other hand, as Friedrich Seiler (1922:286) has remarked, the differences between social classes or groups within a nation can be greater than those between different nations. Moreover, there hardly exists any whole, coherent world view or mentality behind the proverb tradition. Although proverbs do express particular truths, proverbs from the same culture often have contradictory or incompatible messages. This is their natural property as they, like folklore in general, are thought to be polyphonic, that is, various attitudes and norms compete and constant negotiations are going on about the common or ruling position. Nevertheless, there are grounds to assume that this process of negotiation can lead in different directions, and common values and attitudes can receive varying emphasis on the whole. This means that although there is no uniform world view represented by the proverbs, it can be supposed that the proverbs of different groups of people to some extent represent different values and norms which can be regarded as mental differences between these groups.

For the most part, proverbial representations of mentality have been studied with a national focus, ostensibly because most published materials represent the proverb tradition of a given nation. The study of mental differences in a nation should be based either on comprehensive regional or local publications of proverbs – or proverb collections of certain social groups – or on well-organized archive materials. This is impossible in many cases, and paremiologists generally must accept the nation as a relevant unit of mentality research.

My own experiment, a comparative analysis of Russian and Finnish proverbs, is based on published materials, "Sananlaskut" (Proverbs; Laukkanen – Hakamies 1978) and "Russkije poslovicy" (Dal' 1984). The study focuses on the gendered organization of the household, the economy and the society at large, and the relations between the sexes. Using the source literature, I have selected all the proverbs concerning these topics, using a total of 140 Finnish and 339 Russian items.

For systematic analysis this material was divided on the basis of content into thematic groups, and in each group the percentage of the texts was calculated in comparison with the whole material of each nation. Of course, this process of choosing texts, analyzing their content and thematic grouping involves a certain subjectivity, so the results are not to be considered too exact.

The proverbs from both nations share a male point of view: the woman appears as an inferior being designed to obey man. Only the Russian material occasionally provides a female perspective. The following table shows the most prominent differences between Russian and Finnish proverbs. Included are those groups which show a marked dissimilarity between these national traditions.

Table 1. Pronounced differences between Russian and Finnish materials

Theme of the content	Finnish material	Russian material
Woman is troublesome	14	14
Woman is a joy	4	6
Woman keeps house	6	3
Woman is talkative	4	6
Woman is dull	14	4
Woman quarrels	1	7
Woman has to be hit	3	6
Woman's wealth is quickly used up	9	2
Division of labor – woman cannot do man's work	15	2
Woman has her husband as protection	0	2
Love between spouses	0	6
Wife rules husband	6	9
Poor widow	0	6
Widow as a potential spouse	11	4
Wife has to work hard	6	1
Wife's death is no problem	3	0
Wife is nice to take but bad to keep	4	0
Wife has a tough lot	2	4
Total	98 %	82 %

The most salient differences concern the emphasis on economic matters and the division of labor, as well as the lack of Finnish proverbs dealing with emotions in comparison with the Russian material. The Finnish proverbs underline women's inability to do men's work. The Finnish proverbs reveal a profound division between the two sexes with men largely representing the positive qualities and women the negative. The woman is usually referred to with the pejorative term *akka* ("hag") as in proverbs such as *Akka mies aseeton* ("An unarmed man is a hag") or *Akka tieltä kääntyköön, vaan ei mies ikinä* ("An old woman may falter along the path, but never a man".) (Laukkanen – Hakamies 1978:9, 11.) Finnish proverbs depict the widow solely in the role of a potential spouse, whereas Russian proverbs offer a wider array of roles – and often from a female perspective.

Some of the proverb themes require commentary. For example, the rapid depletion of the wife's dowry is a key theme in Finnish proverbs. The theme alludes to the times when wives were economically dependent on their husbands and men had the right to use their wives' property as they saw fit. As the following proverb says, some men apparently exercised this right to excess: *Vaimon perintö kestää tuomaanpäiväst jouluun* ("Wife's inheritance lasts from Thomas's day to Christmas"; i.e., just a few days; Laukkanen – Hakamies 1978:505).

Proverbs about husbands using physical violence to control or discipline their wives are a rare occurrence in the Finnish material. Nevertheless, the few that do depict such violence are rather playful: *Akkoa ja kissoa piteä lyöjä aina kun muulta työltä joutoa, jos ne ei o tehny pahoa nin ne meinoa* ("Cats and wives should be beaten whenever possible – even if they have yet to cause some trouble, they are about to"; Laukkanen – Hakamies 1978:10). Expressions of violence appear more frequently in Russian proverbs, as though such use of force were a normal part of life: *"Subu bej – teplje, zenu bej – mileje"* (Hit the fur – it will be warmer, hit the wife – she will be lovelier; Dal' 1984 I:291).

The results presented in the table in a compressed form may have been distorted by various factors, beginning from the biased collection and publication of the proverbs. Possible causes for misleading analyses have already been noted. Nevertheless, the results can provide us with a sense of the proverb traditions of both nations, which, in turn should correlate with their respective mentalities. Some of the differences between the Russian and Finnish materials could be explained by their differing social history during the 19th century, when most of the proverbs were collected, especially in Russia. After all, because the Russian peasants lived under serfdom, a system which involved considerable violence, their proverbs may convey such attitudes. Also, it can be assumed that the status of the widow has been different in these neighboring countries.

When evaluating the results, the above-mentioned methodological problems and reservations need to be kept in mind. As Westermarck and Kuusi have noted, not all topics are suitable for public discussion. Emotional relations between the spouses may be just one of those delicate issues, as Westermarck had noted.

In conclusion, I would like to claim that proverbs provide relevant and interesting data for mentality studies, as long as the many-sided problems involved with their use are taken into account. The argumentation should mostly be based on a quantitative analysis and from comprehensive materials. Individual proverb types can rarely provide enough evidence about a group's mentality. As an exception and a practical illustration of mentality I would like to draw attention to the following proverb: *Räkänokastakin mies tulee muttei tyhjän naurajasta* ("Man comes from a sniveler, but not from an empty scoffer") – even if the child has a runny nose, he can later be a brave man, but not if he laughs without reason. Can coincidence alone explain its popularity in Finland – over three-hundred archived items collected from all over the country – and rarity or non-existence among the neighboring countries? In fact, there are only two Estonian references to the proverb and no similar proverbs are even known among the neighboring peoples (Kuusi 1985 No. 380). Could the proverb be yet another expression of the Finnish – as opposed to Russian or Estonian – disapproval of openly expressing positive feelings?

Translated by Gregory Watson.

BIBLIOGRAPHY

Basgöz, Ilhan 1990: Proverbs about Proverbs or Folk Definitions of Proverb. Proverbium 7.

Baumgarten, Franziska 1952: A Proverb Test for Attitude Measurement. Personnel Psychology 5.

Dal', Vladimir 1984: Poslovicy russkogo naroda. Hudozestvennaja literatura.

Daun, Åke 1989: Svensk mentalitet. Ett jämförande perspektiv. Simrishamn.

Knuuttila, Seppo 1994: Tyhmän kansan teoria. Näkökulmia menneestä tulevaan. Vaasa.

Koskenjaakko, A.A. 1913: Sananlaskututkimuksia I. Laki, oikeus ja oikeudenkäynti suomalaisissa sananlaskuissa. Suomalaisen Kirjallisuuden Seura. Helsinki.

Krikmann, Arvo 1974: On Denotative Indefiniteness of Proverbs (Preprint 1); Some Additional Aspects of Semantic indefiniteness of Proverbs (Preprint 2). Academy of Sciences of The Estonian SSR. Institute of Language and Literature. Tallinn.

– 1985: Some Statistics on Baltic-Finnic Proverbs. Academy of Sciences of the Estonian S.S.R. Division of Social Sciences. Preprint KKI-36. Tallinn.

Kuusi, Matti 1953: Sananparsien suosionmuutoksia. Virittäjä.

– 1981: Zur Frequenzanalys. Proverbium Paratum 2.

– 1985: Proverbia Septentrionalia. 900 Balto-Finnic Proverb Types with Russian, Baltic, German and Scandinavian Parallels. FFC 236. Helsinki.

– 1994a: Variations in the popularity of Finnish proverbs. Mind and Form in Folklore. Selected Articles. Studia Fennica Folkloristica 3. Pieksämäki .

– 1994b: The Place of Women in the Proverbs of Finland and Ovamboland. Mind and Form in Folklore. Selected Articles. Studia Fennica Folkloristica 3. Pieksämäki.

Laukkanen, Kari – Hakamies, Pekka 1978: Sananlaskut. Suomalaisen Kirjallisuuden Seura. Helsinki.

Leino, Pentti 1970: Strukturaalinen alkusointu Suomessa. Folklorepohjainen tilastoanalyysi. Suomalaisen Kirjallisuuden Seura. Helsinki.

Manninen, Juha 1989: Tiede, maailmankuva, kulttuuri. J. Manninen – M. Envall – S. Knuuttila Maailmankuva kulttuurin kokonaisuudessa. Jyväskylä.

Mikic, Pavao 1989: Zur Auffassung vom Tod in den Sprichwörtern der serbokroatischen und der deutschen Sprache. Proverbium 6.

Obelkevich, James 1994: Proverbs and Social History. W. Mieder (ed.) Wise Words. Essays on the Proverb. New York – London.

Peltonen, Matti 1992: Matala katse. Kirjoituksia mentaliteettien historiasta. Tampere.

Rooth, Anna Birgitta 1969: Ordspråk från södra Sverige. Lund.

Röhrich, Lutz – Mieder, Wolfgang 1977: Sprichwort. Stuttgart. Metzler.

Sarmela, Matti 1974: Folklore, Ecology and Superstructures. Finnish Folkloristics 2. Studia Fennica 18. Helsinki.

Seiler, Friedrich 1918: Das deutsche Sprichwort. Strassburg.

– 1922: Deutsche Sprichwörterkunde. C.H. Beck. München.

Taylor, Archer 1931: The Proverb. Cambridge, Mass.

Vovelle, Michel 1990: Ideologies and Mentalities. Worcester.

Westermarck, Edward 1930: Wit and Wisdom in Morocco. A Study of Native Proverbs. London.

Wulff, Michal 1990: Das Sprichwort Im Kontext der Erziehungstradition. Frankfurt am Main.

Expressions of Love
and Sexuality

ANNELI ASPLUND

Changing Attitudes to Love in Finnish Folk Songs

L ove continues to prevail as one of the foremost themes in today's popular vocal music. In fact, the theme has eclipsed all others since the emergence of this genre of singing in the 1920s. In Finland, modern popular music owes a great deal to the folk songs of the pre-industrial era. A study of these folk songs can reveal how traditional forms had to make way for modern popular music. Initially, popular music became fashionable in the cities, but thanks to the record industry, it also quickly captivated the tastes of rural youth. Since that time, no other subject has been able to usurp the place of love in the lyrics of popular and vocal music (Nordenstreng 1966:36–57).

The depictions of amorous themes in the most archaic folk poetry composed by agrarian folk have generally been characterized as meager and restrained. Although songs conveying an earthy and sensuous exuberance were composed in the Kalevala meter, these are a minority from the most recent layer of poems (Kuusi 1963:390–391; Hako 1963:429). How did the vast gulf between these extremely different attitudes to love (from the Early Kalevala period to popular music) develop? When and how did love emerge as a topical theme in Finnish folk songs? Do the various periods of folk poetry differ dramatically when it comes to notions about family, fidelity, infidelity and emotions in general? I attempt to answer these questions by studying epic poetry from both eastern (Savo) and western Finland, as well as epic poetry from Ladoga and Northern Karelia, which has been published in *Suomen Kansan Vanhat Runot* ("The Ancient Poems of the Finnish People"). My source for the newer Finnish folk songs is the volume entitled *Balladeja ja arkkiveisuja. Suomalaisia kertomalauluja* ("Ballads and Broadsides: Finnish Narrative Popular Songs").[1]

By the 17th century, archaic singing traditions were already beginning to decline in western Finnish folk culture. However, these traditions were best maintained in the eastern parts of the country, i.e., in Savo, Karelia and Ingria. Historical circumstances, such as evacuations, played a significant role in both changing and preserving oral traditions. Nevertheless, the songs – like all traditions – must be analyzed as products of a particular cultural environment. Like their ecosystems, the songs have also undergone structural changes (Sarmela 1994:189). Since areas of eastern Finland have been sanctuaries for some of the country's most ancient pre-agrarian cultural

Myth and Mentality
Studia Fennica
Folkloristica 8, 2002

practices, we can also assume that oral traditions from other parts of Finland have also been preserved in the eastern regions. So far, folklore research shows that the most effective method of investigating the history of a given item of folklore, is to compare the various phases of its development from region to region. In Finland, scholars tend to compare the *runes* (Kalevala metre poems) collected in the western frontiers of Finland, eastern Finland's swidden agricultural regions, and the ancient Kalevala culture of Karelia. (Sarmela 1970:76).[2]

For my present purposes, epic poetry proves more useful than lyric poetry, and hence I touch only lightly on the latter genre.[3]

The Portrayal of Love and the Period Styles of Archaic Finnish Poetry

Period styles of Archaic Finnish folk poetry can only be loosely classified according to corresponding historical developments.[4] The earliest poetic expressions of individual emotions and opinions are from the Early Kalevala period style, about one thousand years ago, and these are largely made up of songs of complaint and cautionary lyric poetry. Some scholars have suggested that the hyperbolic portrayal of emotions may have been incorporated into the poetry from elegiac laments. Although elegies were largely the domain of women, some songs do offer a masculine point of view. The singer of the *Morsiamen moitinta* ("Blaming the Bride") bewails his unhappy lot: instead of marrying a rich and graceful girl, he has wed a woman who is poor, lazy and far from pretty. Happiness in love fails to inspire the singers of this era. Their songs merely give voice to the harshness of daily life. These songs of resignation hardly dwell on hopes for future joy, instead they convey a desire for death (Kuusi 1963:181–192).

The Early Kalevala period style is followed by the Middle Kalevala period style, which is historically associated with the Viking Age. The lyrical themes generally remain the same: poetic expressions of despair and dejection. These songs of complaint were inspired by the sad fates of orphans, the poor, and young brides adjusting to their humble place in the family hierarchy. Most of the songs are about homelessness and the longing for unconditional maternal love. None of the poems depict courtship or love between men and women (Kuusi 1963:260–272).

During the Middle Kalevala period Sampo songs and archetypal heroes began to evolve in the epic genre. These songs are characterized by a masculine, warring spirit particular to the Viking age. The masculine world of epic poems generally has little room for dynamic female figures. However, some songs, such as the song of Ahti and Kyllikki, do have active female subjects. The song depicts the tragedy of the opposing needs and expectations of men and women. A woman's love fails to keep the hero by hearth and home. Seafaring and male camaraderie prevail over Ahti's attachment to his wife. Nevertheless, Kyllikki, a passionate and emotional woman, does bear the responsibility for her husband's departure. Her disenchantment with married life, after her first night with her husband, drives her to commit adultery. Despite the masculine point of view, the portrayal of the female protagonist differs from other contemporary songs and thus signals the advent of a new era in folk poetry. Matti Kuusi remarks on the "highly revolutionary nature of the poem: not only do we have the appearance of a lively female protagonist who speaks, feels, and acts, erotic themes have also have begun to make their way into epic poetry" (Kuusi 1963:216–260; Siikala 1996:180).

The Middle Ages was a time of upheaval in Finland. After all, it was then that the campaign began to convert the pagan Finns to Christianity. The transformations in the spiritual climate subsequently brought about changes in traditional songs. Legendary songs began to make their way to Finland from the west, and their poetic meter, melodies and singing style were modified to suit local singing traditions. In addition, ballads – usually devoted to stories of love – came to Finland largely from Western Europe, but sometimes also from the South and the East. These songs portray Eros as an ardent and destructive fire, destined to lead to tragedy, most often death (Haavio 1952:218–219; Kuusi 1963:273–372).[5]

The prevailing theme in these songs is the love affair between a peasant girl and an unknown seducer. In "The Song of Marketta" Hannus, German of the Isle, seduces the virtuous Marketta, who later gives birth to a child. When is infant abandoned is found, the lovers, instead of admitting to their crime, remain silent. The new-born infant, however, utters the names of its parents. In the song entitled "The Man-Killer", Hannus lulls the household to sleep with his music and then sneaks over to Kaisa. The maiden kills the intruder to preserve her family's honor. "Tuurikkainen's Song" relates the story of a young man on a journey who seduces a young maiden without having any previous knowledge of her identity. Upon realizing that the girl is his own sister, Tuurikkainen commits suicide. "Annikainen's Song" describes how a broken-hearted maiden invokes a powerful storm to drown Kesti, the Hansa merchant who betrayed her. In *Kaloiniemen neito* ("The Killing of the Previous Wife") the Maiden of Kaloiniemi urges her suitor Anterus to kill his wife first. After murdering his wife, Anterus returns to woo the maiden. She rejects him with this disdainful reply: "You killed the woman you married before, and perhaps you'll do the same to me."

These songs impart a harsh and unyielding moral code. The value placed on virtue occasionally goes beyond common sense. For example, Marketta, in the name of chastity, avoids even the most indirect contact with the opposite sex: she refuses to eat bread from a field plowed by a stallion; she will not drink milk from a cow that has been bred, or eat eggs from a hen that has been bred. *Vesitiellä viipynyt* ("The Water Carrier") is a portrayal of extreme parental mistrust: a young woman's parents decline the water she brings to them because they suspect her of dawdling and chatting with a man while running the errand. In the song *Katrin poltto* ("St. Catherine") the female protagonist so fervently wants to preserve her virginity that she would rather be burnt at the stake than be a concubine to Ruma Ruotus (Ugly Herod).

Medieval ballads are also characterized by a spirit of protest against family authority. Devotion to a lover triumphs over obedience and allegiance to kin. A ballad heroine would rather die than marry a loathsome husband chosen by her family. For example, *Inkerin virsi* ("Inkeri's Song") tells the tale of a girl who, despite family pressure, refuses to get married and waits faithfully for the return of her beloved from across the sea. *Myyty neito* ("The Bartered Maiden") depicts a young girl being sold off as chattel to a stranger. She responds by cursing her relatives. In the song *Hirttäytynyt neito* ("The Hanged Maid") a maiden is courted by a boyar's heavy-set son, Riski Riiko. After her mother forces the girl to accept his proposal, the girl hangs herself. Likewise *Taivaanvalojen kosinta* ("Divine Light Courtship") describes a girl's rejection of the man chosen by her family, but chooses instead; a man she already knows and loves.

Family relations are also maligned in ballads such as the *Kuolinsanomat* ("News of Death"). This song juxtaposes a soldier's cool resignation upon hearing of the death of his parents and sibling with the bitter complaint upon the death of his wife. Another good example of the climax-of-relations formula is *Lunastettava neito* ("The Ransomed Bride"); in this case, a girl's materialistic family refuses to pay the ransom to free their imprisoned daughter. Only the girl's beloved is willing to pay the fee for her liberation. The maiden curses her family and blesses her future husband.

The comparison of relations formula in the refrain songs may lay bare a hierarchy of human attachments. The singer's relatives, that is father, mother, sister, brother, and occasionally even more distant kin and his beloved are all up for comparison. In some songs the singer's family members are negatively rendered whereas his beloved is positively rendered; in other songs this is reversed. Regardless, the main stress is on comparison, whether it is a love or hate relationship. Kuusi says "despite their highly regular patterns, these poems, with the exception of actual ballads, convey the power of Eros in a more varied way than any other kind of Finnish folk epic genre" (Kuusi 1977:59–60). Besides offering a portrayal of love, these songs also cast light on the family's significance.

The table (see page 242–243) includes all the songs whose main theme deals with relationships between men and women. Prominent themes in these Kalevala meter songs are the significance of kin: the positive (1) or negative (3), attitude to family, a negative attitude to sexuality (2), and fidelity to the partner (4), or infidelity to the partner (5).

Regarded in this light, medieval songs appear to be heavily laden with Catholic teachings on virtue, i.e., relationships between men and women are regulated by repressive norms on sexuality. Marriage appears largely as a contractual agreement between kin, whereby the preservation of family honor is highly valued. Thus, during the early stages of courtship, young men and women were obliged to consider the interests of their kin. If they dared to ignore family wishes, they had to face the consequences. Nevertheless, the young did protest against these parental principles. Unlike the earlier Middle Kalevala period songs, the medieval epics do dedicate a relatively large amount of verse to amorous themes. Also, the songs appear to have a moral function. Songs about forbidden love were hardly composed for the purposes of mere entertainment: they also served to caution the young, especially girls. As cautionary songs, they appear to express a female point of view; the male protagonist is the cause of the tragedy.

Although epic poetry does undergo some changes in the Middle Kalevala Era in the Medieval Period, lyric poetry basically maintains the same conventions (Kuusi 1963:352–381; Kuusi 1977:50–59). The later medieval songs do exhibit some new features despite the tenacity of worry, sorrow, yearning and death as basic themes. As Kuusi has noted, "love is no longer viewed as the ornamental and tragic theme of ballads or as a passionate attachment to be morally condemned." Instead, these songs now convey a humorous and pragmatic view of life (Kuusi 1963:382). Unlike the pre-Christian days, love is no longer consigned to silence. This era even engendered a number of wanton and lyrical love songs. *Jos mun tuttuni tulisi* ("If the one I know came now") is by far the most memorable because of its poignant and impassioned expression of longing. The song was even translated into German by Goethe (Kuusi 1963:388). Attitudes towards love and sexuality seem to have relaxed during the late Middle Ages. The only obvious example of this found in epic poetry, however, would be *Neito ja lohikäärme* ("The Maid and the Dragon"). This poem is the only known comic ballad composed in the Kalevala meter: a wayward maiden has been condemned to the dragon's lair. Instead of devouring the maiden, however, the beast deems her lover guilty and refuses to harm her.

A New Singing Tradition

During the late 1500s and early 1600s a new style of singing appeared and gradually took the place of the ancient songs of the Kalevala meter. A European stanzaic and rhymed style of singing first arrived on the shores of western Finland via Sweden, and then spread to the eastern regions of the country at the end of the 1700s (Hako 1963:443; Asplund 1981:64–78). Although there were radical changes in style and melody, the rhyming narrative songs maintained their medieval content.

Of particular interest are the songs which were first incorporated into Finnish tradition during the Middle Ages; these were sung in the Kalevala meter and the singers also continued to employ conventional stylistic techniques. Thematically similar songs, such as 'Little Katri' – already mentioned as a Kalevala meter song "St. Catherine" *Katrin poltto* ("The Burning of Catherine"), were composed using new stylistic techniques. Like its counterpart in the Kalevala meter, the version in rhyme also stresses Katri's steadfast virtue. She refuses to be tempted by the king and subsequently dies a martyr's death. *Lunastettava neito* ("The Ransomed Bride") also retains the same main motif as the earlier version: her family refuses to pay the ransom fee, but her beloved does.

The rhymed ballad *Morsiamen kuolo* ("The Bride's Death") and the Kalevala meter *Anteruksen virsi* ("The Song of Anterus") share the same central theme. The main protagonist, a young man, discovers that his bride-to-be is ill. On his way home he sees omens of her death. As he reaches his home, he sees her dead body being borne on the bier. The version in the Kalevala meter ends tragically with the young man stabbing himself. The version in rhyme, however, places greater stress on the young man's grief.

Convinced he will never find another woman comparable to his dead bride, he weeps for seven days and dies on the eighth. The lovers are finally united in the same grave.

In addition to surface and metric differences, there are a few functional differences between the Kalevala meter and rhymed versions of the song. The Kalevala meter song serves as a stark reminder to its medieval audience: those who dare to flout convention will be duly punished. According to Martti Haavio, the main protagonist who "cracks the mystery of virginity", i.e., has a premarital affair (Haavio 1955:360–445), ends up losing his loved one. Another ballad from the same group is a newer song called *Vilhelmi ja Liisunen* ("Vilhelmi and Liisunen"), which is thematically close to *Anteruksen virsi* ("The Song of Anterus"). This song also depicts the tragic death of a protagonist who violates the norm.

The importance of virtue also emerges in three other rhymed ballads: *Kreivin sylissä istunut* ("Sat on the Count's Lap"), *Kriivari ja neito* ("The Clerk and the maid") and *Neito ja metsästäjä* ("The Hunter and the Maiden"). In all three songs, the plot revolves around an encounter between a man and a woman in remote surroundings and subsequent attempts at seduction. The songs close with the maiden either accepting or rejecting the young man. In the first two ballads, after initially refusing him, the maiden gives in to the young man's wishes. In the third, the maiden succeeds in preserving her honor (Asplund 1994:140).

On the other hand, *Morsiamen kuolo* ("The Bride's Death"), like two other similar songs, *Surullinen kirje* ("The Sad Letter") and *Nauru ja itku* ("Laugh and Cry"), underline the value of genuine emotion, romantic love and fidelity. *Kaksi kuninkaanlasta* ("The Two Royal Children") is a narrative borne by the theme of a grand and all-consuming love. Two children of kings fall in love but are separated by a river. The prince decides to swim across the river. As he is attempting to cross the river, a villain extinguishes the lamp lit by the shore to guide him and the youth drowns. *Petetty nuorukainen* ("The Betrayed Youth") is yet another ballad underscoring the themes of fidelity and betrayal. The hero slays his betrothed for falling in love with another man during his absence.

Although the songs discussed so far only range from the sober to the tragic, there are a number of comic ballads in Finnish tradition. These establish an alternative world where prevailing moral values are turned upside-down. The ballad entitled *Myllärin tytär ja kosijat* ("The Miller's Daughter") relates the story of an ingenious young man's seduction of a young woman. In spite of her parents' attempts to safeguard her virtue, the young man manages to have his way with her in the dead of night. In the ballad entitled *Sotamies ja talonpojan vaimo* ("The Soldier and the Peasant's Wife") the stranger who arrives at a house manages to cuckold the owner by ravishing the man's wife. A mother urges her daughter to rebel against convention in *Tyttären kosijat* ("The Daughter's Suitors") and *Naimahaluinen tytär* ("The Man-hungry Girl"). The songs applaud characters who achieve their desires through wit and deception. In these ballads, carnal desires eclipse true love, virtue and fidelity.

Nevertheless, the overturned values of the comic songs paradoxically serve to amplify the message of the more "sober-minded" ballads. Although sly seductions, infidelity and extramarital affairs may evoke laughter, the content and style convey their levity. Thus, they were hardly intended to be taken seriously.

The number of narrative songs still available from this period is rather insignificant compared to those composed in the Kalevala meter, hence making it more difficult to draw conclusions about the songs in rhyme than about the older songs. A perusal of the table, however, may provide some clues about the prevailing values of the era. The themes appear to be fidelity in love (4), and the intensifying emotional aspect of romantic love (7). The importance of virtue is still apparent (2), but views on sexuality have become more realistic. There are no longer prohibitions on singing about sexuality. Singers now feel free to poke fun at virtue, infidelity and sexual relationships in general (8).

The Many Forms of Love in the Broadsheet Ballads

The third layer of Finnish narrative songs are the broadsheet ballads. These songs were first transmitted through the printed word and then were gradually assimilated into the oral tradition. This tradition was so short-lived, however, that there was not enough time for any significant changes to take place. The songs started being published during the 1870s and by the 1920s were already a tradition in decline.[6] Even though these sheet ballads may not fit into a narrow definition of folklore, they functioned just like Kalevala meter poetry once did.

In terms of pattern, the broadsheet ballads are remarkably uniform: Two people of different social classes fall in love (a farm hand, a sailor, orphan, fisherman's daughter, maid, factory worker, etc./an aristocrat, a knight, a wealthy merchant's daughter, a shipmaster, a peasant, a student, etc.). The parents, most often the father, do everything in their power to keep the young lovers apart. Their love is so strong – and it is illustrated in the song through fervent declarations and actions – that the lovers would rather die than be parted. The story often ends in death; another type of ending is that the once hard-hearted parents relent, allow love to run its natural course, and the song ends happily.

Although the content and style of the songs of this period reveal a certain naivete, they are illustrative of the ideals and social realities of the day. Class distinction often emerges as the main point of departure in these songs.

> Example 1:   The boy's name was simply Jake
> a poor young farm hand was he
> but the girl's name was Maria
> a wealthy family's heir.
> (Asplund 1994:278)

Example 2:   A lovely maiden from the manor house
her beloved a low-born servant boy.
(Asplund 1994:356)

The plot is set in motion with the introduction of a conflict-ridden situation: high – low, rich – poor. In these songs the violation of a norm on sexuality is not the cause of conflict; in fact, sexuality receives minimal attention. None of the songs uphold chastity as a prerequisite for marriage. The broadsheet ballads simply underscore the significance of faithfulness in love. This genre of folklore victimizes those who break the sacred promise of love or those who try to stand in the way of true love. The enemies of love are duly punished in the course of the narrative.

Features of Lyrical Songs

These same features appear in erotic rhyming lyrical songs, which were gaining popularity in Western Finland during the seventeenth century. The earliest records of these are from the end of the eighteenth century (Asplund 1981:68–69; Hako 1963:427). Although satire and humor are key features of these plotless one-stanza songs, erotic rhyming lyrical songs are thematically diverse. The songs run the gamut of emotions: love's pleasures are exulted, eternal love is sworn, the beloved is yearned for, unspoken love produces anguish, lovers are betrayed, and abandoned lovers wail and gnash their teeth, etc. That is why lyric songs, as opposed to rhymed narrative songs, are far more illustrative of the gradual shifts in opinion reflecting the structural changes in society. Boasting and fickleness were also popular motifs. A symbol of the new perspective on life could be the "farewell letter" (Hako 1963:427). Such songs depict the young man or woman nonchalantly handing his/her lover a letter of farewell:

Example: The farewell letter is weightless in the rascal's pocket,
even if they were to arrive by the thousands every Friday.

The farewell letter was penned with blue ink
But not handed over with teary eyes.
(Hako 1967:116)

The dichotomy of old love versus new love, even in the farewell letter, embodies contemporary perceptions of love.

Example: The cursed old love I'll cook in tar.
The blessed new love I'll cover with a silk sheet.

The old love's letters were spread out on the table.
With a light heart, I'll take a new one, the other
one I'll leave in the spring.
(Hako 1967:121)

240

The turn of the century broadsheet ballad's characteristic theme, social conflict, is also conspicuous in rhymed lyrics. The juxtaposition of high and low status, wealth and poverty, is a common motif in rhyming lyrical songs.

Example:
    Was I cheap in your eyes or was it my poverty you feared, when you began to love me and then rejected me.

Was it only mockery when you called me your friend? I am so much lower than you are.

I courted the rich one and I courted the poor one
I courted them both
I soon learned that the poor love with the heart
(Hako 1967:76–77)

The emergence of erotic themes in this genre of folklore does not mean that the traditional moral views had disappeared for good. Lyric songs provide us with ample evidence that traditional values nevertheless persisted. Despite their erotic content, these songs were still colored with a cautionary tone. A young woman had to be prudent in her dealings with men, otherwise her reputation would suffer.

Once a pretty maiden allowed a no-good boy to kiss her
And soon she was as common as a bad girl's broom
(Kanteletar XX)

Turn-of-the-century songs express a variety of attitudes to sexual morality. On the one hand, true love has the power to triumph over all and ties of kinship are easily eclipsed by intense erotic attachments. On the other hand, some songs poke fun at fidelity; and characters boast about their faithlessness. Lyric songs are also characterized by similar contradictions. It must be noted, however, that the songs also depict attitudes formed by age and gender, and express group solidarity. Therefore, they are limited when it comes to trying to ascertain prevailing attitudes of the past. In any case, one can assert that the world view of nineteenth-century songs is typified by a state of ferment.

Love and Sexuality

A study of the representations of love from medieval times to the beginning of the 20th century reveals the significance of kin alliances (see table). Medieval songs convey two views of the family: positive (1), kin-centered and negative (3), the late nineteenth century songs are all negative. The family is always rendered unfavorably. In the newer songs, the root of the conflict lies in social differences (6), whereas social differences are a non-issue in the medieval songs. Undeniably, some songs clearly underline class differences, such as *Viron orjan virsi* ("The Serf and the Master"), in which the basic idea is that spiritual wealth outlasts material wealth; in other words, the wealthy landowner goes to hell and his wretched serf enjoys eternal life in heaven. Nevertheless, class differences never emerge as the basic conflict in songs portraying relationships between men and women.

241

TABLE

Central Theme	1 Kin-bound or kin-centered in a positive sense	2 Denial of sexuality Stress on virtue	3 Protest against family authority; Kin-centered in a negative sense	4 Emphasis on the emotions and fidelity
Kalevala meter from the Middle Ages	Kiia's Children Golden Bridge to the Forefather(s) The Suitors from the Sea The Man-Killer Ogoi and the Priest's Song Different burials for the relatives The Unhappy Bride Tuurikkainen's Song Vassilei's Departure The Water-Carrier	The Forsaken Maid Anterus's Song St. Catherine Kiia's Children Marketta's Song The Man-Killer Ogoi and the Priest's Song Tuurikkainen's Song The Water-Carrier Mataleena's Song	Inkeri's Song An Inquiry into Weeping The Useless Bridegroom The Hanged Maid The Bartered Bride The Boy and the Cloud Divine Light Courtship The Thief and the Suitor	Anterus's Song Inkeri's Song News of Death The Ransomed Bride The Man-Killer The Sickly Maiden
Rhymed – since the 1600s		Little Katri (2) Sat on the Count's Lap (6) The Clerk and the Maid (7) The Hunter and the Maiden (8) Vilhelmi and Liisunen (11)		In the Herb Garden (9) The Two Royal Children (10) Vilhelmi and Liisunen (11) The Castle in the Eastern Land (12) The Bride's Death (13) The Sad Letter (14) Laugh and Cry (15) The Girl to be Ransomed (40)
Rhymed – since the 1870s			The Sailor and the Nobleman's Daughter (16) The Message from the Land of Germany (17) Jaakko and Maria (29) Pista and Ilona (26) In the Churchyard of Eura (28)	The Sailor and the Nobleman's Daughter (16) The Message from the Land of Germany (17) Saida and Rikhard (18) Jaakko and Maria (29) Akseli and Hilda (23) The Merchant from India (24) The Wedding in Hades (25) Cruel Piety (27) In the Churchyard of Eura (28) Beneath the Lovely Birch (31)

TABLE

Central Theme	5 Emphasis on the emotions infidelity or other negative activity	6 Protest against social/class differences	7 Romantic Love Protestations of Love	8 Acceptance of Sexuality
Kalevala meter from the Middle Ages	Annikkainen's Song The Death of Elina The Killing of the Previous Wife Kojonen's Song			The Maid and the Dragon
Rhymed – since the 1600s	The Betrayed Youth (32)		In the Herb Garden (9) The Two Royal Children (10) The Bride's Death (13) The Sad Letter (14) Laugh and Cry (15)	The Clerk and the Maid (7) The Miller's Daughter (54) The Soldier and the Peasant's Wife (59) The daughter's Suitors (58) The Man-Hungry Girl (59)
Rhymed – since the 1870s	The Deceitful Bride (29) The Unfaithful Maiden (30) The Girl in the Herb Garden (34) The Valiant Sailor (35) Deceitful Elsa (36) The Revenge of the Factory Girl (37) Darling Emma (38) Jalmari and Hulda (39) Soldier Boy Slender and Maiden Fair (40) Forgotten His Vow (41) Otto and Olga (42)	The Sailor and the Nobleman's daughter (16) The Message from the Land of Germany (17) Saida and Rikhard (18) Jaakko and Maria (29) The Spring Wind from the South (21) Two Girls in the Rose Grove (22) Akseli and Hilda (23) The Merchant from India (24) The Wedding in Hades (25) Pista and Ilona (26) Cruel Piety (27) The Revenge of the Factory Girl (37) Soldier Boy Slender and Maiden Fair (40)	The Sailor and the Nobleman's daughter (16) The Message from the Land of Germany/of the Germans (17) Saida and Rikhard (18) Jaakko and Maria (29) The Spring Wind from the South (West) (21) Two Girls in the Rose Grove (22) Akseli and Hilda (23) The Merchant from India (24) The Wedding in Hades (25) Pista and Ilona (26) Cruel Piety (27) In the Churchyard of Eura (28) The Deceitful Bride (29) Beneath the Lovely Birch (31) The Cross of Ida's Grave (33) The Valiant Sailor (35) The Revenge of the Factory Girl (37) Jalmari and Hulda (39) Soldier Boy Slender and Maiden Fair (40) Forgotten His Vow (41)	

A fundamental difference between the attitudes expressed in songs in the Kalevala meter and the newer layer would be attitudes to sexuality. Kalevala songs value sexual purity (2), forbidden sexual relationships are harshly condemned, and when sex is mentioned, it is to convey a warning. During the age of rhyming songs – the 1600s to the early 1800s – attitudes to sexuality become more relaxed (8), even though earlier values and attitudes are still apparent (2).

After the mid 1800s the value of virtue no longer reigned as a prominent theme. Instead songs issued a warning to those who tried to block the lovers from realizing their dreams or to those who broke the new norm of fidelity. The change ultimately appears as a statement reflecting the contemporary attitude to love. While this sentiment (7) remains absent in the medieval songs, it features plainly in the 19th century songs. Indeed, the themes of fidelity and betrayal (4, 5) are also touched upon in these songs, but the two eras of song still speak of love in a different tone. Romantic love appears to entail promise and emotional commitment; this is a new characteristic which entered into narrative songs along with rhyming songs in the new meter.

Songs and Reality

How do the folkloric messages correspond to historical facts? Matti Sarmela has asserted that when basic groups (relatives, family) were characterized by habitual and intense association and reciprocity, changes in values and attitudes would occur slowly and gradually. Thanks to the Roman Catholic Church's introduction of European cultural influences, the dissemination of new attitudes was accelerated (Sarmela 1969:242). Medieval songs can be illustrative of contemporary values. Although both marriage and courtship took place under the watchful eye of the kin group, evidence of an influx of new ideas about love can be seen in the songs. Thus, the songs convey protest against family authority. Genuine affection and the spiritual dimension of love begin to take priority in the songs.

According to Sarmela, another period of diffusion took place in the 17th century, after which began the formation of reciprocity systems encouraging youthful interaction and solidarity (Sarmela 1969:242; 1994:107–117). This was also a breakthrough period regarding the emergence of Western stanzaic and rhymed songs which began to compete with the traditional Kalevala meter songs. Thus, signs of new values eclipsing the old are apparent in the erotic songs. The involvement of emotions is clearly more visible than ever before.

The 1870s was also the beginning of a third distinct cultural era. The growth of cities and the introduction of new technologies coincided with the early phases of the third type of narrative song. The shift from a kin-centered society to that of integration and solidarity among the younger generation signaled the death of a world view characterized by fatalism and resignation. Unlike their ancestors, the youth of the 1870s appeared to feel a greater sense of agency regarding their emotional life. Emotional and personal preferences replaced material values when it came to choosing a mate (Sarmela 1969:237–243, 265–267; 1994:34–36). The new emotional climate is echoed in late 19th century popular songs.

Finnish narrative songs reflect the development of ways of interaction or forming alliances (marriage ties): 1) the kin-centered era, which was already in decline during the 1600s in western Finland but still described communal life of eastern Finland and Karelia until the end of the 1800s, and 2) the youth integration period, when young people began to embrace folklore corresponding to their own world view.

We must keep in mind, however, that many narrative Kalevala meter songs, in addition to the newer ballads and broadsheet ballads, traveled to Finland from elsewhere and had a role in shaping local attitudes. We may even claim that the values conveyed in these oral traditions were not local. Nevertheless, the new ideas were imparted to a receptive audience. Had the songs meant nothing and served no function to their singers, they would have simply been rejected or modified to suit existing ways of thinking.

It may well be that human lives characterized by close kin relations, sober-minded attitudes to love and sexuality and the power of the church can explain the lack of songs depicting passionate attachments, except for the light-hearted erotic songs found in the most archaic folklore. The comic ballads conveying more light-hearted views of sexuality emerge in Finnish narrative singing tradition only during the period of rhyming song. During this time new values, attitudes and customs began to take hold among the younger generation.

Translated by Leila Virtanen.

NOTES

[1]   The 33 volumes of *Suomen Kansan Vanhat Runot* ("The Ancient Poems of the Finnish People," 1908–1948, abbr. SKVR) contains the central part of collected archaic Finnish folk poetry. The original material is found mainly in the archives of the Finnish Literature Society. Epic poems, lyric poems, wedding poems, songs from annual festivals and incantations from all the different cultural regions of Finland, Karelia and Ingria are published in SKVR. In this study I have used parts VI_1 (Savo), $VII_{1,2}$ (Ladoga-Karelia), VIII (Southwest Finland), IX (Häme), X (Satakunta), XI_1 (Southern Ostrobothnia) and XII_1 (Northern Ostrobothnia). *Balladeja ja arkkiveisuja: Suomalaisia kertomalauluja* (Ballads and Broadsides: Finnish Narrative Popular Songs) (1994) contains the more recent Finnish folk song traditions. The original material compiled for this volume comes primarily from the collections of the Folklore Archives of The Finnish Literature Society and additional materials have been drawn from the Department of Folk Tradition and the sound archive at the University of Tampere. The numbers in parentheses after the title of each rhyming song on the table (page 242–243) correspond to the type numbers used in the work "Ballads and Broadsides: Finnish Narrative Popular Songs" (1994).

[2]   An exemplary product of the comparison of Finnish non-material culture from various regions is the comprehensive Suomen perinneatlas (Finnish Traditional Atlas, 1994). Using a cartographic approach, the work delineates the structural changes that took place during each cultural era.

[3]   I have also decided to exclude the explicitly sexual songs which have clearly pornographic themes. These were composed in both the ancient Kalevala meter and more modern genres of rhymed songs.

[4]	Matti Kuusi formulated the 'period style theory.' He discussed this theory in an article entitled 'Kalevalaisen muinaisepiikan viisi tyylikautta' (1957) and has applied it in *Suomen Kirjallisuus* (Finnish Literature) I (1963). Matti Kuusi presents his 'period style theory' in English in *Finnish Folk Poetry Epic* (1977:44–61).

[5]	When discussing Kalevala meter ballads, it must be noted that the term ballad is used rather loosely, i.e., as a category based on content. See Asplund 1994:810–812.

[6]	The oldest ballad in rhyme surfaced as a broadsheet ballad as earlyas 1683. These ballads, *Pyhä Yrjänä ja lohikäärme* ("St. George and the Dragon") and *Linna itäisellä maalla* ("The Castle in the eastern Land") from 1735 are the only broadsheet ballads to appear so early in the Finnish language. Although some ballads also appeared in the early 1800s, the majority of broadsheet ballads began to be published during the 1870s (Asplund 1994:33–36; see also Hultin 1931).

BIBLIOGRAPHY

Asplund, Anneli 1981: Riimilliset kansanlaulut. A. Asplund – M. Hako (eds) Kansanmusiikki. Suomalaisen Kirjallisuuden Seuran Toimituksia 366. SKS. Helsinki.

–	1994: Balladeja ja arkkiveisuja. Suomalaisia kertomalauluja. Ballads and Broadsides, Finnish Narrative Popular Songs. Suomalaisen Kirjallisuuden Seuran Toimituksia 563. SKS. Helsinki.

Haavio, Martti 1952: Kirjokansi. WSOY. Helsinki.

–	1955: Kansanrunojen maailmanselitys. WSOY. Helsinki.

Hako, Matti 1963: Riimilliset kansanlaulut. Suomen kirjallisuus I. Otava. Keuruu.

–	1967: Suomalaisia kansanlauluja. Suomalaisen Kirjallisuuden Seuran Toimituksia 229. SKS. Helsinki.

Hultin, Arvid 1929–1931: Luettelo Helsingin Yliopiston kirjaston arkkikirjallisuudesta, I–V. Helsinki. Katalog över Helsingfors universitetsbiblioteks samlingar av skillingstryck I–V. Helsingfors

Kanteletar elikkä Suomen kansan vanhoja lauluja ja virsiä. 14. painos. SKS. Vaasa 1982. (1. painos 1840).

Kuusi, Matti 1957: Kalevalaisen muinaisepiikan viisi tyylikautta. Kalevalaseuran Vuosikirja 37. WSOY. Porvoo.

–	1963: Keskiajan kalevalainen runous. Suomen kirjallisuus I. Keuruu. Otava.

–	1977: Finnish Folk Poetry. Epic. An Anthology in Finnish and English, M. Kuusi – K. Bosley – M. Branch (eds). Publications of the Finnish Literature Society 329. SKS. Helsinki.

Nordenstreng, Kaarle 1966: Iskelmätekstien suunta. Sosiologia 3. 1966. Helsinki.

Sarmela, Matti 1969: Reciprocity Systems of the Rural Society in the Finnish Carelian Culture Area. FF Communications 207. Helsinki.

–	1970: Perinneaineiston kvantitatiivisesta tutkimuksesta. SKS. Helsinki.

–	1994: Suomen perinneatlas. Suomen kansankulttuurin kartasto 2. Atlas of Finnish Ethnic Culture 2. Folklore. Suomalaisen Kirjallisuuden Seuran Toimituksia 587. SKS. Helsinki.

Siikala, Anna-Leena 1996: Kalevalaisen mytologian nainen. P. Hakamies (ed.) Näkökulmia karjalaiseen perinteeseen. Suomi 182. SKS. Saarijärvi.

Suomen Kansan Vanhat Runot. Osat VI_1; $VII_{1,2}$; VIII; IX; XI_1; XII_1. Helsinki 1908–1948.

SEPPO KNUUTTILA AND SENNI TIMONEN

If the One I Know Came Now

Modal Contexts and Bodily Feelings in a Folk Poem

Besides studying the lore, folklorists have also put their interpretive skills to work in trying to understand the individual authors and performers of folk songs. Nowadays, instead of regarding an individual person as the definitive origin of a poetic text, scholars view the individual as a participant in a continually unfolding series of creative moments. Many of the elements constituting gender identity are typically based on the dimensions or repetition and variation without the assumption of the existence of an ultimate origin. (cf. Pulkkinen 1998:245–246, 250.)

Our present aim is to turn our attention to the authors, interpretations, and, as a methodological experiment, to the visionaries of the folk poem beginning with the words *Jos mun tuttuni tulisi* ("If the One I Know Came Now"). Within the limits of this article, we aim to observe how the poem has been produced through various interpretive traditions by presenting the above-mentioned poem's textual variation. From the present standpoint, we shall compare and juxtapose past interpretations in order to address previously unanswered questions: do the different variants convey the full extent of the original poet's emotions? Why was a "vicarage maid" ruled out as the author of the poem? Has the poem's original or normal form been successfully reconstructed? If so, how can we account for regional variation? Why has this particular poem become world famous? What sorts of meanings does the poem assume when its singer or ego is believed to be a member of the "other" sex? How are the feelings of the Finnish "Sappho," "the daughter of ice and snow," manifested, and to whom, or to what, are they directed? Can we suppose that the emotional ego of the text is stable (always the same sex, the same age, alive or dead)? By appealing to the abundance of textual and interpretive details, we would like to underline, unlike many writers before us, the ambiguity, density, and mutability of human emotions.

In 1778, the Finnish scholar Henrik Gabriel Porthan (1739–1804) initiated an approach to our topic. In *De Poësi Fennica*, in a chapter on Kalevala meter grinding songs, he also provided the first outline of women's songs in folklore research. Interestingly, Porthan associates the theme of erotic love with a female ego: "Some of the songs treat somber topics, especially in the

Myth and Mentality
Studia Fennica
Folkloristica 8, 2002

realm of morality, while others resemble folk tales and legends, and there are even some songs dedicated to love, a topic which naturally occupies the thoughts of the female sex" (1983:84).

To illustrate his point, Porthan published a poem fragment in which "a bride, attesting to the steadfast nature of her love, declares her willingness to kiss the lips of her beloved, even if they are covered with wolf blood, and to offer him her hand without hesitation, even if he held a snake in his palm" (1983:86; SKVR VI 591, XII 347). In 1799, a student of Porthan, Frans Mikael Franzén, gave two explorers, the Italian Giuseppe Acerbi and the Swede A.F. Skjöldebrand, a complete copy of the poem (Saarenheimo 1974:329; 1992:6; SKVR XII 350). Soon afterwards, Acerbi and Skjöldebrand published their respective travel writings, in 1801 and 1802. Both men presumed the poem's author to be an Ostrobothnian vicarage maid who was expressing her love and yearning for a faraway beloved. The poem in the manuscript in Sakari Topelius's old collection reads as follows:

Jos mun tuttuni tulisi,	If the one I know came now
ennen nähtyni näkyisi!	the one I've seen were in sight
Sillen suuta suikkajaisin,	I'd snatch a kiss from his mouth
olis suu suen veressä,	though his mouth bled from a wolf
sillen kättä käppäjäisin,	I would touch him on the hand
jospa kärme kämmen päässä.	though a snake were in his palm!
– Olisiko tuuli mielellissä,	Had the wind a mind
ahavainen kielellissä!	and the gale a tongue
Sanan toisi, sanan veisi,	it would bring word, take a word
sanan liian liikuttaisi	set an extra word astir
kahen rakkaan välillä.	between two lovers.
– Ennempä heitän herkku-ruat,	I will sooner leave fine foods
paistit pappilan unohtan	and forget rectory roasts
ennenkuin heitän herttaiseni	before I leave my sweetheart
kesän keskyteltyäni	the one I tamed all summer
talven taivuteltuani.	and persuaded all winter.
(SKVR XII 351).	(trans. by Keith Bosley in Honko et al. 1993:315)

Although Porthan does subscribe to the idea of collective creation, especially in the domain of women's folklore, he also regards this particular poem as the individual expression of a speaking subject, the possible author of the poem. Acerbi and Skjöldebrand strongly advocated the latter view.

This is an early variation on the question of the author/subject. This question has long been placed within the dichotomy between collective and individual creation. The background to this reasoning is complex and these value-laden dichotomies are by no means limited to debates in folklore studies. Although today we tend to privilege the individual in defining the creative subject, if possible, we should also remember that most of the world's great inventions (literacy, music, geometry, religions, visual arts, computers, space exploration) are collective efforts and that their significance and practice are continually changing. The longstanding dialogue between the Enlightenment and Romanticism has yielded, among other things, the conclusion that the latter paradigm has generally given rise to theories and hypotheses on the creative consciousness and its traces. Those involved in the debate sought out evidence to show that the unlearned folk were indeed capable of composing simple verses; and, in the best of cases, these were deemed to be of high poetic merit. According to one idea of development, those at the center (the elite) forget whereas those at the periphery (the common folk) remember. This principle continues to inform the geographic-temporal thinking of researchers of folk poetry.

Notions of high and low – and the line that divides them – have been used to make the distinction between individual and collective creativity. In his preface to the *Kanteletar*, Lönnrot not only asserted that the folk poem – unlike the literary poem – could have no identifiable author, but also declared that "as soon as a folk poem was acknowledged as the work of an individual artist, its folkloric value was lost". Despite these claims, Lönnrot, when reading folk poems aloud to Mateli Kuivalatar, was convinced of Kuivalatar's truthfulness when she claimed to have composed those girls'songs as a "young girl".

Collective creation has come under numerous attacks during the past one-hundred years. While some scholars sought to dismiss collective creation as a Romantic fallacy, others were ideologically motivated. In the early decades of the 20th century, the scholars who were contemptuous of the masses arrived at a unanimous agreement: the masses do not create. In *Sammon arvoitus* ("The enigma of the Sampo") E.N. Setälä declared: "Every folk poem has an original but often unknown author." He also roundly condemned Roman Jakobson's and Petr Bogatyrev's (1929) ideas about collective creation. (Setälä 1932:444, 445–449.) In 1949 Martti Haavio had (or attempted to have) the final word in his inauguration lecture, *Kansanrunojen sepittäjät ja esittäjät* ("The Authors and Performers of Folk Poems"). For Haavio, "poems are created by individuals ... there is no such thing as a collectively created poem."

Later on, Matti Kuusi came up with an original solution to the question of authorship. He organized the poems in the logical belief that stylistically similar poems would originate in the same period. His method proved effective: "A distinct and melodious voice rises above the collective din produced by the dozens of songs of complaint from the first centuries of this millennium. This cannot be a communal tune formed by a particular school or period of singing." What we have, in the words of Kuusi, is a brilliant innovator and an unnamed poet: the *Bird Eulogist.* There was another lone voice that he named the *Turku Modernist* and temporally placed her in the Middle Ages. Kuusi was convinced that this bold and emancipated woman, "a black swan among the chicken flock in the City of Turku," had authored two dramatic ballads, *Annikaisen virsi* ("Annikainen's Song") and *Lohi-käärme ja neito* ("The Dragon and the Maid"). "Even if she herself is but a mere illusion, an auditory fiction, her poems are not illusions." (1963:265, 339–340.)

Before proceeding, yet another attempt to grapple with poem authorship deserves mention. The performance-centered approach or performance analysis was a new theoretical shift in folklore studies in the 1970s. Put succinctly, its basic idea is that the "telling is the tale," that is, each oral performance is a unique cultural text. Thus, the question of origins was eclipsed by a discussion on authenticity, and, carried to its most extreme form, the question returned to the author or subject of the performance.

The Urform and Other Affective Interpretations

Scholars have found countless ways to underline the extraordinary nature of *If the One I Know Came Now*. Franzén, Skjöldebrand and Acerbi all marveled at the unaffectedness of this work of art. In the words of Acerbi, "considered as the production of a girl who could neither write nor read, [the poem] is a wonderful performance ... snatching a grace beyond the reach of art." Acerbi characterized this northern vicarage maid as "nature's poet", a Finnish Sappho, who, "amidst all the snows of her ungenial climate, discovers all the warmth of the poetess of Lesbos" (Acerbi 1802:318). Since lyrical love poems rarely appear in the austere Kalevala landscape, folklorists have regarded the poem as the exception that proves the rule. Here, however, the impassioned poetic ego is burning with love's natural fires and is intoxicated by imagination's power. Perhaps scholars drew attention to such an exalted passion to better distinguish this poem from sexual poems. How can our ears discern the difference between the feelings of erotic love and carnal passion, especially as the song was actually sung centuries ago?

Eighteenth-century perceptions of both the poem itself and its possible poet remain with us right up to the present day, especially in the form of general surveys (Haavio 1933:308; Enäjärvi-Haavio 1935:133; Tarkiainen 1943:250; Haavio 1952:7; Kuusi 1963:388–392; Kuusi et al. 1977:10; Karhu 1979:64–65; Apo 1981:59–61; Laitinen 1994:7–10; Virtanen 1988:166–167; Apo 1989:22–23; Timonen 1993:296; see also Virtanen – DuBois 2000:143). Undeniably, even in the early days, folklore scholars were beginning to wonder whether the performer and composer of the song was not one and the same young woman after all. It may well be that even Franzén had given the matter some thought. Indeed, his translation of the poem (1801) included a reference to its author – that she was a native of Ostrobothnia or Savo (Sarajas 1956:303). In any case, through their travel tales, Acerbi and Skjöldebrand conveyed the poem to the world. And, in 1810, the latter's text fell into the hands of Goethe and he, in turn, translated the poem into German and called it "Finnisches Lied":

Käm' der liebe Wohlbekannte,
Völlig so wie er geschieden;
Kuss erkläng' an seinen Lippen,
Hätt' auch Wolfsblut sie gerötet;
Ihm den Handschlag gäb' ich, wären
Seine Fingerspitzen Schlangen.

Wind! o hättest Du Verständnis,
Wort'um Worte trügst Du wechselnd,
Sollt' auch einiges verhallen,
Zwischen zwei entfernten Liebchen.

Gern entbehrt' ich gute Bissen,
Priesters Tafelfleisch vergäss' ich,
Eher als dem Freund entsagen,
Den ich Sommers rasch bezwungen,
Winters langer Weis' bezähmte.
(Kunze 1952:40)

Undeniably, this was remarkable, and the fact of its translation has worked as further testimony to the poem's status as a lyrical treasure in world literature. *If the One I Know Came Now* did much to fuel the male imagination. In fact, in the mid-19th century, a Swedish admirer of the poem, C.G. Zetterqvist, embarked upon a mission to collect as many different translations of it as possible. Thanks to his wide-ranging international correspondence, he succeeded in gathering a total of 467 translations. Although the majority remained in an unpublished manuscript (Zetterqvist 1858), his efforts clearly contributed to the poem's renown. Indeed, one line of research deals with the poem's international reputation, that is, translations of it and its place in literary history (Collan 1843; Krohn 1922; Kunze 1952, 1957; Haltsonen 1961; Weöres 1961; Kunze 1970; Austerlitz 1984; Oinas 1996).

The same version of the poem that Franzén gave to Acerbi and Sjköldebrand and which Zetterqvist had had translated, Lönnrot divided up into four poems (or even more if we want to be precise) and then published them in the *Kanteletar*. Lönnrot believed that the singer, "as skillful singers are inclined to do", had compiled the poem from several verses originally belonging to different poems. (1843; cf. Anttila 1985:194–195; Kaukonen 1984:62–65; 1989:26–27). Thus poem 43 from Book II of the *Kanteletar* resembles the versions assumed to be original forms, which Viljo Tarkiainen (1912), Kaarle Krohn (1920), Martti Haavio (1952) and Matti Kuusi (1963) – to name a few – have constructed. According to Matti Kuusi's verse analysis, the poem's basic form should be the following (390):

Jos mun tuttuni tulisi,	If the one I know came now
ennen nähtyni näkyisi,	the one I've seen were in sight
sille kättä käppäjäisin,	I would touch his hand
vaikk ois käärme kämmenpäässä,	though a snake were in his palm
sille suuta suikkajaisin,	I would kiss his mouth
vaikk ois suu suden veressä,	though his mouth bled from a wolf
siitä kaulahan kapuisin,	I'd climb on his neck
vaikk ois kalma kaulan päällä,	though death were upon his neck
vielä vierehen kävisin,	and to his side I would go
vaikk ois vierus verta täynnä.	though his side were all bloody.

(Adapted from trans. by Keith Bosley, cf. Honko et al. 1993:315–316)

The poem's unique place in literary and folkloristic research is evidenced by the fact that the further its origins recede – both temporally and locally – the more brazen and more sensual the poem begins to appear to contemporary scholars. Could this be an indication of just how powerfully some readers have identified with the absent lover? Have they, however unconsciously, betrayed how they themselves would have liked to have been received, how passionately and openly they would have longed to be loved?

"Not with that sentimental and tenderly affectionate type of lulling, which is actually a rather recent introduction but often regarded as typically Finnish lyric poetry. No, it [the poem] is a raw and powerful expression of those bygone days, when the voice of nature still rang truly and forcefully within the human heart."
(Tarkiainen 1912:26; "those bygone days" he later situated in the early modern era, that is during the 1600s; 1943:250.)

Tarkiainen's analysis of the poem proceeds in a mechanical fashion. In his quest for the poem's original form, he unreflectively discards random or later additions to the poem. For example, Tarkiainen asserts that the lines *Had the wind a mind and the gale a tongue it would bring a word, take a word, set an extra word astir between two lovers* are too tender and placidly wistful to belong to the poem in question. For Matti Kuusi the above lines are also alien to the poem in terms of style and era of composition, especially because of the "the sentimental tone of the final line" (1963:403). Unlike Tarkiainen, Kuusi (390), like Krohn (1922:43–44) and Nuutinen (1961:17–19), considers the presence of *death* ("kalma"), rather than the bear, to be an original element in the poem (*though death were upon his neck; kalma* is a contagious and fatal disease caused by contact with a dead body).

Kuusi also spurns Tarkiainen's vision of a "hot-blooded daughter of the wild forests". Rather, he considers the poem's author to be "a forerunner in the verbal arts of her own day". While Tarkiainen identifies the poem's author and performer as a denizen of the "gloomy and dangerous wilds, whose original vitality was not yet weakened or overanimated by education" (1912:30), Kuusi suggests, albeit tentatively and obliquely, that the author is an epic poet from the late Middle Ages, an ingenious and extraordinary woman, who stands out in the crowd. Kuusi names her the "Turku Modernist". He sees her "leading a group of singing maidens, carrying a rebel flag; she is a virtuoso who favors stark and violent images" (1963:391; later, Kuusi locates her in the 15th or 16th century, 1967:337).

The Turku Modernist's self-knowledge and poetic prowess enable her to detach herself from the subject matter of her art. Thus Kuusi's argumentation proceeds: In *If the One I Know Came Now* she brings erotic passion to Parnassus in a novel way, using the Gothic romanticism of the untamed wilderness instead of the medieval urban imagery in *Annikainen's Song* and *The Dragon and the Maiden*. "We may pause to wonder whether it is possible that such a small and conventional country could produce two such impassioned and dynamic poetesses during the same century, particularly when the songs reveal a mature and absolute command of Kalevala poetry" (1963:391). There are no field notes to support the western Turku Modernist hypothesis, but in light of the traditional folkloristic diffusion theory this detail has only posed a minor problem.

Besides the actual texts, the interpretations and the poem's international fame, little is really known about the poem in question. Despite this lack of information, not only have critics had tremendous confidence when making claims about the poem's original splendor, no one has questioned the gender of poem's speaker or the one spoken of. Oddly enough, the poem has been performed by both men and women; and the one desired has occasionally even been inanimate. "It is hard to imagine what could be discarded or added to this naturally and dramatically expanding series of verses without disrupting its unity or diminishing its force," says Tarkiainen (1912:31). Singers, however, have been inclined to think otherwise. The 217 text versions of *If the One I Know Came Now* that have been collected over a span of nearly two hundred years betray an oral aesthetic: a voice which is incessantly adding and discarding, translating ancient verses and articulating them as interpretations both of the self and the times.[1]

An examination of 18th century sources yields a greater variety of verses than the much celebrated paragon of folk poetry. In fact, as early as 1775, a poem called *Viinasta valitusvirsi, runo raukan kuolemasta* ("A Lament for the Booze, a Poem about a Poor Fellow's Demise") was written down in Savo and later published as a broadside ballad in 1777. The poem is a protest against the prohibition on home spirit distilling. Longed for and sorely missed come evening, alcohol's arrival is eagerly anticipated by the singer: *If you, the one I know came now, the one I've seen were in sight, I'd steal a kiss from a little goblet – – Come still, You, the one I knew, appear before me, you, the one I've seen, before separation descends, death's hour hovers near!* (XV 205, cf VI 730.)

The opening lines of a grinding song published by Porthan depict the measured and knowing speech of Jaakko's wife. The leisurely tone is suddenly interrupted by the shriek of the poem's ego, in her own words, *the old moldy ear.* She utters the following words: *If the one I know came now, the one I've seen were in sight, I'd give a kiss to that one, I'd open my jaws wide. But my dear one cannot be heard, that's why I'm lonesome in the evenings...* The poem closes with an impassioned plea: *come to bed...* (VI 828, XII 409). Porthan suggests that the husband "is apparently on a long journey..." (1778/1983:84). In another grinding song the singer, who is in this case undefined and ungendered, repeatedly invokes various images of desire: if the rivers were flowing with beer, the slaves could also drink! If I sing, I sing forth an oak with golden-tongued cuckoos on its branches! *If the one I know came now, at once I'd give a kiss, throw my arms around the neck.* (XII 396). The essential nature of the "one known" remains unclear. In addition, the wedding poem written down in 1780, a learned adaption of folk poetry, describes future marital bliss with our poem's lines (*You'd give a kiss to that one, open wide your jaws...* IX 27). Ganander's dictionary examples allude to the existence of other old texts of the poem (XV 131) as well as the lines including the word denoting the "one known" used to describe friendships between men (XV 209).

All in all, the 18th century texts show that the theme was then not only already familiar but also subject to change. Because of its thematic flexibility, its verses could be performed on many different occasions, by both male and female, young and old. The singer could express her/his longing for liquor, a lover, or even a close friend. Adding other motifs to this poem could lend new and distinctive tones to the "one known" and the anticipated arrival. Ultimately, the core theme was rather simple, including only the hope of reunion and the image of the kiss.

The later mass of texts intensifies this sense of polyphony. The poem has been written down in Finland – Ostrobothnia (5), Savo (15), Northern and Ladoga Karelia (38), the Karelian Isthmus (53), Häme (2) – as well as beyond the country's borders: Archangel Karelia (5), Olonets Karelia (3), and Ingria (96).

The omnipresent ego has not only a regional but also a gendered voice. Although most of the poem's performers were women (116 texts), there were also a number of male performers (24). Nearly one-hundred of the written records, however, make no mention of the singer at all. Occasionally, the gender of the speaking subject is apparent from the poem, but it is not necessarily the same as that of the singer.

On the surface, the basic theme appears to remain the same from region to region, regardless of the performer's gender. The variation of individual lines, however, is endless. A given performer uses one image, whereas another performer discards that same image; while one performer presents the lines in one order, another performer prefers an alternative order. A precise definition of the theme, that is, which text really conforms to the poem, is far from obvious, particularly if the interpreter chooses to give up a fixed notion of an original form and simply pay attention to the singer.

Polyphony as Significance

Usually the poem begins with the line *If (when) the one I know came now, the one I've seen were in sight*. The person awaited may be a sweetheart, the beloved, a friend, a relative. Accordingly, the form of the wish also varies: *If I believed my darling were coming, If I knew my own were coming*.

Even from afar, be it two *versts* (XIII 3068) or the distance to the moon (III 3729), the speaker can recognize the longed-for one. The form and gait of the beloved are immediately identifiable (VII:2 2364, V:2 288, XIII 3080). In some variants the narrator says that the clothing of the person coming does not matter (XIII 3072, 3074). Furthermore, the arrival of the other brings to mind the thought of one's own departure to meet the other, first from indoors to outdoors – *as mist I'd go out, as smoke I'd go to the yard* (I:3 1434) – and then beyond the yard: *I'd go a verst to meet that one, I'd hurry six miles* (VII:2 2360). The passionate welcome is underlined by its sheer physicality: *another verst on my knees, another on my side* (IV 1000); *I'd slither along on my belly, crawl on all fours* (IV 3952). Sometimes the journey would take one through forests by boat, on skis (VII:2 2356–57); sometimes one would move like a creature of the forest or in an animal form: steal through the woods as a wolf, through the gloomy brush as a bear, through the trees as a squirrel, along the lakeshores as a hare (IV 3952). Some singers proclaim that they will build blue bridges (IV 240), or onion bridges (IV 3165). Nearly all of the singers underline the narrating ego's haste *to tear down the fences and the gates* (III 2760) to allow the friend to come. Here the images may turn violent: *I'd break the brushwood fences, I'd tear down the wooden fences, I'd break the iron fences* (XIII 3077), *I'd roll the stone fences* (XIII 3076), *I'd smash the gates* (IV 310).

Earlier scholars have dismissed the images of hastefully traversing the *versts*, crossing the bridges, and tearing down fences; such images were deemed mere additions to the "real" poem (Tarkiainen 1912 etc.). The archived texts nevertheless do appear to stem from the singer's personal experiences. By way of these images, the performers animate the poem's ego and anticipate the reunion, whose meaning now, as the climax approaches, grows more and more consequential:

No viel mie suuta suikkajaisin
vaik ois suusi suven veressä,

Still I'd steal a kiss
even if your mouth flowed with a
wolf's blood

viel mie kättä roikkajaisin
vaik ois käärme kämmenpäässä.
(XIII 3073)

still I'd grasp the hand
even if a snake were in the palm.

Viel mä kaulaan karkajaisin
vaikk ois karhu kaulan päällä.
(XIII 3074)

Still I'd rush to the neck
even if a bear clung to it.

Hot olis miekku kaglan piällä
sitki mie kaglasta kapuasin.
(KRA 18)

Even if a sword were on the neck
even then I'd throw my arms around the
neck.

Hot olis kalmoilaudu kaglah
sivottu,
täyvelleh kaglah kabuisin.
(II 433)

Even if a funeral bier were
bound to the neck
I'd eagerly climb to that neck.

Tok mie viereen kävisin
vaik ois vierus verta täynnä
lavan laiat lainehtisi.
(XIII 3080)

Come what may, I'd go to the bedside
even if the side was a bloody flood
even if the edges were overflowing.

Tuompa vierehen vetäisin

jos on veitsi vieressäh.
(II 434)

I'd stretch myself out by the side
of that one
even if a knife were by the side.

Vaik ois polvet poikki lyöty
sittenkin polvessa polusin.
(XIII 3090)

Even if the knees were chopped off
even then I'd crawl to those knees.

In all its variation, the poem's key theme never clearly identifies the speaker or the one being spoken of. The language is so simple (*tuttu* = the one known, *ennen nähty* = the one seen before) and so metaphorical (wolf's blood, snake, death, bear in the mouth, in the hand, on the neck) that both the speaker and the one spoken of remain open to interpretation.

Often, the theme is conveyed alone and majestically, without explanations, referring only to the "one known" and "the one seen before," the idea of an arrival, a welcome, and a long anticipated reunion. Thus the poem remains hauntingly enigmatic and lends itself to various interpretive possibilities. (This is the case for over half the texts.) In the others, however, the singers

255

nevertheless combine motifs or transform and give attributes to terms in order to describe the longed-for one. This takes place in all of the texts dating from 18th century; for example, the predicament of the vicarage maid is sparsely but distinctly framed. Because a vast distance separates the vicarage maid from her beloved, only the wind can deliver her regards; she is even prepared to relinquish rectory roasts to be with her beloved. Through the additional motifs and epithets, the singer, or more broadly speaking, the collective ego, which can be regional or gendered, contextualizes the self, the friend and the situation from which he/she speaks. By paying attention to the additional motifs, we can also attune our imaginations to appreciate even the plainest variations of the poem.

Even the most exhaustive study of all the variations cannot change our perception of the poem's essence, that is, the longing or desire for the absent loved one. New data can, however, alter our perception of the ego's situation and the object of desire – and perhaps these convey the texture of the emotions. Only twenty-two texts unequivocally portray the desired individual as a man and the one who desires as a woman; and six have the woman as longed for object and the man as the ego. The relatively common words such as *darling* and *beloved* usually allude to the awaited lover. However, such terms are also used in this poem and in others to denote family members. Some of the texts afford us a spare but poignant glimpse of a 19th century love story. Occasionally, the ego of the poem appears to be unhappily married and longing for another lover (I:4 2220, VII:2 2367). Other times, however, the couple is torn apart by the man's obligation to go to war or military service (IV 4589; KRA 16). One backwoods singer pines for her love, the dark-haired one, and vainly searches for his footprints on the ice; she then expresses her desire with a rich variant of the first line, *If the One I Know Came Now*. At the end she exclaims: *Others are wicked, many are evil, and they wish to tear our love asunder* (VII:2 2358).

A thorough study of the corpus can show the many possible meanings of the word *tuttu*, the one known. The word may indicate Väinämöinen's feelings for the golden maiden he created (VI 40), a man's attachment to spirits (VI 730, KRA 1), a hunter's bond to the hunted (a hare or a bear VI 4959, XII 6848), a person's outlook on his/her good luck (III 1512) or the hosts' relationship to their guests: *And so the fathers lived before, parents treaded the land: they knew the one known by the manner of coming, guessed by the gait, they went a verst to meet...* (XIII 3060, 8109). In the above-mentioned South Karelian texts the cultural ideal of hospitality is underlined through imagery. The friend to be embraced is the one – anyone – who comes to visit the home.

A broader interpretation would include the obvious association between the longed-for one and a dead husband/wife or lover. Ingrian singer Ontropo refers to the poem as the *Song of Widow(er)s* (V:2 2429). Another singer wishes that her darling *would return from the land of the dead* (IV 3814), while another sees such hopes as futile, as the *friend is already in the soil, the beloved lies in the earth's bosom* (IV 3429).

The death theme emerges even more powerfully in the texts collected from Ingria and the Karelian Isthmus; the absent but sorely missed person is a family member: a son or daughter (V:1 1292), a sister (IV 1477), a brother (V:2 1155), a father (IV 2560) or, most often of all, a mother. Usually she is dead, but other times she is simply far away. Because this version is so wide-spread, it cannot be dismissed as merely an individual or local variation. In Ingria it is even stronger than the love song version apparently inspired by literary sources (cf., e.g. Kuusi 1983:170). At least in these cases, researchers cannot ignore the poem's existence and reality as a voiced longing for a family member. There are approximately fifty texts expressing this kind of familial attachment. Although present in many others, it is simply not overtly voiced. How could the standard interpretation of our poem ignore such strong emotions? This may stem from a will to deny any possible sensual attachment to the mother. Kuusi attempted to explain this by referring to a "hidden eroticism" (1994:90). Was he suggesting that a woman, in the name of propriety, would voice longings for her parents or her brother, when she was really thinking about a lover? Moreover, the imagery does not necessarily lend itself to erotic interpretations. After all, emotions are generally, and particularly in this case, expressed through bodily sensations and feelings; so, does it not make sense to use bodily images to communicate feelings for the mother?

Although men did perform the poem, most scholarly writing on the poem has assumed the speaker to be a woman. So far, we have already suggested a number of reasons for this uniformity of opinion. From a methodological standpoint, however, it is also interesting to consider how and with how much confidence we can determine the untold traits of authors and their subjects from the written records of oral poetry. What exactly compels researchers to suppose that the emotions conveyed in the poem were felt by a woman? Is it the direct and wanton way they are expressed, or their alleged lack of control – a lack generally characterized as feminine (Lutz 1988:73–76)? Interestingly, the scholarly efforts to construct the original and normative forms betrays a desire to control and domesticate the poetic imagination. Why have scholars been so reluctant to imagine the absent Other as a woman?

Marc Bloch has devised a regressive method for historical research. In short, this means the study of the unknown in light of the known, requiring the scholar to move through various temporal dimensions, but without altering the past to resemble the present, or interpreting the past to suit the researcher's contemporary needs (1976:35–47). The method is an adaption of the contrafactual hypothesis, whereby an alien notion – one that runs counter to factual knowledge – is inserted into the past, and thereafter the interpretive consequences of this alien introduction are analyzed. In a semiotic framework there is a commutation test, which, according to John Fiske, has two central functions: with it one can recognize the differences which produce meaning, and it also serves to determine that meaning: "The technique involves changing a unit in the system and assessing the change in meaning, if any, that has occurred. Normally the change is made imaginatively, and the meaning of the changed syntagm assessed the same way." (1990:109.) The last remark is especially intriguing because it suggests that the test is useful even regarding the present article.

In an article entitled *World Poetry* Matti Kuusi states that the erotic song of longing is one thematic domain of folk lyric poetry which retains its popularity regardless of context – the contemporary music industry or ancient stone dwellings. He does wonder why Solja Tuuli's (Sauvo Puhtila) hit song *En enää vaieta mä voi*, 1967 ("I can no longer hold back") has failed to usurp the literary place of *If the One I Know Came Now;* and why Tuuli's song would have never captured the the the attentions of Franzén, Goethe and Tarkiainen (1994:91). And why not? Because the desire for worldly fame has never animated folk poetry and folk authors. Such renown is actually created by scholars and marketing experts, and even they do not always distinguish between a phenomenon's commonness and popularity.

From the above perspective, today's hit songs qualify as contemporary folk songs. The popularity of individual pieces from either genre has never been easy to predict in advance or to explain in retrospect. The first platinum record in Finland (over 100 000 copies sold) was Erkki Junkkarinen's LP record *Ruusuja hopeamaljassa* ("Roses in a Silver Cup") in 1976. The song's tune was originally composed by Hannes Konno and some of the lyrics date back to the 1930s. Eugen Malmsten recorded it in 1937. The lyrics for the first verse were written by actress Dagmar Parmas (her male pseudonym was Ari Saarni), who is regarded as the first Finnish female pop lyricist. In the version performed by Junkkarinen, the second verse was penned by Lauri Jauhiainen. If one listens attentively, one can hear that the gender of the speaker changes midway through the song.

Your red roses I placed in a silver cup. Only the most beautiful of them I pinned to my breast.
Sun ruususi punaiset laitoin hopeamaljahan. Vaan kauniimman ma niistä taitoin ja pistin rintahan. (DP)

Now the silver vase blooms with your beloved roses. Whenever they catch my eye, they glow for me.
Nyt hopeamaljassa hohtaa nuo ruusus' rakkahat. Kun katseeni milloin ne kohtaa ne mulle hehkuvat. (DP)

As your lips glow, they gild your crimson cheeks, they fuel the fire of love, that set your kiss...
Kuin huules hehkuvat ne kultaa sun purppuraposkillas, ne lietsovat lemmen tulta, jonka sytytti suudelmas. (LJ)

While Parmas's verses convey the absence of the giver of the roses (the man who is being talked about), Jauhiainen foregrounds him as the subject, the one gazing admiringly on the woman's lustrous lips and crimson cheeks. As far as we know, no one objected to the text's subtle gender shift and it did nothing to undermine the song's popularity. In the world of popular music female songwriters have often used male pseudonyms and vice versa, which is only a part of the larger issue of concealing authorship. On the other hand, in many folk songs "boys" may easily replace "girls" and "girls" may just as easily replace "boys," depending on who is singing. There are also many songs in which the speaker's gender has no significance, but, as we have already seen, *If the One I Know Came Now* does not fall into this category. Tarkiainen has noted that in one variant, "it appears as though a male singer had mixed up the song's original conception and imagined the one arriving as a woman, speaking of 'the sway of a graceful hem'"(1912:12). As is evident from the quotation, "the original conception" does not include this kind of possibility any more in Tarkiainen's or in that of any other interpretation (cf. *Kanteletar* II, 42).

If we insist on seeing the poem's speaker as a male, an alternative interpretation may be in order. In other words, "the friend, the one seen before" might just be a woman. Would snakes, wolves, death and blood hold the same significance when attributed to an absent, wished-for woman? Would we still be talking about an erotic song of longing and its natural passion? Or would we regard the text as a sexual poem, one performed mainly by male singers to male collectors of folklore? Folklorists' interpretations have generally gone this route: men and women want different things and likewise want to be loved in different ways. From a psychocultural perspective this may be true. Indeed, the same text is often interpreted differently, depending on the performer and the context.

Satu Apo's study of the so-called "black" sexual poems, an exclusively male genre, underlines how the female body is depicted with disgust and horror: "The vagina is compared to a dog's or wolf's snarling mouth or an open wound. The wound metaphor is often linked to menstruation. – I have rarely encountered such a blunt articulation of male terror when confronted with female sexuality as in these archaic oral poems" (1995:16; cf. also 1998:67). These references can be clearly associated with some of the lines of the poem in question, perhaps even too easily, if we include Apo's observation that – according to eastern Finnish songs – female genitals were made of animal parts: "the flesh of a grouse and partridge, but above all, the mouth of a wolf, the paws of a bear, and the tongue of a fox" (1998:76). If we defy convention and regard the speaker as a man, the poem may emerge as a profound demonstration of man's devotion, i.e., to be near his beloved he is willing to ignore warnings, taboos, and even risk death.

From nearly the opposite perspective of the example above is the following motif in which "the male sex pays homage to the vagina" (Apo 1995:17): *In all her glory, the Cunt sat on the castle window clad in white stockings – the priest took off his cap, the king his crown, the peasants kneeled to the ground* (XV 414). This is not an exclusively folkloric theme; in fact, it is also depicted in European visual arts. The Triumph of Venus, a miniature wood painting apparently made by the 14th century master of Taranto, is just one example. It is a portrayal of six legendary lovers (Achilles, Tristan, Lancelot, Samson, Paris and Troilus) in an oval-shaped ring kneeling before a nude Venus. Golden rays extend from the goddess' genitals, extending to the lovers' faces – and perhaps as some kind of stream of desire back to the object of the gaze. (See Gowing 1987.) Within a mythological context, the painting parodies representations of stigmatization. It also beautifully exemplifies the politics of the gaze and desire.

Sexual and religious elements have been combined in folklore in more complex ways than those already mentioned. For example, the vagina which, according to folk narratives, is made of butter, and pig meat has also been described as *the big hole made of an angel, the tongue from Jesus's flesh* (XV 414). Lotman writes that the texts recall intensified knowledge and experiences: "The text's relationship to the cultural context may be metaphorical, when the text is considered as a substitute for the entire context ... or the relationship may be essentially metonymous when the text represents the context in the same way as a given part represents the whole" (1989:153– 154).

Textual and Contextual Visions

Let us return to the poem's potentially female voice: what do snakes, wolves, bears, blood and death actually signify to a woman? Only one singer, Oksenja Mäkiselkä, has graced us with an interpretation. Mäkiselkä suggested that the image of the mouth dripping with wolf's blood denotes the lover's anger "Even if he was so angry" (KRA 11). As far as we know, the other singers said nothing.

Undeniably, the poem's long history of masculine readings is coming to halt. A significant number of women scholars have already offered alternative interpretations. Trying to ascertain the nature of the poem's ego, i.e., just what kind of woman she was, no longer seems of interest. Although female scholars describe the richness of variation, they do not dwell on it; rather, their studies have focussed more on the exploration of the poem as a metaphorical expression of feeling.

Anneli Nuutinen (1961), for example, indicated a variety of themes related to the poem. However, her main objective was, in the study of variation, to find the poem's ancient core, which, in her view, was formed in the 11th century at the latest. Although reunion was possibly part of that core, Nuutinen claims that the death motif was the most powerful (cf. Krohn 1922, 1923 and Kuusi 1963:390); furthermore, death is interestingly linked to folk belief: "death is contagious, if one is afraid, or if one touches a corpse or sleeps in a bed in which the deceased has lain" (19). All touched by death would pass death on to whoever in turn touched them. In Nuutinen's view, the poem depicts the fatal risk the poem's ego is willing to take. This interpretation sounds even more plausible if we briefly pause to think of the deathly touch of AIDS transmitted by blood in our own day and age. The poem's grave message could prompt one to think, could I, and for whom, and could I say, in this way: if... and even if...

Lotte Tarkka thus conceptualizes the images: predators, death and blood are symbols of strangeness, of Otherness. The poem conveys the speaker's longing to transcend the feeling of separation and confront that strangeness, whatever it may be: he/she tries to unite "this world and the underworld, the familiar and the strange, the known and the unknown, the seen before to the unforeseen, the living and the dead, man and woman" (1994:261–262). The basis for this type of desire and the nature of these distinct entities to be united vary depending on the circumstances. For example, female and community experiences of separations and unions are manifested in poems about weddings and falling in love. To the young bride, her future husband

and his family appear as predatory strangers, (the bridegroom is a wolf, the father-in-law a bear, the brother-in-law an adder, see, e.g. Ilomäki 1994:247 and Siikala 1998:185). Upon leaving her childhood home, it too becomes a strange and threatening place; the snake beer offered to her after marriage symbolizes her estrangement from her natal home (VII:2 998, 1000 etc.). The irony of marriage is that it initially turns the young woman into a stranger to both households. Knowing this, one can easily imagine her words: "I risk all of this by touching him".

Brita Polttila approaches the poem's key emotion, the burning longing for the Other, by describing the deathly attributes. "The profundity of the series of images was discernible to me only after seeing it within the framework of ancient folk beliefs," asserts Polttila. Snakes, wolves, and bears are thus linked to the mythical cosmology of the world of the dead, to *Manala's* reptiles and beasts of prey; blood and death allude to the absent beloved's struggle against death, even in *Tuonela*: "In the entire cosmological dimension the sequence of images does not only reveal the feelings of the bereft, but also the feelings of the one who is missed" (1982:15–17). The song clearly appears to articulate the feelings of widow(er)s and orphans. Polttila does not stop at this, however, but through 18th century grinding songs tries to construct the poem's possible origin as a pre-Christian ritual for appeasing the spirit of wheat, dough or milk: by grinding, baking or churning, the wheat and the milk would "die"; in ritual poetry it was hoped that these "mothers" would return, be resurrected. It was only later on, after the structural shift in economy took place, that the poem become a profane lyrical demonstration of longing for a lover or relative (1991:101–111).

Anna-Leena Siikala (1998:181–186) offers an interpretation framed within the Savo tradition, with particular emphasis on passionate love's "power to break day-to-day commitments." Unlike romantic love, erotic passion poses a threat to social organization and responsibility. Thus it endangers both the community and those who experience it. The lovers' fulfilment can be followed by death – either their physical death or a social demise. In the poem, this passion and the risks it poses are conveyed with mythical images. Like the shaman, who has access to powerful words and uses them to beckon his magical helpers – snakes, bears, wolves and iron fences, the lover in his own altered state of consciousness gains the power to destroy the barriers (symbols of social order) keeping him/her from the object of his desire.

Despite the shifts in emphasis, women scholars have chosen to analyze the poem by drawing from mythological accounts of the other world. But how far off could that ancient world beyond the horizon be? The focus of the interpretation should also be turned to the texts and to the synchronic, experiential relationships between possible contexts. Thus, in addition to articulating the researcher's views, we could render the voices of the singers more forcefully.

If the author of the poem had been the epic poet, the extraordinary woman of genius, the learned "Turku Modernist" of the late Middle Ages, as Kuusi suggests, the range of inspirational sources could be broadened to include the visionary poetry and the artistic traditions of mysticism depicting the Passion of Christ. From such a perspective, the "one known" and the "one seen before" would be Christ, the beloved, merciful, beckoning, suffering, dying and rising from the dead – the Son of God. Johan Huizinga's research on late medieval religious sentiments and images of religious ecstasy reveals an interesting paradox. Even though the Church itself tolerated blatantly carnal expressions of love for God, it harshly condemned all forms of immorality, sensuality, and debauchery. Particularly Christ's wounds and the glowing red blood may have stirred the imagination. "Catherine of Siena was one of the saints who drank from Christ's bleeding side". Death was a refuge, and the animal symbols (snakes, wolves, lions) could just as well be Apostolic heavenly signs as bad omens from the Book of Revelations (1989:259–265; see also Setälä 1996:185–189). Could the "Gothic Romanticism of the wild backwoods" have been inspired by religious literature and iconography? After all, if all is borrowed, why not these as well?

In principle, the "one known" and "the one seen before" may have referred to any absent or longed-for person, an object of desire. Every single line carries emotional significance; and, omitting any of them will not lead us to the ultimate and original emotional core, or the authentic experience. The fact that the poem's individual lines can be found in varying contexts as early as the 18th century does not necessarily mark the process of decay. Perhaps we must assume that the lines in their textual connections are part of a signifying process which remains mysterious to us. Has individual creativity found its expression as a transition from one context of significance to another in the manner of the commutation test? If so, a new meaning of a text would also be an origin in Severino's view: "Every beginning involves a changing into something else and every change involves a becoming something else, thus beginning"; "the burning log in the hearth approaches the origin of ash." (1997:128) For folkloristics this could be a challenging way to reflect upon the process of origins, i.e., placing it within the context of change rather than an unreachable horizon.

According to Tor-Björn Hägglund, "an individual's apprehension of exterior facts is based on personal understanding and completely personal/ subjective aims"; thus creative activity can be regarded as "an attempt to influence the already existing real world and chain of events and change them"; from this follows that "the result of creativity is not the creation of something totally new but a modification of what already exists" (1991:54– 55). In other words, synaesthetic emotional processes lend meaning to their objects by exterior sense impressions and psychophysically dense and evermoving contexts.

When trying to appreciate emotional contexts and possible sources of inspiration, a study of 18th century religious iconography may be in order. This kind of art surely reflected the meanings of desire, promise, and fulfillment in the minds of congregation members. Up till now, church paintings have, especially in folklore research, been used mainly to provide a visual background to the texts, or, in some cases as an aid in temporally locating a poetic motif (see Haavio 1935; Kuusi 1963, esp. 273–397; Klemettinen 1997). However, when congregation members were also authoring their own poems, the singers must have also assigned meanings to the texts in religious contexts. Surely, it is plausible that Christ's sufferings, which were visible on church walls, would have been conveyed in lyric poetry as a personal relation between images and those who gaze upon them. How can we deny the emotional impact such paintings must have had on church-goers, particularly people who had no other access to representational images. Mikael Toppelius (1734–1821), a church painter from Northern Finland, was known for his skill in familiarizing Biblical artistic traditions (see Mähönen 1975 and Kari – Ruotsalainen 1989).

The serpent is ever-present in Biblical imagery. To cite just a few examples, the snake plays a key role in creation narratives, wanderings in the desert, and, of course, in the standard horrific images of Hell. Church walls were covered with images of wolves, gaping mouths, blood, wounds, and death; there were also a number of depictions of bountiful Communion tables (*I will sooner leave fine foods and forget rectory roasts before I leave my sweetheart*), and images of the fence being lowered before the one seen before Christ is taken down from the cross. Interpretations of this kind do not ultimately seek to see how the pictures and the text correspond, but rather the possible meanings that can be derived from such combinations. Nevertheless, we can say with conviction that most people that were familiar with, say, the religious art of Emanuel Granberg (1754–1787) and Mikael Toppelius, also knew one or more variations of the song in question. Generally, the above cited lines about fine delicacies and the vicarage roast have been regarded as alien to the true poem, but some researchers have indeed presented views to the contrary. Eero Saarenheimo, for example, regards the banquet images as a balancing element. "And why would the rejection of the vicarage roast not be the expected type of zealousness to some experts?" (1992:7).

A consideration of 17th and 18th century religious ceremonies renders the poem's emotional import more understandable. For a start, we could contemplate the mysticism about the Bride of Christ, an extraordinary love theme depicted in both sermons and hymns. No distinction was made between men and women, or between individual or collective subjects. Once inside the stately church structure, with its walls flickering with Biblical images, how did the individual feel when the entire congregation and the parish clerk chanter sang, for example, a hymn composed by Abraham Achrenius (1706–1769)? This hymn illustrates the emotional intensity of religious love: *Dearest Jesus, Jesus Dear, Lamb of God, Thou let thyself be slain, To thee I offer myself, Thou art my beloved bridegroom! Before Beloved God I am thy bride, I pray that I can stay by your side! Blessed, blessed, blessed is he, who is beckoned to the wedding and communion of the Lamb, he, who is beckoned to the wedding and the communion.* The concrete imagery of bodily suffering, death, and redemption are entangled with the promise of touching the body and blood of Christ. This aspect of mysticism has been one of the forms of Christian mentality right up to our own day. *Let your open wounds be my nest, my solace, my fortress and haven until I can come to kiss them* (Songs and Hymns of Zion 1953, numbers 106 and 111; both are placed under the heading of Food Hymns).

A broader study of Kalevala poetry could be undertaken in terms of Christian mythology and meditations, not only through the poem *If the One*

I Know Came Now; after all, there are a number of Christian verses in the archaic Finnish-Karelian poems. In fact, the powerful co-existence of old and new is precisely what has led to the syncretic richness of Finnish-Karelian folk culture. Väinämöinen and the other bygone heros are accompanied by the child who is born, the man who suffers, dies on the cross, and rises from the dead – the figure of Christ. The Son of God is divinely distant and yet physically approachable; he slips into the world of humanity, can almost be touched, and is thus a figure for the singers to identify with.

The idea of the mystical and physical encounter between the poem's ego and Christ is, to some degree, comparable to poems about the conception and birth of Christ. In these poems, the ego, the Virgin Mary, is impregnated by eating a red berry. This act of consumption may correspond not only to Annunciation iconography, but also to an actual physical conception, personally experienced by the singer. For the most part, images of death and suffering are not present here unless accompanied by references to the berry's red juice and the occasionally explicitly uttered belief that Christ *made red lingonberries from his own blood* (I:2 1098). Thus, the story of Christ's suffering is familiarized and easily graspable in terms of everyday life. *The Messiah,* which is essentially a narrative depicting the Passion of Christ, proceeds in the following fashion: Christ is pierced by a thousand swords, rises from the dead, etc. (VII:2 1077), washes away his blood in a holy river (VII:2 1071, 1076–1077). Incantations against disease invoke the healing liquids: *Jesus's red blood and Mary's sweet milk* (VI 3416); an incantation to stop the flow of blood alludes to Jesus's bleeding wounds (VI 3446) and how Mary stopped the flow with her beautiful hands, her thick thumbs. In light of the some of the old archival data, "the one known" can imply an emotional and physical closeness to Christ who sends a thousand of those known before, a hundred heros of God to help those who pray (VII:4 1594–1595). The texture of the poems combines the supplicating ego/self with categories of the sacred and the profane: *Jesus my father, the Virgin my mother, I the son of the Virgin Mary, a piece of Jesus's flesh, two pieces of liver* (VII:3 901). Is it not plausible that these poetic images were inspired by the church paintings portraying Christ, Mary, and the angels?

The Ingrian variants describing the reunion with the mother lend further depth to Christian readings of the poem. In Ingrian poetry as a whole, the mother holds a prominent place. Occasionally, she even attains a God-like status. The feminine ego finds in the mother and/or in God her own origins, the mystery of her birth and how they determine her happiness and the direction of her fate. In the present tense the songs render the mother Christ-like in her absence from the world of the living; she is dissociated from the profane. Nevertheless, she is emotionally everpresent, the most familiar of all beings; she is the persona always spoken to and passionately longed for. Like *If the One I Know Came Now*, many other poems deal with the themes of the mother's death and the subsequent feelings of being orphaned by developing the wishful images, such as the return from the land of the dead or rising from the grave; mythical journeys are made in the blink of an eye, birds' wings fly, the ego uses his/her hands to dig the mother from the grave. Thus, the images of clasping the hand of the mother, in spite of the snake in it, embracing her in spite of the bear or death around her neck, are not strange at all, on the contrary, they are self-evident.

Matti Kuusi (1994:89–90) writes that Ingrian women have discarded the lines describing unseemly maternal encounters. However, there are exceptions. For example, when Larin Paraske first dictated the poem to a collector she omitted this pair of lines, but when she sang it she added them. She also performed a short poem beginning with the line *If the One I Know Came Now*, but without the encounter or the lines referring to the hand, mouth, neck or side. These she associated especially with the mother. Paraske's mother poem is in many ways interesting in that she combines the mother and the one known themes in the same text; nonetheless, the reunion is clearly one with the mother. To whom does Paraske refer as the one known here and in other texts remains ambiguous. Perhaps she directly expresses here what other singers left unvoiced, that is the simultaneous presence of many interpretations and levels of experience, and the disappearance of borders. This is a characteristic of mystical experiences which, according to Terhi Utriainen, include "crossing, destroying and inversing of gender difference and the desire that is fixed in this difference ... Some mystics momentarily show the heterosexual matrix as a polymorphous kaleidoscope" (1998:144). Thus sang Larin Paraske:

Tietäisin emon tulleeva	If I knew my mother were coming
hopiaisen tien tekisin,	I'd pave a silver road
hopiasillat seisattaisin,	I'd build silver bridges
hopiapatsaa'at panisin,	I'd erect silver pillars
oron sillalle vetäisin,	I'd lead a stallion along the bridge
oron selkään mie satulan,	with a saddle on his back
hopialoimen lautasille!	a silver blanket on his hindquarters.
Virstan vastaan mie mänisin,	I'd go a *verst* to meet (her)
puolet matkat polvillaini	half-way on my knees
veräjii mie purkamaane,	to tear down the gates
aitoi availemaane.	to open the fences.
Jos ois suu suven veressä	If the mouth bled from a wolf
mie vaan suuta suikkajaisin,	I'd still steal a kiss
tahk ois kärme kämmenpäässä	or if a snake were on the palm
mie vaan kättä kääppäjäisin,	I'd still grasp that palm
jos ois kalma kaklan päälle	if death clung to the neck
mie vaan kaula'a rappaisin,	I'd still throw myself at the neck
taihk olis vieruus vertä täynnä	or even if the side were all bloody
mie vaan viere'en kävisin.	Still I'd go to the side.
Jos miun tuttuin tulisi,	If the one I know came now
ennen nähtyin näkyisi,	if the one I've seen were in sight
tuntisin tutun tulosta,	I'd know the way of walking
astunnast on arvajaisin,	I'd guess it from the gait
kypäräst ja kinttahast,	from the cap and the mittens
kaikest on keso-kalusta.	from all the summer clothing.
(V:3 88–88a)	

The poetic simultaneity re-emerges with regard to modalities. The singers never say: *When s/he comes*. They say: If s/he came now. The one known does not exist in the poem's present tense. Nor does s/he come. The only sure site of reunion is in a vision, that is, within the poetic domain.

From this perspective the poem conforms to the utopian vision that runs through the entire corpus of Kalevala lyric poetry; the poem can be considered representative rather than exceptional (Timonen 1992). The utopian image denies what is and focuses on what could be. The simple sign, *If,* often functions as a linguistic gate, opening a view to the conditional and what could be possible and thus to the desired. Utopia is dynamic; not only does the poem provide a glimpse of it, but it renews already existing reality, creating something else altogether. For example, it eliminates the absence of the loved one by establishing new intimacies. Moreover, it defies distances, by crossing them: *Had the wind a mind and the gale a tongue it would bring a word, take a word, set an extra word astir between two lovers.* Often, as in the poem, the encounter enables a utopian journey transcending all obstacles.

"Hope is the opposite of security; hope is not confidence," says Ernst Bloch (1989:16–17). To various degrees, utopia always also contains, as a hint or an expression, dystopia: the category of danger, the risk of destruction. It is the sounding board of courage and joy that sustains utopia. The utopian vision functions most dramatically when its opposite is clearly in sight – at the moment when it unites the two poles of reality, not just the good, but also the bad.

The poetic and emotional force of *If the One I Know Came Now* emerges in the dialogue between hope and fear. As malevolent as the physical incarnations of evil – a snake, wolf, blood, or death – appear to the ego, the utopian vision responds with equal force; with the images of earthly love, and maintaining itself it transcends dystopia. It is precisely the nature of visions – be they poetic, dramatic, musical, or visual – to juxtapose the most peculiar details and seemingly incompatible things. Keeping such a polyphonic principal in mind, we ought to refrain from organizing the lines historically and geographically, particularly for textual material whose lines keep shifting into ever-new arrangements.

The Bodily Nature of Feelings

If we had concluded that the entire corpus – well over two hundred texts – could easily yield an infinite number of valid interpretations, we would have come full circle to no avail. Rather, we have tried to show that not all previous interpretations, not even the ones put forth in this paper, are equally intriguing or worthy of further consideration. Origins are no longer accessible to us. Nevertheless, the obsessive desire to capture the original – a hunger that gnaws away at those of us studying the past – is a refusal to let that which is lost rest in peace.

Ruth Benedict maintained in both her research and writing an aim to present her object of study from various points of view. Her style of scholarship was to try and persuade her reader by juxtaposing or placing in contact the familiar and tame with the wild and exotic. Termed articulation, this technique enables the reader to ask, among other things, what sort of impact does the proximity of the various elements have upon one another.

What happens when they change places? Benedict suggests that human nature is defined by its multiplicity, and thus its environments traces and cultures, should always be described from a number of varying perspectives. Interestingly, these methodological ideas have now gained currency after a long period of silence. Hélène Cixous's use of poetical writing as a research method is one fine example. "The other in all his or her forms gives me *I*. It is on the occasion of the other that *I* catch sight of *me*; or that *I* catch *me* at: reacting, choosing, refusing, accepting. It is the other who makes my portrait. Always. And luckily." (1997:13.)

One of the purposes of this paper has been to seek the dimensions of emotional expressions and relations conveyed in *If the One I Know Came Now*. Keeping the various interpretive approaches in mind, it has been fruitful to observe how, and above all, where earlier scholars have placed and distanced the feelings projected from the texts. More often than not, scholars have raised this poetic expression of love or passion to a lofty and lonely pedestal. Were they trying to prevent the poems from being sullied by collective and peasant images of love? This circular interpretation has always led to the same conclusion: although only a few archaic folk poems are devoted to love, there is no dearth of vulgar sexual songs.

Studies of *If the One I Know Came Now* show how feelings have been considered to be located "inside" the individual subject, and the emotions correspondingly located within a symbolic realm ("between" people). Indeed, the older interpretations made no distinctions between individual feelings and social emotions. According to this, the poem's fictive subject feels love within himself/herself, and the text's if-even-so assurances awaken in the performer/listener/reader a feeling of its power, depth, and authenticity. Margot L. Lyon approaches the ambivalence of interpretations dealing with feelings and emotions in a novel manner. Moreover, she explores the kinds of arguments used within research to present feelings and emotions as secondary and peripheral in relation to knowledge. Lyon asserts that in social relationships emotions are contextualized through the body, and thus they renew themselves and enliven experiences.

But how can one approach and interpret the bodily nature of feelings when they have typically been deemed immaterial? Upon hearing our discussion, social psychologist Kari Vesala proposed a "rhetoric for dealing with the mystery of experience" (Letter 13.12.1996). As an experiment, he related the poem and its interpretive visions to Thomas Mann's *Magic Mountain*. Hans Castorp goes to the sanitarium "to meet his consumptive friend (the one known with blood flowing from his side) by finding a focus of the disease also in himself. He befriends the mystical Clavdia, another convalescent at the sanatorium. For Hans she is an intriguingly older and maternal "one known." Her mere presence leads to a meeting of minds:

> What an immense festival of caresses lies in those delicious zones of the human body! A festival of death with no weeping afterward! Yes, good God, let me smell the odor of the skin on your knee, beneath which the ingeniously segmented capsule secretes its slippery oil! Let me touch in devotion your pulsing femoral artery where it emerges at the top of your thigh and then divides farther down into the two arteries of the tibia! Let me take in the

exhalation of your pores and brush the down – oh, my human image made of water and protein, destined for the contours of the grave, let me perish, my lips against yours!
(Mann 1996:337.)

Underlining the bodily nature of emotions could yield new, concrete and earthly interpretations of folk poetry. Poems do not ask to be remembered. The original lines live within us.

Translated by Leila Virtanen.

NOTE

[1] Throughout this article we have indicated the volumes and poem numbers for those texts found in *Suomen Kansan Vanhat Runot* (The Old Poems of the Finnish People = SKVR).

BIBLIOGRAPHY

Acerbi, Giuseppe 1802: Travels through Sweden, Finland, and Lapland to the North Cape in the Years 1798 and 1799. London.
Ala-Könni, Erkki 1961: "Jos mun tuttuni tulisi" -runoon liittyvä sävelmistö. Kalevala-vuosikirja 41:221–226.
Anttila, Aarne 1985 [1931]: Elias Lönnrot. Elämä ja toiminta. SKS. Helsinki.
Apo, Satu 1981: Kansanrunous. K. Laitinen (ed.) Suomen kirjallisuuden historia: 13–95. Otava. Helsinki.
– 1989: Suullinen runous-vuosisatainen traditio. M.L. Nevala (ed.) "Sain roolin johon en mahdu". Suomalaisen naiskirjallisuuden linjoja: 21–28. Otava. Helsinki.
– 1995: Naisen väki. Tutkimuksia suomalaisten kansanomaisesta kulttuurista ja ajattelusta. Hanki ja jää. Helsinki – Hämeenlinna.
– 1998: "Ex cunno Come the Folk and Force". Concepts of Women's Dynamistic Power in Finnish-Karelian Tradition. S. Apo – A. Nenola – L. Stark-Arola (eds) Gender and Folklore. Perspectives on Finnish and Karelian Culture. Studia Fennica Folkloristica 4:63–91. Finnish Literature Society. Helsinki.
Asplund, Anneli cf. Nuutinen
Austerlitz, Robert 1984: A Finnish Folk Poem, its Yakut Translation, Goethe, and Other Personalities. Turks, Hungarians and Kipchaks. A Festschrift in Honor of Tibor Halasi-Kun. Journal of Turkish Studies 8:1–9. Harvard University. Harvard.
Bloch, Ernst 1989: The Utopian Function of Art and Literature. Selected Essays. Translated by Jack Zipes and Frank Mecklenburg. MIT Press. Cambridge.
Bloch, Marc 1976: The Historian's Craft. Manchester University Press. Manchester.
Cixous, Hélène – Calle-Gruber, Mireille 1997: Hélène Cixous Rootprints. Memory and Life Writing. Routledge. London – New York.
Collan, Fabian 1843: "En Finsk Runa, öfversatt på alla verldens språk". Helsingfors Morgonblad n:o 44.
Enäjärvi-Haavio, Elsa 1935: Lyyrilliset laulut in Haavio, Martti 1935:112–175.
Fiske, John 1990: Introduction to Communication Studies. Second edition. Routledge. London – New York.
Gowing, Lawrence 1987: Paintings in the Louvre. Stewart, Tabori & Chang. New York.
Haavio, Martti 1933: Suomalainen muinaisrunous. Suomen kulttuurihistoria 1. Heimoyhteiskunnan ja katolisen kulttuurin aika: 280–354. Gummerus. Jyväskylä.
– 1935: Suomalaisen muinaisrunouden maailma. WSOY. Porvoo – Helsinki.

- 1949: Kansanrunojen sepittäjät ja esittäjät. Virittäjä 53:1:6–15.
- 1952: Laulupuu. Suomen kansan tunnelmarunoutta. WSOY. Helsinki.
Haltsonen, Sulo 1961: C.G. Zetterqvist ja suomalainen runo. Kalevalaseuran vuosikirja 41:208–220.
Honko, Lauri – Timonen, Senni – Branch, Michael 1993: The Great Bear. A Thematic Anthology of Oral Poetry in the Finno-Ugrian Languages. Poems translated by Keith Bosley. Finnish Literature Society. Helsinki.
Huizinga, Johan 1989 [1923]: Keskiajan syksy. Elämän- ja hengenmuotoja Ranskassa ja Alankomaissa 14. ja 15. vuosisadalla. WSOY. Helsinki.
Hägglund, Tor-Björn 1991: Tuonelan eteisessä. Psykoanalyyttinen tutkimus ihmisen luovuudesta ja suojautumiskeinoista kuoleman edessä. Pohjoinen. Oulu.
Ilomäki, Henni 1994: Song in Ritual Context: North Karelian Wedding Songs. A.-L. Siikala – S. Vakimo (eds) Songs beyond the Kalevala. Transformations of Oral Poetry. Studia Fennica Folkloristica 2:236–249. Finnish Literature Society. Helsinki.
Jakobson, Roman – Bogatyrev, Petr 1974 [1929]: Folklore som en särskild form av skapande. Jakobson, Roman, Poetik och lingvistik. Litteraturvetenskapliga bidrag valda av Kurt Aspelin och Bengt A. Lundberg. Norstedt. Stockholm.
Karhu, Eino 1979: Suomen kirjallisuus runonlaulajista 1800-luvun loppuun. 1. Kansankulttuuri OY. Helsinki.
Kari, Risto – Ruotsalainen, Matti 1989: Kirkkomaalarit. Mikael Toppeliuksen ja Emanuel Granbergin taide. Otava. Helsinki.
Kaukonen, Väinö 1984: Elias Lönnrotin Kanteletar. SKS. Helsinki.
- 1989: Elias Lönnrot ja Kanteletar. SKS. Helsinki.
Klemettinen, Pasi 1997: Mellastavat pirut. Tutkimus kansanomaisista paholais- ja noituuskäsityksistä Karjalan Kannaksen ja Laatokan Karjalan tarinaperinteessä. SKS. Helsinki.
Krohn, Kaarle 1920: Muinaisrunoja laulusta – surusta – lemmestä. Ruusu-sarja 6. WSOY. Porvoo.
- 1922: Goethes "Finnisches Lied". Laographica VI:41–44.
- 1923: Vanha runo. "Jos mun tuttuni tulisi". Valvoja-Aika 1:28–30.
Kunze, Erich 1952: Goethes "Finnisches Lied". Studia Fennica VI:39–57.
- 1957: Jakob Grimm und Finnland. FF Communications No. 165.
- 1970: Nachklänge von Goethes "Finnischem Lied". Die Versionen von Geibel und J.G. Seidl sowie ahd. und mhd. Bearbeitungen. Neuphilologische Mitteilungen LXXI:3:372–378.
Kuusi, Matti 1963: Suomen kirjallisuus I. Kirjoittamaton kirjallisuus. Otava. Helsinki.
- 1967: A lírai népdalok datálásáról – általános megjegyzések és egy finn példa. (Auszug: Zum Datierungsproblem der lyrischen Volkslieder. Theoretische Beobachtungen und ein finnisches Beispiel). Ethnographia LXXVIII:3:324–340.
- 1983: Maria Luukan laulut ja loitsut. Tutkimus läntisimmän Inkerin suomalais-perinteestä. SKS. Helsinki.
- 1994: World Poetry. Kuusi, Matti, Mind and Form in Folklore. Selected Articles. H. Ilomäki (ed.) Studia Fennica Folkloristica 3:88–95. Finnish Literature Society. Helsinki.
Kuusi, Matti – Bosley, Keith – Branch, Michael 1977: Finnish Folk Poetry. Epic. An Anthology in Finnish and English. Finnish Literature Society. Helsinki.
Laitinen, Kai 1994: Literature of Finland. An Outline. 2nd ed. Helsinki. Otava.
Lotman, Juri 1989: Merkkien maailma. Kirjoitelmia semiotiikasta. SN-kirjat. Helsinki.
Lutz, Catherine A. 1988: Unnatural Emotions. Everyday Sentiments on a Micronesian Atoll & Their Challenge to Western Culture. The University of Chicago Press. Chicago – London.
Lyon, Margot L. 1995: Missing Emotion: The Limitations of Cultural Constructionism. Cultural Anthropology 10:2:244–263.
Lönnrot, Elias 1908 [1843]: En Finsk Runas Öde. (Ur ett bref till Fabian Collan.) J. af Forselles (ed.) Elias Lönnrots svenska skrifter 1. Uppsatser och öfversättningar: 243–248. Svenska Litteratursällskapet i Finland. Helsingfors.
- 1966 [1840]: Kanteletar elikkä Suomen kansan vanhoja lauluja ja virsiä. 13. painos. SKS. Helsinki.

Mann, Thomas 1996 [1924]: The Magic Mountain. A Novel. Translated from German by John E. Woods. Vintage Books. New York.

Mähönen, Reino 1975: Kirkkomaalari Mikael Toppelius. Suomen Muinaismuisto-yhdistyksen aikakauskirja 78. Suomen Muinaismuistoyhdistys. Helsinki.

Nuutinen, Anneli 1961: "Jos mun tuttuni tulisi." Unpublished manuscript: seminar paper, S 87. Department of Folkloristics, University of Helsinki.

Oinas, Felix 1996: "Kui see mu tuttav tuleks". Uusi tölkeid. Looming 5:655–657.

Polttila, Brita 1982: Lauluja rakkaudesta ja kuolemasta. M. Polkunen – A. Viikari (eds) Suomalaisia kirjailijoita. Kirjailijat kirjailijoista: 9–17. Tammi. Helsinki.

– 1991: Taivaan mereltä. Tammi. Helsinki.

Porthan, Henrik Gabriel 1983 [1778]: Suomalaisesta runoudesta. Translated and foreword written by Iiro Kajanto. SKS. Helsinki.

Pulkkinen, Tuija 1998: Naisyhteisö: subjektius, identiteetti ja toimijuus. J. Kotkavirta – A. Laitinen (eds) Yhteisö. Filosofian näkökulmia yhteisöllisyyteen. SoPhi. Yhteiskuntatieteiden, valtio-opin ja filosofian julkaisuja 16: 239–251. Jyväskylän yliopisto. Jyväskylä.

Saarenheimo, Eero 1974: Giuseppe Acerbi ja suomalainen kansanrunous. Kalevalaseuran vuosikirja 54:326–339.

– 1992. Kansanrunoutemme tärkein kirjaanpano. Bibliophilos 4:5–7.

Sarajas, Annamari 1956: Suomalaisen kansanrunouden tuntemus 1500–1700-lukujen kirjallisuudessa. WSOY. Helsinki.

Setälä, E.N. 1932: Sammon arvoitus. Otava. Helsinki.

Setälä, Päivi 1996: Keskiajan nainen. Otava. Helsinki

Severino, Emanuele 1997: Kärsimys, kohtalo, kapitalismi. Loki-kirjat. Helsinki.

Siikala, Anna-Leena 1998: Oliko savolaisilla tunteita? J. Pöysä – A.-L. Siikala (eds) Amor, genus & familia. Kirjoituksia kansanperinteestä: 165–192. SKS. Helsinki.

Siionin Laulut ja Wirret. 1953. Oulu.

Skjöldebrand, A.F. 1986 [1801–1802]: Piirustusmatka Suomen halki Nordkapille 1799 [Voyage pittoresgue au cap Nord]. Translation in Finnish, foreword and comments by Kerkko Hakulinen. Helsinki.

Suomen Kansan Vanhat Runot (SKVR) I–XV. 1908–1997. SKS. Helsinki.

Suomen Kansan Sävelmiä IV: 1 (Inkerin runosävelmät), 2 (Karjalan runosävelmät). Publ. Armas Launis. 1910, 1930. SKS. Helsinki.

Tarkiainen, V. 1912: "Jos mun tuttuni tulisi". Suomi IV:11. SKS. Helsinki.

– 1921: Viisi Kantelettaren runoa. Kalevalaseuran vuosikirja 1:100–112.

– 1943: Tunnelmarunous. V. Tarkiainen – H. Harmas (eds) Suomen kansalliskirjallisuus: valikoima Suomen kirjallisuuden huomattavimpia tuotteita. III. Vanhaa kansanrunoutta julkaistuna alkuperäisten kirjaanpanojen mukaan, 242–257. Otava. Helsinki.

Tarkka, Lotte 1994: Other Worlds – Symbolism, Dialogue and Gender in Karelian Oral Poetry in A.-L. Siikala – S. Vakimo (eds) 1994: 250–298.

Timonen, Senni 1992: 'Utopian' Ideas in Women's Poetry. R. Kvideland (ed. in collaboration with P. Laaksonen, A.–L. Siikala – N. Storå) Folklore Processed in Honour of Lauri Honko on his 60th Birthday 6th March 1992. Studia Fennica Folkloristica 1:214–224. Finnish Literature Society. Helsinki.

– 1993: Love in Honko et al. 1993:287–298.

Utriainen, Terhi 1998: Ruumis, kuolema ja pyhä sana -ruumis kohtalona ja ilmaisuna keskiajan naismystikoilla. T. Koskinen (ed.) Kurtisaaneista kunnian naisiin. Näkökulmia Huora-akatemiasta:130–158. Yliopistopaino. Helsinki.

Vesala, Kari 1996: A letter to Seppo Knuuttila and Senni Timonen 13.12.1996.

Virtanen, Leea 1988: Suomalainen kansanperinne. SKS. Helsinki.

Virtanen, Leea – DuBois, Thomas 2000: Finnish Folklore. Studia Fennica Folkloristica 9. Helsinki: Finnish Literature Society in Association with the University of Washington Press, Seattle.

Weöres, Gyula 1961: Suomalaisten kansanlaulujen varhaisimmista unkarinnoksista. Kalevalaseuran vuosikirja 41:227–239. Helsinki.

Zetterqvist, C.G. 1858: Anthologie philologique. MS, Finnish Literature Society, Literature Archives. Helsinki

Sources of Poems

The following list includes all texts of *If the one I know came now* regardless of who (a friend, beloved, darling, mother, father, etc.) is being spoken of, the opening line, or whether the poem appears to have a literary source. Apparent copies of the same texts (VI 591, XII 347–348:1, 350 = XII 351; XII 348:2, 407–409, 411 = XI 828; III 104 = III 3643; VII[2] 2361 = VII[3]L 327) are not included in the total presented in the article. For about 20 of the texts marked with asterisks the link to our poem is a question of interpretation as they only contain the opening lines and the lines describing the distance to the meeting (If..; I'd go a *verst*...). All the texts not marked with an asterisk contain images (snake / wolf's blood / bear / death / blood) that we believe belong to the core of the poem. In addition to the four melodies mentioned by Ala-Könni (1961:222, 224), the notes taken on the poem in relation to melodies are the archive texts 2a and 5–7 as well as Skjöldebrand's travel book (1986:45).

Published in The Old Poems of the Finnish People (SKVR):

I[3] 1433–1434; I [4] 2220*; II 433–434; III 104, 974–975, 1512*, 2525, 2638, 2760, 3643, 3729*; IV 240*, 305*, 310*, 416*, 835*, 936, 1000–1001, 1044, 1477, 1490, 1539*, 1709, 2113, 2165, 2169–2172, 2365, 2373, 2465*, 2487, 2546, 2560, 2635, 3156, 3165, 3312, 3332, 3429, 3535, 3645, 3814, 3952, 4059, 4589*; V[1] 1233*– 1234*, 1292; V[2] 288, 420*, 735, 1143*, 1144–1145, 1146*, 1147, 1148*–1149*, 1150–1152, 1153*–1156*, 1157, 1158*, 1159–1163, 1246*, 1250, 1251*, 1253*–1254*, 1259*, 1605*, 2429;V[3] 88, 521*, 681*–682*; VI 40, 591–593, 594*–595*, 596, 609, 613*, 730, 828*, 4959, 6511*;VII[1]252*; VII[2] 2321, 2354–2357, 2357a*, 2358– 2360, 2361*, 2362, 2363–2364, 2365*, 2366, 2367*, 2368–2370a, 2640*;VII[3]L 327*; IX[1] 27*, 56; XII 347, 348*, 350–352, 396*, 407*–409*, 411*, 6848; XIII 1598*, 1793, 1930, 3060–3063, 3064*–3065*, 3066–3067, 3068*, 3069, 3070*, 3071*, 3072*, 3073–3082, 3083*, 3084, 3085*, 3086–3091, 3282, 3283*, 3284, 3290*, 3291, 3293*, 3295*, 3656, 8102, 8109, 10680*, 10704*, 10806*, 10807; XV 131*, 205*, 601, 1332, 1335–1336.

Unpublished, The Folklore Archives of the Finnish Literature Society (KRA):

ARCHANGEL KARELIA: **1.** Uhtua. Ievala 704. 1931. OLONETS KARELIA: **2a–b.** Rukajärvi. Borenius e 525–526. 1877 (Suomen kansan sävelmiä IV, 2:626, 625). SAVO: **3.** Nilsiä. Karhu 4909. 1936; **4*.** Nilsiä. Karhu 4881. 1936. NORTH KARELIA: **5*.** Nurmes. Borenius e 421b. 1877 (= Boreniana II:24); **6.** Liperi. Savokarjalainen Osakunta, Hällström 147.1877 (= Malisto/Hannikainen 43 = Borenius e 640> Suomen kansan sävelmiä IV, 2:618) **7.** Liperi. Savokarjalainen Osakunta, Hällström 146.1877 (= Malisto/ Hannikainen 43 = Borenius e 639> Suomen kansan sävelmiä IV, 2:290). LADOGA KARELIA: **8.** Korpiselkä. Potschareff 72. 1909; **9.** Suojärvi. Haavio 172. 1932; **10.** Suojärvi. Haavio 302. 1921–33. **11.** Suistamo. Haavio 2061. 1935; **12.** Suistamo. Kärki 989. 1942; **13.** Suistamo. Kärki 963. 1942; **14*.** Suistamo. Kähmi KRK 143:9. 1935; **15*.** Suistamo. Martiskainen KJ 36:15390. 1957; **16.** Salmi. Haavio 1575. 1934; **17.** Salmi. Toiviainen KRK 154:286. 1935; **18.** Salmi. Toiviainen 353. 1937–39; **19.** Impilahti. Hainari & Hagan 26. 1913/1943; **20.** Uukuniemi. Toiviainen 574. 1939. SOUTH KARELIA: **21*.** Heinjoki. Borenius 6:705. 1876; **22.** Lumivaara. Sääski 6356. 1956; **23.** Hiitola. Alhava 215. 1956; **24*.** Metsäpirtti. Klaus KJ 8:2147. 1957. INGRIA: **25.** Keltto. Alava VIIIB s. 11. 1894; **26.** Central Ingria. Haltsonen 194. 1930; **27.** Liissilä. Kärki 214. 1907; **28*.** Tyrö. Borenius e 129. 1877 (>Suomen kansan sävelmiä IV, 1: 199); **29.** Narvusi. Aili Laiho 2272. 1937; **30.** Narvusi. Niemi 856, 1938; **31.** Narvusi. Aili Laiho 2251. 1937; **32.** Narvusi. Lukkarinen 472f. 1909; **33*.** Narvusi. Launis 395. 1903 (>Suomen kansan sävelmiä IV, 1:608).

TARJA KUPIAINEN

The Forbidden Love of Sister and Brother

The Incest Theme in Archangel Karelian Kalevala
Meter Epic

According to Claude Lévi-Strauss (1969:24), the incest taboo marks the
fundamental and universal transition from nature to culture. This
transition appears in various ways in world mythologies. Even though incest
is a highly frequent mythic theme and motif (Kluckhohn 1969; Brewster
1972:5–9, 15–22), myth scholars have generally ignored the topic (Meletinskii 1987:26). The incest theme emerges most clearly in Finnish Karelian
Kalevala meter poetry in the so-called *Sisaren turmelus* ("Ruined Sister")
poems, which depicts a young man's seduction of his sister. The *Kalevala*
features a sexual relationship between a sister and brother in Kullervo's
story (poems 31–36). This article focuses on the variants collected in the
1800s from Archangel Karelia and those published in *Suomen Kansan Vanhat
Runot* ("Ancient Poems of the Finnish People") (SKVR I$_2$, 954–992). Since
my study deals primarily with the poetic manifestations of the incest theme,
a brief summary of anthropological theories of incest and incest prohibitions
is in order.

The Incest Taboo in the Study of Culture

Anthropologists have studied incest as a cultural, social and biosocial
phenomenon. Most studies, however, have placed more emphasis on the
incest taboo than on incest itself; since the latter is less visible and more
difficult to define (Willner 1983:135–138; Spain 1987:627–628; cf. Syndergaard 1993:127; Roscoe 1994:49–50). Incest has evolved into a cultural
metaphor for the archetypal evil (Twitchell 1987); like cannibalism, incest
has been regarded as the ultimate sin (Syndergaard ibid.). Nevertheless, incest
definitions have often been limited to explanations of the origin and
significance of incest prohibitions.

Claude Lévi-Strauss has paid considerable attention to incest in his work
The Elementary Structures of Kinship (1969:3–51) in which he presents a
hypothesis of the incest taboo as a marker of the human transition from
nature to culture. He classifies three types of theoretical approaches to the
understanding of incest: rationalist, psychological and sociological (ibid.:2–
25). According to the first theory, the incest taboo stems from the belief that

Myth and Mentality
Studia Fennica
Folkloristica 8, 2002

continued intermarriage between kin spells genetic catastrophe. Evolutionary theorists of the 19th century, such as E.B. Tylor, H.J.S. Maine and L.H. Morgan, were advocates of this rationalist view.

Like his contemporaries, Edward B.Tylor viewed incest as the ultimate manifestation of sexual anarchy. Incest prohibitions, therefore, existed to impose order on sexual anarchy: this paved the way for the shift from unruly (feminine) nature to (masculine) patriarchal culture. At the same time, the incest taboo consolidated male social dominance over women. Although Taylor did not explicitly associate the origins of the incest taboo with his theory of marriage, he was convinced that people had either to seek mates outside their kin group or be doomed to ethnic extinction (an essential choice between "marrying out" or being "killed out"[1]; thus, Tylor allies the incest prohibition with the rationale behind exogamy (Fox 1980:4–5; Weiner 1992:70).

G.P. Murdock (1961:289) has argued against biological justifications for the incest taboo. Thus, if the outcome of sexual relations between kin was indeed genetically disastrous, then why do prohibitions not apply to close kin outside the nuclear family; or, when they do, why are they not applied equally? (see Malinowski 1982:416–433; Lévi-Strauss 1969:42–51, 119–133; Roscoe 1994:52–53.) Recent medical and sociological debates seem to have arrived at the consensus that although the source of the incest taboo lies in biology, its transgression steps into the realm of culture. The biological theory is further sustained by the fact that the incest taboo exists among all primates, and is not confined to human beings (Erickson 1993). Moreover, this helps to explain why some societies accept cross cousin marriages but prohibit parallel cousin marriages: as cultural beings, humans may "illogically" defy a natural and genetically inherent prohibition. This need not preclude the social nature of the incest taboo or the theory that incest draws the line between nature and culture.

Advocates of the psychological theory claim that the incest taboo is a logical extension of the so-called natural aversion for incestuous relations. From a psychological perspective, people who have been raised together as siblings in close proximity naturally feel no sexual attraction for each other. The most renowned representative of this position is Edward Westermarck. He based his theory on the principle "... that there is an innate aversion to sexual intercourse between persons living very closely together from early youth, and that, as such persons are in most cases related, this feeling displays itself chiefly as a horror of intercourse between near kin" (Westermarck 1891:320).

Lévi-Strauss (1969:18) disagrees with Westermarck. He argues that it makes no sense to prohibit an activity which fails to occur in nature. Freud (1989:148–149) challenged Westermarck with a similar "Frazer-like" comment: why prohibit an activity for which people would have no inclination? Arthur P. Wolf (1993), who has cautiously taken up Westermarck's position, bases his argument on the analysis of the Chinese adoption and marriage system and research on kibbutz life (see Spiro 1958; Kaffman 1977).[2] Wolf and Huang (see Wolf 1993) have divided traditional Chinese marriage customs into two main types: 1) parents adopt a bride for their son while he is still a child, 2) bride and groom meet for the very first time at the wedding ceremony. According to their findings, couples who were raised together as children were less fertile, and more prone to adultery and divorce. Moreover, the research that Wolf cites shows that members of the same kibbutz rarely intermarry. On the other hand, according to Malinowski, in Trobriand communities, where incest was most severely forbidden, incestuous desires for one's sister or brother were known to surface in dreams (Malinowski 1982:331–334). Thus, Malinowski's research would undermine the Westermarckian view that incest prohibitions are cultural reflections of an innate and natural aversion for incest (Westermarck 1922:198, 203–204). It is more likely, however, that Malinowski's field description says more about suppressed desires for the forbidden.

We know that consanguineous marriages between siblings were commonplace among ordinary Egyptians up until 300 A.D. when the practise disappeared under the sway of Roman law and Christianity (Hopkins 1980). Keith Hopkins (ibid.:352–353) tentatively concludes that Egyptian sisters and brothers married each other simply because they wanted to; these highly endogamous marriages had nothing to do with familial or social pressures. Moreover, it was also common practise for siblings to marry each other in Sumerian, Inca, Hawaiian and Dahomey aristocratic families. These examples thus undermine the general assumption that incest prohibitions *always* apply to members of the opposite sex within the nuclear family whether the community be endogamous or exogamous, matrilineal or patrilineal (Murdock 1961:1–22, 285, 266; Weiner 1992:66–97). Nevertheless, such exceptional cases further bolster the argument that incest prohibitions regarding siblings are indeed needed since growing up in close proximity does not necessarily preclude sexual attraction.

According to Lévi-Strauss's (1969:19–23) third theory, notions of incest and its prohibitions are purely social phenomena and have no valid biological foundations. Furthermore, even if biological explanations can be found, they should be deemed meaningless. Lévi-Strauss is not alone in his analysis of incest. The subject has earlier been explored by, e.g. Herbert Spencer, J.F. McLennan and Émile Durkheim.

Lévi-Strauss dismissed biological explanations for their inadequacy and lack of genetic evidence. He rejected psychological theories because he was convinced that there was no reason to forbid the unthinkable. Like other sociological theorists, Lévi-Strauss agreed that the incest taboo was a phenomenon which was both social and universal.[3] From his perspective, however, the incest taboo is more than just a human survival strategy because its significance resides in its cultural and social purpose (Lévi-Strauss 1969:23). Although Murdock (1961:297) also underlined the social nature and significance of the incest taboo, he did not explicitly deny its biological roots; nevertheless, he did imply that biological factors were less important than social ones.

The human aversion to incest stems more from a potential social threat than from any genetic risks. The marriage of cousins in the United States, for example, hardly poses a real threat to the genetic future of the family, but it does threaten its social harmony; and, after all, the family has been the basic unit of American society (Twitchell 1987:1–10).

Incest Taboo between Siblings

Incest and incest prohibitions have much more to do with cultural and social principles than with biological or medical facts. Lévi-Strauss considers the incest taboo a fundamental transition from nature to culture. Its origins are neither wholly natural nor cultural. Instead of simply seeing the taboo as a mixture of cultural and natural elements, Lévi-Strauss sees the incest taboo as a fundamental leap from nature to culture (Lévi-Strauss 1969:24). Thus he aligns himself with Freud's (1989) assertion that the origin of culture lies in the primeval crime: Oedipal parricide to gain sexual access to the mother. According to Lévi-Strauss, the incest taboo establishes the route from the natural fact of kinship based on blood to contractual kinship and the social fact of marriage. Nature determines mating, but culture shapes and regulates marriage. In other words, nature determines the union through mating, but at the same time culture determines its written and unwritten rules (Lévi-Strauss 1969:32). Incest appears as a mediator between culture and nature, and thus functions as an agent between the two without fully belonging to either one.

However rare, cases of incestuous relations within the nuclear family – such as those already mentioned along with even more extreme violations of the taboo – do exist[4]; and the incest taboo is the most universal norm to regulate sexual or other conduct. Incestuous relations between parents and children are considered unnatural and looked upon with revulsion. Sexual intimacy between mother and son, or grandmother and grandchild are sure to arouse disgust (see Shepher 1983:165–168); such relations are considered immoral, contrary to nature, or occasionally as "a merely ridiculous possibility" (Malinowski 1982:441). According to Malinowski (ibid.:429–443), the worst possible form of incest in the Trobriand Islands was the sexual relationship between brother and sister. Regarded with fear and loathing, its prohibition was the first moral rule; sexual relations between siblings were strictly prohibited.

The seafaring Trobriand Islanders were not the only people to condemn sibling incest as the most vile and horrific form of sexual activity. In many societies, the consequences of an incestuous relationship are commonly held as unfortunate. Traditional belief narratives attest to this view. Such a union's offspring – idiots, witches or vampires – would be unwanted and regarded as a danger to the community. According to an ancient Persian belief, paradise was lost due to an incestuous relationship between a brother and sister (Brewster 1972:3–4). Although incest is nearly universally forbidden to ordinary mortals, myths often tell us that the first human beings or the first people of a clan were indeed siblings (see Malinowski 1979:83–134; 1982:416–433, 452–474). Thus, many societies and their social organizations can be traced back to an incestuous relationship between a sister and brother. For instance, in the ancient kingdom of Hawai'i sibling incest occured in the highest rank, among the rulers while it was strictly tabooed for anybody, else (see e.g. Valeri 1985).[5]

In societies where fathers are socially distant or not considered close kin, the bond between brother and sister is especially significant and hence

275

surrounded by prohibitions. A woman's closest male relative is her brother. The brother's duty is to protect and provide for his unwed sisters. In such communities, a boy's closest male relative is not his biological father, but his maternal uncle. There is a special term to differentiate the maternal uncle from other adult males (see Malinowski 1979:40–48). The Finnish language has a special term for the maternal uncle – *eno* – but not for the paternal uncle; the latter is merely an uncle, *setä*: Jussi-*eno* invariably refers to a maternal uncle, but Jussi-setä may be either a paternal uncle or just an acquaintance to a child or a younger person. If indeed a man is obliged to see to the well-being and welfare of his sister, that is, to be her social father, a sexual relationship between them would radically disrupt the social system. On the other hand, if the maternal uncle is the closest male relative, in Freudian terms the primeval crime would not be to kill the father, but to kill the mother's brother and then marry the sister (Malinowski 1979:74–82).

Cross-cultural studies have shown that relationships between siblings are especially intense in pre-industrial societies (Cicirelli 1994). Hence, sibling solidarity is a compulsory behavioral norm into which people are socialized from an early age and which continues throughout adulthood (ibid.:13). Many anthropologists contend that exogamy is inextricably connected to incest prohibitions regulating the brother and sister relationship; in other words, exogamy could be regarded as simply a logical extension of the taboo (Seligman 1950) or that the taboo is the logical extension of exogamy (Malinowski 1982). So far, the evolutionary assumption that there is a link between the incest taboo and marriage systems has been challenged by few scholars in anthropology (however, see Weiner 1992:73–83; Ortner 1996:83–93).

Myths tell us that incest and cannibalism are decidedly non-human activitites which distinguish human beings from common beasts; hence the incest taboo is viewed as the first step towards human culture or civilization (Syndergaard 1993:127). Incest myths serve to validate and renew a society's most fundamental social structures. Moreover, myths explain and justify why members of the society must conform to certain marriage norms. Often the violation of such a rule leads to anarchy, disrupting both the social and the cosmic order. For example, according to some texts from the Karelian Isthmus, incest makes the flowers wilt, the land barren, the doors of the new town fortress howl, and the robbers begin to run wild.

Tuo poika Tuurettuisen	As the son of Tuurettuinen
ajoi neitonsa keralla,	drove with his maid,
ulvoi ukset uuen linnan,	the new town doors howled
vinkuivat Viron veräjät	the gates to Estonia wailed
tuota neittä naitaessa.	as he made love to the maid.
---	---
Poika vasten vastaeli:	The boy replied:
"Makasin oman sis'oni,	"I slept with my own sister,
Lemmen tyttären lepäsin.	"I laid the daughter of Lemmi."
Alkoi ryöstäjät rypeä,	Robbers began to run wild,
aina arvaajat ajella,	all the clerks to drive,
notkui suuret Suomen sillat	Finland's big bridges sagged

Tuurittuisen karjan alla,
Lemmittyisen lehmäkarjan,
maata puski mamman sarvet,
maata Mairikin utarat.
Tuo on poika Tuurittuinen,
tuo sanoi sanalla tällä:
Ei noita veroista vieä,
ei oteta oprakasta
eikä restistä reväistä,
vieähän sis'on vihoista,
kun makasin oman sis'oni,
Lemmen tyttären lepäsin.

under Tuurittuinen's beasts,
Lemmittyinen's cattle,
the cow butted the ground,
Mairikki's udder nudged the earth.
It's that Tuurittuinen boy,
he said with these words:
Those are not taken for taxes,
not for poll-taxes
not lost for dues,
they'll pay the sister's wrath ,
since I slept with my own sister,
laid with the daughter of Lemmi.

(SKVR XIII$_1$, 1130, anonymous, Sakkola. Ahlqvist 1854; cf. SKVR XIII$_1$, 1125, 1126)

Kun sie sisaren sokasit,
pilloit neion viattoman,
siitä kukat kuihtumahan,
maa mustaksi maatumahan,
puut pulskat poistumahan.

When you blinded your sister,
deflowered the innocent maid,
the flowers wilted,
the land moldered black,
vigorous trees vanished.

(SKVR XIII$_1$, 1127, anonymous, Rautu, Sumpula. Leino 1892)

A master singer from Latvajärvi in Archangel Karelia, Miihkali Arhippainen (Perttunen) sang about a boy who seduced a girl by charming. It is possible that Miihkali's seducer is shamanistically skilled: by his songs the *sampo*, the magical device gets its words (see SKVR I$_3$, 1278) and his horse is described as a mount of a wiseman (see Siikala 1992:95; SKVR I$_1$, 58a, 156, VII$_1$, 137). Thus, incest occurs in the mythic world.

Avasi sanasen arkun,
virsilippahan viritti
poikkipuolin polvillahe,
tuosta sampo sanoja soapi,
umpilampi ahvenia,
meri pieniä kaloja.
Neiti korjahan kohosi,

"Voi polosen päiviäni,
voi ankehen aikojani,
kuin makasin emoni lapsen,
rinnakkoho riuvuttelin."

Vesi on selvä selkäluulla,

sampi suuri lautasilla,
tuosta noijat vettä juopi,
lappalaiset lainuoli.

He opened the chest of words,
tuned the box of songs
across his knees,
thus the sampo wins its words,
the barren pond its perches,
the sea its small fishes.
The maid climbed into the sledge,

"Oh, my days of despair,
oh, my times of woe,
when I laid with my mother's child,
slept with my own sibling."

The water is clear on the wide horseback
the vast and placid pond,
the witches drink its water,
the Lapps swallow it.

(SKVR I$_2$, 979; cf. 979a)

As we have already seen, both Malinowski and Lévi-Strauss have been intrigued by sibling incest and the prohibitions placed on the brother and sister relationship. According to Malinowski (1982:440), the sister is at the heart of all that is sexually forbidden – she is a symbol of it. Lévi-Strauss takes a similar position. While he defined woman as the sign of marital exchange, he saw the sister as the sign of seduction: as an object of personal desire, she represents both the power and denial of sexual instinct (Lévi-Strauss 1969:496). Thus the brother denies his sexual attraction for his sister by giving her to another man in marriage, who, in turn, hands his own sister over to another man. Ultimately, the sister's function is to establish ties of exchange between men. In short, Lévi-Strauss's theory of marriage means that men trade sisters to obtain wives for themselves. A woman remains as "a sign and value" of male reciprocal responsibility. Nonetheless, Lévi-Strauss (ibid.) refuses to see the sister as a mere object: after all, through marriage, it is she who establishes a bond between men.

Kinship in Finnish Karelian Cultures

Finnish or Karelian marriage customs and kinship systems have received a fair amount of ethnographic and historic attention. Over the years, the topic has been explored by a number of scholars: e.g. Väinö Voionmaa (1915:365–516), Väinö Salminen (1916), I.K. Inha (1921), Juho Lukkarinen (1933), Uno Harva (1938; 1940–1941; 1947), Matti Sarmela (1969; 1978; 1981; 1994), Jouko Suurhasko (1977), Aili Nenola (1981), Maija-Liisa Heikinmäki (1981) and Unelma Konkka (1985). Lukkarinen devoted a chapter of his book to marriage customs regarding close kin and the attitudes to such marriages. Harva (1938; 1947) analyzed family relations by examining Uralic kinship terms. He also turned to folk poetry in his study of avoidance behavior within families (Harva 1938:305–307). Suurhasko's work is a comprehensive account of Karelian wedding customs. He has observed that weddings and funerals emphasize the importance of the ancestral kin group. Generally, according to Suurhasko, individuals in Karelian traditional communities belonged first and foremost to their kin group. This group has also been highly influential in village communities, whereas the state or socio-political organization had far less significance (Suurhasko 1977:161; see Itkonen 1921:29).

Oral history tells us that marriage between relatively close kin was common in Archangel Karelia; there are even claims that first cousins used to marry each other in "bygone days" (Lukkarinen 1933:23). Many Archangel Karelian songs acknowledge the intense and profound nature of the sibling relationship: girls' song about their love and yearning for their brothers (e.g. *Veion tuomiset*, "Brother's Presents" SKVR I$_2$, 1211–1214; SKVR I$_{4,2}$, 2210, 2210a). Not only does Karelian Kalevalaic poetry give expression to the relationship between sister and brother, a number of texts also feature a mother's devotion to her son. Karelian singers appear to have remained rather silent, however, about the bond between father and son. In the *Ruined Sister* poem and *The Lemminkäinen Song* the mother is her son's closest relative and her main function is to help him. In both poems the father appears only as a fugitive and a former villain who had established a farm on the Island. These fathers are basically absent and their only link to their sons is the fact that the boys seek refuge on his island property. The family relations in the poetic realm may be survivals or allude to a more ancient kinship system (see Siikala 1992:274). It is quite possible that the Finnish Karelian kinship system was patrilocal but matrilinear. Interestingly, the Trobriand Island community studied by Malinowski was patrilocal and matrilinear; and sexual relations between brother and sister were strictly prohibited (Malinowski 1979; 1982).

In Karelia the youngest son customarily remained on the family farm and inherited the ancestral land. His duty was to take care of his parents and his unwed sisters (Harva 1947:70–71). According to some Archangel Karelian narratives the sixth youngest daughter was allowed to marry her brother, but there is no evidence that this was actually practised. On the Finnish side of the border, in Juva, however, there is mention of a couple who lived as man and wife and had the same father. Karelians, however, tended to intermarry within their own community, and cross cousins often married each other. Finns and Karelians regarded marriage to a local person as the best alternative, and childhood friends would often marry each other; this obviously runs counter to Westermarck's theory. Most probably, clergymen condemned marriage between kin as sinful, and this clerical censure had an impact over time; the same type of development took place in Finland (Lukkarinen 1933:23–33). Uno Harva (1940–41:32), however, asserted that the ancient Karelian institution of marriage was no doubt exogamous: villages were made up of extended kin groups and the villagers could not intermarry, so the men sought their partners beyond their own villages and kin groups.

In both Ingria and in Karelia it was not out of the question for a young woman to wed a complete stranger. Lukkarinen described this type of marriage as a "quick wedding". According to Lukkarinen's research, even as late as 1912, a young man from Vuonninen, in Archangel Karelia, had asked for the hand of a girl he had never seen until the day he made his proposal. That same evening, a wedding would be arranged and the youngsters would consummate the marriage late that very night. Lukkarinen (ibid.) himself witnessed a similar case in Repola, Olonets Karelia, during an Orthodox church festival, and Inha (1921:133; see also ibid.:143) mentioned that the games played during these festivals provided ample opportunity for fast friendships often leading to marriage proposals and weddings, even though the young people had never even set eyes upon each other before taking part in the festivities.

Although marriage and leaving one's own home community was far from the happiest moment of a Karelian girl's life, an even worse fate was spinsterhood – to be an unwanted "leftover" (Inha 1921:228). Landowning parents did not consider it very important for youngsters to get acquainted before their wedding day: the parents and kin group decided whom a girl could marry, and often, whom a boy could court (Lukkarinen 1933:41; see Itkonen 1921:31–32; Ruoppila 1937:322; Harva 1940–41:34; Vuoristo 1992:91). Youthful courtships and weddings were the concern of the entire kin group. The offspring of the prosperous families had no choice: they had to seek their spouses from other wealthy families (Inha 1921:228).

*Forbidden Love: Incestuous Relations between Brothers
and Sisters in Archangel Karelian Epic Poetry*

In the Archangel Karelian *Ruined Sister* poem a young man unwittingly
seduces his own sister and is forced to flee his home. Usually, variants of
the poem begin with the youth on his way to pay taxes, bets or tithes. The
revenge theme of the Kaleva Boy, however, is conspicuously absent in the
texts describing the purpose of the journey (SKVR I$_2$, Kellovaara 954, 956,
Miinoa 968, 969, 969a, Niskajärvi 971, Kivijärvi 976, 977, Latvajärvi 979,
979a, 980). Another common narrative turn in the texts on sibling incest is
the girl's adamant refusal to climb into the boy's sled; her resolve quickly
gives way, however, as the boy cajoles her with coins or precious metals.
The girl is motivated by greed instead of infatuation or passion. In Archangel
Karelia these features appear in all but two of the aforementioned texts
(SKVR I$_2$, 979, 979a)[6] in which the boy uses sorcery to charm the maiden
and fills a barren pond with fish.[7]

As an example of Archangel Karelian songs I present a text written down
by D.E.D. Europaeus in 1845; the singer's name was Gostja Ondreinen and
he was from the village of Suurijärvi[8] (SKVR I$_2$, 960). The above-mentioned
themes are all included in this text. The most prominent ones are the journey,
the seduction, the sister's guilt, the brother's hope for redemption, and his
final exile. In this text the person who commits the crime of incest is called
the Kalova Boy and the blue-stockinged gaffer's son; both epithets refer to
heroes from the *Kalevala*, such as Lemminkäinen and Kullervo. Later, it
becomes apparent that the young man's father is Köyrötyinen, the wrathful
Tuiretuinen (cf. Tuurikkainen). Ondreinen's song says nothing about the
purpose of the boy's journey. Along the way, the boy meets a group of girls
and decides to take the most attractive one for himself. The song underlines
the passive nature of the girl. She neither acts nor expresses her wishes: she
is merely a lovely souvenir that the Kalova Boy picks up along his journey.

Se kaunis Kalovan poika,	The beautiful Kalova Boy,
sinisukka äiön poika,	the blue-stockinged gaffer's son,
sinisukka hienohelma,	the blue-stockinged dandy,
hivus keltani koria,	with yellow curls and good looks,
hyppäsi hyvän selällä,	mounted a good horse,
hyvän laukin lautasilla.	a fine saddle-horse's back.
Ajoa karettelevi	He drove easily
noilla Väinön kankahilla,	through those heaths of Väinö,
ammoin raattuja ahoja.	the glades tilled long before.
Neitoset kisaelevi	The maids were dancing
noilla Väinön kankahilla,	on those heaths of Väinö,
ammoin raatuilla ahoilla.	the glades tilled long before.
Se kaunis Kalovan poika	The beautiful Kalova Boy
katso parvesta parahan,	picked the finest of the flock,
tukkapäistä turpehimman.	the most splendid bare-locked one.
Sen hän koopi korjahansa,	That one he snatched into his sleigh,
rekehensä reusoali.	stole into his sledge.
(SKVR I$_2$, 960)	

The youth seduces and has his way with the maiden. Only after their amorous encounter does it occur to him to ask the maiden her name. Horrified, the boy realizes that he has ravished his own sister. He rushes off at once to lament his fate to his mother. He asks his mother where a boy who has defiled his own sister could find a safe refuge. The mother suggests that he metamorphose into a tree or a fish, but he rejects these suggestions because they would mean the end of him. Neither mother nor brother expresses any concern about the fate of the sister.

Ajoa karettelevi	He drove easily
noit' on Väinön kankahia,	through those heaths of Väinö,
ammoin raattuja ahoja,	the glades tilled long before,
käsi oron ohjaksissa,	with one hand he held the stallion's reins,
toinen neitosen nisuissa.	and the other the maid's nipples.
Siinä neitosen makasi,	There he had his way with the maid,
tinarinnan riuotteli.	slept with the tin-breast.
Alko tuossa suella:	He began to ask:
"Mit' olet sukua suurta,	"Tell me of your great family,
mitä rohkieta rotua?"	and your brave race?"
"En ole sukua suurta,	"I am not of a great family,
enkä rohkieta rotua,	not a brave race,
laps' olen köyhän Köyrötyisen,	I'm a child of a poor Köyrötyinen,
tytär tuiman Tuiretuisen."	a daughter of a stern Tuiretuinen."
"Voi minä poloinen poika,	"Oh, woe is this poor boy,
Voi poika polonalainen,	how this boy deserves pity,
kuin makasin maammon lapsen,	since I slept with my mother's child,
siuotin oman sisaren."	laid with my own sister."
"Oiot maamo kantajani!	"Oh-o mother who bore me!
Kunne sie minua käset	Tell me where I can go
pillojani piilemähä,	to conceal my crimes,
pahoja pakenemaha?"	to flee my bad deeds?"
"Poikuono nuorempani!	"My son, my younger boy!
Mene männyksi mäkehe,	As a pine go in the hill,
katajaksi kankahalla."	as a juniper in the heath."
"Lempo sinne lähtenee!	"Let the devil go there!
Kuin on männyksi mäellä	As a pine in the hill
katajaksi kankahalla,	as a juniper in the heath,
usein katajakangas	often the juniper heath
kaskipuiksi kaaellaha,	is destined in for slash-and-burn,
halmeheksi hakkaellah.	cleared to be a glade.
Oiot maamo kantajani!	Oh-o my mother who bore me!
Kunne sie minua käsket	Where do you tell me to go
pillojani piilemähä,	to conceal my crimes,
pahoja pakenemaha?"	to escape my bad deeds?"
"Mene koivuksi or'olle."	"As a birch go the marsh."
"Lempo tuonne lähtenee!	"Let the devil go there!
Usein oronen koivu	Oft a marsh-birch
pinopuiksi pilkotaha,	will be felled for firewood,
halkoloiksi hakkaellah.	chopped up for burning.
Oiot maamo kantajani!	Oh-o mother who bore me!
Kunne sie minua käset	Tell me where I can go
pillojani piilemähä,	to conceal my crimes,
pahoja pakenemaha?"	to flee my bad deeds?"

"Poikuoni nuorempani!
Mene hau'iksi merehen,
sii'aksi Silojo'ella."
"Lempo tuonne lähtenee!
Kuin menen hauiksi merehen,
sii'aksi Silojo'ella:
mies musta no'en näköinen
seki verkkoja kutoo,
vei on verkkonsa veteh,
hau'in surman sammaleh.
Missä saapi, siinä syöpi.
Oiot maamo kantajani!"

(SKVR I₂, 960)

"My son, my younger boy!
As a pike go to the sea,
as a powan go the to placid river"
"Let the devil go there!
As a pike if I go to the sea,
as a powan to the placid river:
a man as black as soot
who makes nets,
cast his nets into the water,
a death swamp for a pike.
Where he catches, there he eats.
Oh-o mother who bore me!"

Finally, the mother tells the boy to seek refuge on an island, a favored hiding place. His father has also used the island while on the run and during his exile established his own farm there. While in exile the boy builds himself a boat. The boat is no ordinary vessel and the building process, its golden bow and its bronze paddle are further testimonies to its uniqueness (see also SKVR I₂ 957, 959, 960a, 961, 965, 970, 974, 980). The Kalova Boy seats himself in the stern and begins to paddle. This is an extraordinary voyage: the boat's mythical dimension allows its passenger to travel from the prosaic world of the living to the Underworld. The texts collected in Archangel Karelia usually display more mythical elements than those texts from the southern singing areas, i.e., Karelia Isthmus and Ingria (Siikala 1987:16). The tendency is obvious in the texts of the *Ruined Sister* poem.

"Mene saarehen selälliseh,
puuttomaha luotoseh,
siell' ennen isäsi piili,
joll' on piili, jolla säily."
Se kaunis Kalovan poika
vesti päivän, vesti laian,
vesti toisen, vesti toisen,

kolmantena kokan asetti,
päivät honkoja hakevi,
huoparia huolittaa:
Voi sie minun puinen pursi
venyt vestälmyksillesi,
lahot lastumuksillasi.
Lykkäsi venon vesille,
100 laian lainehille,
itse istusi perähän,
kokan kultasen nojahan,
melan vaskisen varahan.
Laskea karittelevi
saarehen selällisehen,
puuttomahan luotosehen.
Saarehen saantoa pitävi.

"Go to island on the open sea,
to the islet barren of trees,
to where your father hid,
where he hid, and thus survived."
That beautiful Kalova Boy
whittled all day long, whittled a board,
whittled yet another day, whittled another board,
the third day he positioned the prow,
some days he looked for logs,
he primed a paddle:
Oh, you my wooden boat
you will reach your full size,
your chips will rot.
He pushed the boat to the waters,
the hundred-boarded to the waves,
he himself sat in the stern,
with the golden prow's serivce,
with the copper paddle's aid.
He sailed easily
to the island on the open sea,
to the islet barren of trees.
He stayed on course to the island.

Itse sano, noin pakasi:	He himself spoke and talked:
"Onkos saarella sioa,	"Is there space on the island,
onkos maata saaren maalla,	land on the island's mainland,
veteä venoista maalle,	to beach a boat on the land,
purtta kuivalle kumota?"	to overturn a vessel on dry earth?"
"Ompa saarella sioa,	"There is indeed space on the island,
jos saisit 100 venoista,	even if you had a hundred boats,
jos tulis 1000 purtta,	even if there would come a
	thousand vessels,
isäis saamille teloille,	on the grounds your father has gained,
vanhempas varustamille."	your parent has built."
(SKVR I$_2$, 960)	

On the island, the young dandy becomes quite a ladies' man and proceeds to seduce the female islanders. This activity severely tries the tolerance of the island's menfolk, however, and thus the fathers, brothers and husbands from all 80 houses thirst for revenge. The young man once again climbs into his mythical vessel and allows it to take him where it will.

Se kaunis Kalovan poika	The beautiful Kalova Boy
---	---
---	---
100 on neioista makasi,	slept with a hundred of the maids
1000 kunnan tukkapäitä	with a thousand of the bare-locked ones
yhtenä kesäissä yönä.	during a single summer night.
Yhen tunsi 10:stä,	He knew, one out of ten,
2 kaikesta sa'asta,	two out of a whole hundred,
1000 3 tunsi	three out of a thousand
piikoa pitämätöntä.	maidens left untouched.
Se kaunis Kalovan poika	The beautiful Kalova Boy
kävi yhtä huomenessa	one morning he visited
taloja 80.	eighty houses.
Ei ollut sitä taloa,	There was not one house
kuin ei 3 urosta,	without three men,
jotka miekkoa hioo,	sharpening their swords,
tapparata tahkoaapi	and grinding their hatchets
miun poloisen pään varalle.	for my poor head.
Se kaunis Kalovan poika	The beautiful Kalova Boy
lykkäsi venon vesille,	pushed the boat to the waters,
100 laian lainehille,	the hundred-boarded one to the waves,
itse istusi perähän.	he himself sat in the stern.
(SKVR I$_2$, 960)	

The youth drifts to the dark North to a man-devouring village. He has wandered further and further from his home. In the North he takes a job as a shepherd and the text evolves along the lines of the Kaleva Boy's revenge theme. His employer – a woman – offers bread she has baked containing a rock, on which the boy breaks his knife. The enraged boy takes his revenge by herding the cattle into the swamp and the bears to the "manor". When his employer goes to milk the cows, she finds savage beasts instead. Ondreinen's song proceeds in a similar vein to the Kaleva Boy's slash and burn theme, and the boy continues with his journey to the workshop of Ilmarinen the

Smith. He asks Ilmarinen to make him a sword. Once he gets a weapon to his liking, the Kalova Boy goes to clear the forest for cultivation. He fells trees as far as his voice can carry. Woodland clearing (slash and burn) is yet another intriguing theme in Finnish and Karelian folk poetry, but my focus here is on the incest theme.

Laskea karettelevi	He sailed easily
pimiähän Pohjolahan,	to dark Pohjola,
miesten syöjähän kylähän.	the man-eating village.
Palkkasihen paimeneksi.	He was hired as a shepherd.
Isänt' ois hyvätapanen,	The master would be well-mannered,
emänt' on pahatapanen,	the mistress is ill-mannered,
leipo on kivestä leivän,	she baked bread from a stone,
palaseksi painelee.	and disguised it as a tidbit.
Se kaunis Kalovan poika	The beautiful Kalova Boy
veälti veitsensä kiveh,	thrust his knife in the stone
kasahutti kallivoh.	struck it against the rock.
Se kaunis Kalovan poika	The beautiful Kalova Boy
tuosta suuttu, tuosta syänty,	then turned angry, and then furious,
tuosta viikoksi vihastu.	and raged for a week.
Kaiken karjan suohon sotki,	All the cattle he sent to the swamp,
vasikan sorkat vajotti,	a calf's hooves he drowned,
ajo karhut kartanolle.	drove bears to the farm.
Isäntä savua panevi,	The master makes smoke,
emäntä lypsylle tulee.	the mistress comes to milk.
Karhut karju kartanolla.	The bruins rumble around the ranch.
Se kaunis Kalovan poika	The beautiful Kalova Boy
astu seppolan pajahan.	strode to the smith's forge.
"Oi seppo Ilmarinen,	"Oh smith Ilmarinen,
takoja ijän ikuinen!	eternal forger!
Ta'os miulle tarpehia,	Forge me some tools,
ta'o miekka miestä myöten,	forge a sword fit for a man,
kilpi kantajan mukahan,	a shield seemly for its bearer,
tappara tasateränen.	a hatchet with a tidy blade.
Lähen kasken kaatantahan,	I am off to slash and burn,
halmeen hakkoantaha."	to clear away the woodland."
Hyvä puu kerralla mänevi,	A good tree needed one stroke,
kerta huonoa pitävi.	one stroke for a bad one.
Lempo tuota raatanee!	Let the devil have this drudgery!
Se kaunis Kalovan poika,	The beautiful Kalova Boy,
hän on nousi kannon päähän:	he climbed to the top of a stump:
Kuin huhu kuulunee,	As far as my call can be heard,
sini kaski kaatukoon.	let the slash and burn be done.
(SKVR I$_2$, 960)	

In Finnish-Karelian poetry, the incestuous brother usually goes by the name of Tuiretuinen, Tuurituinen, Tuurikkainen or Keyretyinen Boy. In Archangel Karelia his name is frequently Kullervo or Kulerva (SKVR I$_2$, 962, 972, 973, 974, 983, 984, 985, 985a, 986, 987, 989, 990, 991), and in the *Kalevala* it is Kullervo who seduces his sister. In Kaarle Krohn's (1903–1910:707–711) analysis of the *Kalevala* poem cluster, the sister seducer is the son of wrathful Tuurikkainen or Tuiretuinen. Krohn concentrates on seeking the origins of the tradition and overlooks the incest theme. In many of the Archangel Karelian texts the hero of the *Ruined Sister* poem gets a name like Lemminkäinen or other allusive epithets and names like *liedon Lieran pojan* ("wanton son of Liera"); *sinisukka Äijön pojan* ("blue-stockinged son of Äijö")[9] (SKVR I$_2$, 955, 957, 957a, 958, 959, 960, 960A, 961, 962, 964, 966, 970, 972, 979, 979a). In Kalevala meter poetry, Lemminkäinen and Kullervo are mischievous heroes who constantly wage war against the community, so it is no wonder that their "list of bad deeds" also includes incest (see Honko 1979:66). On the other hand, in Archangel Karelia the seduction of the sister has been linked to the text dealing with the Kaleva boy's revenge (SKVR I$_2$, 908, 911, 912, 914, 916, 917, 922, 923, 924, 934). For the sake of clarity, from now on I will use the name Kullervo to refer to the hero.

Liminality in the Ruined Sister Poem

Since the poem begins with Kullervo undertaking a journey on horseback to pay tithes or taxes, we may conclude that the poem was originally composed in a provincial setting during the Middle Ages (Kuusi 1980:229). The cultural context in which the poetic texts were written down, however, was 19th century Archangel Karelia. Kullervo is clearly a product of culture. Moreover, as a domesticated beast, the horse is a cultural means of transport vital to both farmers and itinerant pedlars; taxes or tithes are payments required by society. On the other hand, we may recall that the horse also has a mythic link to the Underworld; usually, however, the mythic horse can be identified by epithets referring to its otherworldly nature such as the *Horse from Hiisi* (sacrificial grove) or the mountain. The mythical horse is either a shamanistic helper animal or a means of crossing the border between this world and the next (Siikala 1992:199). For example, in the Sampo cycle, before the creation of this world, Väinämöinen rides a straw stallion or a beanstalk steed (e.g. SKVR I$_1$ 58, 58a). In the *Ruined Sister* poem, however, the hero takes another mythical means of transport – a boat – to reach the Underworld.

During the course of the voyage Kullervo meets an enchanting maiden. Generally, this encounter takes place on the clear blue sea (SKVR I$_2$, 954, 956, 959, 960A, 964, 965, 969, 969a, 971, 972, 973, 974, 976, 977, 978, 978a, 979, 979a, 980, 982, 991; SKVR I$_4$, 1192). According to mythical thought, water often functions as a liminal or marginal element (Turner 1978:245–246; Haavio 1992:166–192), and the nature of the voyage is such that the person occupies no particular place. During the voyage, the person is obviously in motion, so it is impossible to state his precise whereabouts. Indeed, both definitions of space – the open sea and the voyage – are indicative of a liminal state. Lévi-Strauss (1986a) regards water as an element both natural and cultural; thus, like incest, water functions as a mediator between nature and culture. Raw, uncooked food is natural, whereas cooked food is a product of culture. Essential for cooking, water is used to turn a natural product into something culturally useful (Lévi-Strauss 1978:477–495). Thus, the water images of the poetic texts attain further symbolic weight. Even before the crime of incest takes place, the water images work to foreshadow Kullervo's crossing from this world to the next, from culture back to nature.

The person in a liminal state is moving from one place to another without really being in either place. Hence, during the voyage the person occupies an undefined space (see van Gennep 1960) and can pose a serious threat to both himself and the environment (Douglas 1989:94–113). In the *Ruined Sister* poem this marginal and dangerous zone – dangerous because of its ambiguity to the individual and society – provides the setting for the most heinous crime – incest. Some texts even further stress liminality by continually referring to the "ambiguous" nature of the place (SKVR I$_2$, 954, 958, 959, 976, 977, 978, 980).

Interestingly, the texts of *Väinämöinen's Leavetaking* feature yet another reference to incest: a nameless orphan, the future leader or chief of the people, accuses old Väinämöinen of sleeping with, and thus shaming, his own mother (SKVR I$_1$, 682, 690, 691, 692, 693, 694, 695a, 695b, 697, 697a, 698).

Puhui poika puolikuinen:	A half-month-old boy spoke:
"Oi on vanha Väinämöinen,	"Oh old Väinämöinen,
eipä sinua sillonkaan,	you weren't driven away,
eipä sillon suollen vuottu,	you weren't sent to a swamp,
eikä tangolla tapettu,	you weren't slain with a stake,
makasit oman emosi,	when you laid your own mother,
rinnalla riuvottelit	slept by her side
rannalla meren karisen."	on the shore of the rocky sea."

(SKVR I$_1$, 695a, Martiska Karjalainen, Vuonninen, Lonkka. Lönnrot 1834)

The site of this Oedipal crime – if indeed it is mentioned – is usually on hilly ground (SKVR I$_1$, 682, 690, 692, 693, 694), by a rocky seashore or out on the open sea (SKVR I$_1$, 695a, 695b, 697, 697a). As in the Archangel Karelian *Ruined Sister* poem, the latter locations thus endow the poem with a liminal flavor. On the other hand, hilly ground also alludes to the Underworld, particularly if we recall the rocky hill of the North, i.e., the place where diseases are driven in incantations (Siikala 1992:153–164). To validate such a claim, however, still requires further research.

In Archangel Karelian poems the wide open sea usually appears as a signifier of place and is repeated throughout the narrative. Sometimes it literally refers to a lake or a sea. Regarding the *Ruined Sister* poem, however, such images are probably employed because of their established place in Kalevalaic epic language. Therefore, we have little reason to believe that the singer would have consciously manipulated his or her choice of words to underscore liminality or to foreshadow a strange event.

If we choose to follow Lévi-Straussian logic, we could say that the narrative itself, instead of the singer or the demands of the performance, has chosen the necessary narrative components (Lévi-Strauss 1990:631–632; also 1986b, 206–230 and 1987:146–194). In other words, the singer unconsciously selected metaphors of liminality. Although the open sea often appears in Archangel Karelian poetry, its frequency is hardly coincidental. In the *Sampo* poem, for example, the open sea occasionally surfaces in descriptions of the journey to the North, i.e., to the World of the Dead (SKVR I₁, 22, 36, 38, 58, 62, 64, 83b, 92, 93, 100).

Kullervo flees the scene of the crime and takes refuge on an island. In Kalevalaic poetry, the island emerges as a highly traditional haven for fugitives: Kullervo's father also once sought asylum there; and, like his father before him, Lemminkäinen will hide on the island after murdering the owner of Päivölä (SKVR I₂, 703, 704, 712, 724, 729, 742, 746, 757, 757A, 759, 766, 766a, 773, 781, 789b, 791a, 803, 810, 811, 816, 828, 834). During his sojourn, Kullervo, like Lemminkäinen, takes full advantage of the company of young female islanders. Both Kullervo and Lemminkäinen possess sexual powers far beyond ordinary human limits:

Se kaunis Kalovan poika	The beautiful Kalova Boy
---	---
---	---
100 on neioista makasi,	slept with a hundred of the maids
1000 kunnan tukkapäitä	with a thousand of the bare-locked ones
yhtenä kesäissä yönä.	during a single summer night.
Yhen tunsi 10:stä,	He knew, one out of ten,
2 kaikesta sa'asta,	two out of a whole hundred,
1000 3 tunsi	three out of a thousand
piikoa pitämätöntä.	maidens left untouched.
Se kaunis Kalovan poika	The beautiful Kalova Boy
kävi yhtä huomenessa	one morning he visited
taloja 80.	eighty houses.
(SKVR I₂, 960)	

Väinämöinen, however, does not go to the island to hide or to make amends for his exposed crime; rather, he is given an even more severe punishment: the falls into the most heinous places imagineable, and from there escape is impossible (SKVR I₁, 682, 690, 692, 693, 695a, 697, 697a). The punishment recalls Christian repentance or Purgatory, and has thus prompted many folklorists, since the days of Elias Lönnrot, to liken Väinämöinen's judge to the Christ child (Krohn 1903–1910:483–487; 1928:167–183).

On the other hand, regarding *Väinämöinen's Leavetaking*, Domenico Comparetti questioned the notion that the folk singers simply added Christian symbolism to the songs. After all, their songs generally allowed "Christian and pagan names and notions to mingle and overlap quite randomly" (1892:123). Although we may accept the canonical view, i.e., the songs attest to the replacement of pagan beliefs with Christian values, when it comes to the *Kalevala*, such a notion may be inapplicable for interpretations of the oral traditions of Archangel Karelia. From another standpoint, we could even say that Väinämöinen, through his incestuous act, reverts back from culture to nature. As a part of nature, he is no longer a fitting leader, and thus must be exiled from the community.

Sister Seducer on the Run

After committing murder, Lemminkäinen travels for three days and three nights to the Island. His boat is specially crafted for the voyage (see SKVR I₂, 703, 724, 766, 781, 791, 791a, 808, 809, 810, 811, 816, 828). Likewise, the texts often depict Kullervo constructing his own vessel or they stress the unusual features of the boat: the paddle is bronze and the bow golden (ibid.: 954, 957, 959, 960, 960a, 961, 962, 964, 965, 972, 973, 974, 977, 986, 988, 989, 991). The hero cannot go to the Island by just any vessel; reaching the Island requires an exceptional craft. After all, the Island is no common hiding place, its unique constitution renders it akin to the World of the Dead. In some Archangel Karelian Sampo cycles, the Island may even exist before the actual creation of the world; in these texts, the island floats alone in a primeval sea (see e.g. SKVR I₁, 83a, 121–123). Nevertheless, the Island need not always be equated with the World of the Dead.

While exiled on the Island, Kullervo does retain some contact with the human world. In fact, he is living on the land his father has tended (SKVR I₂, 957, 959, 960, 960a, 961, 962, 964, 965, 972, 973, 974, 984, 985a, 986, 989, 991). The hiding place is depicted as a faraway island and a treeless islet. The texts tell us that it is closer to the North – the man-eating village – than to Kullervo's home region. Once again, since his popularity with the women of the Island has fueled the rage and jealousy of their menfolk, Kullervo must flee for his life (ibid.:962, 965, 972, 973, 974, 985a, 986). If the North refers to the Land of the Dead (see Siikala 1992:132–146), the Island could be regarded as a place in between, a place half-way between this world and the next. On the other hand, mythical thought and history does not clearly distinguish between this world and the next (ibid.:145), and this ambiguity is also present in the *Ruined Sister* poem.

After his carefree days on the Island come to an end, Kullervo strays even farther away from his home, i.e., the present world. His wanderings take him to the North where he finds work as a shepherd for a smith's wife. The once heroic and boastful youth accustomed to knives of gold and silver has taken a social fall. Not only has he turned into a lowly shepherd, to add insult to injury, he is now under the employ of a woman. His degradation is complete when the smith's wife offers him a loaf of bread with a stone inside it. In Archangel Karelia, as in all of Karelia, bread has held a unique and favored place in the peasant economy. Not only was bread the most highly valued form of nourishment to the Karelians, it was also handled with extreme respect; Karelians considered bread to be more sacred than other foods, and children were taught to eat it with reverence (Lukkarinen 1918:102–103; Kemppinen 1977:103–105). Placing a stone inside dough to be baked would have been a grievous – if not a downright blasphemous – violation of the norm.

In the Archangel Karelian texts of the *Revenge of Kaleva-Boy*, the stone-filled bread is always offered to the incompetent slave (e.g. SKVR I₂, 928, 935, 936, 937, 945, 946, 951). The youth "jabs" the stone with his knife and breaks his most essential tool. The destruction of his knife infuriates the highborn-boy-turned-shepherd so much so that he casts a spell on the unfortunate woman's farm animals, and thus the cattle and sheep turn into wolves and bears. Finally, he drives the predators to the house where they attack the treacherous wife and rip her to pieces. The woman dies for breaking the boy's knife. The knife is more than just a cutting implement; rather it is sign of manhood and the last concrete link to his own family and cultural heritage (see Kupiainen 1996).

The Ballad of Sister and Brother

More often than not, scholars have overlooked the portrayal of gender relations and the incest theme in the *Ruined Sister* poem. This is rather odd, after all, the incestuous crime is the poem's most striking episode and its climax. Instead, folklorists have simply stressed its western origins and that it was featured in the *Kalevala*'s Kullervo story. Although Kaarle Krohn initially studied the poem through the name of the incestuous brother, he soon turned his attention to questions of origin. Where does "wrathful boy Tuurikkainen" or "naughty child Tuurituinen" come from? Krohn then concludes that the Finnish and Karelian variants of the poem are of Scandinavian origin. He supported his hypothesis with mention of Danish narrative of brother and sister incest in a ballad called *'herr Tor'* (Krohn 1903–1910:707). Another Danish song tells about the Truels sisters, three girls who sleep in and end up being late for church.[10] The girls devote so much time to dressing up and adorning themselves that the rest of the household leaves without them. Since they are in a hurry, the girls take a short-cut to the church. Instead of taking the (safe) road, they take a (dangerous) path through the woods where they are raped and murdered by bandits. In the Norwegian text Torgjus has two daughters: on Sunday morning one of the girls wants to sleep late and dress up more than the others. As she rushes to church, the lazy, conceited sister meets three bandits who give her a beating. The outlaws are later revealed to be the girl's long-lost brothers (ibid.:709–710).

According to Krohn, the tradition originated in Scotland. The Scottish versions feature three sisters who take turns gathering wildflowers. While in the forest, the two eldest sisters are taken by surprise by a lone outlaw. Because both girls refuse to marry him, the outlaw murders them. Only the youngest sister has the wit to threaten him with the revenge of her three brothers. When he asks her the names of her brave brothers, he realizes that they are his own siblings. Upon this discovery, the outlaw throws himself upon his sword. (Krohn 1903–1910:710–711.) In his usual fashion, Kaarle Krohn tries to locate the origin of the tradition and to trace its eastward route to Finland and Karelia. He used to be more keen on finding thematic similarities with European oral traditions than on seeing the tradition's significance within the community from which it had been collected. Krohn understood the poems as autonomous objects moving from culture to culture. He did not appear to be interested in the actual people who composed and used such oral traditions, never mind their own views of their traditions. Like his contemporaries in the newfound discipline, Krohn, as a matter of course, paid attention to the contents of tradition; its internal not external regularities and interactions. Hence, he failed to explore the interaction between tradition and the social reality of the given community. (Nenola 1986:179–185.)

Scandinavian and Scottish songs of incest display no mercy for wayward young women. Girls who violate the unwritten rules of their society get just what they deserve. A respectable girl must make it to church on time like everyone else instead of simply lingering at home before the mirror; in other words, vanity is a vice and modesty a virtue. Likewise, in the Finnish Karelian tradition, frivolous-mindedness brings the girl to ruin: the boy coaxes the girl into his sled by showing her his gold-laden purses and silver knives. The moral of the story comes through loud and clear: the girl is clearly at fault and is fully deserving of her punishment. (Syndergaard 1993:135–136.) Dazzled by his silver and gold, the girl climbs into the boy's sled. She abandons the familiarity and safety of her own cultural home for a marginal space where she is profoundly on her own. Flouting conventional manners, the girl falls into an amorous encounter before even taking the time to learn about his family background. Thus the tragic course is set and their true identities are revealed much later.

Larry Syndergaard (1993:134–136) asserts that the incest taboo is one of the most profound intersections between gender and culture. According to his research on English and Scottish folk ballads, the genre's casualties are invariably female. If characters do experience physical or mental anguish, it is the female characters who always suffer more than their male counterparts. The incestuous affair ends with the death of the sister; if indeed both brother and sister die, the sister is the first to die. In these folk ballads the sister generally pays for her moral lapse with her life whereas her brother pays with his sanity. Although the young man is granted a slim chance for redemption, his sister is not. Likewise, Kullervo's life is spared even if he is forced to leave his home community and/or give up his worldly belongings. The sister's lot is a tragic death or she is forgotten completely; tradition consigns the fate of the sister to silence (Makkonen 1996:85–86).

Heroic epics and ballads, however, have different functions. The ballad was originally a narrative dance song about love and death, whereas a heroic epic was a communal story about a celebrated culture hero. Nevertheless, incestuous gender themes may be similar in both ballads and heroic epic poetry; and thus both genres may shed light on the gender system of the given community.[11] In the *Ruined Sister* poem, the young girl decides, without parental permission, to run off with a handsome young stranger, and thus the tragedy takes its course. Had her elders found out in time, the catastrophe could have been avoided. Moreover, had the female protagonist behaved in the demure manner befitting a young maiden instead of surrendering to lust and vanity, there would have been no tragedy. Ultimately, responsibility lies with the girl, for she should have rejected the stranger's advances. The tradition underlines the girl's guilt by giving the boy a chance to redeem himself while leaving his sister to meet her doom. Even the girl's own mother appears indifferent to her fate. She simply preoccupies herself with finding refuge for her son.

The Silenced Fate of the Sister

None of the texts depicts the fate of the female protagonist. Presumably, the girl suffers more than just a little shock. Not only has a girl from an esteemed family slept with a complete stranger, she has also made love with her own brother. Her shame is great and retrieving her honor is difficult if not impossible. Archangel Karelian poetry shows no sign of possible punishments or repentance for the female protagonist.

It is difficult to determine a fate which has been silenced. Folk poetry, however, can provide us with some clues. There are narratives providing accounts of "ruined maidens" or girls who participate in "inappropriate" sexual relationships. These narratives depict girls who have had love affairs with casual strangers or who have otherwise indulged in sexual experiences contrary to the norms and expectations of their society. The poem of *Marketta and Hannu* or *Marketta and Anterus* (see e.g. SKVR VII$_1$, 699–757) is one good example: an excessively virtuous maiden (e.g. she refuses to eat fertilized chicken eggs, or to drink milk from a cow who has been bred) suddenly gives her love to a handsome stranger. Soon enough, her passionate love affair yields her an unwanted pregnancy which she keeps secret. When the time to give birth draws near, she stealthily makes her way to the sauna. After giving birth, she hides the infant under the benches. The baby can hardly remain a secret for long and is soon found. Since the infant has no parents, the leader of the community neither accepts it as a member of the community nor does he give it a name. The mystery is solved, however, when the newborn speaks out and reveals the identity of the parents. The ruined bride is forced to answer to her shameful deed. Once virtuous to excess, the maiden who rejected all the local suitors is rightfully punished and exposed as a hypocrite.

An examination of the *Hanged Maid* texts can help us to appreciate the fate of Kullervo's sister. The Archangel Karelian texts recount the story of not only an unwelcome suitor, but of a completely unacceptable being for a spouse. The suitor called *Osmotar, Osmo, Osmoinen, Kaleva* or *Kalevatar* demands the female protagonist for himself. *Osmo* is highly ambiguous in character. On the one hand, the name referred to a virile suitor in the wedding songs, but on the other hand to a beast of the forest, such as a bear or wolverine (Nirvi 1982:55–73); and the suffix *-tar* indicates femininity. These texts also allude to an uneven or lopsided sexual relationship. In the *Anni tyttö, ainu neiti* ("Hanged Maid") poem ('maiden Anni, the only girl') goes to the woods to collect bath whisks for her family. Osmotar rises from wet ground in the woods and proposes marriage to the girl. The creature orders the girl to live with him, dress in humble clothes, and to avoid all other potential suitors:

"Kasva neito miussa mielin,   "Grow, maiden, to please me,
älä muissa sulhasissa,   not the other bridegrooms,
kasva kaijoissa sovissa,   grow in narrow dresses,
veny verka voatteissa,   grow tall in broadcloths,
kasva leivän kannikoilla."   grow with a crust of bread."
(SKVR I$_1$, 209 Marppa Joussei's daughter Hänninen, Kliimo's wife, Miinoa, Varonen 1886)

The girl hurries home in tears and laments the loss of her precious jewels:

"Kirpoi risti rinnaltani,
kultalangat kulmiltani,
hopielangat vyöni päistä."

(ibid.)

"The cross slipped from my breast,
the golden ribbons from my brow,
the silver ribbons from the tip of my
belt."

The mother ignores her daughter's tears and tells her to go into the storage shed on the hill to dress up in her finest clothes and prepare herself for her wedding day. At first she obeys, but then chooses to defy her mother's orders after all. Since she does not want a husband – particular such an undesirable one – she chooses the worst possible alternatives:

"...Kolm' on aittoa mäellä,
astu aittaan mäellä,
avaos parahin aitta,
syö sie siellä vuosi vuota,
tulet muita vuolahampi,
toisen vuoen sian lihaa,
kolmas kuorekakkaroita;
pane arkku arkun päälle,
lipas lippahan lomahan.
Avas sie paras arkku,
kimahuta kirja kansi,
pane päälle parainta,
ripeintä rinnoillasi."
Anni tyttö, aini neiti
astu aittaan mäellä,
avasi pahimman aitan,
tuli muita sirkiempi,
tuli muita vuolahampi;
avasi pahimman arkun, ---"

"...Three are the sheds on the hill,
step to the shed on the hill,
open the best shed,
there, eat butter for a year,
you will grow plumper than the others,
the next year eat pork,
and the third, smelt pies;
pile chest upon chest,
case on top of case.
Open the best chest,
let the bright lid fly open,
put on the best things,
the most gorgeous on your breasts."
The girl Anni, the only maid
stepped to the shed on the hill,
opened the worst shed,
grew prettier than the others,
grew plumper that the others;
opened the worst chest, ---"

(SKVR I$_1$, 233, anonymous Uhtue, Lönnrot 1834)

From the worst chest she pulls out a girdle and uses it to hang herself. Death is the only way for the girl to save herself from the grasp of Osmotar. After three years the mother goes to the storage shed expecting to find her daughter beautiful and mature enough for marriage. Instead, a dead body awaits her, and she bursts into tears. The tears turn into rivers, trees, and cuckoos which mournfully call for abandoned and nameless children. In the poetic realm, at least, the girl does not die barren; the tears that flow in her name animate the natural world, investing it with new and possibly even more fruitful life (Tarkka 1994:264).

A Young Woman's Crime and Punishment

Although not obvious at first glance, the characters, themes and motifs in the *Hanged Maid* and the *Ruined Sister* do share common elements. An inappropriate and thus shameful sexual liason means that neither of the female protagonists can return to her home community. Firstly, both girls are culpable of straying from home and are punished for allowing themselves to be 'spoiled' (or ruined), i.e., sexually unclean. In addition, the fate of the hanged maid closely parallels that of Kullervo's sister. Both girls unwittingly find themselves in forbidden or otherwise inappropriate sexual acts, after which they are banished from their own cultural roots and lose their position in their own community, and neither can return. By the end of the narrative, both girls are doomed to leaving the home and culture familiar to them; this type of exile could be regarded as the ultimate punishment for violating the sexual norms of the community. Although exile is a suitable way out for a young man, it is difficult – if not inconceivable – for a young woman.

Only a small number of positive female figures can be found in the whole poetic corpus now under consideration. For the most part, female characters were often associated with notions of otherness and strangeness. Only Kullervo's mother and the mother figure in the *Hanged Maid* poem have a few redeeming qualities. Although Kullervo's mother expresses no concern for her daughter's emotional and social recovery after her traumatizing incestuous affair, she appears as an understanding and loving mother to her son. She passively rejects her daughter, but actively helps her son. The mother of Anni Girl, on the other hand, orders her daughter to prepare herself for marriage despite the girl's terror of her future husband. Only after the girl's suicide can the mother appreciate the extent of her daughter's anguish. The mother attempts to atone for her daughter's tragedy through a poetic lament.

Masculine heroes are generally aided and understood by their mothers in Kalevala meter poetry. Lemminkäinen's mother first tries to prevent her son from going uninvited to the Päivölä celebrations to start an argument, but the boy defies his mother's advice and goes to the party in which he kills the owner of the Päivölä farm. Lemminkäinen runs back to his mother's apron strings, and the mother advises her son to go to hide his crimes on the Island. Kullervo's mother wastes no time worrying about her daughter's fate, but instead does all she can to find a safe refuge for her son.

Kullervo's sister and the smith's wife both wreak havoc in narratives primarily about masculine heroes. Kullervo's sister's sexuality acts as a disruptive force, while the smith's wife's higher social status – as the masculine hero's employer – upsets the social order. The *Ruined Sister* poem can also be read as a narrative aimed at validating and reinforcing a social order which favors male authority, power and action. A woman's sexual assertiveness is destructive to the general scheme of things. The smith's wife pays a heavy price for her failings as an employer. Anni Girl and Kullervo's sister dare to venture beyond their own home environments and pay with their lives. Although the fate of the sister is left unspoken, she apparently shares the same fate as Anni. Traditional narratives deny female characters the opportunity for life beyond their home villages. Return is impossible: once she has left, i.e., violated the social norms, she is no longer welcome to come back home. The tradition underlines the dangers lurking beyond the home community; it is a place where no one will protect her and she cannot protect herself. Therefore, she will be considered fair game. The male protagonist appears and hunts her down. By daring to enter a dangerous, i.e., strange and unknown area, she gets "spoiled". Her identity as a bare-headed maiden changes to that of a "used" bitch. A ruined maiden can no longer assume the role of a respectable bride.

The Sister: A Dangerous Victim

In traditional Finnish and Karelian societies the men wielded more power than the women; and, it goes without saying that they were physically more powerful as well. Moreover, women were enculturated to submit to male authority. Oddly enough, when it comes to so-called feminine crimes – which female characters have either unknowingly committed or have been violently coerced into committing – tradition ascribes the guilt to its female protagonists (Nenola 1986:166–193; Syndergaard 1993:135–136). In the Archangel Karelian texts of *The Revenge of Kaleva-Boy*, a poem sometimes linked to the *Ruined Sister* poem, a female character is even severely punished for providing a man with unsatisfactory food. By leaving the aftermath of the incest untold, the guilt of Kullervo's sister is rendered in a more subtle manner. The silence about the sister's destiny highlights her guilt and shame.

The moral culpability of female characters is far from unusual in Kalevala poetry. A similar tendency of moral reproach appears in the *Ahti and Kyllikki* poem or in the *Song of Mataleena*.[12] In the former poem, not only is Kyllikki portrayed as guilty for the loss of her husband, but also because her warring husband risks his life by embarking on yet another expedition of conquest. If Kyllikki had behaved herself in a way befitting a good wife and stayed near home and hearth, she would have saved her marriage and the life of her husband. The *Ahti and Kyllikki* poem and the texts of the *Hanged Maid* poem, like the *Ruined Sister* poem, obliquely caution women to stay close to home to ensure their own safety and the balance of their entire environment (Nenola 1986:113–114).

In the *Ruined Sister* poem, the narrative harshly obscures the fate of the sister. She has existed solely as an object of male desire and sexual gratification. Unfortunately, the man turned out to be her own brother. Nevertheless, the sister bears the burden of guilt through silence. Her own vanity has led her to adorn herself before going to the village and her greed compels her to accept a ride from a young stranger: a respectable woman would have rejected him. Tradition forgives the fallible man, but forgets the fallible women.

A brief consideration of another Kalevala meter poem, the *Singing Match*, may further elucidate the sister's social position. The poem tells of two men of wisdom who engage in a contest. Joukahainen, a young shaman, challenges Väinämöinen, the wisest shaman of them all. The two engage in a battle of wits which is played out in the realm of song. Joukahainen is the loser. By promising his sister's hand in marriage to the old shaman, however, he does manage to save his own life. Not only does the sister salvage her brother's honor and his life, she also functions as a bond between the two men. Joukahainen's mother rejoices upon hearing about this prestigious addition to the family; indeed, his presence will raise her status in society. The sister's lot is quietly to accept what is to come. Nevertheless, as Lévi-Strauss has written, the community perception of the woman is far from insignificant: she is not just a passive object or merely a means of exchange; in fact, she has a vital and active role as a link between kin groups (Weiner 1992:73–97).[13]

Even though a young Karelian woman would have spent most of her existence, since early childhood, being groomed for married life, her lot was not necessarily a bleak one. In most cases, the identity of her future mate was no secret. Indeed, her parents and kin group would have spent years inculcating her regarding the most appropriate future husband. What is most heart-breaking about both the *Singing Match* and the *Hanged Maid* poems is the fact that the suitor is not the one the girl has been expecting, but another new, surprising and inappropriate alternative. What is tragic about both the *Singing Match* and the *Hanged Maid* is the sudden change in plan. Neither girl will wed the suitor she has been expecting. Instead, she must suddenly accept a new – and inappropriate – alternative.

In Lévi-Straussian terms, it is her participation in the incestuous act which causes Kullervo's sister to lose her important function in the community. No longer the rejected object of her brother's sexual desire, she is now a sexual subject. The sister can no longer act as a means of exchange; her potential as a suitable wife has been lost.[14] The sister appears as a threat to the entire human (masculine) organization. Because she has endangered the entire society, she is muted. The masculine tradition silences the woman who breaks the system based on exchange. The fact that tradition abandons her to her fate without an explicit condemnation makes her all the more significant. Her significance is underlined by silence. The sister emerges as a central figure and force at the climax of the poem.

Kullervo is exiled and loses his worldly belongings; his sister's fate is obscured, but we can assume she is dead. As an exile, the young man must live as a nameless and kinless pariah. His crime has estranged him from his own community and his own identity. The breakdown of the family signifies the discord caused within the larger kin group. Thus, the harmony of the entire community has been broken, for villages traditionally were made up of extended families. (Harva 1940–41:32.) The sister has functioned as a catalyst for both individual and communal destruction. Undeniably, Kullervo regrets seducing his own sister – *not* because of what happens to her, but what happens to him. His sorrow arises from self-pity.

Also the mother's sympathy lies with her son. As a ruined or spoiled woman, the sister has lost her opportunity to become a suitable wife to anyone, and thus she would have to live with her brother because the brother's duty is to take care of his unwed sisters (Harva 1947:70–71). But in this case it is not possible because the brother has been forced to suffer because of his sister. The sister has threatened the communal order and been punished for it. She has paid for her crime with her life. Tradition wastes no words on the sister's fate. Indeeds, words are needless for such a self-evident outcome. The sister has no place to hide.

Translated by Leila Virtanen.

NOTES

[1] E.B. Tylor presented this well-known view in an article dealing with research methods for the study of the development of institutions (1888). McLennan, however, stressed the need for exogamy ("marriage out") in his study of the "primitive" marriage (1865).

[2] Kaffman (1977:216) challenges the assumption denying the possibility of heterosexual relationships evolving between people who have grown up together. Melford E. Spiro has not drawn his conclusions from research that proves that men and women who have been raised together since early childhood are disgusted by the notion of physical intimacy together. On the contrary, he states that the kibbutz research indeed supports incest theories which do not deny the possibility of sexual tension between people who have lived together since early childhood (Spiro 1987:83).

[3] Lévi-Strauss (1969:9–10) is aware of the Egyptian practice of consanguineous marriage. The existence of this practice, however, does not rule out the universal nature of the incest taboo because the incest prohibition still applied to some members of the immediate family or wider kin group, even in ancient Egypt.

[4] Although there are also accounts of consanguineous marriages among the Japanese Ainu, their kinship systems remain somewhat unclear, i.e., who is defined as a true sibling.

[5] Sigmund Freud (1989) regarded the beginning of culture as the crime of parricide committed by the son to gain sexual access to the mother. He derived his theory from the Oedipus myth.

[6] In Arhippa Perttunen's song the girl refuses twice. Upon the boy's third attempt to entice her, however, she joins him without needing much more persuasion (SKVR I$_2$, 978, 978A).

[7] The "closed pond" is a place in which diseases transmitted in water are released. One should never drink from such a pond or consume its fish; otherwise one will catch the curses sent to the pond (Paulaharju 1924:66). Generally, boasts about property or skills do not appear in the texts connected to the Kaleva Boy's theme of revenge.

[8] The songs recorded in Suurijärvi, Liedma, Jyskyjärvi and Piismalahti all refer to the young man guilty of incest as *sinisukka, hienohelma* ("blue-stockinged, fine-dressed"), *sinisukka Äijön poika* ("blue-stockinged Äijö's son"), *liedo Lemminkäinen* ("wanton Lemminkäinen or Kullervo, the son of Kaleva") (SKVR I$_2$, 958, 959, 960, 960a, 961, 962, 964, 965). In these songs the boy does not invite or coax the girl to join him on his journey; he simply forces her.

[9] *Sinisukka Äijön poika* ("blue-stockinged Äijö's son") is also a reference to Kullervo (SKVR I$_2$, 962, 972, 983, 984, 985, 985a, 986, 987, 989, 991).

[10] Often in Ingrian songs the girl meets Tuurikkainen while on her way to church (see SKVR V$_1$, 840): *Poik' oil tuiman Tuurikkainen, /Lemmettyisen liekuttama, //Nei'ot kirkkoon männiit, /pursiit punahammeet, /siniviitat viilättiit.* ("It was that son of stern Tuurikkainen/cradled by Lemmettyinen, //Maidens went to church/with their red skirts/ and their blue robes").

[11] Anneli Asplund (1994) points out that the themes of the *Ruined Sister* poem are reminiscent of those in ballads. Nevertheless, even though the form and plot content are typical to the ballad, the poem does have mythic elements.

[12] In Finland, the *Song of Mataleena* has only been recorded during the Ritvala Whitsuntide festival. It has never been recorded in Karelia, but a few texts have been collected in Ingria. Only a few texts of the *Ahti and Kyllikki* poem have ever been collected: two come from Archangel and the other two from Olonets Karelia.

[13] Annette B. Weiner has studied the Melanesian cultures of the South Pacific. She has observed that the close relationship between brother and sister is more significant than the incest prohibition on that relationship. Ultimately, it is the brother's role to defend and to protect his sister (the same kind of role is also evident in Kalevala meter poetry and even in old Karelian court records). Weiner has further stressed the sister's economic and political role as a marker and guardian of certain "inalienable

possessions". Thus, a woman's seemingly subjugated and passive role may appear quite different when viewed from within.

[14] Lukkarinen (1918:88) describes the Archangel Karelian marriage as a direct and honest trade involving a buyer, a seller, and a piece of merchandise", in other words, the suitor, the girl's relatives and the girl herself, "a young hen (chick) for sale" (also Inha 1921:141–142).

BIBLIOGRAPHY

Asplund, Anneli 1994: Balladeja ja arkkiveisuja. Suomalaisia kertomalauluja. Suomalaisen Kirjallisuuden Seura. Helsinki.

Brewster, Paul G. 1972: The Incest Theme in Folksong. Folklore Fellows Communication No. 212. Academia Scientiarum Fennica, Helsinki.

Cicirelli, Victor G. 1994: Sibling Relationships in Cross-Cultural Perspective. Journal of Marriage and the Family 56:7–20.

Comparetti, Domenico 1892: Der Kalewala oder die traditionelle Poesi der Finnen. Historisch-kritische Studie [u]ber den Ursprung der grossen nationalen Epopöen. Halle.

Douglas, Mary 1982: Natural Symbols. Explorations in Cosmology. Pantheon Books. New York.

– 1989 (1966): Purity and Danger: An Analysis of Concepts of Pollution and Taboo. London.

Erickson, Mark 1993: Rethinking Oedipus: An Evolutionary Perspective of Incest Avoidance. American Journal of Psychology Vol. 150:411–416.

Freud, Sigmund 1989 (1913): Toteemi ja tabu. Eräitä yhtäläisyyksiä villien ja neuroottisten sielunelämässä. Suom. Mirja Rutanen. Love kirjat. Helsinki.

Fox, Robin 1980: The Red Lamp of Incest. Hutchinson, London – Melbourne – Sydney – Auckland – Johannesburg.

van Gennep, Arnold 1960 (1909): The Rites of Passage. Transl. from the French by Monica B. Vizedom and Gabrielle L. Caffee. Routledge – Kegan Paul. London – Henley.

Haavio, Martti 1935: Suomalaisen muinaisrunouden maailma. WSOY. Porvoo.

– 1992: Esseitä kansanrunoudesta. Suomalaisen Kirjallisuuden Seura. Helsinki.

Harva, Uno 1938: Suomensukuisten kansain sukulaisnimistön rakenne. Virittäjä 1938: 297–310.

– 1940–41: Naimatapojemme historia. Kalevalaseuran vuosikirja 20–21. WSOY. Porvoo.

– 1947: The Finno-Ugric System of Relationship. Transactions of the Westermarck Society. Vol I:52–74. Ejnar Munksgaard. Copenhagen.

Heikinmäki, Maija-Liisa 1981: Suomalaiset häätavat. Otava. Helsinki.

Honko, Lauri 1979: Perinteen sopeutumisesta. Sananjalka 21:55–76.

Hopkins, Keith 1980: Brother-Sister Marriage in Roman Egypt. Journal for Comparative Study of Society and History Vol. 22:303–354.

Inha, I.K. 1921: Kalevalan laulumailta. Elias Lönnrotin poluilla Vienan Karjalassa. Toinen painos. Kansanvalistusseura. Helsinki.

Itkonen, T.I. 1921: Suomensukuiset kansat. Tietosanakirja-Osakeyhtiö. Helsinki.

Kaffman, Mordecai 1977: Sexual Standards and Behavior of the Kibbutz Adolescent. American Journal of Orthopsychiatry 47:207–217.

Kalevala 1849: The Finnish National Epic. Compiled by Elias Lönnrot. Suomalaisen Kirjallisuuden Seura. Helsinki.

Kemppinen, Iivar 1977: Kadonnut Karjala. Karjalaisen talonpoikaiskulttuurin pääpiirteet. Joensuu.

Kluckhohn, Clyde 1969 (1960): Recurrent Themes in Myths and Mythmaking. A. Murray (ed.) Myth and Mythmaking. Beacon, Boston.

Konkka, Unelma 1985: Ikuinen ikävä. Karjalaiset riitti-itkut. Suomalaisen Kirjallisuuden Seura. Helsinki.
Krohn, Kaarle 1903–1910: Kalevalan runojen historia. Suomalaisen Kirjallisuuden Seura. Helsinki.
– 1928: Kalevalastudien VI: Kullervo. Folklore Fellows Communication No. 76. Suomalainen Tiedeakatemia/Academia Scientiarum Fennica. Helsinki.
Kupiainen, Tarja 1996: Piiloutuneet merkitykset: tutkimus vienankarjalaisesta ja inkeriläisestä Kalevanpoika-mytologiasta. Perinteentutkimuksen lisensiaatintutkimus/Licenciate thesis on Folklore Studies. Manuscript, University of Joensuu.
Kuusi, Matti (ed.) 1980: Kalevalaista kertomarunoutta. Suomalaisen Kirjallisuuden Seura. Helsinki.
Leach, Edmund 1973:Structuralism in Social Anthropology. D. Robey (ed.) Structuralism: An Introduction. Clarendon Press. Oxford.
Lévi-Strauss, Claude 1966: The Savage Mind. Trans. by George Weidenfeld. The University of Chicago Press. Chicago.
– 1969 (1949): The Elementary Structures of Kinship. Trans. from French by James Harle Bell, John Richard von Surmer and Rodney Needham. Beacon Press. Boston.
– 1978 (1968): The Origin of Table Manners. Trans. from French by John and Doreen Weightman. Jonathan Cape Limited. London.
– 1986a (1964): The Raw and the Cooked. Transl. from French by John and Doreen Weightman. Penguin Books. Harmondsworth. Middlesex.
– 1986b (1958): Structural Anthropology 1. Transl. from French by Claire Jakobson and Brooke Grundfest Schoepf. Penguin Books. Harmondsworth. Middlesex.
– 1987 (1973): Structural Anthropology 2. Transl. from French by Monique Layton. Penguin. Books. Harmondsworth. Middlesex.
– 1990 (1971): The Naked Man. Transl. from French by John and Doreen Weightman. University of Chicago Press. Chicago and London.
Lukkarinen, Juho 1918: Vienan Karjalassa. Karisto. Hämeenlinna.
– 1933: Suomalaisten naimatapoja. Aineksia suomalaisten kansojen avioliiton historiaan I. Suomalaisen Kirjallisuuden Seura. Helsinki.
Makkonen, Anna 1996: Sinulle: romaani joka ei uskalla sanoa nimeään tai: Nainen, kapina, kirjoitus ja historia. Suomalaisen Kirjallisuuden Seura. Helsinki.
Malinowski, Bronislaw 1979 (1927): Sex and Repression in Savage Society. Routledge – Kegan Paul. London and Henley.
– 1982 (1929): The Sexual Life of Savages in Norht Western Melanesia. An Ethnographic Account of Courtship, Marriage, and Family Life among the Natives of the Torbriand Islands, British New Guinea. Routledge – Keagan Paul. London, Boston, Melbourne and Henley.
Mauss, Marcel 1990 (1928): The Gift. The Form and Reason for Exchange in Archaic Societies. Trans. by W. D. Halls. Routledge. London.
McLennan, J. F. 1865: Primitive Marriage. Black. Edinburgh.
Meletinskii, E. M. 1987: The Incest Archetype in the Folklore Tradition (Especially in the Heroic Myth). Soviet Anthropology – Archeology Vol. 26:21–29.
Murdock, George Peter 1961 (1949): Social Structure. The Free Press. Macmillan. London and New York.
Nenola, Aili 1981: Inkeriläiset itkuhäät. M. Sarmela (ed.) Pohjolan häät. Suomalaisen Kirjallisuuden Seura. Helsinki.
– 1986: Miessydäminen nainen. Naisnäkökulmia kulttuuriin. Suomalaisen Kirjallisuuden Seura. Helsinki.
– 1994: Folkloristiikka ja sukupuolitettu maailma. J. Kupiainen – E. Sevänen (eds) Kulttuurintutkimus. Johdanto. Suomalaisen Kirjallisuuden Seura. Helsinki.
Nirvi, R.E. 1982: Petojen nimitykset kosinta- ja häärunoissa. Suomi 123:3. Suomalaisen Kirjallisuuden Seura. Helsinki.
Ortner, Sherry B. 1996: Making Gender. The Politics and Erotics of Culture. Beacon Press. Boston.

Paulaharju, Samuli 1924: Syntymä, lapsuus ja kuolema. Vienan Karjalan tapoja ja usko-
muksia. Kalevalaseuran julkaisuja 2. WSOY. Porvoo.

Perander, Johan J. F. 1872: Tragillisesta peri-aatteesta Kullervo-runoissa. Kaikuja
Hämeestä I:133–143.

Roscoe, Paul B. 1994: Amity and Aggression: A Symbolic Theory of Incest. Man Vol.
29:49–76.

Ruoppila, Veikko 1937: Sakkulan vanhat häätavat. Virittäjä: 322–331.

Salminen, Väinö 1916: Inkerin kansan häärunoelma muinaisine kosimis- ja häämenoineen.
Suomalaisen Kirjallisuuden Seura. Helsinki.

Sarmela, Matti 1969: Reciprocity Systems of the Rural Society in the Finnish-Karelian
Culture Area: with Special Reference to Social Intercourse of the Youth. Folklore
Fellows Communications No. 207. Suomalainen Tiedeakatemia/Academia
Scientiarum Fennica. Helsinki.

– 1978: Vienalaiset lauluhäät. Kalevalaseuran Vuosikirja 58. WSOY. Porvoo & Helsinki.

– 1981: Suomalaiset häät. M. Sarmela (ed.) Pohjolan häät. Suomalaisen Kirjallisuuden
Seura. Helsinki.

– 1994: Suomen perinneatlas. Suomen kansankulttuuri kartasto 2: Folklore. Suomalaisen
Kirjallisuuden Seura. Helsinki.

Seligman, Brenda 1950: The Problem of Incest and Exogamy: A Restatement. American
Anthropologist 52:305–316.

Setälä, E.N. 1910: Kullervo-Hamlet. Valvojan Kalevalan 75-vuotinen muistio: 3–22.

Shepher, Joseph 1983: Incest. A Biosocial View. Academic Press. New York and London.

Siikala, Anna-Leena 1987: Myytti ja historia eeppisessä kansanrunoudessa. M. Linna
(ed.) Muinaisrunot ja todellisuus. Suomen kansan vanhojen runojen historiallinen
tausta. Historian ystäväin liitto XX. Helsinki.

– 1992: Suomalainen šamanismi. Mielikuvien historiaa. Suomalaisen Kirjallisuuden
Seura. Helsinki.

SKVR (1908–1948): Suomen Kansan Vanhat Runot. Suomalaisen Kirjallisuuden Seura.
Helsinki.

Spain, David H. 1987: The Westermarck-Freud Incest-Theory Debate. An Evaluation
and Reformulation. Current Anthropology Vol. 28:623–645.

Spiro, Melford E. 1958: Children of Kibbutz. Harvard University Press. Cambridge.

– 1987: Culture and Human Nature. B. Kilborne – L. Langness (eds) Theoretical Papers
of Melford E. Spiro. The University of Chicago Press. Chicago – London.

Suurhasko, Jouko 1977: Karel'skaja svadebnaja obrjadnost': konec XIX-nacolo XX v.
Nauka. Leningrad.

Syndergaard, Larry 1993: Incest Ballads in the English and Scottish Popular Ballads:
Pattern and Meaning. Southern Folklore Vol 50:127–141.

Tarkiainen, Viljo 1909: Kullervo-aihe Suomen kirjallisuudessa. Valvojan Kalevalavihko
II, III:231–246.

Tarkka, Lotte 1994: Other Worlds – Symbolism, Dialogne and Gender in Karelian Oral
Poetry. A.-L. Siikala – S. Vakimo (eds) Songs Beyond the Kalevala. Transformations
of Oral Poetry. Studia Fennica Folkloristica 2, Suomalaisen Kirjallisuuden Seura.
Helsinki.

Turner, Victor 1978 (1974): Dramas, Fields, and Metaphors. Symbolic Action in Human
Society. Cornell University Press. Ithaca – London.

Twitchell, James B. 1987: Forbidden Partners. The Incest Taboo in Modern Culture.
Columbia University Press. New York.

Tylor, E.B. 1888: On a Method of Investigating the Development of Institutions; Applied
to Laws of Marriage and Descent. Journal of the Royal Anthropological Institute, Vol.
18:245–269.

Valeri, Valerio 1985: Kingship and Sacrifice. University of Chicago Press, Chicago.

Voionmaa, Väinö 1915: Suomen karjalaisen heimon historia. Kansanvalistusseura. Helsinki.

Vuoristo, Sakari 1992: Iivo Marttinen, Vuokkiniemen kansanperinteen suurkerääjä. Suomi
167. Suomalaisen Kirjallisuuden Seura. Helsinki.

Weiner, Annette B. 1992: Inalienable Possessions. The Paradox of Keeping-While-Giving. University of California Press. Berkeley, Los Angeles – Oxford.

Westermarck, Edward 1891: The History of Human Marriage. Macmillan and co. London and New York.

– 1922: The History of Human Marriage. 5th edition, rewritten. Vol. 2. Allerton Book Company. New York.

Willner, Dorothy 1983: Definition and Violation: Incest and the Incest Taboos. Man Vol. 18:134–159.

Wolf, Arthur P. 1993: Westermarck Redivivus, Annual Review of Anthropology. Vol. 22:157–175.

ANNIKKI KAIVOLA-BREGENHØJ

Sexual Riddles

The Test of the Listener

Riddles are among the most outspoken expressions of folk eroticism. Nevertheless, the use of sexual vocabulary is rare in riddles, unlike in other forms of erotic folklore. Until recently, few sexual riddles have been published; in most cases they have for reasons of propriety been forgotten. One rare exception was the Finnish clergyman Christfrid Ganander, who, in 1783, published the first collection of Finnish riddles, *Aenigmata Fennica*. Ganander appreciated the value of living tradition and did not censor his publication. In preparing a new edition of his book, however, he was obliged to remove 39 riddles that were deemed banal and inappropriate. These included riddles alluding to the Church and some forms of sexuality. Examples of puritanical publishers abound (see Hart 1964:138–141). The most renowned among them is Archer Taylor, who, in the chapter headed Erotic Scenes in his work *English Riddles* (1951:687–688), includes innocent answers to sexual riddles but omits those with a double meaning. The following riddle type 1425–1428, most obviously of a sexual nature, has, however, escaped Taylor's sieve:

> Something round, split in the middle
> Surrounded by hair, and water comes out. – Eye.
> (ER 1425)

It has quite rightly been pointed out that bashful publishers have been responsible for the squeaky clean yet misleading image of folklore as something that is almost antiseptically devoid of sensuality (Launonen 1966: 374). Yet this is a living tradition, and one still in use: sexual riddles and jokes are not merely a bygone form of entertainment, since they continue to be popular among both adults and children (see Brown 1973 for examples).

Sexual riddles generally fall into two expressive types. A common type of sexual riddle evokes seemingly sexual images and arouses erotic fantasies without employing even a single "naughty" word (e.g. "Spread open the fuzz, stick a bare thing in" or "What four-letter word begins with **f** and ends with **k**, and if it doesn't work you can use your fingers?"). But because the image inevitably suggests a sexual answer, the respondent is surprised when offered the innocent answer "hand in mitten" (FR 161) or "fork" (Dundes –

Myth and Mentality
Studia Fennica
Folkloristica 8, 2002

Georges 1962:225). Riddles with explicitly sexual or vulgar answers referring to sexual intercourse or the male or female genitalia are far rarer (e.g. "Buried when alive; Pulled out when dead. – Penis". Hart 1964:149). In any case the answer is always unexpected, and this surprise element is in fact regarded as typical in obscene folklore and in jokelore in general (Dundes – Georges 1962:221).

> The old lady pitted it an'patted it; The old man down with his breeches an' at it. – She made up the bed, and he undressed and got into bed.
> (Boggs 1934:321)

> Spread open the fuzz, stick a bare thing in. – Hand in mitten.
> (FR 161)

The next riddle, however, hints at the male sexual organ:

> About six inches long, an' a mighty pretty size; Not a lady but will take it between her thighs. – The lefthand horn on a lady's side saddle.
> (Boggs 1934:323)

And the true referent of this riddle is the female sexual organ:

> An odd girl whose private parts are very soft. – Banana.
> (Blacking 1961:22)

Among the most popular innocent answers to Finnish riddles are churning and draw well, in which a long object plunged deep into a vessel greatly misleads the guesser. One expert on the riddle tradition writes:

> 'A woman on the ground, a man in a tree, a man's balls in woman's mouth' was a typical riddle because every household had its draw well. I recall that the girls would try to answer these suggestive riddles quickly if they happened to know the answer so that the boys would not have time to smirk.
> (SKS. K.Harju AK 2. 1966)

The vocabulary and imagery of sexual riddles center around expressions suited to double entendre (Harleman Stewart 1983: 47). Sometimes an innocent answer seems so contrived as to be inconsistent (e.g. the riddle about the man's penis).

Swedish riddles draw a distinction between male and female actors. The man represents sexual egocentrism, male assessments and concepts of women and women's sexual properties, reactions and behavior. By contrast, if a woman appears as main character in a riddle, she is receptive and passive. (Lövkrona 1991:272–273.) The following riddle may be regarded as the ultimate in active and passive sexual relations:

> Father's was stiff when he came in, and he laid it on mother's hairy thing, but when mother awoke father's was slack and mother's hairy thing was wet? – Father came home when mother was sleeping and laid his stiff frozen gloves on mother's woolly cloth. When mother awoke the gloves had melted and the woolly cloth was wet.

As a rule, however, sexual riddles are dominated by the act, not its performers. As means of expression sexual riddles usually stick to the middle of the road, deliberately presenting the image in an ambiguous manner. At the same time they nevertheless incite their listeners to sexual fantasy. Stylistic flaws are thus easy to identify. Most often the reason for the blunder is that the inventor of the riddle makes the mistake of describing things too graphically, so that the image loses its ambiguity, e.g.:

Uncle's prick stands at the door to Auntie's quim. – Well bucket and well.
(FR 927)

From cunt to cunt it snaps. – Pot hooks.
(FR 1154)

Whereas the most wide-spread sexual riddles in the Folklore Archive of the Finnish Literature Society run to more than 500 variants, the two examples I have quoted appear only twice. Both the stylistic error and the circulation indicate that the riddler was not wholly competent as an image inventor; these riddles never gained much popularity.

There is, however, another possible interpretation. Outspoken sexual images of precisely this type are dominant in, for example, Mari riddles. They may in fact represent a type of sexual riddle that was never even intended to have a double meaning.

Many erotic riddles are international, though it is difficult to achieve a clear sense of their distribution and frequencies in view of the small volume of material published so far. Suggestive riddles used to be regarded as age-old ritual questions (Schultz 1912:96), but also as relatively recent lore flourishing at the end of the Middle Ages and the beginning of the modern era. It is thought that they were invented by itinerant scholars in the 16th century (Peuckart 1938:107).

The Traditional Contexts and Users of Sexual Riddles

We do have some information on the contexts in which traditional sexual riddles were used. Among groups of young people this lore has always clearly functioned to raise the erotic temperature. In the farming community there were some jobs done by the young people of the village together, and these situations provided a setting for the transmission of oral tradition. V.E.V. Wessman (1940:183) described the verbal merry-making of a Finnish working community as follows:

In the autumn the malt was sweetened in a malt sauna and spirits were brewed. Usually the work was done by the young girls from the farm. It was a laborious job, because it had to be watched over day and night. Nevertheless, the time passed quickly, because as soon as the boys caught a whiff of the malt, they sought out the girls and helped them pass the time by dreaming up all sorts of pranks. One popular form of entertainment was posing riddles for the girls to answer. And the boys were indeed sharp: for many riddles lead one's thoughts to something that would make the girls blush and giggle although the object to be guessed might well be something as innocent as a tobacco pipe or a spoon, or such legitimate pursuits as weaving, spinning or father eating lingonberry porridge out of a bowl in mother's lap. Other riddles were less 'risque'.

The posing of sexual riddles was particularly popular among men. Often it was a way of cultivating the tradition of both the sex and the occupational group, as the following description illustrates:

> Nowadays riddling sessions take place while the men are pausing for a cigarette, enjoying a moment of free time, or while in their living quarters. The riddles tossed about are seldom the old traditional ones of the Finnish people. Instead, the popular ones are those criticized as being vulgar and obscene, such as "What do a woman and a guitar have in common? –Both are fingered at the hole".
> (SKS. O. Mäkelä AK 12.1966.)

When it comes to performing sexual lore, same sex groups appear to be far less inhibited; furthermore, this form of lore strengthens the group's cohesion (Virtanen 1988:215). Men and women may have used riddles for different purposes. By turning our attention from a Finnish milieu to the Spanish village of Monteros, we clearly see that riddle distribution divides the populace by class as well as sex. "Riddles show themselves to be a popular form of spontaneous verbal entertainment among men and women of the working class and women of the elite. There is a definite tendency for working-class men to tell riddles more than any other single group and for male members of the upper class virtually to refrain from riddling at all. There is a moderate amount of riddling among women of all social ranks, though, as I have said, it is more common among elite women." (Brandes 1980:128.)

Sexual riddles are, according to Stanley Brandes (1980:133), the single most common riddle type that has come to be known in Monteros. Both men and women know and tell pretended obscene riddles. Nevertheless, content determines the riddler: men tend to tell riddles evoking male physical attributes, while women tell those concerning the female anatomy. Both genders may pose riddles suggesting copulation. Examples of riddles posed by men are:

> By day hung, by night pressed tight. – The cross-bar of a door.
> (cf. ER 1744a, FR 843)

> I put it in red and I take it out red. – The pepper.

Examples of women's riddles are:

> I went down to the market, I bought a young girl, I raised her skirt, And I saw her thing. – A head of lettuce / compared here to a young girl; the outer leaves are the skirt/.

> A chap came: He put it in me, He removed it from me; Ask God that He do well by me. – A male nurse giving an injection.
> (Brandes 1980:133–135.)

The occasion on which women, too, may freely participate in the posing of such riddles is the olive harvest important to the village community. Otherwise women – and Brandes underlines "especially elite women – merely use this folkloric device as a means of expressing otherwise taboo desires and concepts while safely keeping this slight degree of licentiousness within the secret confines of their homes". Sexual motifs are normally to be avoided between unrelated men and women in Monteros. Pretended obscene riddles give men a chance "to expose their genitals verbally and to evoke images of the sexual act in the presence of women whom they covet but cannot otherwise take." (Brandes 1980:133–136.) Brandes refers to Sigmund Freud's analysis of "smut" (i.e. obscenity) in humor. Freud (1960:97) writes, among other things: "... smut is directed to a particular person, by whom one is sexually excited and who, on hearing it, is expected to become aware of the speaker's excitement and as a result to become sexually excited in turn..." Brandes sees in Freud's analysis an explanation for why men and women cultivate sexual riddles as "a subtle means of displaying their own sexual organs".

Posing sexual riddles has been regarded as a way of wielding male power. However, this power may not be only confined to men. Perhaps women have power, too, at least the power to tease men. Inger Lövkrona (1991:277) conjectures – though she does not have any ethnographic accounts at her disposal – that women in a farming community, where there was strict demarcation between men's and women's jobs, might tease men encroaching on their territory. As a tool they might use sexual riddles with images in which the male organ acquires endearing, humorous and provocative names.

Some folklore collectors mention that women were in the habit of interrupting a game or changed the topic of conversation as soon as anyone began asking sexual riddles.

> ... I remember the women would not let some riddle be asked to the end but put a stop to it and interrupted so that it never got asked.
> (SKS. Aino Hanhisalo AK 2. 1966.)

Women's chastity is also underlined:

> The farm hands and day laborers were bolder at asking more obscene ones, whereas the mothers and serving girls were more respectable.
> (SKS. Olea Hirvonen AK 3. 1966.)

This information on the use of riddles dates from the extensive collection of Finnish riddles made in 1966 and throws light on the situation in the early decades of the 20th century. But are the details of women's attitudes necessarily as straightforward as this? Where was the limit to the presentation of sexual lore? Let us regard this question in terms of Finnish and Swedish folklore.

An examination of answers to sexual riddles (Finnish Riddles 1977) yields somewhat surprising results: a considerable proportion of them deal with women's life and labor on the farm. 40% of the answers refer to the women's domain on the farm, and only 15% to that of men. 45% refer to the agrarian way of life in general and are sexually neutral. The corresponding figures for all Finnish riddles are, by way of comparison, 24%, 23% and 53%, respectively. Sexual riddles thus clearly allude to women's work (cf. also Lövkrona 1991), but the same cannot be said of those not referring to sexuality. Could the reason for this be that women were considered the target for sexual riddles and sexual implications were hidden in the images familiar to them?

The invention of a riddle begins with the answer, for which an image is devised as a means of circumlocution. Does the fact that the answers to sexual riddles clearly tie in with the women's domain mean that the inventors and users of riddles were – contrary to what has been claimed above – for the most part women? Some scholars (Olsson 1944:10 and Wessman 1949:viii) have stressed the role of women as users of sexual riddles. Their cursory claims do not, however, contain any clear documentation and are limited to collecting situations and not to the use of riddles. On the other hand, we may also ask whether the tradition was in fact one of teasing invented and cultivated by men. To my mind we still have too little information to permit a conclusive answer.

But why do the ethnographic accounts so often underscore women's objections to sexual riddles? This may be a case of a late change in attitude. V.E.V. Wessman notes in the foreword to his publication of riddles:

> Women are just as daring as men at asking 'improper' riddles. Even young girls may, though sometimes giggling and blushing, pose riddles with a double meaning, or turn their faces away as they hand in a paper bearing a suggestive text.
> (Wessman 1949:VIII).

This is also the impression created by the puritanical general view of the role of women given in the descriptions submitted for the collection project in 1966.

Sexual folk tradition is not confined to riddles alone and ranges from shanty-like songs sung by men to make their work easier to outspoken or erotic sexual sayings familiar to both genders, anecdotes, fairy tales, and the songs sung by young people to accompany dancing. Mixed groups of adults have from time immemorial cultivated open and risqué sexual humour, so why not sexual riddles too, which, being ambiguous, are far more exciting? We do, however, have very few descriptions and facts about what people talked about when they got together and the type of language permissible on a given occasion.

One must exercise caution when trying to assess the moral attitudes reflected in early 20th century accounts of riddling. After all, this was a period of intense public enlightenment on all fronts: elementary schooling, the workers' movement, the youth association movement, the temperance movement, the farmers' associations, the country women's associations and many others. These were all efforts, at least in the West, not only to instruct people for their own good, but to clean up their language and morality. What is more, the very act of sending material to the largest folklore archive in the country must have acted as quite a filter. One female collector, who did admittedly also sent in some sexual riddles she had noted down, made the following observation:

If the local people ever found out that I had written such things to you, they should say I was quite abnormal. They would never believe that you would want to know anything vulgar ....
(SKS. Helmi Mäkelä AK 12. 1966)

Many communities had clear restrictions on the use of sexual lore. It was apparently common practice to forbid sexual riddles in the presence of children.

Although country children knew all about animals' mating and giving birth, it was the rule rather than the exception for them to be completely ignorant about the sex life of men and women and the way babies were born (Ruoppila 1954:94–98). Modesty presumably obliged people to refrain from asking riddles that might have led to any awkward questions when children were around.

The limits on the use of sexual lore depend very much on the culture and are often influenced by, for example, religion, the position of women in the community, and on whether sex is regarded as a favorable resource or as a potentially dangerous activity in need of regulation. In some cultures, sexual insinuation may be a natural part of everyday discourse. Don V. Hart (1964:139) reports that in the Philippines such talk was not considered vulgar or obscene but that it reflected "an amiable attitude that puts normal sexual behavior on the same level as other pleasant activities such as scratching and yawning". Riddle games can also be directly related to sexual socialization, as among the Quechua-speakers of Peru. Billie Jean Isbell and Fredy Amilcar Roncalla Fernandez (1977:22–25) insist that they see a direct correlation between the search for one's sexual identity and the creative manipulation of metaphors in riddles, insults and songs. The young person well-versed in these traditional genres is considered more intelligent than the one who is not. Someone who is innovative with riddles, insults and songs is also believed to be a good sexual partner. Unlike in western pre-industrial communities, Quechua children are also familiar with sexual metaphors even though they are too young to engage in sexual relations.

The performance of sexual riddles is, however, as a rule confined either to set situations or to groups of the same age or gender. For example, in the British West Indies sexual lore was an integral part of funeral rituals, the aim being to stress at a time of crisis that the living emerges from the dead. All can take part in the wake, so sexual lore is not restricted to any particular group. (Abrahams 1968:155–156.) Among the Venda of Africa, however, young people only asked sexual riddles among their friends, and never within earshot of adults (Blacking 1961).

Erotic Teasing

The sexual riddle, according to the Finnish accounts, was not only a means of charging the atmosphere, but also a way for young village men to test the tolerance of a new serving girl. The girl had to be on her guard: showing anger, overt shock or taking part in the jest were to be avoided:

307

Then I went into service in the village of Kytösyrjä in Impilahti ... It was an ancient custom for all the young men of the village to come and take a look at any new serving girl. They introduced themselves, under all sorts of names. One said he was Mr. Emptypants from Helsinki. When I refused to flirt with them, they began asking each other dirty riddles. In some of the riddles, the question was innocent but the answer was naughty. With others it was the other way round. Then it was best not to get caught up in their talk. Otherwise, they would soon say you had a dirty mind. Their aim was to trip the girl up in her speech. The boldest one always asked the questions, the others answered and laughed. If the girl did not join in, she could not show she was offended. It would only have made things worse. If she joined in, she had to be sure she could hold her own. It was no use trying unless she really knew what she was about. If she pretended she had no idea what they were talking about, she was more likely to be left in peace, they lost interest in teasing her. But if she let them see she was angry, it went on and on. I saw it happen with a day worker from the farm.
(SKS. Elsa Jaatinen AK 6. 1966.)

The above account describes a new member's initiation into a community; the atmosphere is sexually charged, the males tease the newcomer and test her behavior. Erotic teasing remains part of the living workplace tradition, and the butt of the joke is often a younger member of the opposite sex.

Embarrassment often goes hand in hand with teasing, and only the smart and lucky victim comes out with honor. Teasing is regarded as a masculine tradition, a way to amuse, embarrass or insult a woman (Simmons 1956:1). But women are also capable of it. The following quotation, though brief, from an answer given to a Finnish riddle collector is typical:

... the riddles are from the Rajala shoe factory at Kankaanpää, where a worker called Aili Kivelä put them to the young men working alongside her.
(SKS. O. Mäkelä AK 12. 1966)

Sexual riddles have also been a means of testing the norms of the individual and community, of blurring and breaking them. These means are still in use, despite the transformation of the riddling tradition. I was once subjected to just such a test when spending the night with my husband at the home of one of our informants while we were doing fieldwork. During our numerous previous visits we had grown accustomed to a mode of conversation tinged with sexual joking and innuendo. This was particularly marked during the local masking-tradition period, when the donning of a mask gave the wearer greater liberty to speak out and to grope. I nevertheless had to hide my astonishment when, over breakfast, our host, who was about my age, asked with a grin: "How did you sleep?" Noting the look on his face, a warning bell began to ring, but I briskly replied: "Very well, thank you." "How did you sleep?" our host repeated, and when I failed to give him the answer he expected, added: "Did you sleep like me, with balls between your legs?" Although such jokes can be a form of flirtation, the way they are received depends largely on the listener and the mode of presentation. The same joke may be perceived as vulgar and offensive or simply as an acceptable way for adults to create an erotically charged situation. Stanley Brandes

(1980:135–136) emphasizes the use of power attached to sexual joking. Sexual exchange is in his opinion, too, in its mildest form no more than flirting, but "when carried to excess, a form of verbal rape".

The Use of Riddles Today

Many true riddles survive only in books and archives. There is, however, always an exception to prove the rule. The following riddle, already included in the *Aenigmata Fennica* published in 1783, was recently sent in to the Folklore Archives:

> Stick, wet, loose, pull, if it doesn't fit then lick the end. – Needle and thread. (FR 770)

The riddler was a 22-year-old woman student at a domestic science college who put the riddle to her fellow-students during one of their breaks. Although sexual riddles still remain part of the oral tradition, new riddle formulae are to be found more often than the traditional ones. The following riddle jokes were noted down in 1990 (background information in brackets):

> Why did Sarah laugh? – God was trying her. (16-year-old girl; riddle known since the 1940s)

> What happened when the seven dwarfs saw Snow White in the shower? – Seven up. (13-year-old boy; riddle very popular; varies)

> What do men and matches have in common? – They both catch on just as easily. (16-year-old girl)

> What did the leper say on coming out of the brothel? – Now I've lost it!

The formulae of these riddle jokes are familiar from joking questions and there is little new in their contents, either. Representing more recent lore is the copy tradition rapidly spreading from one country to another. Among the numerous jokes is the following:

> It was the first time as I recall, one evening in May, you gave it me, My mother was hiding and watching it all, My very first time with her own eyes to see. It was an experience beyond compare. You pushed it between my lips, I swear, I could feel it, feel it, all of it there. I coughed and I spluttered, I thought I would choke, So great was the feeling that nobody spoke, The first time you gave me – my very first smoke. (19-year-old girl)

These sexual riddles, likewise the visual ones that follow, are from an unpublished collection by Ulla Lipponen.

Items of copylore often have direct counterparts in neighboring countries, but the origin of this 'poem' is unknown. There is, however, nothing new about the link between smoking and sex (Dundes – Pagter 1975:202–203). Although this is not a proper riddle, the false expectation effect is exactly the same as in sexual riddles.

Sexual riddles are not told merely for fun or as a means of teasing someone; they are also a conscious means of making a protest and violating fusty or outdated behavioral norms. America witnessed a fashionable wave of sexual riddles in the late 1960s (Bauman 1970) instigated by a parodic secret society calling itself The Turtles. The society had its own mocking slogan and initiation rites, during which the following four riddles were as a rule posed:

1. What is it a man can do standing, a woman sitting down, and a dog on three legs? – Shake hands.

2. What is it that a cow has four of and a woman only two of? – Legs.

3. What is a four-letter word ending in 'k' that means the same as intercourse? – Talk.

4. What is it on a man that is round, hard, and sticks so far out of his pajamas that you can hang his hat on it? – His head.

The most important thing was not for the respondent to find the right 'innocent' answer but to amuse the initiated by giving a sexual answer that was laughingly proven to be wrong. The aim of the lore was, among other things, to promote conviviality among drinkers in restaurants and pubs and to embarrass friends in a good-humored way. It was common for men to ask women the riddles. Sexual riddles helped to break the conversational ice, and thus the situation was charged with sexual tension. Richard Bauman, in his studies of riddle joking, considered that fundamentally this institution also parodied the initiation rites of various fraternal orders in America (Masons, fraternities, etc.), for their serious rites were likened to the mock rites of The Turtles. (Bauman 1970: 21–25.)

Even today, the erotic riddle can be an apt way of dealing with sexual taboos. In spring 1989, a 27-year-old Israeli student of folkloristics in Jerusalem (R.D.) wrote down the riddles put to her by a man living in the same mixed student hostel. There were 26 in all, and they were all sexual in theme. The material was provided by Galit Hasan-Rokem, Senior Lecturer at the University of Jerusalem. Why riddle jokes rather than, say, political jokes, R.D. wondered. By discussing this with her student friends, she found that the sexual riddle can break the ice in awkward or formal situations. But it is also a neutral way to talk about a delicate issue. One informant claimed that sexual riddles are also a means of expressing hidden feelings. Such a jest amuses the listeners more than any other. These riddles were not, however, only a men's tradition, for R.D. herself asked her friends the same riddles in order to decide how easy or difficult they were to guess. The material shows just how tempting the mere taste of the forbidden fruit is; besides, a subtle hint, as opposed to an obvious statement, is often far more effective when it comes to creating a erotically charged atmosphere. There was, however, a limit to sexual jokes in the student community, too, since they were never asked when there were strangers present. A sexual riddle may well incorporate some other joking point. The Israeli riddles were often spiced with ethnic humour:

What does a Georgian have that is long and hard? – His name and the first class at school.

Why does a Polish woman close her eyes during the sexual act? – Because she can't bear to see someone else enjoying something.

Why do Israeli men come quickly? – Because they've got to run and tell the lads.

What do you call an English woman's nipple? – The tip of the iceberg.

These riddles can only be appreciated by the listener familiar with the stereotypes: the stupid Georgian with a long name, the sadistic Pole, the childish and boastful "Israeli" man, and the frigid English woman. Ethnic stereotypes are not, however, always international, so there is a limit even to joking. Many of the riddles popular among students were also culture-specific, that is they referred to contemporary Israeli politics, culture and everyday life.

Children and young people also test each other, adults and the limits of norms via sexual riddles. The border between the forbidden and the permissible is elastic and clearly changes over time. The following description, published in 1955, illustrates a Filipino boy's boldness and desire to tease: "The riddle contest may proceed smoothly...until some naughty boy would pop up with a riddle having a double meaning such as the following Tagalog: 'The spear-thrust has not yet been aimed, but the wound gapes widely open.' "Of course, this would at once arouse a cry of objection.../and/ some bold girls would make a comeback... The arm of your father is surrounded with boils." (This is the answer.) (Manuel 1955:152).

In the early 1970s a group of junior schoolchildren wrote down the riddles they could remember for me during one school lesson. Among them were the following sexual riddles:

Why are fire engines red? – You would be too, if you had your hose pulled.

What is the ultimate miracle? – A drunk knocks up a telephone pole and the operator has twins.

In an anthology of children's lore, which was published in 1987, the fire engine riddle appears in the following variation:

Teacher: Why does a cow have a long face? Little Johnny: Well you would too if you had your tits pulled twice a day!

Other sexual riddles in the anthology employ the popular "what's the difference" and "what" formulae.

What's the difference between a man and a woman? – Nothing really. They look the same from behind and slot together at the front.
(Lipponen 1987).

When the presenters of the riddles are children aged 8–10, the shift in sexual lore from a means of raising the erotic temperature to the level of childlike, daring entertainment is clear. These riddles are children's way of showing off to their friends just how much they know about the subject in question.

Far more daring are the sexual riddles contained in the anthology edited by Carsten Bregenhøj (1988), where the point of the joke may be aimed at, for example, homosexuals.

Do you know why gays don't like space? – Because it's endless.

Once upon a time, adults tried to protect children's ears from all manner of sexual insinuation. Nowadays, however, those in need of protection may be the parents, for they are shocked at their children's use of vulgar language and the attitudes thus reflected. The most astonishing thing as far as the adult is concerned is that the same riddle may amuse the adult and the child in early adolescence who is testing his limits. In addition to providing entertainment, the riddle is for the child often a way of transgressing the norms, of testing adults' tolerance and weighing up the various manifestations of sexuality. Although some sexual lore is shared by different age groups, adults usually conceal their knowledge in the presence of youngsters, or at least the fact that they are amused by sexual humour. The double standard of morality is ready and waiting.

One explanation for today's risqué sexual lore is perhaps the general laxity in the way people speak. Sex is also fed to us, by the media for example, in a way that was once unheard of. We may, on the other hand, wonder how people living in the cramped living conditions in rural society, with large families all sleeping in the same room and even in the same bed, could possibly be ignorant of the facts of life. Sex has in any case ceased to be taboo. Nevertheless, limits still exist, for verbal exchange with sexual overtones is cultivated chiefly as the lore of peer groups.

Sexual Picture Puzzles and Spoonerisms

From time to time there is a fashionable wave of picture puzzles (Preston 1982 and Roemer 1982). As with riddle jokes, only the person who sets the puzzle as a rule knows the answer, which always gives an amusing twist to a simple visual expression. Only a small proportion of picture puzzles are mildly sexual, such as this one – one of the oldest – which its presenter learned while living in a student hostel in 1959.

Picture (1) 1. 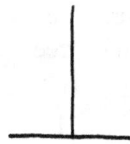 2.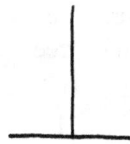

3.  4.

5.  6.

The picture proceeds in stages, and each stage is followed by the question "What's this?". No. 5 shows a mushroom, no. 6 big sister in the bath. In children's lore this final picture has been modified as

Picture (2)

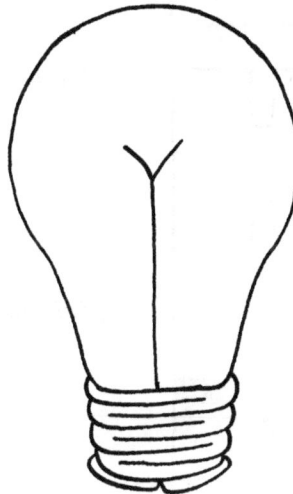

the answer to which is "Sister pulling her tights on" (Lipponen 1987:72). Danielle M. Roemer (1982:194) presents a version of this picture in which the explanation is "A fat lady seen from behind pulling up her girdle".

The following pictures are taken from Finnish children's lore and depict Marilyn Monroe behind a tree.

Picture (3)

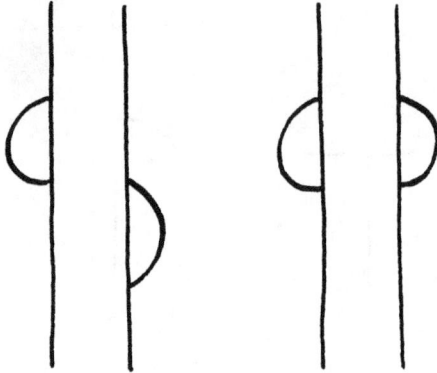

In American lore the curvaceous woman is sometimes Dolly Parton (Roemer 1982:193). Adults also amuse themselves by drawing picture puzzles. Again, some lore is shared by children and adults alike, but the following series appeals more to adults at least somewhat familiar with the plays of William Shakespeare. It is called "Shakespeare's Plays" and it was drawn in 1987 by a woman of about 40 Ulla Lipponen met on a bus.

Pictures (4)

1. The Merry Wives of Windsor

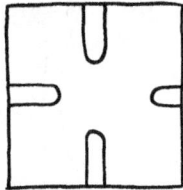

2. Much Ado About Nothing

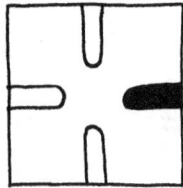

3. Othello

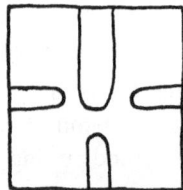

4. Midsummer Night's Dream

The picture here says more than a thousand words. What makes them into a riddle is precisely the fact that the image conjures up two answers. The giver of the "right" interpretation is chastised on hearing the answer. The pictures are presented as a series, so that the clash between "naughty" pictures and world classics affords cumulative pleasure.

Another popular form of contemporary word play close to riddling is the spoonerism. Alan Dundes and Robert B. Georges give some examples of this type of verbal jesting in an article entitled "Some Minor Genres of Obscene Folklore" (1962:222):

> What is the difference between a nun and a girl in a bathtub? – The nun has hope in her soul.

> What's the difference between a chorus girl during the day and a chorus girl at night? – A chorus girl during the day is fair and buxom.

The question part of the riddle always begins with the opening formula "What's the difference between". The answer is just as innocent, until the initial sounds have been reversed. A spoonerism is a transposition usually of the initial sounds of two or more words. The point lies in the answer, and the listener must know what to do in order to appreciate the joke.

Waln K. Brown distinguishes the two processes that have to be executed in order to discern the ultimate answer. As examples, he uses the following riddles:

> What's the difference between a well stacked broad in the day and the same chick in the night-time? – In the daytime she's fair and buxom.

> What's the difference between a skinny broad and a counterfeit dollar bill? – A counterfeit dollar bill is a phony buck.

"First, certain letters must be transferred from word to word, thus: **f**air and **b**uxom, **ph**ony **b**uck. Second, the whole answer must be put into place: "In the daytime she's fair and buxom; in the night-time she's bair and fuxom" and "A counterfeit dollar bill is a phony buck; a skinny broad is a bony phuck." (Brown 1973:96.). On hearing the question the respondent cannot know it is a play on words and is thus at the mercy of the riddler. But on grasping the answer to the first riddle, the experienced respondent will have grasped the cognitive model and will know how to solve the next spoonerism.

The potential for playing with spoonerisms depends on the structure of the language, which has yet to be investigated. The Finnish language, for example, seems to lend itself almost endlessly to pairs of innocent words which, when reversed, produce a crude result dealing with sex or feces. There are even some stories in Finnish children's lore containing pairs of words resulting in a daring sexual expression. Adults also amuse themselves with spoonerisms, but at textural level, which is untranslatable.

Spoonerisms draw on the same sexual images as real riddles, since the result of twisting the words is always left to the listener to guess. If he laughs, he has understood the joke.

Conclusion

The material I have presented here covers a time span of almost a hundred years. Obviously both the sexual imagery and the use of riddles have during this time changed many times over. The examples take us from town to country and from an agrarian to an urban milieu, and the users of the riddles have been heterogeneous in the extreme. Sex, which was, judging from the descriptions, once both secret and forbidden, is now open to all in numerous different manifestations. It would never occur to anyone to accuse another of an overactive or dirty mind for guessing a sexual riddle "correctly", unless of course such accusations were a vital part of the game. But, so far, we know virtually nothing about the use of sexual lore among, for example, different social classes.

On the subject of love, or the emotions in general, riddles remain silent. This is a genre that, as regards the scale of emotions, gives frank expression to pure sensuality and sexuality. Sex education and the prevalence of representations of sexuality have not robbed the subject of its charm. A masterly double entendre still has the power to amuse even if it is vulgar, but at the same time it reflects the attitudes of the community and the figures of speech assimilated by people in different communities. The "coarseness" of the metaphors depends on, for example, the time and the situational context. Something that may today appear obscene may not have been in its time. It nevertheless appears to be clear that the people made to look stupid were the women who tried to prevent sexual riddles from being asked. The concept of obscenity and propriety may also vary from one group to another. Perhaps sexual jokes are also a way of assessing the tensions and tones inherent in sexuality. Sexual riddles both ancient and modern constitute easily recognizable semantic chains testing the listener by playing with words, while examination of sexual referents from different angles is a constant source of new variations. All sexual riddles have one thing in common: the right answer is always in a sense the wrong one.

Translated by Susan Sinisalo.

BIBLIOGRAPHY

Abrahams, Roger D. 1968: Introductory Remarks to a Rhetorical Theory of Folklore. Journal of American Folklore 81:143–158.

Bauman, Richard 1970: The Turtles: An American Riddling Institution. Western Folklore 29:21–25.

Blacking, John 1961: The Social Values of Venda Riddles. African Studies, Vol. 20, No. 1:1–32.

Boggs, Ralph Steele 1934: North Carolina White Folktales and Riddles. Journal of American Folklore 47:289–328.

Brandes, Stanley 1980: Pranks and Riddles. S.Brandes (ed.) Metaphors of Masculinity. Sew and Stratus in Andalusian Folklore. Philadelphia.

Bregenhøj, Carsten 1988: Blodet droppar, blodet droppar. Skolbarns humor. Helsingfors.

Brown, Waln K. 1973: Cognitive Ambiguity and the Pretended Obscene Riddle. Keystone Folklore 18:89–101.

Dundes, Alan – Georges, Robert A. 1962: Some Minor Genres of Obscene Folklore. Journal of American Folklore 75:221–226.

Dundes, Alan – Pagter, Carl P. 1975: Work Hard and You Shall Be Rewarded. Urban Folklore from the Paperwork Empire. Austin, Texas.

FR: Finnish Riddles. see Virtanen – al. 1977.

Freud, Sigmund 1960: Jokes and Their Relation to the Unconscious. New York.

Ganander, Christfrid 1783: Aenigmata Fennica. Suomalaiset arvotuxet Wastausten kansa. Helsinki.

Harleman Stewart, Ann 1983: Double Entendre in the Old English Riddles. Lore and Language 3:39–52.

Hart, Don V. 1964: Riddles in Filipino Folklore. Syracuse.

Isbell, Billie Jean – Fernandez, Fredy Amilcar Roncalla 1977: The Ontogenesis of Metaphor: Riddle Games among Quechua Speakers Seen as Cognitive Discovery Procedures. Journal of Latin American Lore 3:19–49.

Launonen, Hannu 1966: Varas menee aittaan. Suomalainen Suomi 6:374–379.

Lipponen, Ulla 1987: Kilon poliisi ja muita koululaisjuttuja. Helsinki.

Lövkrona, Inger 1991: "Dä river å ravlar unner kvinnornas navlar..." Gåtor och erotik i bondesamhället. J.Frykman – O.Löfgren (eds.) Svenska vanor och ovanor. Stockholm.

Manuel, Arsenio E. 1955: Notes on Philippine Folk Literature. University of Manila Journal of East Asiatic Studies 4:137–153.

Peuckert, Will-Erich 1938: Deutsches Volkstum in Märchen und Sage, Schwank und Rätsel. Berlin.

Preston, Micharl J. 1982: The English Literal Rebus and the Graphic Riddle Tradition. Western Folklore 40:104–121.

Roemer, Danielle M. 1982: In the Eye of the Beholder. A Semiotic Analysis of the Visual Descriptive Riddle. Journal of American Folklore 95:173–199.

Ruoppila, Veikko 1956: Kansa lastensa kasvattajana. Helsinki.

Schultz, Wolfgang 1912: Rätsel aus dem hellenischen Kulturkreise. II. Leipzig.

Simmons, Donald C. 1956: Erotic Tone Riddles. Man 56.

SKS: Finnish Literature Society.

Taylor, Archer 1951: English Riddles from Oral Tradition. Berkeley.

Virtanen, Leea – Kaivola-Bregenhøj, Annikki – Nyman, Aarre 1977: Arvoitukset, Finnish Riddles. Suomalaisen Kirjallisuuden Seuran Toimituksia 330. Helsinki.

Virtanen, Leea 1988: Suomalainen kansanperinne. Suomalaisen Kirjallisuuden Seuran Toimituksia 471. Helsinki.

– 1990: Huoraksi nimittely suomalaisessa perinteessä. A. Nenola – S.Timonen (eds) Louhen sanat. Kirjoituksia kansanperinteen naisista. Suomalaisen Kirjallisuuden Seuran Toimituksia 520. Helsinki.

Wessman, V.E.V. 1940: Finlands svenska folkdiktning 4. Gåtor. Helsingfors.

www.ingramcontent.com/pod-product-compliance
Lightning Source LLC
Chambersburg PA
CBHW081736270326
41932CB00020B/3291